1993

CLINICAL SUPERVISION

CLINICAL SUPERVISION

COACHING FOR HIGHER PERFORMANCE

EDITED BY

Robert H. Anderson
Karolyn J. Snyder

IN COLLABORATION WITH

John M. Bahner
Jean M. Borg
Mary Bullerman
Emily Calhoun
Letitia Carr
John H. Fitzgerald
Noreen B. Garman
Mary Giella
Carl Glickman

Nelson L. Haggerson
Douglas D. Hatch
Helen M. Hazi
Karen Hosack-Curlin
John J. (Jack) Hunt
Robert Krajewski
Arthur J. Lewis
Theodore Micceri

Lore A. Nielsen
Edward Pajak
Barbara Nelson Pavan
Donovan Peterson
Jo Roberts
Gerald Skoog
Myndall Stanfill
Joyce Burick Swarzman

TECHNOMIC
PUBLISHING CO., INC.

LANCASTER · BASEL

Clinical Supervision
a **TECHNOMIC**®publication

Published in the Western Hemisphere by
Technomic Publishing Company, Inc.
851 New Holland Avenue
Box 3535
Lancaster, Pennsylvania 17604 U.S.A.

Distributed in the Rest of the World by
Technomic Publishing AG

Printed in the United States of America
10 9 8 7 6 5 4 3 2 1

Main entry under title:
    Clinical Supervision: Coaching for Higher Performance

A Technomic Publishing Company book
Bibliography: p.
Includes index p. 389

Library of Congress Card No. 92-85468
ISBN No. 0-87762-968-4

CONTENTS

V

INTRODUCTION

WHY A BOOK LIKE THIS?

Clinical supervision, or that dimension of educational supervision that focuses particularly on examining and improving actual classroom behaviors, is almost always included in discussions of how the workers within schools (and other professional environments) can be helped toward more effective and appropriate performance. Within the literature that examines and advocates the reformation and/or betterment of schooling, there is invariably reference to, or at least implicit inclusion of, the necessity for retraining, reeducating, or redirecting teacher efforts through inservice, consultative, coaching, or supervisory services. Prominent in all such discussions is the presumed value to teachers (and others) of guidance that is based upon the authentic involvement in their day-to-day performance by colleagues in observational/analytical roles.

Since the term first entered the literature in the 1960s, clinical supervision has been the subject of at least a half dozen books, has been described in full or partial chapters in at least twenty supervision textbooks, and has been elaborated in over 200 articles or monographs. These elaborations have included historical, philosophical, legal, procedural, technical, pedagogical, curricular, and evaluative dimensions, along with many references to the numerous skills needed by the practitioner in a great variety of settings.

Another possible title for this book would be "Clinical Supervision Landscapes," since we have attempted to describe clinical supervision as broadly as possible across the many "landscapes" on which it can be found. The landscapes metaphor, originally used in education by Maxine Greene, was first applied to the field of education in 1985 by Thomas J. Sergiovanni, one of the most thoughtful and creative contributors to the literature of educational leadership. Our effort to embrace that metaphor as we designed this volume and selected a group of authors whose expertise and interests cover a very wide spectrum, was therefore inspired to some extent by Sergiovanni's insight.

That no volume exists whose purpose is to examine the ever-widening landscapes of clinical supervision was noted about two years ago by a group of educators who have been heavy contributors to the leadership literature. This group, later augmented by others invited into the project, therefore dared to launch an effort to describe these landscapes, and their effort has resulted in a book that will, they hope, enable others to view clinical supervision with deeper understanding and greater clarity.

This book has two audiences in mind. Much of the largest audience includes practitioners in the field: supervisors, directors, principals, department heads, team leaders, and all others whose roles include responsibility for assisting others to sharpen their skills through (clinical) coaching. One goal of the twenty-seven contributing authors was for this to be the kind of a book that school leaders will want to keep on or near their desks for frequent and ready reference.

A smaller but equally important audience includes professionals who are enrolled in graduate courses in educational leadership, particularly in supervision, and who are either preparing themselves for coaching/supervisory roles or seeking to enhance their skills in the helping functions. Therefore a related goal of the authors was for this volume to be chosen by some professors as the official text for their course, and by all professors as a supplementary text or at least a major reference book.

For both audiences, this volume seeks to offer a balanced mix of substantive and practical suggestions. Throughout these pages the more serious scholar will encounter the theoretical frameworks and the philosophical orientations that undergird the practices for which the label "clinical supervision" and the correlated term "coaching" have come to be commonly used. Interwoven with this background information are explanations of what clinical supervision and coaching are all about, and how classroom teachers (and others) can be guided toward more effective practice with tools and approaches that are known to have transformational capability.

There is a broad range of experiences and insights that the twenty-seven contributors have brought to this work. About one-third currently occupy practitioner roles in the public schools. Several are long-time veterans in the development of clinical supervision, while others are in the latest generation of researchers who continue to probe the fields of supervision, coaching, and staff development. It is hoped that the breadth and range of their experience, in the aggregate, will have resulted in a useful overview of the landscapes they seek to understand.

Very significant, we think, is that despite the diversity in their backgrounds and notwithstanding their slightly differing orientations and perceptions, these authors are very much in agreement on basic issues and on the role that clinical supervision can play, and has played, in the enhancement of professional practice.

Responses to some important practical questions tend to appear, and reappear, in these chapters:

(1) Do expert teachers, as contrasted with neophytes and others with less experience, really need to be coached and supervised?

(2) Is a truly collegial relationship possible between the supervisor and the teacher?

(3) What are the moral dimensions of supervisory behavior?

(4) What does the supervisor need to know about legal issues and legal decisions related to clinical practice?

(5) What connections are there between efforts at school renewal and restructuring, and the daily work of coaching?

(6) In what ways can teachers and supervisors implement the full five-stage observation cycle given the tight time constraints in most schools?

(7) What are the most essential conditions if clinical supervision is to flourish?

(8) What guidelines are there for effective communication between coaches and teachers?

(9) How can people take stock of their readiness to engage in clinical supervision practices?

(10) How does clinical supervision take into account the reality of different needs and different contexts within different schools?

(11) What are the various models of supervisory practice that fit the definition of "clinical"?

(12) Why are terms such as "metacognition" and "technical coaching" used in discussions of good supervision?

(13) Peer coaching, mentoring, collegial assistance: are these concepts all the same? How do they relate to supervision?

(14) In what contexts, beyond those found in public schools and classrooms, are the concepts of clinical supervision being put to good use?

(15) What does the supervisor need to know about the research bases that help us to understand effective classroom instruction?

(16) What sorts of skills should be emphasized as future teachers are prepared, and as supervisors work with teachers in service?

It is to be hoped that meaningful and satisfying answers to these and other important questions will be found by the reader in the twenty-three chapters that follow. At the very least, the authors hope that the reader will come to appreciate that clinical supervision is found within many different educational landscapes, and that it has the potential to be a very significant force in the improvement of school services to children.

CLINICAL SUPERVISION LANDSCAPES

During the past several decades, "clinical supervision" has moved to center stage as an approach to enhance the performance of teachers and others in professional roles. Although being a true professional requires that one be fully capable of making appropriate decisions and providing high-quality services, it also requires that one be in constant pursuit of better understanding and more efficacious methodologies. In nearly all fields of endeavor, growth in knowledge and in operational expertise depends in large measure upon interaction with other workers in a common search for improvement. The lone-wolf professional is rapidly disappearing from the American workplace, and cooperative problem solving and productive effort is emerging as the normal working pattern.

More so than most human service professions, teaching has long been defined as a lone-wolf activity. Architecture defines the classroom rather rigidly as an insulated space with one teacher in charge, and the tradition of self-contained teaching is firmly established in the minds of most teachers. Because of this, teachers are unaccustomed to the sort of mutual dialogue for which terms like mentoring, peer coaching, and collegial assistance are coming into use. Because supervision in the past has been predominantly an inspectorial, top-down, compliance-oriented function, teachers are also unaccustomed to regarding supervisors as colleagues with whom one-on-one relationships are possible. Within the landscapes they occupy, however, teachers are finding new opportunities for cooperating and for enlarging and enriching their repertoires, as well as their views of what is possible. Prominent in these new landscapes are practices associated with the term clinical supervision.

In this opening section of the book, five chapters provide not only an historical perspective but also several contextual perspectives. Chapter 1 traces the emergence of the clinical supervision cycle as an outgrowth of efforts to equip beginning teachers with the ability to analyze and modify instructional behaviors. It also shows how the development of team teaching created new opportunities, especially within a staff development framework, for the uses of that cycle in program improvement. The chapter then looks at the perceptions and definitions of clinical supervision, as found in the general literature of supervision, and concludes with some brief observations about the research.

In the second chapter, Snyder proposes that today's challenge to supervisors is the transformation, not the mere modification, of schooling. Developing greater human resources within a stimulating work culture represents a major goal in this transformation process. The ability to address problems cooperatively, within a variety of partnerships, becomes an essential skill for all workers. Snyder examines the shift that is underway from an outmoded management paradigm toward one geared to releasing the creative energies of workers. Her discussion of the changes taking place in the business world, including efforts to develop a common vision, leads to a review of clinical supervision and coaching as "essential components" of a dynamic work culture. She concludes that clinical supervision is a powerful tool in all efforts to restructure schools.

Garman and Haggerson, in a thoughtful review of philosophic considerations, identify (at least the potentiality of) clinical supervision as a moral endeavor. Recognizing that practitioners inevitably "embody" certain skills and philosophic orientations that influence their actions, Garman and Haggerson urge that striving for wisdom be acknowledged as the essence of clinical supervision. The supervisor is a moral agent, as indeed he/she should be in a democratic society. Clinical supervision, they note, also provides both the subject matter and the context in which to practice what Shon defines as reflection-in-action. As a moral agent, the supervisor has certain attitudes and characteristics including collegiality, caring for and caring about, and collaboration. Their chapter emphasizes that supervisory practice must be based on compassion, wise understanding, and moral judgment. Caring and moral wisdom are therefore the cornerstones of clinical supervision.

The contribution that clinical supervision can make toward establishing the school as a center of inquiry is developed in the fourth chapter by Glickman, Calhoun, and Roberts. They note that clinical supervision is often "misapplied" as a tool for mandating prescribed practices, whereas it can and should be used as individual assistance to teachers seeking to "learn more about their capabilities to provide good education." They identify the spirit of clinical supervision as a problematizing, action research endeavor around the moral work of teaching and learning, and urge that this spirit be reclaimed within an inquiry-oriented and democratically operated school environment. Their chapter will help readers to appreciate how, in an inquiry-oriented school, clinical supervision can best be put to work as a positive force for instructional improvement.

Following this is a chapter by Hazi, showing how legal issues and legal decisions impact on the field of instructional supervision, particularly in its clinical dimension. Ways in which supervisory practice tends to be limited by legislation, litigation, and regulations are examined. These limits are of two kinds: those due to the lack of legal definition (of which she provides four examples) and those due to legal-based incidents of practice, such as grievances about frequent visits or the use of laptop computers.

Hazi begins with an effort to demystify "the law" for readers, drawing on her personal experience as a practicing supervisor. Her conclusion is that supervisors must carefully monitor developments that could affect their status, and she suggests that they may be better able to maintain their ranks where their roles are differentiated from other public school roles, e.g., through certification.

ROBERT H. ANDERSON

Clinical Supervision: Its History and Current Context

HISTORICAL BACKGROUND

In the American experience with schooling, beginning with the colonial period in the seventeenth century, supervision has been mostly concerned with monitoring the work and behavior of teachers and their students, thereby ensuring that schools and classrooms are/were in compliance with the community's expectations. In the earliest times, such monitoring was done by laypersons, usually government officials (e.g., town selectmen), and the inspectorial visits focused not only upon the diligence with which specific tasks were being performed but also upon the physical conditions in the schools, for which teachers in those days generally had custodial responsibilities. There was a very strong emphasis upon religious ideals and moral character in teachers and pupils alike, and the personal lives of teachers were generally controlled no less stringently than were their work behaviors.

In the various literature that helps us to visualize what it was like to be a teacher, even through the early decades of the twentieth century, there is little evidence that the administrative apparatus of school districts played a psychologically supportive or professional development-oriented role. More often, it would seem, the apparatus kept teachers under strict surveillance and there was little effort beyond the monitoring to enable teachers to expand their pedagogical repertoire and increase in professional wisdom. In the rare cases where supervision as a helping/enabling function was provided, it was usually connected with a larger effort in the school or district to improve the curriculum or embrace a presumably superior method of teaching or of organizing classrooms. The teacher under conventional circumstances did not

5

receive much help of the sort for which terms like "clinical supervision" or "peer coaching" are now used.

In the mid-nineteenth century, as towns and cities grew and there was a concomitant growth in the size and complexity of schools, there emerged roles such as the "head teacher" or "principal teacher," and these persons in addition to handling administrative or managerial duties sometimes served as advisers to their colleagues. By the first quarter of the twentieth century, the office of Superintendent of Schools had become established, and in the larger districts the superintendent's office was expanded to include a variety of "special supervisors" whose expertise in subject matter was utilized in the significant curriculum changes that were introduced. Less often did these "supervisors" have an impact on instructional procedures per se, and in fact prior to the 1920s the literature of supervision was very vague, general, and by current standards naive.

Public education after World War I became both a larger and a more complex enterprise, and within an educational literature growing in both quantity and quality there was a lively sub-literature of supervision. The Association for Supervision and Curriculum Development emerged as a major organization after World War II, and in that same period "supervision" matured as a field of study and as a component of pre-certification graduate work. It was not until the 1950s and early 1960s, however, that what is now called clinical supervision emerged as a major topic. Up until then, the textbooks, articles, and even manuals dealing with supervision had very little to say about how to help teachers to reflect upon their daily instructional behaviors through the in-class collection of data about observed events, and through subsequent interactions. This is not to say that the literature was devoid of concern for the well-being and the developing skills of teachers, but rather points out that there was a big gap waiting to be closed, or a big hole to be filled, with respect to the technologies for accomplishing such purposes.

As with almost all inventions or "breakthroughs," Clinical Supervision (CS) was born at a time when hundreds if not thousands of educators were wrestling with questions about how to help beginning as well as veteran teachers to grow in skill and understanding. It was also a time, as noted, when the literature of supervision was "ripening." Most observers seem to agree that it was Morris Cogan of Harvard University who first conceived the idea of a several-stage cycle and who chose to use the term "clinical supervision" for it. In his 1973 book of that title, Cogan described his struggle to get the adjective "clinical" accepted in view of its sometimes-negative medical connotations. The term did survive, although in its current usage it identifies a number of other direct-observation-based systems (e.g., microteaching, Hunter-style supervision) that vary from the Cogan model.

For the most part, the chapters in this volume draw upon or refer to the definitions and descriptions of clinical supervision provided by Cogan and his associates, notably Robert Goldhammer.

HARVARD-NEWTON/HARVARD-LEXINGTON

Cogan was administrator of the secondary school teacher education program at Harvard in the 1950s, and as such was concerned with helping apprentice teachers through their student teaching experience. Robert Anderson, from 1954 onward, had the corresponding responsibility for directing the elementary school preparation program. In 1955, Harvard launched what became widely known as the internship program. Its components were an intensive six-week summer school (in Newton, Massachusetts) which included student teaching; a subsequent semester as a full-time, salaried intern teacher; and a semester of full-time graduate study. The interns were employed in pairs by one of the nine cooperating school districts, one to teach in the fall semester and one to teach in the spring semester.

In the Harvard-Newton Summer School, each classroom was managed by a master teacher, selected from across the country because of an outstanding reputation, serving under the direction of Harvard faculty members. Out of economic necessity the apprentice teachers were assigned in groups of four or five to each master teacher, whose class generally had thirty or more (voluntary, tuition-paying) pupils so that each of the apprentices could have small-group as well as total-class teaching experiences. At the elementary level, a class of thirty-five pupils seemed desirable because each of the five apprentice teachers could therefore work at times with a subgroup of seven pupils, e.g., in reading or math.

The pupils, in both the elementary and the secondary programs, attended class in the mornings only, and afternoon time was used by the apprentice groups for planning and reflection, as well as for a methods course (e.g., The Teaching of Mathematics, or Elementary Language Arts). It was in this nurturant setting, during which the apprentices had both the opportunity and the obligation to observe each other at work and to provide feedback, that the "cycle" of clinical supervision was born: pre-observation conference, observation, analysis, and strategic planning by the observer group, post-observation conference, and postconference review. The Harvard faculty members and the master teachers, in managing this exciting activity, gradually evolved intricate ways of thinking about each stage in the cycle and came up with a number of strategies and "ground rules" for increasing the value and the productivity of each event in the sequence.

By happy coincidence, 1955–1956 was also the period when the brilliant dean of Harvard's Graduate School of Education, Francis Keppel, challenged his faculty to help define and implement a (new) idea called "team teaching." Cogan and Anderson were among those who responded, seeing the enormous potential for teacher growth and development (among other things) in an arrangement that would significantly increase professional discussion and interaction. In 1957 the first team-teaching program was launched in an elementary school in Lexington, under Anderson's direction, and secondary school models soon followed. By 1960, the idea had spread widely across the country and there was recognized to be a great need for preparing elementary and secondary teachers and administrators to participate in teaming more effectively. Harvard responded to this need by creating a team-focused summer program in Lexington, similar in some ways to the Harvard-Newton program. Beginning in 1961 and continuing for five summers, the Harvard-Lexington Summer Program (HLSP) provided the ultimate laboratory within which clinical supervision was developed and demonstrated.

In brief, teams of 100 or more pupils were organized under the general direction of a senior faculty member called the team leader (a top expert in team teaching), who coordinated the "apprentice team teaching" done by three groups of teachers and administrators, usually nine in number, who rotated between the functions of planning, teaching, and observing (one week in each role, and then again one week in each role). All of the apprentice team members, by the way, were experienced professionals representing school systems co-sponsoring the program.

During the week of curriculum planning, each team was advised by Harvard faculty members with expertise in the disciplines (Math, Science, Social Sciences, Language Arts, etc.). The planned program was then taught to the pupils within a team-teaching framework, under the direction of the team leader. Meanwhile, the observation team, under the direction of Morris Cogan and some of his supervision doctoral students, spent each day going through several five-stage "observation cycles" with the members of the teaching team.

To recap, on any given day one-third of the experienced graduate students would be doing team curriculum planning, another third would be teaching the curriculum previously planned, and the other third would be practicing and developing their skills as clinical supervisors. And as at Harvard-Newton, the afternoon hours were used in part for lectures and discussions, and in part for team activities.

Robert Goldhammer, one of Cogan's doctoral advisees and later Cogan's colleague at the University of Pittsburgh, served for two summers in HLSP as an observation team leader, and his notes and tapes from observation cycles provided the basic material first for his doctoral dissertation and later for his 1969 book, *Clinical Supervision*. Since Cogan's volume with the same title did not appear until 1973, it was the Goldhammer book that gave clinical supervision its first visibility and in effect launched a generation of both commentary and practice.

There were of course a great many other scholars and practitioners who contributed significantly to the development of "helping" supervision (as contrasted with "judging" supervision). What is already known about direct supervisory assistance to teachers as of 1992, and what will come additionally to be known in the years ahead, derives from hundreds of people and places not identified in the above brief history. However, what happened somewhat serendipitously in one place, during one period of time, seems to have had a unique impact on the field.

THE LITERATURE ON CLINICAL SUPERVISION

Twenty-four supervision textbooks published since approximately 1982 were recently searched for references to clinical supervision. In about half, there is little or no mention of the topic. On the other hand, several of the more recent volumes do contain sections, or even chapters, in which clinical supervision is examined in some detail.

Daresh (1989), for example, includes a chapter in which he presents underlying assumptions, development of an appropriate climate, stages of the clinical supervision cycle, and limits of clinical supervision. The author observes that CS's "use in a school is always contingent upon the extent to which a climate of openness and trust exists in that school between supervisors and teachers. The model may be used only when teachers and supervisors share a fundamental respect for each other" (p. 230).

Lovell and Wiles (1983) also provide a full chapter about CS, in which concepts, assumptions and the process of CS are detailed. The authors call attention to nine obstacles or pitfalls that they believe need to be explicated and discussed. These are: (1) human and material resources, especially *time*, must be provided; (2) not everyone needs continuous clinical supervision, and other arrangements (e.g., peer supervision, group CS, and self-supervision) must also be used; (3) supervisors must have sufficient understanding of, and skills in, CS for it to be effective; (4) teachers also need the prerequisite skills and understanding; (5) CS should not be used as an evaluation system for personnel decisions; (6) rigid and inflexible use of CS can be inimical to the well-being of individual teachers; (7) trust and mutual respect must first be established; (8) supervisors can't always see things as they really are, and teacher feedback is often needed to reshape data; and (9) tension and fear must be recognized and eased (pp. 181–182).

In a thirty-six page chapter appropriately entitled "Helping Teachers on a One-to-One Basis," Oliva (1989) identifies clinical supervision as a "structured approach to formative evaluation," and proposes that the instructional supervisor will serve as the formative evaluator whereas the administrator will serve as the summative evaluator. The emphasis on evaluation, which seems to contradict the message in the chapter title, is unfortunate, but overall the chapter is one of the most inclusive discussions of clinical supervision that is available. Cogan's early contribution is explained. A section on the supervisor's role acknowledges the identification of clinical supervision by Goldhammer et al., as a teaching activity, and notes that Acheson and Gall (1987), by contrast, picture the supervisor as primarily a facilitator. Noting other orientations, such as the curriculum development emphasis by Mosher and Purpel (1972), he observes that the dual roles of many supervisors, helper on the one hand and evaluator on the other, presents a serious problem. The clinical supervisor, Oliva concludes correctly, has less difficulty with this problem because of the helping, face-to-face relationship he/she has with teachers.

In a lengthy and very useful section on the prevailing models of clinical supervision, Oliva pays appropriate tribute to one of the earliest writers in the field, George C. Kyte, who in 1930 while not actually using the label "clinical" suggested a three-phase supervision process (planning, getting the most out of the observation period, and analyzing the teaching observed) that in Oliva's words "anticipated the clinical approach thirty years later" (p. 482). Of much interest is what Kyte wrote about each of the three phases, especially the second involving observation devices and instruments. The profession may well be grateful to Oliva for discovering Kyte's long-forgotten but remarkably contemporary work and devoting four pages to a summary of it.

Beach and Reinhartz (1989) provide a seven-page section on clinical supervision within a chapter on "Models of Supervision." They refer to reviews of research findings about the effectiveness of clinical supervision, including (1) teacher preference for close and supportive supervision; (2) general agreement with the basic assumptions of CS; (3) preference for CS over traditional supervision; (4) capacity of CS for changing teacher behaviors in desired directions; (5) tendency of CS supervisors to be more "open" and "accepting" than traditional supervisors in post-observation conferences; and (6) the preference of beginning teachers for more direct supervision, contrasted with the preference of experienced teachers for nondirection.

Beach and Reinhartz emphasize the necessity of a collegial, collaborative relationship between supervisors and teachers as an essential prerequisite to success. They note that by linking professional growth with everyday classroom events, CS "provides supervisors and teachers with the philosophical and methodolial framework to improve student performance" (p. 162). They observe that teachers and supervisors proficient in the use of CS become "better at diagnosing instructional skills and offering suggestions for improvement" (pp. 162–163).

In a chapter prepared for the landmark ASCD yearbook, *Supervision of Teaching* (Sergiovanni, 1982), Garman (see Chapter 2) provides a thoughtful overview of CS. An associate of both Cogan and Goldhammer during the years when the University of Pittsburgh was literally the intellectual and operational headquarters of CS, Garman traces the evolution of CS (including, in a footnote, the etymology dating to the seventeenth century of the term "clinical"). She examines the knowledge base and the constructs and concepts of supervision and then develops the concepts of collegiality and collaboration. Hers is a call for depth and richness in the interactions that CS stimulates. She reports a study in which were identified at least five different "modes of inquiry" necessary for supervisory practice: discovery, verification, explanation, interpretation, and evaluation.

As is recognized in nearly all of the recent writings about CS, and especially regarding the related phenomena known as peer supervision, peer coaching, mentoring, tutoring, and collegial assistance, helping teachers to assume greater responsibility for improving their own as well as colleagues' instructional skills is now seen as a high-priority objective in American schools. One of the best statements about "collegueship in supervision" was provided by Alfonso and Goldsberry in the ASCD yearbook (Sergiovanni, 1982). These scholars note that there must exist a larger, ongoing, comprehensive plan for instructional improvement if efforts at peer or colleague supervision are to be productive. They observe, however, that teachers usually work in isolation ("one of the tragedies of American education," p. 91) and that very little feedback on teaching performance is usually provided within the minimal supervision that exists, so that collegueship efforts probably provide a form of help that is not available elsewhere.

Three advantages of collegueship are claimed: (1) it mobilizes human resources of the school in a joint effort to improve instruction; (2) it provides long-overdue recognition and a sense of personal achievement; and (3) it makes the introduction of instructional innovation more likely. The process requires, however, that leadership be provided by the supervisory staff as teachers develop patterns of collegueship. That clinical supervision is one of the mechanisms that "emphasizes and works to develop collegial relations between supervisors and teachers" is noted (p. 98).

Sergiovanni and Starratt (1988) provide a thoughtful chapter that examines "Clinical Supervision and Teacher Evaluation." The authors state that "since clinical supervision in all its forms involves making informal judgements about teaching, teacher evaluation is inevitably involved in the process" (p. 350). They go on to note that teachers generally disdain evaluation, and therefore they disdain supervision, which they perceive to be a "hidden" form of evaluation. In the chapter, CS is defined as a "partnership in inquiry," and an "in-class support system."

"The heart of clinical supervision is an intense, continuous, mature relationship between supervisors and teachers with the intent being the improvement of professional practice" (all quotes on p. 357). The authors discuss the concept of an "education platform," the ingredients of which are what one believes is possible, what one believes is true, and what one believes is desirable (p. 361). The platform concept is then discussed in relationship to CS, it being noted that teachers sometimes are unaware of the contradiction that there may be between their espoused platform and the assumptions, beliefs, and theories that actually guide their classroom decisions and behavior.

Glickman (1990), another of this volume's authors, devotes eleven pages to a discussion of CS, in a section that is part of a chapter entitled "Direct Assistance to Teachers." Included in the CS discussion is commentary on coaching, seen as a peer use of CS, in which it is emphasized that for peer supervision to be successful there need to be, in addition to agreement and voluntarism, components addressing the purpose of the coaching, the training that participants require, the scheduling provision of necessary time, and various monitoring activities, including troubleshooting.

Glickman's chapter then discusses some other means of direct assistance, with examples illustrating unplanned, sometimes emergency-oriented occasions that call for supervisors to be readily accessible in order to deal with short-term issues. He proposes that supervisors should try to "check in" with teachers (each day if possible) and also set aside some weekly times for conferences on immediate matters. In addition, supervisors should seek to delegate (i.e., refer questions or problems to other specialists in the school) more often in order to better meet needs that arise.

Glickman also addresses the differences between direct assistance and formal evaluation. Since teachers have historically had little non-evaluative supervision and since they therefore tend to mistrust the use of classroom observations and other direct assistance that purports to be helping and formative, creative ways are needed to resolve the dilemma of evaluation and supervision. He notes that there is some evidence that teachers would like to be observed more often, to receive more feedback, and to talk more with other professionals about teaching. Some procedures for helping teachers to accept more direct assistance, as suggested by Glickman, include the effort to separate marginal from competent teachers and to provide a longer-term evaluation-free system for the latter while providing "needs improvement" services for the former. He urges, as do many others, separate roles for those who evaluate and those who supervise.

In his summary, Glickman notes that failure to provide clinical supervision and other forms of assistance gives a very wrong message to teachers, to the effect that their work is unimportant and an isolated life (keep your doors shut and your problems to yourself) is good enough.

Another standard supervision textbook of interest is by Tanner and Tanner (1987). The Tanners open their discussion of CS with reference to its Harvard origins, and in doing so credit Harvard's President Conant with proposals as early as 1963 for bringing preservice teacher education to the graduate level, where "a coherent theoretical-research base (could serve) as a guide for intelligent practice" (p. 180). They also mention Conant's 1963 proposal that "the supervision of students in the practice-teaching phase of their preparation be conducted under the direction of the clinical professor whose status would be 'analogous to that of a clinical professor in certain medical schools' " (p. 181). The "clinical professor" in this proposal would be a highly skilled and experienced classroom teacher who also holds rank as a university professor. The analogy to medicine, in Conant's mind, derived from a view that the developing sciences undergirding instructional practice are no less complex or important than the developing sciences that undergird medicine, and the clinical professors in both instances serve as intermediaries between the basic sciences and the future practitioner.

Turning to CS and the various definitions of it, the Tanners describe CS as systematic but not rigid, and (in a variety of versions) more democratic than the traditional supervisory process. They agree with various researchers, however, that although CS has gained wide acceptance in the literature, it is not widely employed. They observe that CS tends to be a personalized-consultative approach, rather than a participative-group system in which schoolwide and districtwide problems are addressed cooperatively and systematically by all involved. The focus is on classroom instruction (micro-curricular) rather than on curriculum design, development, and evaluation, which become upper-tier macro-curricular concerns. CS also concentrates, they observe, on the study of overt classroom behavior, and may leave inferential and other approaches undetected. As a general criticism, the Tanners express concern that CS does not usually lead to the solution of wider curriculum and educational problems (faculty philosophy and psychology, curriculum articulation, coherent general curriculum, long-term curriculum outcomes, etc.), and they claim that with its counseling focus CS does not touch sufficiently upon many of the substantive problems that are faced by teachers and students.

The Tanner analysis reflects the tendency of some supervision generalists to see CS as a competitive approach to their broader-gauged work, rather than as a useful and valid subset of the larger field called supervision. This is unfortunate, because the adjective "clinical" has been intended by most proponents of CS to imply "a fraction of" as well as "a particular and focused aspect of" supervision. CS should be, as many advocates see it, a respected and powerful part of the larger efforts that are made to improve school programs and help teachers to grow in skill and understanding. The CS literature therefore is best seen as an exciting chapter within the broad literature that deals with supervision writ large. The visibility and the resonance of CS within that literature serves to remind those who do write large that the study and the use of hands-on, direct assistance to teachers has been all too often neglected in the past and now deserves a prominent place in the supervisory scheme of things.

Related Literature

In the past decade there has been a steady flow of journal articles, conference reports and handouts, monographs, association publications, and other materials dealing with clinical supervision and associated topics such as coaching, mentoring, and other forms of collegial assistance. The authors of these materials are not only university-based scholars, but also practitioners who report their direct experience with CS and the various instruments and/or procedures that they have discovered to be useful. In the chapters that follow in this volume, the flavor and substance of these materials is well represented.

It is primarily within the periodical literature that research information first becomes available, and therefore in preparing this volume we maintained a monthly check up to press time to be certain that no new or unexpected signals were being received. With some confidence we are able to report that the chapters in this volume speak accurately to the current status of CS research and therefore to prevailing views of CS as a tool for improving educational programs through staff development.

Research

A comprehensive current summary of research findings about "Clinical Supervision and Coaching" was prepared by Snyder and Anderson (1990) with the assistance of seven of their doctoral students at the University of South Florida. Selected and summarized were forty-two reports, two of which (Hosack-Curlin, 1988 and Nielsen, 1988) are on coaching and have been elaborated in Chapters 13 and 15 of this volume. Many of these reports deal with the questions already identified in the textbooks mentioned above. There is frequent reference to the dilemma faced by principals and other administrative officers in separating their motives and their behaviors with respect to teacher evaluation from their motives/behaviors vis-à-vis assisting and helping. That it is (perceived to be) difficult to find sufficient time for CS and/or coaching activities is a pervading concern, and several authors refer to the essentiality of training and practice for principals, mentors, and coaches if the assisting activities are to be productive. For these and related reasons, many of the comments about CS and coaching are found within articles examining staff development, for which "human resources development" is an emerging label, as a crucial function.

An impression one gets from this literature is that teachers, although often cautious and reluctant at the onset, respond with increasing enthusiasm to the growth-inducing opportunities that are inherent in CS, especially when it involves interactions with peers. Supporting evidence is found in the report by Cawelti and Reavis (1980) who state that attitude changes, high levels of openness, and increased accepting behaviors result from CS practices. They also note that the high frequency of supervisory visits correlates with high ratings of supervisory service by teachers.

It may interest readers to know that much of the commentary and research about CS derives from members of a small national Council of Professors of Instructional Supervision (COPIS). This group, formed in 1975, meets twice annually and its weekend-long annual conferences provide a forum for sharing ideas and debating issues. From the beginning, the place of CS within the larger field has been constantly on the agenda. It was in the aftermath of the 1989 conference, in which tribute was paid to the memory of Robert Goldhammer, that work on this volume was begun.

Papers presented at COPIS conferences are frequently published in

Wingspan (see "References" section), the February 1990 issue of which featured reports on CS. One of these papers, by L. Anderson, pulled together nine concepts synthesized from the major writings and dialogues. In brief, and paraphrased, these are: (1) deliberate systematic inquiry into classroom instruction; (2) focus on improving the teaching/learning process; (3) planned supervision objectives; (4) reliance on objective data; (5) pattern analysis; (6) flexible methodology; (7) role and function delineation; (8) essentiality of training for clinical supervisors; and (9) productive tension within a nurturing climate.

It remains the fact that CS, no less than the broader field of general supervision (Alfonso and Firth, 1990), has yet to be fully examined and understood. CS is still in its early stages of development, but its structural elements seem to make sense, and it appears to stimulate fruitful thought about quality educational services to children. That its use apparently also has many beneficial side effects, such as breakdown of the self-contained isolation of teachers and the emergence of a productive work culture in schools, is worth celebrating. All the same, an overall and authentic appraisal of CS as a positive force on the American educational scene awaits further research and discussion. Our hope is that this volume will be a major contribution to such pursuits.

REFERENCES

Alfonso, R. J. and G. R. Firth. 1990. "Supervision: Needed Research," *Journal of Curriculum and Supervision*, 5(Winter):181–188.

Anderson, L. A. 1990. "Clinical Supervision Concepts," *Wingspan*, 5(February): 35–38 (see also below).

Beach, D. M. and J. Reinhartz. 1989. *Supervision: Focus on Instruction*. New York: Harper and Row.

Cawelti, G. and C. A. Reavis. 1980. "How Well Are We Providing Instructional Improvement Services?" *Educational Leadership*, 38(December):236–240.

Cogan, M. L. 1973. *Clinical Supervision*. Boston: Houghton Mifflin.

Daresh, J. C. 1989. *Supervision as a Proactive Process*. New York: Longman.

Glickman, C. D. 1990. *Supervision of Instruction: A Developmental Approach, Second Edition*. Boston: Allyn and Bacon.

Goldhammer, R. 1969. *Clinical Supervision: Special Methods for the Supervision of Teachers*. New York: Holt, Rinehart and Winston.

Kyte, G. C. 1930. *How to Supervise: A Guide to Educational Principles and Progressive Practices of Supervision*. Boston: Houghton Mifflin.

Lovell, J. T. and K. Wiles. 1983. *Supervision for Better Schools, Fifth Edition*. Englewood Cliffs, NJ: Prentice-Hall.

Mosher, R. L. and D. E. Purpel. 1972. *Supervision: The Reluctant Profession*. Boston: Houghton and Mifflin.

Oliva, P. F. 1989. *Supervision for Today's Schools, Third Edition*. New York: Longman.

Sergiovanni, T. J., ed. 1982. *Supervision of Teaching*. ASCD 1982 Yearbook. Alexandria, VA: Association for Supervision and Curriculum Development. See Chapter 3: Garman, N. B. "The Clinical Approach to Supervision," pp. 35–52. See also Chapter 7: Alfonso, R. J. and L. Goldsberry. "Colleagueship and Supervision," pp. 90–107.

Sergiovanni, T. J. and R. J. Starratt. 1988. *Supervision: Human Perspectives, Fourth Edition*. New York: McGraw-Hill.

Snyder, K. J. 1988. "Clinical Supervision," *Encyclopedia of School Administration and Supervision*. Phoenix: Oryx Press, p. 261.

Snyder, K. J., R. H. Anderson, et al. 1990. *Managing Productive Schools Research Base*. Tampa: Pedamorphosis, Inc., 5:24–27. (see also below).

Tanner, D. and L. Tanner. 1987. *Supervision in Education: Problems and Practices*. New York: Macmillan.

WINGSPAN: The Pedamorphosis Communique. For information write to Pedamorphosis, Inc., P.O. Box 271669, Tampa, FL 33688-1669.

KAROLYN J. SNYDER

2

Schooling Transformation: The Context for Professional Coaching and Problem Solving

Educational institutions today are taking bold steps to alter the effects of schooling upon both professionals and students. The tough reform models of bureaucratic control and "absolutes" advocated in the 1980s now are giving way to development-oriented partnerships within and across institutions, as many role groups address together the challenges of schooling. Restructuring is a response to environmental challenges of doing more with less, and its success requires attention to fresh questions about schooling outcomes and to aggressive development strategies.

A major management challenge during these turbulent times is to develop greater human resources primarily for becoming highly skilled at addressing problems cooperatively within a variety of partnerships. School-based management, one current dimension of reform, will succeed to the extent that all professionals, both within and outside the school, become retooled for an era of shared decision making and networking, and where development efforts focus on student success. As educators raise new questions about the social outcomes of schooling, new collective visions of schooling will be born that will lead to more powerful work structures and processes. The focus of current reform efforts tends to center around meeting the needs of a full range of students, and includes the challenges of dropouts, at-risk students, learning disabled children of all kinds, and children from single parent or dysfunctional families. Tomorrow's schools are likely to be built around the premise of "Every student a winner, every day," which is a relatively new aspiration for schools. Graded class structures and curriculum, and isolated learning and competition practices that interfere with this aspiration could and should disappear during the pursuit of more powerful schooling practices.

This chapter seeks to examine the organizational context for planning and institutionalizing clinical supervision and coaching efforts. The "gotcha" approaches to clinical supervision, like other punitive control patterns, have yielded few gains in student success patterns. A swing of the reform pendulum to empowerment approaches, giving teachers responsibility to help solve schooling problems, is likely to have a positive effect if all levels of professionals within a school district work together as partners. Consequently, new knowledge and skills for shared problem solving and decision making are likely to become a major staff development focus in the next decade. Professional educators can better meet most schooling challenges given a foundation in the current knowledge base about productive work cultures, and the function of clinical supervision or coaching within an organization's development.

The context of professional teaching and coaching in an era of transition is the focus of this chapter. If the learning context is to be restructured to enhance student success, then the work context for professionals also will require significant alterations. The research literature of business and industry, social and behavioral sciences, and schooling will be examined for guidance about developing work cultures that stimulate performance. What is known about productive workplaces and their effect on performance is already being used by many school districts to restructure work relationships for adults and students alike, making use of resources both within and outside the organization. Education institutions are experiencing a paradigm shift from the bureaucratic models that control for lower levels of compliant performance, towards the empowerment models that unleash talent, and enhance and expand performance for individuals and their organizations.

At the very root of the paradigm shift, from compliance to proactivity, is a realization that teachers have for too long been treated as blue collar workers, in need of basic direction, structures, and controls. Instead, the teacher as partner in policy making now is being viewed as critical to the success of schooling. In their reform efforts, many administrators are rethinking the role and function of teachers, realizing that as line managers teachers provide fresh and vital perspectives (Conley, Schmidle, and Shed, 1988).

In the search for structures and processes that will transform schooling outcomes, partnerships will be required of schools, districts, state education agencies, universities, and local businesses and social agencies. Breaking out of the single-institution model of reform is necessary for preparing schools for a new century. To facilitate student success, four striking features of schooling are likely to evolve from restructuring efforts: (1) a community of learners, where teachers, students, parents, and other resources from the district and the community will become co-involved in learning; (2) interdependence between the school and community, where students work together to solve problems in the community, becoming part of its development during schooling years; (3) a problem-solving and service orientation to learning, where students learn how to address real challenges by using multiple resources, and by continuing work activity until the problem is solved or new service patterns are in place; and (4) a community of caring and support, where the professional staff addresses multiple levels of human need for students, moving beyond a fix on cognitive development and performance.

REFORM PERSPECTIVES

Reform efforts during the 1980s were guided by a rather simplistic view of the cause and effect relationship between good teaching and student achievement. Many states, such as Texas, adopted tough curriculum guidelines, and placed rigorous expectations upon school districts for certain levels of student performance. Hence, the results of a curriculum-control approach to reform have been disappointing. The underlying but erroneous assumption was that clear statewide standards of achievement, if controlled, would eliminate many schooling problems.

Some states also adopted rigorous teacher evaluation systems, based in part upon the effective teaching research findings (e.g., Texas, Florida, South Carolina, and Georgia). It was assumed that if teaching expectations were grounded in research and made explicitly clear to all professionals, and if evaluation systems were in place to weed out low-performing teachers, many schooling problems would be corrected. However, the results of such teacher-evaluation approaches to reform also have been disappointing.

Other states, such as Minnesota, approached school reform quite differently and focused instead on improving the school as a unit. It was assumed that if teachers and principals would address the problems unique to their schools, schoolwide learning patterns would be altered. This approach has been more successful. Research over the past decade confirms that a school-based approach to reform can alter achievement patterns significantly (Snyder, 1988a).

During the 1980s, many well-advertised management best sellers appeared in popular book store chains, giving the public for the first time a glimpse inside corporate America's best companies. What emerged from that exploding literature was a view of productive workplaces that was not consistent with most school reform efforts. The effective schools research also began to identify many organizational work conditions that appear to influence school productivity and outcomes. This emerging knowledge about organizational culture and its effects upon performance has provided energy and direction for new approaches to school reform.

Concurrent with the appearance of the management best sellers in the marketplace, and the publication of effective schools research, the relatively new field of Human Resources Development (HRD) blossomed. Within productive workplaces, correlations have been found between continuous professional development and organizational productivity. Hence, HRD approaches now are altering management practices and organizational performance throughout America. School districts as well as corporations are focusing more attention on the development of more powerful systems of employee selection, development, appraisal, and compensation. In many successful enterprises there exists a fundamental belief in the importance of continuous professional development (for all role groups) for responding to a changing marketplace. What is especially new in staff development is attention to the relatively recent literature of "work culture" within which there is an emphasis upon altering the prior patterns of isolation and competition in the direction of collaboration and partnership.

CORPORATE TRANSFORMATION

Restructuring, empowerment, and entrepreneurship are characteristic of major efforts throughout corporate America to transform the workplace and its effects on products and services. Schools are one among many service agencies in the community, and as such are responding to the same social conditions and service needs as other agencies and businesses. Three scholarly works provide a portrait of a cultural transformation that is sweeping the American workplace, and offer perspectives on the context within which clinical supervision is likely to enhance school transformation. Kilmann and Covin (1988) focus on the nature of corporate transformation, its dimensions, causes, and responses. Peters (1988) describes the ways in which management has been turned upside-down in the best companies, responding to redefined purposes. Kanter (1989) explores restructuring as giant corporations learn to develop new response capacities.

To begin, Kilmann and Covin, in *Corporate Transformation* (1988), observe that the corporate world today is experiencing a transformation of purpose, role relationships, and responses to the environment. They conclude that corporate transformation is "a process by which organizations examine what they were, what they are, what they will need to be, and how to make the necessary changes." They also note that transformation indicates the fundamental nature of change taking place, in contrast to a mere linear extrapolation or evolution from the past. Basic to success with tossing out the old structures and inventing more powerful forms, is a growing realization of the limitations of the old bureaucratic structures, for they no longer are sufficient to support the greater demands for market responsiveness. The implications for educational reform are striking. Attention only to areas of improvement is unlikely to lead educators to the new work structures that are needed for schools to respond to the needs of today's marketplace. Different product and service standards today are requiring a totally different approach to management and the organization of work.

The results of the Kilmann-Covin research on corporate transformation lead to several conclusions. Corporate transformation, they note, is a serious, large-scale change that demands new ways of perceiving, thinking, and behaving by all members of the organization. Transformation is:

- a response to environmental and technological changes
- a new model of the organization of the future
- based on dissatisfaction with the old and a belief in the new
- a qualitatively different way of perceiving
- expected to spread throughout the organization at different rates of absorption
- driven by management

- ongoing, endless, and forever
- orchestrated by inside and outside experts

Transformation, then, is a response to environmental changes that demands a fundamentally new approach to solving problems. Many schools and school districts now are asking fresh questions about the central focus of schooling and what is needed to address mounting challenges. Among the hurdles for schools are dysfunctional families, drug and substance abuse, violence and suicide, racism, crack babies, child care, and diverse cultures. Moreover, questions also are being addressed for the new structures and programs needed to help all student populations. When these challenges are examined by local educators, the reform and restructuring agenda becomes more clear.

The question arises, "How does transformation occur in an organization?" Peters' book, *Thriving on Chaos* (1988), describes ways in which management practice in the best companies has been turned upside-down in relation to new definitions of purpose and outcomes. Greater attention is being given to creating total customer satisfaction. In so doing, management is pursuing fast-paced innovation, and achieving flexibility by empowering people. Rather than denying the need for it, the best managers are coming to love change, and as a result new views of leadership are emerging at all levels of the organization. Realizing that the old bureaucratic models are too restricting, managers are designing new systems for a work world that is more positive and responsive to client needs and demands.

Peters also predicts that the winners (organizations) of the future will be "flatter" (people working more in collaborative arrangements rather than in hierarchical ones), more quality and service conscious, more responsive to customer needs, faster at innovation, and capable of making more productive use of highly trained and flexible people. Hustle, he notes, is becoming a key strategic principle for responding to the customer. "Piloting everything" will become a way of life as programs and partnerships are formed to solve pressing problems.

The ways in which people work under new forms of management are equally noteworthy. The basic structural unit or building block of new organizations, Peters observes, is the self-managed team. In some places a team structure is being designed for workers who manage and are accountable for their own productivity. Rather than following policy books, common visions of excellence are replacing old control mechanisms and guiding performance as workers are empowered to tackle pressing organizational challenges. A horizontal style of management often is created as leaders empower others to act and grow in support of a cause that both leaders and followers find worthy. Control tends to be paperless, as the shared vision, remarkably high standards, recognition of performance, and mutual trust form the glue that transforms the performance of organizations.

In education's paradigm shift from the bureaucratic models of policy, budget focus, fixed programs and services, schools and school districts begin to develop a new look. Structures for co-involvement evolve, where educators begin to address challenges schoolwide and district-wide. Managers shed many control patterns and become facilitators and even cheerleaders while providing direction and reinforcement to development efforts. Ad hoc groups of staff members and community members, often working across schools, thrive as problems are tackled with fresh knowledge, perspectives, and resources. A climate of pride evolves from successful problem solving and from piloting new programs, and piloting becomes a major strategy for invention and institutionalization. The neatness and predictability of work structures in traditional work cultures disappears as more dynamic forms are shaped in pursuit of challenges.

How do organizations learn new work patterns? Kanter, in *When Giants Learn to Dance* (1989), documents the ways in which large corporations are developing new capacities to respond to changing market conditions and to create the future. Discussing the same corporate phenomena as Peters, Kanter focuses attention on restructuring and on developing partnerships, both of which are necessary, she notes, to the new "corporate dance." When corporations ask basic survival questions, such as "What should we be doing in the next decade?" the growing response is to alter the basic goals of the organization and restructure the ways in which people think and work internally, across the company, and with external partners. The core of the post-entrepreneurial management revolution, she notes, is how to do more with less (p. 52). The dynamic that enables restructuring to work is a management focus on developing new synergies (work groups whose members cross units and represent different orientations and perspectives); companies are opening their boundaries to form new alliances across organizations. The focus is on developing programs of investment in the future.   *147,970*

The Pillsbury Company, Kanter reports (p. 109), appointed a synergy czar to bring in resources from various units to create a "value multiplier effect." American Express even has a rewards program for the achievement of synergy czars in managing the outcomes and productivity of synergies (p. 112). Post-entrepreneurial companies are developing synergies across units with all levels of workers. These new structures are more focused and leaner, and they develop cultures where people pull together to achieve something new.

Characteristics of restructuring, then, include an entrepreneurial thrust, where emphasis is placed on innovation; a new organizational shape is formed, deal making and partnerships become a way of life, and new structures are designed to handle new relationships. Partnerships, one dimension of restructuring, are among the most powerful configurations in the workplace today. Kanter observes that boundaries become blurred as resources are pooled, opportunities are exploited, and workers from across units and institutions become increasingly interdependent. Successful partnerships are an investment in the future where workers integrate, where a chain of command can rarely be found, and where decentralization allows support structures to be formed to protect and encourage development.

The new productivity paradigm of schooling is likely to place its development focus on student needs, rather than on teachers and curriculum (maintenance paradigm), or even on schools as a unit (paradigm shift to collaboration). Schools are likely to evolve into full-service units for the community, forming partnership arrangements with parents, social agencies, and cottage industries. Hence, students are likely to work cooperatively in their learning (paradigm shift) and actually provide services and produce products for the community (new productivity paradigm). With a shift to the student as worker, teachers and others will play more of a management role in facilitating student development and productivity. Democracy will thrive each day as students and staff learn to function in learning communities that are interdependent with the social context of the school. Entrepreneurs and partnerships across agency boundaries will thrive as ways are invented to help every student succeed daily as a participant in a productive democracy.

In summary, the focus of transforming corporations, when reading these three works, is not on survival or even minimal improvements, but rather on shaping the future. Kanter observes that the best corporations are competing for the global corporate olympics, and in so doing cannot afford to support programs that do not add value to the central purpose. Services must either be restructured to add value, or eliminated. Given a clear purpose, people are pulling together to create something new, working beyond job descriptions, and as a result are transforming the workplace, and its effects, services, and products.

Many school systems also are asking tough new questions about overall purpose. In so doing, the old goals of housing and sorting students for twelve years are giving way to student-success-driven systems. Many of the bureaucratic traditions of grading, grouping, teaching, curriculum, and promotion and retention are being replaced with new more flexible outcome-driven systems for student success. In the process, many are inventing bold new ways to make use of resources in achieving redefined purposes and strategies. Restructuring requires continuous corporate learning and adaptation as challenges are addressed. What seems clear is that tight definitions of performance (staff and students) appear to be but relics of the old maintenance paradigm. In their place attention is given to shared visions, professional development, creativity, and thinking and acting in bold ways with all kinds of partners. Performance appraisal is beginning to appear more like a graduation celebration, focusing on inventions and accomplishments, rather than the dreaded announcement of deficiencies. New questions now are being raised about motivational factors that stimulate creative and productive performance that will help to shape better forms of schooling.

DEVELOPING A COMMON VISION

No clear blueprint to the future exists for any enterprise, including schooling. The future will be invented either by bold and creative educators, or by the business community as it takes on an increasing number of schooling functions. Dreams about the future state of an organization now are viewed as necessary for breaking out of disabling traditions. A vision, however it evolves, has the power to lift workers outside current conditions and constraints to capture collective energy. Visions function to attract human energy similar to a magnet (Kouzes and Posner, 1988), and are the license for daring leaders to invent the future. A vision both attracts energy and also serves as a beacon to control the direction of the growth process. Peters (1988) suggests that a vision acts as a compass in a wild and stormy sea, and like a compass, it loses value if it is not adjusted to take account of its surroundings.

An historical backdrop for visioning is important, for it builds upon the strengths of an organization. Dreaming about future ideals plays an important function in restructuring, for it honors the past as people remember and builds upon great events in their history. Dreaming also considers current realities as images are invented for more ideal states. In this sense, the past is affirmed, and with it the self-concept of those who are to shape the future. Thus, not only is the history of the organization built upon, but also the capacities of those who work in the present (who may have shaped the past) to transform the present.

Peters (1988) observes that the process of developing a vision and values is messy, and involves working convincingly with images of the future that are presently known, and, out of the journey together, future visions of greatness evolve. Bennis and Nanus (1985) argue that a vision must be repeated time and again, incorporated into the organization's culture, and reinforced through the strategy and decision-making process. As the vision grows the image must evolve to address the needs of the entire organization and be claimed by all important actors. In fact, the vision must shape the new social architecture in the organization. Principals confirm the evolutionary nature of vision building, reporting that a vision unfolds continuously as the staff walks down the "school development road" together.

Fundamental to the success of reform efforts is the task of developing a common vision, school by school. In a 1989 report by the Brookings Institution (Chubb and Moe, 1990), evidence was presented from 500 high schools that no correlations were found between student achievement and any of the variables on which school reformers have been concentrating time, effort, and money (e.g., curriculum standards and teacher evaluation systems). The authors conclude that the major causes of student achievement are student ability, school organization, and family background: in that order of importance (p. 140). What matters is whether everyone in the school has a clear vision of what is to be accomplished and their role in achieving that goal. Autonomy has the greatest influence on the overall quality of school organization; everyone must have the authority to make the decisions necessary to carry out responsibility in the overall scheme. Teachers in successful schools were free to tailor their practices to the needs of their students.

Chubb and Moe argue that if public schools are ever to become substantially more effective, the institutions that control them must also be changed.

NOURISHING ORGANIZATIONAL CULTURES

In recent years, we have come to learn that culture is so powerful a force in the workplace that it either stimulates or represses performance (Kanter, 1983). Attention needs to be given in education settings to develop a nurturing work context so as to enhance professional performance. In this section we shall examine dimensions of culture: definition, purpose, content, outcome and effects, and management.

There are many definitions of culture. Kilmann and Covin (1988) argue that culture is the invisible force behind the tangible and observable in any organization, a social energy that moves people to act. Culture provides meaning, direction, and mobilization. Another perspective is to consider culture as the influence system that determines the outcomes of competent performance (Snyder, 1988a). It is further argued that work culture is that psychological and social force within an organization that determines the direction and quality of work (Snyder, 1988b). Deal (1986) simplifies the discussion by contending that culture is "the way we do things around here."

The function of organizational culture is to keep people moving in a common direction (Deal, 1986). Lane and Murphy (1989) suggest that effective school cultures represent an integration of people, cultural context, and administrative commitment that revolves around a critical core of values. These three factors interact in a circular process of mutual, reinforcing interdependence from which effective outcomes evolve.

Since culture is a powerful force that influences the quality of performance in organizations, what then are its tangible dimensions? Many scholarly works on productive enterprises in business and industry were analyzed in search of common themes (Snyder 1988b). Four themes emerged from the study that provide clarity about the common dimensions of culture within productive workplaces: (1) stretch goals and symbol systems, (2) group sharing and networking, (3) reward and recognition, and (4) empowerment and entrepreneurial opportunity. It appears that these four dimensions of culture are interdependent features and do not exist in isolation from each other. Stronger cultures have all four features, while weaker cultures have only two or three dimensions. Many schools now are finding that the development of these four culture dimensions nurtures and stimulates teachers and others to stretch beyond job parameters and tackle the thorny school problems.

In a more recent review of the literature on organizational culture, the following overall themes and patterns were observed: "The culture of an organization is shaped by management and directs the energy system toward its outcomes. In productive organizations, a cohesive culture stimulates people to stretch and perform in unpredictable ways toward common ends; and, applauds risk taking and creativity for transforming conditions and outcomes" (Snyder and Anderson, 1990).

What then is the function of management in developing productive cultures? And further, how does the development of culture relate to effective professional job coaching and problem solving? Deal and Kennedy (1982) contend that principals can improve school culture by getting to know the culture, determining ways in which the school culture may be encouraging or undermining educational performance, and providing opportunities for people to reexamine values that need to be changed. Principals in effective schools, observe Iannacone and Jamgochian (1985), focus their energies and resources on clearly defined basic purpose and culture building. To change the school's culture, a principal creates conditions under which staff members will want to change work patterns, then involves them in planning and implementing that change (Snyder and Anderson, 1986).

PRODUCTIVE WORK CULTURES

Changing the work culture of schools presents perhaps the greatest management challenge of all in restructuring efforts. Altering cultures of isolation, regression, negativism, minimalism, and apathy is difficult but possible, and in its place there need to evolve patterns of collaboration, common purposes and goals, celebration, partnerships, continuous development, and synergy.

Peters (1988) castigates those who perpetuate the entrenched, inflexible hierarchies and the glacial unresponsiveness that have left established American companies vulnerable. In his view, decentralization of everything needs to occur, including information, authority, and strategic planning, and a culture must be established that nurtures innovation and experimentation. Until the work culture of schools controls for student and staff success, very little will change in achievement patterns. Managing a productive work culture is essential to transformation, and through decentralization and retooling efforts is well within the reach of school leaders.

Culture is a force that influences the behavior patterns of a group of people over time, and produces an accumulation of shared values as well as myths and histories. A work culture is a subsystem of organizational culture: the way work is conducted. The concept of work culture has been recently confirmed by Parkinson (1990), and includes organizational planning, staff development, program/services development, and organizational assessment. Four major dimensions of work culture provide a focus for school management and development, and draw their focus from over 500 studies of productive organizations (Snyder and Giella, 1987; Snyder and Anderson, 1990). The four work culture dimensions, and the supporting research themes are summarized below.

Organizational Planning

Productive organizations are driven by a few stretch goals identified through shared decision-making strategies. Goals are then subdivided into tasks and assigned to both permanent and temporary work groups and teams. Groups cooperatively develop action plans to accomplish their tasks. Within a group context, individuals establish performance goals that specify their intended contributions to the school's success. The resulting organizational plan becomes the major focus for work, development, and assessment activity.

Staff Development

In productive organizations, plans are made for knowledge and skill acquisition important for achieving goals. Staff members make workshop plans as they anticipate their collective needs and seek the best available resources. An important finding is that teachers' development processes are creatively stimulated when some form of coaching follows a workshop (Joyce and Showers, 1982). Further, when work groups (the building blocks of successful organizations) are provided with skill-building opportunities, the capacity for shared inquiry and problem solving is enhanced. Collaborative forms of quality control extend beyond coaching and are viewed as developmental, providing adjustment opportunities for the organization.

Program Development

When educators examine the student learning challenges they face, better solutions evolve from making use of the current knowledge base on instruction and learning. From the works of Bloom (1976) and others, we know that students master knowledge and skills to the extent that the following conditions exist: (1) instruction is matched with readiness levels, (2) instruction is guided by clear expectations and procedures, (3) active and interactive task engagement is managed, and (4) positive reinforcement and correctives are provided to ensure certain levels of mastery. Solutions to learning problems occur when leaders facilitate problem solving and development activity and generate the necessary resources.

Organizational Assessment

Productive organizations have complex assessment systems that measure the success of goals. Work groups assess the results of their work; individual staff members are assessed for their contributions to expected organizational outcomes; and student assessment data serve as a feedback measure for improving the instructional program. Assessment data in productive organizations provide a feedback loop for short-range planning and long-range growth targets.

CLINICAL SUPERVISION: ONE DIMENSION OF A WORK CULTURE

Clinical supervision and coaching are essential components of the staff development dimension of the work culture, which focuses on enhancing performance problem solving. Coaching is a data-based technique that enables staff members to learn new skills, to modify practices, to solve problems together, and to develop basic skills.

Coaching is also a problem-solving process for enabling professionals to become increasingly responsive to student needs. Clinical supervision functions interdependently with school goals, staff development, program development, and organizational assessment activity, and as a mediating variable in the school development process, it is likely to have noticeable effects on learning. Linked with school goals and the development of new professional capacities, coaching has the potential for transforming performance.

The focus for coaching is likely to shift in the future, away from predictable teaching behaviors for all situations, toward situational patterns with variable student populations and contexts. Emphasis will be given to technical coaching for learning new strategies, and also to problem solving for enhancing the capability of pilot programs to nurture student success. If more students and student populations are to succeed in schools of the future, then coaching will have a continuous dual challenge: (1) to enhance professional performance in general, and (2) to provide a data base for professional problem solving in the workplace. Attention to the basics of teaching (or performing for other role groups) will direct coaching efforts only for beginning teachers, where the coaching will be routine for three or four years. For the additional twenty-five to thirty years for a teacher (or other professional), coaching activity is more likely to be productive when directed to a data base for shared professional problem solving.

When viewed within the broader construct of culture, we might conclude that coaching is likely to influence student success to the extent that teachers participate in identifying schoolwide stretch goals and symbols; have opportunities to share regularly with colleagues and to network with peers across institutions and functions; are rewarded and recognized for gains in performance and learning problems solved; and work in a context in which there is empowerment to solve problems routinely, and to tackle large challenges where risk is involved and the stakes are high.

It is within the context of a dynamic work culture that coaching has the greatest potential to flourish and to influence performance patterns. Coaching structures permit access to the work context and to numerous opportunities for observation, data collection, analysis, feedback, and problem solving. Hence, it may be one of the most powerful dimensions of the work culture for inventing viable programs for at-risk populations, for enhancing the professional performance of educators, and for transforming outdated and inappropriate professional patterns. Without the backdrop of the work culture dimensions of shared school planning, staff development, program development, and school assessment, the effects of coaching are likely to be minimal. In this volume, coaching is viewed as the pivotal practice for shaping exemplary professional behaviors for an age of schooling transformation, and is seen as a major dimension of a productive work culture.

SUMMARY

The intent of this chapter has been to examine the context of coaching, both historically and conceptually. Current reform efforts are shifting attention to a school development orientation, which is reinforced by the research literature of successful organizations. Corporate transformation is evolving throughout American institutions as new questions are being asked about the future. Restructuring work and learning patterns is essential to the invention of new, more viable schooling futures, and will result in a transformation of the ways that schools conduct their business.

A shared vision is replacing policy manuals and bureaucratic procedures as schools develop new capacities for influencing learning. Within a work culture of shared goals, networking, partnerships, professional development, and program renovation, clinical supervision plays a dynamic function. Clinical supervision is helpful within an organizational culture that both expects and celebrates bold new ventures and their success. Coaching is an essential dimension of a work culture for shedding unproductive work habits and programs for all student populations and for transforming schooling structures, processes, and outcomes. New and more powerful work behaviors can be shaped over time through peer and supervisory feedback and problem solving. Collective attention to solving performance challenges can alter the learning patterns of a school. To this end, clinical supervision is a powerful restructuring tool.

REFERENCES

Bennis, W. and B. Nanus. 1985. *Leaders: The Strategies for Taking Charge.* New York: Harper and Row.

Bloom, B. S. 1976. *Human Characteristics and School Learning*. New York: McGraw Hill Book Co.

Chubb, J. E. and T. M. Moe. 1990. *Politics, Markets and America's Schools*. Washington, DC: The Brookings Institution.

Conley, S. C., T. Schmidle and J. B. Shedd. 1988. "Teacher Participation in the Management of School Systems," *Teachers College Record*, 90(Winter):259–280.

Deal, T. E. 1986. "Deeper Culture: Mucking, Muddling and Metaphors," in *Corporate Cultures: Research Implications for Human Resource Development*, J. C. Glidewell, ed., Alexandria, VA: American Society for Training and Development, pp. 49–57.

Deal, T. E. and A. A. Kennedy. 1982. *Corporate Cultures: The Rites and Rituals of Corporate Life*. Reading, MA: Addison-Wesley Publishing Co.

Iannocone, L. and R. Jamgochian. 1985. "High Performing Curriculum and Instructional Leadership in the Climate of Excellence," *NASSP Bulletin*, 69(May):28–35.

Joyce, B. and B. Showers. 1982. "The Coaching of Teaching," *Educational Leadership*, 40(October):4–9.

Kanter, R. M. 1983. "Change Masters and the Intricate Architecture of Corporate Culture," *Management Review*, 72(October):18–28.

Kanter, R. M. 1989. *When Giants Learn to Dance: Mastering the Challenges of Strategy, Management and Careers in the 1990s*. New York: Simon and Schuster.

Kilmann, R. H. and T. J. Covin, et al. 1988. *Corporate Transformation: Revitalizing Organizations for a Competitive World*. San Francisco: Jossey-Bass.

Kouzes, J. M. and B. Z. Posner. 1988. *The Leadership Challenge: How to Get Extraordinary Things Done in Organizations*. San Francisco: Jossey-Bass Publishers.

Lane, B. A. and J. Murphy. 1989. "Building Effective School Cultures through Personnel Functions: Staff Acquisition Processes," *Journal of Personnel Evaluation in Education*, 2(August):271–286.

Parkinson, A. 1990. "An Examination of the Reliability and the Factor Structure of the School Work Culture Profile," dissertation, University of South Florida, Tampa.

Peters, T. 1988. *Thriving on Chaos: A Handbook for a Management Revolution*. New York: Alfred A. Knopf.

Peters, T. 1989. "Peters' Principles," in *CIO* (August):13–18 (an interview by A. E. Alter).

Snyder, K. J. 1988a. *Competency Training for Managing Productive Schools*. San Diego: Harcourt, Brace and Jovanovich.

Snyder, K. J. 1988b. "Managing a Productive School Work Culture," in *NASSP Bulletin*. 72(November):40–43.

Snyder, K. J. 1988c. "Moving Beyond Teaching Competence to Professional Partnerships," editorial in *Florida ASCD Journal*, 5(Spring):5.

Snyder, K. J. and R. H. Anderson. 1986. *Managing Productive Schools: Toward an Ecology*. San Diego: Harcourt, Brace and Jovanovich.

Snyder, K. J. and R. H. Anderson. 1988. "Blueprints for Your Great School Transformation: Stop Tinkering and Start Altering," *School Administrator*, 45(December):18–23.

Snyder, K. J. and R. H. Anderson. 1990. "Managing Productive Schools Research Base," Tampa: Managing Productive Schools Training Programs.

Snyder, K. J. and M. Giella. 1987. "Developing Principal's Problem Solving Capacities," *Educational Leadership*, 45(September):38–41.

NOREEN B. GARMAN
NELSON L. HAGGERSON

3

Philosophic Considerations in the Practice of Clinical Supervision

In the world of supervisory practice philosophy is remote, if not absent, from mainstream discourse. Textbooks and coursework in supervision generally ignore philosophic considerations. Practitioners often complain that the lofty abstractions of philosophers and social theorists are difficult to translate into practical guidelines that influence everyday action. Practice is thought of as separate from the philosophic abstractions of the academic world. In part this may be a consequence of the way in which practice is construed. As Sergiovanni (1982) pointed out, "mainstream thought continues its quest to develop a science or technology of classroom supervision embedded in the measurement and evaluation disciplines." The technology metaphors suggest that there are behaviors and guides that can be "applied" to our practice. In writing about practice, many authors use technological language, and it is this construal of practice that fosters the "application mentality," that is, we think of concepts and skills as being applied to supervisory action.

It is our position that a more useful way to think about practice is to say that we, as practitioners, "embody" certain skills and orientations that influence our action in lived experiences. Furthermore, supervisory practice has to do with social interactions. Two people are continually talking to one another, taking positions, attempting to communicate, to convince each other by their stance and counterstance. It is in the stance and counterstance of the participants, the way in which we articulate our mental and emotional positions adopted *with respect to something*, that we can begin to understand the nuances of supervisory practice. For our purposes, it is useful to consider that each one of us comes to our judgements and actions through our philosophic orienta-

37

tion. In other words, we embody philosophic positions that influence our action.

In this chapter we discuss the notion of orientation as it relates to supervisory practice. We argue in the first section that philosophic considerations are not lofty abstractions, but rather that they exert influence on the stance we take in particular situations. In the second section we draw from moral philosophy and posit that clinical supervision is a moral endeavor and that the clinical supervisor is a moral agent.

PHILOSOPHIC ORIENTATION

Philosophic orientations are embedded in our everyday conversations. For instance, in the teachers' cafeteria the other day there was an interesting conversation between a teacher and principal. The previous day they had attended an all-day workshop about cooperative learning. The principal asked the typical supervisor question, "How did you feel about the workshop?"

The teacher said, "Well, first of all, I loved getting away from the building and the kids . . . right about now I really needed the break and the other teachers were interesting to talk to. About the cooperative learning model . . . well I have some mixed feelings. You know, I do project groups in my class, the kids work together on a project in small groups, and I really like the way it goes . . . but I don't have the groups competing against each other. In the cooperative learning model, the groups compete against one another. I really don't agree with that."

The principal said, "Well, you know, the cooperative learning model comes from research. They have hundreds of studies to prove that the competitive model really works better."

The teacher said, "Yeah, well I suppose I can't argue with research, but, well I know what works with my kids." Then she paused. "You know, what really gets me about this stuff . . . every time we have one of these days, we hear about ideas from research and it makes me feel like what I do in my class doesn't really count very much. The message is, we better start doing something from the workshop. And then you come into class with clinical supervision to see whether we're doing it or not."

The principal answered, "Well, I suppose that's what professional development is. All professionals, like lawyers and doctors, keep upgrading their skills as long as they're in practice."

In the lunchroom conversation we hear a teacher's expression of delight in being away from the classroom, the relief from the daily routine of schooling, of being able to converse with colleagues. We learn that she uses her own form of cooperative learning yet questions the external model being offered in the name of research. We hear her trying to say that the workshop format and subsequent supervision diminishes what she does as a teacher. We hear a principal who needs to support his position by appealing to the authority of research. He may, indeed, be frustrated by the skepticism—and often resistance—generated from teachers about their own progress. (Doctors and lawyers continue to learn without such resistance, he implies.)

If we go a bit deeper into the interpretation we begin to enter the realm of philosophic considerations. The differences reflected in the teacher/supervisor conversation can be attributed to philosophic considerations often referred to as different "ways of knowing." Each of us comes to our judgements and actions through our philosophic orientation. The term "orientation" refers to the specific ways in which an individual looks at the world. On the surface, it includes the notions of point of view, perspective, a person's outlook in relation to events and ideas.

Van Manen (1977) reminds us that "underlying every orientation is a definite epistemology, axiology, and ontology." These high-sounding philosophic terms literally mean that a person's orientation is composed of what he/she believes to be true, to be valuable, and to be real. "An orientation," Van Manen says, "has the uncanny quality of encapsulating the person who has learned to adopt it." In supervision the issue of epistemological legitimacy is a critical one. Each person's orientation provides him/her with rules for legitimacy in action. In the lunchroom conversation, for instance, one can ask, where does the legitimacy reside in a particular "model" of cooperative learning? The teacher appeals to pragmatic authority when she uses her experience in saying, "I don't believe that competition is the best approach" while the principal evokes scientific authority, responding with "research says," in his claim for legitimacy.

In this scenario the stance of the teacher is grounded in her pragmatic sense. She "knows" what works through her years of experience in the classroom. The principal's scientific counterstance may be a result of his concern that the teacher's way of teaching from experience is narrow and habitual and he would like to see her change her perspective. On the other hand, the principal may be heavily invested in his own position. He was "inserviced" in a particular teaching model and is linking his version of clinical supervision to this model. Furthermore, in his mind his clinical supervision skill depends on his "knowing" what good teaching is.

There is a substantial difference between these two positions. They are not mere differences of opinion, but rather epistemological conflict. That is, the differences grow from what each takes to be true (knowing from experience vs. scientific legitimacy). In this case, it is the principal, as supervisor, who is on shakier ground. His scientific "knowing" about teaching is limited to brief inservice training. He may have been told about the research, but the chances are he would not have read the "hundreds of studies" he refers to. Yet, in this scenario, the teacher with a pragmatist stance (I know from experience) and the principal with a scientific realist counterstance (I've learned what good teaching is) are participants in one of the most common dialogues in clinical supervision.

In the typical dialogue mentioned above, there are also ontological considerations based on one's philosophic orientation. Ontological considerations are those that explore the nature of existence. They are concerned with what it means to *be* (Palmer, 1962). Heidegger (1962) calls ontology the phenomenology of being. Within this notion is the issue of reality—what we take to be the "real world" of our existence.

The significance of one's reality orientation in supervision is poignantly revealed in an article entitled "Observations" by Jane Juska (1991). In it she describes her experiences with her principal as he observes her classroom. Her lesson on the day of observation focuses on logs that students have prepared, with written comments about their reading. She has them working in small groups to discuss their log entries. As she describes her supervisor, "From his station at the desk nearest the door, my principal writes furiously, his notes already covering three pages of yellow foolscap." In her writing she recognizes the proclivity of her principal to see her class through his own lens and laments, "all these scientific techniques that have so helped the business world can also help students learn, my principal has been told." She expresses genuine caring for her principal and understands his position, yet in a poignant wish she says:

> I want him to stop writing and simply sense the rightness or wrongness of what's happening in my classroom. I want him to say to me, when it's

true, "I liked being in your classroom. It's a safe place for students to learn. I could see them thinking." And then I want him to *write that down* on those state forms so that everyone knows that teaching is not a scientific activity: that real learning happens inside a student, not outside; and that intelligence, intuition, sensitivity, and common sense are vital tools for teachers and administrators alike. (p. 470)

Jane Juska is expressing her concern as an ontological explanation, wishing that the principal might see, however dimly, her reality of the classrom events. While she feels that she is able to see her classroom through her principal's eyes, she doesn't think that he has seen it through hers. She would like him to consider the different sense of being, of becoming part of the flow of the learning energy that she felt with her students. In her final statement, Jane Juska reveals the irony of her discovery. "Now, as I write this," she says, "it occurs to me that my principal's job ought to be the same as the one I gave my students: to observe, record, and then react as a human being." She is asking for her supervisor to find a way of coming to know the world she considers real, the world that reflects her orientation.

STRIVING FOR WISDOM

In the previous section we have posited that one's philosophic orientation influences one's actions. In supervisory exchanges the stance and counterstance of the participants embody these powerful positions. The consequences of supervisory exchanges represent the success or failure of clinical supervision. In order to face each situation, then, it is imperative that the supervisor have a sense of his/her philosophic orientation and recognize that it is in striving for wisdom that these matters are addressed. [It is interesting that the term "philosophy" derives from two Greek words: *philia* (love) and *sophia* (wisdom).] Wisdom is the quality upon which the supervisor must draw for action. One vivid entry (*Random House Dictionary*, 1987) defines wisdom as "knowledge of what is true or right coupled with just judgement as to action." We would add that "what is true or right" should be taken as tentative, reflective knowledge rather than certainty.

Clinical supervision is about relationships, and schools, as bureaucratic institutions, support hierarchical relationships. Those of us who write about clinical supervision try very hard to accommodate, discourage, or discount the hierarchical nature of the supervisor-teacher relationship. But even when two colleagues get together to observe each other's lessons, the hierarchy prevails. Within this situation it is the teacher's performance, her/his professional lifeblood that is being scrutinized and challenged. The responsibility of the supervisor is to recognize that the teacher, as a human being, occupies a position of absolute value, one who can never be used as a means to an end, but who constitutes an end in himself/herself, one who has intrinsic dignity and worth. It takes all the caring and wisdom a supervisor can muster to meet the moral responsibility of this charge. Because of this basic nature of clinical supervision, then, we posit that clinical supervision is a moral endeavor and the clinical supervisor is a moral agent (as is the teacher) in the school.

CLINICAL SUPERVISION AS A MORAL ENDEAVOR

We base our contention that clinical supervision is a moral endeavor on the premise that educating children, youth, and adults is itself a moral process. As Dewey said, ". . . the educative process is all one with the moral process, since the latter is a continuous passage of experience from worse to better." Clinical supervision is, of course, a part of the educative process, hence part of the moral process, and it has a special mission of its own which is also a moral endeavor. That is, clinical supervision is concerned with one person meeting with another person (or persons) in an educational setting, with the intention to promote the professional growth of the teacher, or, as some prefer, to improve instruction through some form of action. Inherent in what we have said here is the fact that in the role of supervisor one has to make judgments about another person. Hence, the supervisor, in carrying responsibilities accruing to the process of supervising, is a moral agent. The so-called success of clinical supervision is dependent upon relationships among persons, as well as knowledge of and about teaching, learning, and subject matter.

The Supervisor as Moral Agent

We are using the traditional notion that to consider an action moral (or immoral) there is both an intention to act and an action toward "better" as opposed to "worse."[1] For our discussion here, we are assuming that the ongoing and primary "good" of an individual is growth towards responsible freedom (some are using the term "empowerment," but we prefer "responsible freedom"), and that this is balanced by the primary and ongoing "good" of society which is social justice. In these days of rampant individualism, we also look toward a "community" of responsibly free individuals who treat one another in socially just ways. Growth toward responsible freedom, social justice, and community, then, become the criteria of morality with the educative supervisory processes.

The clinical supervisor, acting as a moral agent in this venture, then, is responsible not only for the improvement of mathematics or language instruction, but for the moral progress of the teacher, the students, and her/his self. Sergiovanni and Starratt (1988) add to this list of responsibilities that of "directing moral action at the school as a moral entity." That is, they suggest that the supervisor has responsibility for striving for policies that promote the desired moral goals, and, at the same time, to work for the abolishment of policies that are repressive, or stand in the way of common goals.

A poignant issue of morality for the clinical supervisor, be they in a staff or line position, is that of authority which manifests itself in control. It is obvious that some supervisors use their authority to attempt to control the actions of the teacher; it is less obvious when the supervisor manipulates the teacher to do what the supervisor wants, but does so in a "democratic" way. The morality issue that arises here has to do with the goal, the intention, the action, and the consequences of the action.

Let's take the case of the principal (supervisor) who said, "Well, you know, the cooperative model comes from research. They have hundreds of studies to prove that the competitive model really works better." As well as having the responsibility to know what those researches were, of knowing whether they possibly generalized to this situation, the supervisor has to consider what to do if the teacher refuses to follow the suggestion or order. Does he threaten her? Try to persuade her to change? What if she calls him in to observe again and presents con-

---

[1]Intentionally keeping a student in ignorance that prevents growth toward the "better" is a form of immorality. Repression that keeps a teacher from doing something he/she knows works in a classroom, and intentionally keeps him/her from acting in a responsibly free way according to conscience, is another illustration of the "worse," hence immorality.

vincing evidence that her hunch was correct, at least for her current situation? Does he change his rating? What if he goes back to his office and opens up a new issue of a research journal which contradicts "what research said" in the last journal, or what the last entrepreneur who "inserviced" him said? Why must he have his way when the teacher has a different view, anyway? What happens to teacher morale when the teacher tells the other teachers in the lounge about the situation, about that "so and so dictator," about having to do what she knows won't work? What does all of this have to do with morality? The morality in this case has to do with the intentions and the actions with which the principal asserts his authority and control.

Keeping in mind the responsibilities and considerations of the clinical supervisor as moral agent, we now ask, "What approaches are called for which might make the relationships 'better,' i.e., more moral?" We consider them in the next section.

Clinical Supervision as a Moral Endeavor in a Democratic Society

Does all of this seem overwhelming? Perhaps, but in the larger picture it is really the processes of democracy that we are talking about. Those who become overwhelmed at the responsibilities of democracy give way to a dictatorship of one form or another, be it in the school, or in local, state, or national governments. Hence, we make no apology for advocating that we consider clinical supervision as a moral endeavor. What, besides the goals (criteria) of responsible freedom, social justice, and community, characterize our notion of the moral processes of supervision?

Reflection-in-Action

Schon (1983) has given us a current definition and many examples of "reflection-in-action." It means inquiring about our actions and our tacit knowing, and how we put them together in our practice. It means inquiring about our roles and our strategies and guessing what might work better, trying out our hunches, inquiring about what we have done, doing it again. This is actually a current way of using what Dewey wrote about as the "scientific method." The latter term has been greatly distorted from its earlier use by Dewey.

In 1920 Dewey wrote *Reconstruction in Philosophy*, in which he made the case for the subject matter of philosophy and the distinctive mission of philosophy growing out of "stresses and strains in the community life in which a given form of philosophy arises, and that, accordingly, its specific problems vary with the changes in human life that are always going on and that at times constitute a crisis and a turning point in human history." In keeping with the notion that philosophy derives its mission from the context in which we live and work, we are suggesting that supervision as a moral endeavor provides both the subject matter and the context in which to practice reflection-in-action. In other words the moral issues of authority and control, repression and emancipation, and freedom and social justice that we face in supervision are subject to the same reflection-in-action processes as are the knowledge issues with which we deal.

Schon (1983), taking the lead of Dewey, has not only elaborated the notion of reflection-in-action, but has written about the nature and education of the reflective practitioner. He began his important work, *The Reflective Practitioner*, with reference to the crisis of confidence in professional knowledge, and has said, in general, that this crisis cannot be solved from "on high," or by applying principles from the social sciences, but through reflection-in-action, in our practices. Like Dewey, Schon does not want to separate moral problems and issues and apply some esoteric philosophic analysis to them. They deserve and demand reflection-in-action, too.

Sergiovanni and Starratt (1988) refer to this process of reflection-in-action as "transactional supervision." They say:

> Transactional supervision takes place within an individual supervisory episode and within an organizational context. On an individual basis, that initially will involve what we have called the heuristics of moral action, namely the exploration of and agreement upon those procedures, ground rules, guidelines which both parties will follow in order to maintain the exchange on a moral plane. Once those are agreed upon, the supervisor and colleague must follow through and maintain those basic values of honesty, fair play, loyalty, etc. . . . . It means that the integrity of each person will be respected and their sense of professional autonomy honored. It also means that the supervisory episode will serve the larger purposes of the school, so that the transaction ultimately benefits the education of the children involved as well as serves some of the instrumental goals of the school, such as the improvement of good order

in the school and improved communication between teachers and curriculum directors. (pp. 222–223)

A major contribution of Sergiovanni and Starratt's (1988) transactional supervision to clinical supervision as a moral endeavor is that its very name indicates moral action, exploration by those involved in the ways they will establish and maintain their exchange of ideas, methods, and skills on a moral plane. It puts emphasis on negotiations, agreements, and ground rules—not on who is in power or what is the established hierarchy within the supervisory process. This leads to a question, however, of what might happen in case of irresolvable conflicts.

Irresolvable Conflicts

What happens when all forms of reflection-in-action that we generally think of, leave the supervisor (and teacher, school policy makers, et al.) with an irresolvable conflict? Can the supervisor force the issue and still act morally? In general such a question leads us to think about "sanctions."

Since our domain of operation is largely in the public schools we can't invoke the traditional religious (moral) sanctions to bring incompetence into line, nor do we want to invoke the sanctions of a patriarchal or hierarchical organization—the sanctions of demotion, of alienation, or humiliation—on those who are in irresolvable conflict. So what do these conditions regarding moral sanctions mean in supervisory relations in a democratic society?

We take our first cue from Dewey (1970) who advocates that the appropriate action in case of irresolvable conflicts is that which produces the "least undesirable results." In other words we need to look at and discuss the big picture, and be as certain as possible that what sanctions we use produce the best possible results for all concerned.

Another source that serves to provoke our thoughts, albeit providing mainly for the legal foundations of our society, is the federal Constitution. An early part of the Constitution provides for actions and structures protecting the "general welfare" of the people (society, community, etc.). The next to the last part of the Constitution is known as the Bill of Rights. It protects the rights of individuals in our society. When there is an irresolvable conflict between the general welfare and the rights of the individual, the Supreme Court ultimately decides which shall prevail. Our history shows that Supreme Court decisions are not only a function of interpretations of the law and the Constitution, but interpretations within a given time, at a given place. Those interpretations are often reversed or changed, given another set of conditions, circumstances, and judges.

Supervisors, acting as moral agents, need to provide and advocate similar ways to handle irresolvable moral conflicts, e.g., review committees, professional ethics committees, and due process procedures, many of which are in place through teacher contracts. These committees should be guided by the basic criteria of responsible freedom, social justice, and community, and their actions should adhere to the principle that their decisions should produce the least undesirable results.

Attitudes and Characteristics of the Supervisor as a Moral Agent

Collegiality

The term "collegiality" refers to the posture of the persons who become involved in supervision. It is a particular frame of mind one brings to educational encounters. Colleagiality, while often misused, is a prime attitude of those engaged in supervision as a moral endeavor, and provides a language for the degree of involvement in the supervisory encounter. These may also be thought of in terms of degrees of morality in the orientation we are describing here. They are: the "alienated critic," who has no disposition toward collegiality; the "neutral observer," who is neutral about the feelings of others in the encounter and who may lack compassion for others; the "connected participant," who has faith that together the supervisor and teacher can discover the kind of contributions they make to each other; and the "organic member," who is energized by being involved with other and self, and makes important contributions, discovering never-imagined potential in the supervisory relationship (Garman, 1982). The person in the supervisory relationship may be, in Bartell's (1982) terms, synergistic in their relationship. That is, the relationship is complementary.

Caring for and Caring about

Noddings (1984), Sarason (1985), and Hult (1980) discuss collegial relationships in terms of "caring." Hult (1980), using the works of Mayerhoff, Rogers, and others, writes in terms of "caring for" and "caring about." Caring about is a "given" to those in the helping professions, as it is in clinical supervision. The supervisor cares about teachers, about children, about teaching and learning, and about herself/himself. Caring for is something that can be taught and learned. It includes the human relations knowledge and skills that allow the practitioner to show empathy, to show concern, and to be a helper in the helping professions and in supervisory relationships. The caring process, according to Mayerhoff (Hult, 1980) is "helping the other to grow, where growing is understood as the development or actualization of self." These caring attitudes and processes are essential characteristics of the supervisor as moral agent.

Sarason (1985) came to the conclusion in his career-long studies that caring and compassion, while murky concepts, are essential characteristics of all clinicians. On the "worse" side of the morality continuum is lack of compassion. "It is the combined flaws of ignorance and lack of compassion that prevent us from making meaningful connections with those whom we find disagreeable" (Garman, 1982).

Collaboration

"Collaboration" describes the nature of the involvement between or among the people working in an educational alliance. An "educational alliance" includes at least four levels of involvement: nonworking involvement; working-acceptance involvement; involvement with genuine participation; and involvement with organic participation. These, too, are characteristics of supervision as the moral scenario presented here (Garman, 1982).

CONCLUDING STATEMENT

Ultimately supervisory practice is about carrying through a course of action based on compassion, wise understanding, and moral judgment. These are the basic attributes of the clinical supervisor. As we have mentioned, *philia* (love) and *sophia* (wisdom) form the etymology as well as the metaphor of the term philosophy. Caring and moral wisdom are the cornerstones of clinical supervision. It is up to the supervisor to help create the conditions for such a venture.

REFERENCES

Bartell, S. 1982. "In Support of Grounded Theory: One Researcher's Experience," *Review Journal of Philosophy and Social Science*, 7:1–2.

Dewey, J. 1957. *Reconstruction in Philosophy*. Boston: Beacon Press (original edition, 1920 by H. Holt & Co.).

Dewey, J. 1970. *Characters and Events: Popular Essays in Social and Political Philosophy, Vol. 2*, J. Ratner, ed., New York: Octagon Books.

Garman, N. 1982. "The Clinical Approach to Supervision," in *Supervision of Teaching, Chapter 3*, T. Sergiovanni, ed., Alexandria, VA: Association for Supervision and Curriculum Development, pp. 35–52.

Heidegger, M. 1962. *Being and Time*. New York: Harper & Row.

Hult, R. 1980. "On Pedagogical Caring," *Educational Theory*, 29(3):237–243.

Juska, J. 1991. "Observations," *Phi Delta Kappan*, 72(6):468–470.

Noddings, N. 1984. *Caring: A Feminine Approach to Ethics and Moral Education*. Berkeley: University of California Press.

Palmer, R. 1962. *Hermeneutics: Interpretation Theory in Schleiermacher, Dilthey, Heidegger, and Gadamer*. Evanston, IL: Northwestern University Press.

1987. *Random House Dictionary of the English Language, Second Edition, Unabridged*. New York: Random House Publishers.

Sarason, S. 1985. *Caring and Compassion in Clinical Practice*. San Francisco: Jossey-Bass Publishers.

Schon, D. 1983. *The Reflective Practitioner: How Professionals Think in Action*. New York: Basic Books.

Sergiovanni, T. "Supervision and Evaluation: Interpretive and Critical Perspectives," paper at the Council of Professors of Instructional Supervision Fall Meeting, November 12, 1982.

Sergiovanni, T. and R. Starratt. 1988. *Supervision: Human Perspectives, Fourth Edition*. New York: McGraw-Hill.

Van Manen, M. 1977. "Linking Ways of Knowing with Ways of Being Practical," *Curriculum Inquiry*, 6(3):205–229.

White, M. 1981. *What Is and What Ought to Be: An Essay on Ethics and Epistemology*. New York: Oxford University Press.

CARL D. GLICKMAN
EMILY CALHOUN
JO ROBERTS

4

Clinical Supervision within the School as the Center of Inquiry

SPIRIT AND BODY

Clinical supervision as it is generally being used for observing and giving feedback to individual teachers falls far short of its potential to effect school change. Goldhammer (1969) and Cogan (1973) originally wrote about clinical supervision as a collegial, team endeavor to support teachers in complementing and reinforcing each other for attaining a higher purpose in education. One cannot help being moved by the first chapter of Goldhammer's classic work *Clinical Supervision*. In this chapter, in painfully direct terms, he wrote about the lack of moral underpinnings of public school teaching. Clinical supervision was, in his mind, to be a process to help teachers become more aware of themselves, their students, and the nature of teaching and learning. Issues of value, goodness, and collective actions to rectify public education were at the heart of the work.

More than twenty years later, clinical supervision is most often promoted as a tool, consisting of procedural steps, with an identified template of classroom observation measures, and guidelines for operating postconferences to establish teacher competence. Using clinical supervision as a mechanism for evaluating an individual teacher's worth is to keep the body and lose the spirit of the original endeavor. In the reemergence of perceived public school inadequacies and cries for restructuring, decentralizing, and professionalizing the work of teachers and schools, the spirit of clinical supervision as a problematizing, action research endeavor around the moral work of teaching and learning needs to be reclaimed. The body may become less important as the spirit seeps into the everyday, ongoing work of inquiry-oriented and

51

democratically operated school improvement efforts. Indeed, the spirit may even supersede the term "clinical supervision." After all, what Goldhammer and Cogan believed to be important was to find ways of involving teachers and schools in raising questions about their present practices and to have avenues for exploring answers to possible improvement.

THE SCHOOL AS THE CENTER OF INQUIRY

Each faculty member in an inquiry school functions like a member of an exploratory team who supports his/her colleagues in accomplishing the goals of the mission. Just as good teachers attend to the individual and social growth of students, so does a staff member in an inquiry-oriented school accept individual responsibility for improving learning in his/her classroom and collective responsibility for improving the learning environment for all persons in the school. The work of inquiry schools is a stream of posing questions, making decisions, and posing more questions about current instructional practices. Such work is not normative in most schools (Glickman, 1990). To bring about such instructional dialogue, a school must be aware that individual and collective decisions about what is worthy to teach and how to improve teaching and learning are integral parts of their ongoing existence. With awareness must come support, coordination, and preparation so that talk turns into ideas, and ideas turn into actions.

A major function of clinical supervision should be to integrate ideas into classroom actions with schoolwide endeavors of curriculum development, staff development, action research, program evaluation, and group development. Let's be clear: clinical supervision as a format for working with individual teachers that is separate from the overarching educational goals of the schools, can perhaps help improve some individual classrooms but will reinforce the separation and fragmentation of school effort. The real spirit of clinical supervision as a critical inquiry practice around teaching and learning can help with a school's moral direction and give cohesion, support, and thrust to its actions.

This chapter provides an orientation for linking clinical supervision with group activity toward common school goals, staff development programs, and curriculum development. The focus of school development in this chapter is on altering teaching and learning patterns within the complex fabric of work activity to enhance student learning.

Most educational reform efforts make great noise, stay around for three to five years, and make no enduring, structural changes in classroom and school teaching (Cuban, 1989). However, the spirit of clinical supervision used in the context of the entire school has the promise to move reform into the classroom.

CLINICAL SUPERVISION AS STRUCTURAL SUPPORT FOR SCHOOL IMPROVEMENT

Bemoaning the mediocrity of American schools, reports of the early 1980s sparked a series of legislative initiatives, regulations, and mandates aimed at improving school operations. For more than two decades, educators have been subjected to periodically tightened external controls, all of which have implied that local teachers and administrators are the source of school problems. The result of such legislative reform has been little improvement in student learning and an increase in the dropout rate.

In the past few years, an empowerment reform movement has been gaining ascendancy (Wise, 1988), and site-based management, restructuring, and shared governance have placed the local school at the center of inquiry. In such a bottom-up view of school reform, one that supports deregulation and a variety of approaches determined by teachers and administrators, professional educators are seen as the primary instructional decision makers in the school. They must be given choice and responsibility to make collective, informed decisions about teaching practice. True restructuring in our schools can come about only through grass-roots efforts by educators who themselves are seen as the solution rather than as the problem for improving education. In the same way, clinical supervision as proposed here reflects internal control, instead of external authority.

We propose a return to the spirit of clinical supervision to include not only direct instructional assistance to teachers, but to acknowledge teachers as providers of these clinical supervisory functions for each other, and to use the process as a subset of what becomes part of individual schoolwide improvement.

CLINICAL SUPERVISION: DEFINITION, GOALS, AND ROLES

Clinical supervision—generally outlined as a sequence of pre-conference, observation, post-observation analysis, postconference, and critique—may be more accurately viewed as a form of direct assistance which ensures that teachers are involved as part of a collective staff, receive feedback, and are not left alone. It has been shown that teachers who receive the most classroom feedback are also most satisfied with teaching (Dornbush and Scott, 1975; Natriello, 1982). Yet, teachers generally receive little supervisory support, and when they seek it, they tend to prefer the assistance of fellow teachers rather than those in formal supervisory or administrative roles (Lortie, 1975). Since teachers seek out each other for assistance, a recent development is to take advantage of this natural tendency and use it as a support for school improvement. Clinical supervision is used in inquiry schools under such terms as peer supervision, peer coaching, and reflective partners.

Clinical supervision can provide a structure for promoting school improvement. Clinical supervision can become a powerful way to look at what goes on in classrooms and in the school, as well as a powerful way to support schoolwide staff development, including transfer of training into classrooms after shared learning experiences (Joyce and Showers, 1988). Clinical supervision is also a way to support and assess curriculum changes. Multiple initiatives can become cohesive instead of fragmentary. As teachers learn to implement new curriculum, teaching materials, and activities, clinical supervision can be used as a process for shared feedback and curriculum revision. The clinical supervisory process helps people understand each other, reinforce what they believe about education, formulate further questions about classroom practice, decide what to promote, talk about instruction, receive feedback that is not evaluative, and gather data related to instructional improvement.

In an inquiry-oriented school, clinical supervision is position free, standing beyond the implications of hierarchical superiority and inferiority embedded in traditional supervisory practices. Teachers, supervisors, and administrators—through professional development, peer assistance, professional reflective practice, or shared governance—can facilitate clinical supervision activities because the underlying spirit of this approach connotes a process of working together and of expanded awareness, not a process of working "on" or "over" someone. It is far different from the traditional view of supervision.

In an inquiry-oriented school, the role of those in official leadership positions is to assist in articulation, provide resources, and coordinate the support of purposeful activity. Through formal organizational roles, an educational leader can provide focus, structure, and time for teachers to be engaged in dialogue, debate, research, decisions, and actions about instruction. Without focus, teachers will not discuss teaching, because it has not been an accepted norm for discussion in most schools. Without structure, there are no clear apparatus, procedures, and rules for how decisions are made and implemented. Without time, there is no functional or symbolic expression of the fact that teachers have the capacity to make collective and wise instructional decisions on behalf of students.

Clinical supervision is often misunderstood or enacted merely as a program for the evaluation of teachers. While its format can be a useful tool for teacher evaluation, it becomes clinical evaluation, not clinical supervision. More often it becomes perceived in this way.

> For much of my career, supervision has been a highly personalized, position specific relationship, usually unpredictable but rulebound, undefinable but strict, and worthless, except for trying to get what one wants. (personal communication from a teacher of eighteen years)

Those who originated clinical supervision intended it to be a supportive process that has as its goal the improvement of student learning through purposeful interaction among faculty members. This clinical supervision process is a way in which teachers and formal leaders can engage in mutual problem solving relevant to individual students, groups, and classes; can plan and conduct classroom-based research to answer real world questions; and can experiment with instructional innovations that have great potential. The process of clinical supervision in its problematizing, inquiry, action research approach to classroom teaching is a subset to the process of engaging teachers in decisions about schoolwide teaching.

WALKING INTO THE INQUIRY SCHOOL

In schools where teachers and teaching are valued, there exists joint planning, frequent observation of instruction, and joint analysis of instruction. There is someone for teachers to talk with about immediate and long-range instructional concerns, and there is someone(s) who nurtures and helps create an intellectually stimulating environment for the teacher.

Usually, there is a school leader or leaders (principal, assistant, instructional lead teacher, department head, grade level chair, etc.) who serves as a link to school or central office administration and other external resources (Hall and Hord, 1987). As a professional resource, the leader(s) can be a catalyst for change by setting the stage for instructional success (Pajak, 1989). They work with teachers to ensure that various instructional tasks are linked together to support the educational goals of the school. Direct assistance to teachers is connected to curriculum development, staff development, action research, and group development. As a result, persons do not see these various tasks competing with each other, but see them instead as complementary tasks for providing collective thrust to accomplishing the educational goals of the school.

In the public schools we have worked with for the past seven years, we have seen documented success in student achievement and attitudes, improvement in teachers' critical thought and school climate, and increased parent satisfaction. The results of these efforts—currently involving twenty-eight elementary, middle, and secondary schools in our Program for School Improvement (PSI) and League of Professional Schools (LPS)—indicate that clinical supervision can be a powerful tool of inquiry goal setting and unifying efforts of implementation of instructional innovations.

The schools, via their school councils, operate a shared governance system that involves teachers as majority stakeholders and chairpersons of schoolwide instructional initiatives (Glickman, 1990). The premises of decision making that each of our schools learn to operate are:

(1) Everyone in a school who wishes to be involved in the schoolwide decision-making process can be.

(2) Anyone who does not wish to be involved in such decision making, does not have to be.

(3) Once a decision is made, all in the school must support the implementation.

The beginning decisions are ones of setting educational priorities. This is done by school councils and ad hoc study groups who grapple with questions about data and action research.

(1) What data are already in existence in our schools that could better inform us about the current effects of our instructional program on students?
(2) What other data would we like to gather about the current effects of our instructional program on students that would help us further in setting priorities?

The answers to question number one tend to be more quantifiable (standardized tests, course success rates, retention rates, climate surveys, attendance, parent surveys). The answers to question number two tend to be more observational and qualitative (classroom observations, student exhibits, student portfolios, student interviews). The use of clinical supervision by peers is a way of gathering baseline observational data of what each individual teacher has set as classroom teaching priorities and what has been transpiring as experimentation in each classroom.

After the data-gathering and goal-setting processes are complete and the school has clear goals, then the action planning by the shared governance process takes place. The answers to the following questions are discussed, debated, and resolved.

(1) What curriculum changes are needed?
(2) What inservice do we need for ourselves?
(3) What types of group sharing and problem sharing are needed as we implement schoolwide change?
(4) What forms of clinical assistance do we need to provide for each other?
(5) What further data do we need to collect to inform us of our effect to achieve our goals?

Therefore, in the action research and planning phase, clinical supervision becomes a way for individual teachers to receive feedback on classroom efforts to achieve schoolwide instructional priorities.

If the reader follows this line of reasoning, clinical supervision becomes a way to support the individual teacher's growth in communal activity. This does not mean that every teacher will make the same changes. It does mean that every teacher will be challenged to think through school priorities, design individual activity within the school priorities, and be assisted with other sets of eyes and minds, to help clarify, refine, assess, and think through future actions. The spirit of clinical supervision as a reflective action research activity guides individual teachers to study their own aims, their actions, and their effects on students within the context of school aspiration.

Hopefully a few examples will illustrate this. An elementary school prioritizes having students learn to transfer knowledge across subject areas. It makes curricular changes to integrate subject matter and uses a clinical process among peers as part of the observations to assist teachers in the implementation of integrated curriculum. A middle school desires that students learn to be more cooperative, and so it engages in a two-year staff development program using cooperative learning strategies, and clinical supervision is used to transfer training of the cooperative learning strategies into the classroom. A high school becomes committed to students learning to behave according to moral and democratic principles, and clinical supervision is used as a process to give feedback to teachers as they attempt new ways to involve students in greater decision-making responsibilities in their classrooms. Another high school values students learning to be risk takers and sets up a clinical process to assist teachers to identify, implement, and support their own risk taking in their classrooms.

MAKING THE POSSIBLE, PROBABLE

The examples are endless. The difference is that inquiry schools use clinical supervision as individual assistance to teachers to learn more about their capabilities to provide good education. Conventional schools often misapply clinical supervision as a tool to mandate and prescribe teacher practices. Inquiry-centered schools use a clinical process as part of the formal districtwide policies involving professional development, as part of their school-based staff development allocations, and as part of informally arranging for teachers to work together.

What these schools have in common, is not what they do, but how they do it (Fullan, 1990). Inquiry schools recognize teachers as equals (with administrators) in decisions about educational worth, support debate over instructional issues, and implement decisions (not without controversy). These schools "test" themselves to see if their decisions are correct, they collect data on changes in students, and they reassess and adjust their plans as they find themselves moving toward or away from their goals. Informed judgment, rather than external prescription, is their mode of decision making. Most importantly, inquiry about professional work, with all of its trials and tribulations, engages educators' minds and souls and infuses a school with the sense of what is possible. Recapturing the original spirit of the clinical process helps make the possible, probable.

REFERENCES

Cogan, M. 1973. *Clinical Supervision*. Boston: Houghton Mifflin.

Cuban, L. 1989. "The 'At Risk' Label and the Problem of Urban School Reform," *Phi Delta Kappan*, 70(10):780–784, 799–801.

Dornbush, S. M. and W. R. Scott. 1975. *Evaluation and the Exercise of Authority*. San Francisco: Jossey-Bass.

Fullan, M. G. 1990. "Staff Development, Innovation, and Institutional Development," in *Changing School Culture through Staff Development*, B. Joyce, ed., Alexandria, VA: ASCD.

Glickman, C. D. 1990. *Supervision of Instruction: A Developmental Approach, Second Edition*. Boston: Allyn and Bacon.

Goldhammer, R. 1969. *Clinical Supervision: Special Methods for the Supervision of Teachers*. New York: Holt, Rinehart and Winston.

Hall, G. E. and S. M. Hord. 1987. *Change in Schools: Facilitating the Process*. Albany: State University of New York Press.

Joyce, B. and B. Showers. 1988. *Student Achievement through Staff Development*. New York: Longman.

Lortie, D. C. 1975. *School Teacher: A Sociological Study*. Chicago: University of Chicago Press.

Natriello, G. "The Impact of the Evaluation of Teaching on Teacher Effect and Effectiveness," paper presented at the annual meeting of the American Educational Research Association, New York, March, 1982.

Pajak, E. 1989. *The Central Office Supervisor of Curriculum and Instruction: Setting the Stage for Success*. Boston: Allyn and Bacon.

Wiggins, G. 1989. "A True Test: Toward More Authentic and Equitable Assessment," *Phi Delta Kappan*, 70(9):703–713.

Wise, A. 1988. "The Two Conflicting Trends in School Reform. Legislated Learning Revisited," *Phi Delta Kappan*, 69(5):328–333.

HELEN M. HAZI

5

The Legal Dimension of the Practice of Clinical Supervision

Beginning with *Brown v. Board of Education* and continuing in the three decades that have followed, public education has been subject to legal interpretation and limit. During the 1960s and 1970s educators went to the courts to attempt to remedy problems with teacher rights, free speech, desegregation, school funding, and malpractice. While the courts were once considered to be the central focus for such reform, state boards of education and legislatures have become key actors in school reform of the 1980s. Certification, competency testing, career ladders, and increased graduation requirements have been among the reform activities enacted by the states in the name of upgrading teaching quality and student achievement.

During these same decades legislation, litigation, and regulation have accumulated in various states to indicate that supervisory practice has not escaped legal interpretation and limit. Although supervision may not always have been the target, limits to practice have, nonetheless, been a consequence.[1] With a vigilant watch and careful analysis, these limits can be spotted in a state.

---

[1]Although it is beyond the scope of this chapter to explicate how supervision is indirectly affected, one example might briefly illustrate. Career ladder and teacher preparation programs were popular initiatives in the 1980s to address the perceived problem of teacher quality. When such initiatives are in place, teacher evaluation practices are consequently changed, since instruments are needed to identify those who can exit programs or ascend ladders. Since evaluation and supervision are inextricably linked, such instruments become woven into local supervisory practice. Also, some states intentionally disguise evaluation reform as a supervision initiative to diminish the threat evaluation poses to teachers (e.g., in Pennsylvania see Garman and Hazi, 1988). Along with this same tide, clinical supervision has become a popular practice for its promise of helping to improve teaching practice (sometimes with little or no cost).

The purpose of this chapter is to present examples of limits on supervisory practice in general and clinical supervision in particular. There are two kinds: limits due to lack of legal definition, and those due to legal-based incidents of practice. Because of the increased activity of grievants, litigants, legislators, and state boards, those concerned with the practice and preparation of supervisors can no longer believe that law and policy represent marginal influences to be dealt with from time to time. Rather, we should realize that the field of instructional supervision has a legal dimension to its practice.

Before I present examples of limits, I'd like to attempt to demystify "the law" for those who believe that only trained lawyers can understand it. (Indeed, some of my colleagues in the Council of Professors of Instructional Supervision are always amazed to learn that I am not yet a lawyer.) I've made a transition in how I think law relates to the field of supervision.

When I was a practicing supervisor, I was excluded from collective bargaining (being "neither fish nor fowl," neither management nor teacher), yet I faced a contract that had limits on my practice. No one consulted me about contract provisions on observations, curriculum committees, or the inservice council—all integral aspects of my practice! I viewed the law (at that time, collective bargaining law) as some force external to my practice, and thus beyond my control, as it has been characterized by some writings in the field.[2] I was alienated because I did not always understand litigation, legislation, and regulation. I was angry because judges and lawmakers—who were not members of my profession—issued decisions and formulated rules that controlled my practice. Also, by viewing law as some external force, I only paid attention when it impacted my practice, and tended to see only isolated incidents.[3]

[2]In general, references to law and legal issues in writings of the field have been scant over the years. Prior to the 1960s there was little, if any, mention of how law affects practice, since it was only during this decade that educators saw an increase of legislation and litigation concerning education. Commencing with the 1960s, law gains mention as a social force (e.g., Van Til, 1965), and writers like Eye et al. (1971) and Harris (1985) give law a place in their work, albeit minor. As a result of the increased regulation of school reform efforts, writers like Alfonso et al. (1981), Rubin (1982), and Tanner and Tanner (1987) begin to include information on how specific laws impact supervisory practice in their writings about the field.

[3]In some instances, the legal dimension of supervisory practice is conspicuous by its absence. For example, writers like Glickman and Bey (1990) omit it from their recent synthesis of research on supervision in both inservice and preservice settings, as does Pajak (1989) in his development of a proficiency examination for supervisors.

Now I'm teaching at a university and practicing supervision by observing administrators as they prepare for practice. I'm also doing research[4] which allows me to see beyond an individual's practice. Now I think about law as a dimension of supervisory practice like its history and techniques. I see that laws cumulatively contribute to the overall evolution of supervision over time — its definition, its knowledge base, and its practice.[5] Law defines, as well as limits, a field. Although it may not always be apparent to the casual observer how law shapes practice in a state, its continual monitoring will, nonetheless, demonstrate that it does. This chapter will show some of law's cumulative effects on the field of instructional supervision.

LIMITS DUE TO LACK OF LEGAL DEFINITION

A legal definition explains a role or function, and demonstrates how that role differs from others. It provides a legal identity or standing before the law. Legal definition becomes critical when supervisors challenge employment practices such as their own demotions and layoffs in court. An analysis of school codes in selected states reveals considerable confusion about their role and function.

An explicit definition for public school supervisors is more likely absent in school codes. When supervisors are mentioned, it is usually by affiliation with administrators, with teachers, or with other employees.

---

[4]More specifically, I have identified national trends in the legal definition of supervisor (Hazi, 1982, 1984), administrator competency testing (Hazi, 1986a), supervisory certification (Hazi, 1985a), educational malpractice (Hazi, 1986b), and have followed the saga of West Virginia's school finance case, which prescribed the state's curriculum (Hazi, 1983, 1985b, 1989a). I have also explicated critical incidents of practice, such as a legal control of supervisory practice through collective bargaining agreements (Hazi, 1980), a teacher evaluation movement in Pennsylvania, i.e., the Madeline Hunter movement (Garman and Hazi, 1988), scientific practices in teacher evaluation (Hazi and Garman, 1988), grievances filed against a supervisor in New Jersey (Hazi et al., 1990), and the use of a performance-based pay instrument in Florida (Hazi, 1989b).

[5]Nolte (1984) estimates that it can take at least one generation before the impact of some laws can be seen. He uses civil rights as an example:

> First, a minority individual or class of deprived individuals challenges its treatment in court and wins. Second, a period of time elapses during which the decision is being enforced and new adjustments made in the treatment of the minority individual or class. Finally, over time, the new value is accepted by the majority and enacted into law through majoritarian legislation by the Congress or the various legislatures, becoming in effect official governmental policy on a national scale. (p. 99)

Most often supervisors lack an identity that distinguishes them from other public school employees. Instead, they are "legally appended" to others and represent the "lost tribe" of public school professionals (Hazi, 1984).[6]

One example of the importance of legal definition comes from the past. Because of the stigma attached to supervision as fault-finding in the 1930s, there was for many years a boycott against the use of the word "supervisor" in job titles (Spears, 1953). In addition to a boycott, in West Virginia supervisors were legally outlawed from the schools.

In the midst of the Depression of 1933, the County Unit Act, which consolidated the 391 school districts into the fifty-five that West Virginia has today, also intentionally banned supervisors from the public schools: "In no case shall the board of education have authority to employ a supervisor, whether by that name or any other name" [*Supplement to the West Virginia Code of 1932*, 1933 (see "References" section)]. The intent of this legislation was to help eliminate extra administrative personnel affected by school consolidation (Scott, 1954).

After 1941, when the West Virginia legislature deleted this provision, supervisors could become employed once again. However, it was not until 1949 that the legislature provided for their lawful employment by

---

[6]Some might think that certification regulations provide supervisors with a legal identity. However, an analysis of these regulations indicates the opposite. Although all but nine states issue certificates that cover supervisors, a profile of regulations shows supervisors are more often generalists with a certificate that includes "supervisor" in the title, who have taught at least three years, who have averaged thirty hours of course work, and who possess any masters degree. Thus, certification regulations portray supervisors as administrators rather than as a specialty distinct from administration (Hazi, 1985a).

Collective bargaining law has also added to the confusion of legal identity, since supervisors are usually defined in labor as:

any individual having authority in the interest of the employer to hire, transfer, suspend, layoff, recall, promote, discharge, assign, reward, or discipline other employees or responsibly direct them or adjust their grievances; or to a substantial degree effectively recommend such action, if in connection with the foregoing, the exercise of such authority is not merely routine or clerical in nature but calls for the use of independent judgment. (Hazi, 1982)

Thus, some states have ambitious definitions of supervisors in school codes, yet quite explicit definitions of supervisors in collective bargaining statutes, with never the 'twain meeting. There has, as yet, been no incident that has brought these two separate laws in juxtaposition where their conflict would become apparent. Perhaps future efforts that challenge site-based management practices may provide a forum to examine this legal tension.

the following: "The board, upon the recommendation of the county superintendent, shall have authority to employ such general and special supervisors or directors of instruction and of such other educational activities as may be deemed necessary" [*The West Virginia Code of 1949*, 1949 (see "References" section)].

When a definition was issued in 1969, supervisors were provided with standing and an identity that differentiated them from other public school professionals. A supervisor is "the professional educator who, *whether by this or other appropriate title* [emphasis added], is responsible for working primarily in the field with professional and/or other personnel in instructional and other school improvement" [West Virginia School Code, 18A-1-1-(3)]. Because of this definition, supervisors in West Virginia have a competency test and special certification that differentiates them from teachers, principals, and superintendents. The phrase, "whether by this or other appropriate title," within the current definition is a reminder that supervisors were once legally outlawed in the state regardless of job title.

Although this incident seems distant and moot, four contemporary examples address the importance of legal identity. Although the first example refers to teachers, and not supervisors, it serves to illustrate one effect of omission from legislation. Recent legislation in West Virginia protects retired public employees from losing their pensions when they serve on public boards. Retired public employees can retain their pensions while on boards, as long as they refuse the per diem pay. Because "teachers" (and other public school positions like supervisors) were not specifically mentioned in the bill, retired teachers cannot serve on boards of education without losing their pensions ("Pension law excludes teachers . . .," 1990).

Another example is from California, the first known state to mandate a type of supervision through legislation. This example illustrates that law has the power to promote a type of practice. In 1982, California enacted legislation for administrator training and evaluation and promoted clinical supervision:

> Any school district, county superintendent of schools, or consortium of those entities shall be eligible for funds in order to establish an administrator training and evaluation program, which shall provide to school administrators support and development activities designed to improve *clinical supervision skills* [emphasis added]. (Hazi, 1987, p. 16)

The bill came from a task force report on the improvement of preservice and inservice for public school administrators and may have been advocated by the state's association for administrators and departments of education. When the bill was written, clinical supervision was thought to have meant a general process in which a principal helps teachers to grow and reviews their performance; not a specific set of assumptions about teachers and techniques excluding other types of supervision.[7]

Although it had come to have a generic meaning in legislation, it served to promote a specific version of clinical supervision in practice. Because of the popularity of Madeline Hunter, her version of clinical supervision became promoted in administrator training in California. Her version came to be used in the evaluation—not supervision—of teachers. At least two teachers were dismissed in the state when they did not follow her model of teaching, and ultimately the state teachers' association issued a warning urging teachers not to submit to any form of clinical supervision that had teacher evaluation as its hidden objective (Hazi, 1987).[8]

A third example of the effects of lack of definition is found in contracts. Supervisory practice can be legally defined and circumscribed by teacher collective bargaining contracts. An analysis of selected contracts in Pennsylvania revealed many detailed statements regarding teacher evaluation, staff development (or inservice), and the curriculum. For example, contracts specified the number and content of inservice days, the involvement of teachers and their association in planning inservice, the provision of orientations and supportive help for new teachers, teacher attendance at conferences and workshops, details about school visitations, and incentives for professional study (Hazi, 1980).

Ironically, provisions such as these can be included in teacher contracts because of a legal "catch 22." The courts have indicated that any item not explicitly defined or prohibited by state statute can be bargained. Because state statutes fail to explicitly define the instructional

[7]This is what gave rise to the East and West Coast versions of clinical supervision. The West Coast version became associated with Madeline Hunter who ascribed to the belief that supervision was synonymous with evaluation (for a representation of this belief see Hunter, 1988). The East Coast version became associated with Morris Cogan and Robert Goldhammer who fashioned their own conceptions as they worked with beginning teachers involved in the Harvard-Lexington MAT programs.

[8]Another case of teacher dismissal using Madeline Hunter's techniques was *Moran* (see Hazi and Garman, 1988).

supervisor, these matters can be legally defined in teacher contracts (Hazi, 1980).

A final example of the limits created by lack of definition is from *Carnahan v. Rochester City School District and the Rochester Teachers' Association*. This New York case shows that because of lack of legal definition, supervisors have limited employment rights.

During the 1986–87 school year the Rochester School District established the "Peer Assistant Review" program, a program that would release teachers to work as mentors to train and assist first-year teachers and tenured teachers experiencing difficulty. The Association of Supervisors and Administrators of Rochester (ASAR) filed suit in December 1986 against the school district and teachers' association, claiming twenty-two mentor teachers were performing supervisory and administrative tasks without the proper credentials and in violation of state regulations governing mentor programs. According to the lawyer for the district, administrators felt like "stepchildren" of the debate over improving teaching (Hazi, 1988).

The ASAR was in favor of the mentor teacher concept, but opposed how it was implemented. According to Pat Carnahan, a spokesperson for ASAR, this New York school district had a reputation for severely cutting back and eliminating supervisory positions. With the introduction of the mentor teacher program, they feared that more supervisory positions would be eliminated. Administrators were also angry that the district released the very best teachers to serve as full-time mentors, when they were supposed to teach at least 60 percent of the time, according to state guidelines. New teachers were also supposed to be released 20 percent of the time to work with mentors, but in Rochester they taught full time.

The district also created a review panel that replaced administrator evaluations. The panel selected the mentors and evaluated both mentors and new teachers. The collective bargaining agreement stated that program participants would not be evaluated in any other way. Thus, because of the way Rochester is operating its mentor teacher program, supervisors and administrators do not render judgment about the performance of new and some veteran teachers, and do not work with beginning teachers as part of their practice.

A state judge ruled against the Rochester ASAR, finding that administrators experienced "no harmful effect" from this program and that there was nothing in state regulations "which set forth the rights, privileges, or duties conferred by that certification, or that those rights, duties, or privileges are exclusively within the province of certified administrators" (Hazi, 1988, p. 28). This ruling confirms the finding that in some states a statutory basis for the practice of supervisors is absent, making them vulnerable in times of reduction in force and when new roles like the mentor teacher are born.

LIMITS DUE TO LEGAL-BASED INCIDENTS

Thus far we have seen that supervisory role and practice can be abolished, promoted, bargained, circumscribed, and limited due to lack of definition. Another type of limit occurs due to legal-based incidents of practice, i.e., "those incidents of educational practice that are connected to law by virtue of some binding document such as a collective bargaining contract, school board policy, or state law" (Hazi, in press). The first legal challenge against the use of a state observation system and grievances filed against a New Jersey supervisor are two such incidents that limit supervisory practice.

In *Sweeney v. Turlington* a Florida teacher challenged the use of the Florida Performance Measurement System (FPMS), an observation system with twenty-one discrete behaviors identified from the teacher effectiveness research. Maryanne Sweeney challenged its reliability when she was denied the title of Associate Master Teacher and $3,000 in Florida's Master Teacher Program because of a low score on the FPMS (Hazi, 1989b).

Maryanne had received ratings of "above average" and "exceeds expectations," but these annual evaluations from her principals played no part in determining that she was a superior teacher for merit pay purposes. She had also passed her subject exam, the other requirement for merit pay, scoring well above the minimum in the 86th percentile. And, in the opinion of her three observers, she was "well prepared" and "presented a very good lesson." Unfortunately, their opinions did not matter, since they were merely data collectors and were not to render judgment about her teaching performance (Hazi, 1989b).

Despite the testimony of her observers, the use of the instrument was upheld and her petition was denied, making the FPMS the first observation instrument to withstand legal challenge.[9] Ironically, this case reveals that supervisors can be disenfranchised from judging the teaching act. The observer's role is narrowly defined as: "cod[ing] what the teacher does in the classroom. . . . It's not what the coder thinks of the teacher, but what the teacher does in the classroom" (Hazi, 1989b, p. 223). Observers turn their coded FPMS forms over to a machine that calculates the teacher's score. Thus, a computer—not the observer—mathematically renders judgment about the teacher's lesson.

It is also the computer that determines whether improvement is possible. A computer calculates what is called the "hypothetical third observation score," based on two previous scores. This hypothetical third score indicates whether a teacher has a chance to improve and thus warrants a third observation.

Since the observer is disenfranchised from the judgment process there is an unnecessary dichotomy set up between observation and judgment. At the heart of this dichotomy is the assumption that judgment computed arithmetically is error free, sound, and is thus more fair than human judgment. In *Sweeney v. Turlington* an observer's role can be redefined from that of rendering independent judgment to that of merely collecting data.

A second legal-based incident concerns a curriculum coordinator in New Jersey who tried "doing supervision" in an evaluation-only school system and found grievances filed against her. Although the teachers did not win all grievances, the teachers' association achieved success by calling into question some supervisory practices and limiting others. Teachers were threatened on two fronts: teaching and curriculum (Hazi et al., 1990).

Among the many duties found in her job description, the curriculum coordinator was charged to "maintain high expectation of performance for the staff and other personnel" and "evaluate staff effectively." As part of her practice, she conducted both formal and informal observations of beginning teachers and tenured teachers in difficulty. For informal observations she held pre-observation conferences, let the teacher establish the day and time of her observation, and used her own observa-

---

[9]The FPMS was soon eliminated from use with inservice teachers because of the hundreds of other complaints received like Maryanne's. The FPMS is currently used in Florida only with beginning teachers. However, its popularity should not be underestimated, since it has been used as a prototype in other southern and southwestern states.

tion form to decrease the threat of evaluation and to give teachers more control over the process. When conducting formal observations, she was one of a team of three.

One grievance was about the number of evaluations and whether a visit counted as a formal or informal evaluation. The supervisor visited nontenured teachers ten times, while state regulations required only three. Although the supervisor's intent was to help, the teachers' association saw her action as harassment and intimidation. The supervisor constructed her own forms and claimed these visits to be informal rather than formal. The teachers' association claimed a supervisor in a classroom can only mean one thing—an evaluation. They recommended that all evaluations be "recalled and destroyed including all copies."

According to the New Jersey School Code, the association was justified in its request because supervision and evaluation are considered legally synonymous. The school code specifies the following: "Each district board of education shall adopt a policy for the *supervision* of instruction, setting forth procedures for the observation and *evaluation* of all nontenured teaching staff members . . ." [emphasis added] [Section 6:3-1.19(c)]. Thus, the school code precluded the coordinator from doing observation in the name of "helping" (Hazi et al., 1990).

Another grievance was over the use of a laptop computer. The supervisor subscribed to the technique of script taping, claiming that it helped her to write the observation narrative. The teachers' association claimed that the use of the computer "causes a disruptive and distracting atmosphere in the classroom" and "is intimidating and extremely distracting to the overall educational process." They also claimed that "evaluation is incorrect because the supervisor is not observing the whole interaction in the classroom, she is just observing the audible, therefore staff members are being deprived of professional advantage without just cause." Although this practice did not violate state law or the contract, their argument was convincing and the supervisor was asked to eliminate the laptop computer!

Another grievance concerned the initiation of pre-observation conferences. According to this supervisor, she initiated them "to structure the observation in favor of the teacher." However, the teachers' contract specified that only the teacher could initiate a preconference: "*At the request of the teacher*, a pre-observation conference may be held to enable the evaluator to become aware of the instructional period" [emphasis added]. The teachers won again!

The supervisor was also charged to "organize, disseminate, explain, align and direct the curriculum." To carry out this job duty, she worked with teacher committees to write curriculum guides, the first ever in their district. When she refused to allow a social studies teacher to spend three marking periods on the Civil War and cover the rest of U.S. History in the remaining one marking period, the teacher filed a grievance on curriculum pacing, which was found in favor of the supervisor.

This case study illustrates that in times of school reform teachers are protective and view all supervisory practices as suspect, regardless of the intent. Practices—such as more frequent visits, pre-observation conferences, and use of a laptop computer for data gathering—which can help provide more fair and honest evaluations, may also be curtailed in order to protect teachers against the possibility that they might be used to hurt or dismiss them. This case also illustrates that if supervisors are required to evaluate teachers as indicated in their job descriptions, quasi-legal documents, they cannot adopt a few well-intentioned techniques, hoping to minimize the threat associated with the responsibility.

CONCLUSION: WHAT OF THE FUTURE?

Because of the conveyances of law, aspects of supervisory practice can be promoted, bargained, circumscribed, redefined, and curtailed. Most dramatically, the role of supervisor can also be legally abolished. Such limits can occur by omission (i.e., because of oversight) or by commission (i.e., by intentional acts of exclusion).[10] Regardless of intent, the decades of the 1970s and 1980s have provided supervisors with the grounds to carefully monitor legal-based incidents of practice and the contents of legislation, litigation, regulation, and collective bargaining agreements in the 1990s, since they may one day serve to limit aspects of supervisory practice in their respective states.

What of the future of supervision in general and clinical supervision in particular? As school systems (especially the small and the rural) cut

---

[10]The terms omission and commission are used especially to describe acts associated with affirmative action.

funds in times of recession, we will see fewer individuals called supervisors. Instead, we may see more teachers performing supervisory functions like those in the Rochester City School District. Barring economic hardship, supervisors may be better able to maintain their ranks where they are differentiated from other public school roles by definition and where state departments of education closely monitor certificates held by school employees.

As clinical supervision becomes even more popular, it will be common to see aspects of its practice appearing in contracts and state regulation as the rule rather than the exception. For example, in southeastern states the technique of "scripting" teacher and student talk in the class appears to be becoming a standard practice (SREB, 1990).

As long as statewide instruments such as the FPMS are the vehicle for teacher evaluation, observers will continue to overestimate their ability to help teachers improve. However, long-term training in clinical supervision for both teachers and administrators holds the most promise for reuniting observation and judgment.

We will undoubtedly see more instances where the courts will be deciding issues of practice, especially around teacher evaluation. Supervisors in general and those espousing clinical supervision need to more carefully assess school climate before introducing new techniques. As long as teacher evaluation remains a high-stakes activity, inextricably linked to supervision, teachers will protect themselves and their jobs from supervisors who use seemingly helpful, but foreign, practices.

REFERENCES

Alfonso, R. J., G. R. Firth and R. F. Nevile. 1981. *Instructional Supervision: A Behavior System, 2nd Edition*. Boston: Allyn and Bacon, Inc.

Eye, G., L. Netzer and R. Krey. 1971. *Supervision of Instruction, 2nd Edition*. New York: Harper and Row.

Garman, N. B. and H. M. Hazi. 1988. "Teachers Ask, Is There Life After Madeline Hunter?" *Phi Delta Kappan*, 69(9):669–672.

Glickman, C. and T. Bey. 1990. "Supervision," in *Handbook of Research on Teacher Education*, R. Houston, ed., New York: Macmillan.

Harris, B. 1985. *Supervisory Behavior in Education, 3rd Edition*. Englewood Cliffs, NJ: Prentice-Hall, Inc.

Hazi, H. M. 1980. "An Analysis of Selected Teacher Collective Negotiation Agreements in Pennsylvania to Determine the Legal Control Placed on Supervisory Practice," doctoral dissertation, University of Pittsburgh, *Dissertation Abstracts International*, 41:2423A.

Hazi, H. M. 1982. "Should Labor Law Define Instructional Supervision?" *Educational Leadership*, 39(7):542–543.

Hazi, H. M. 1983. "Judge Defines Quality Education for Schools," *Educational Leadership*, 41(1):68–69.

Hazi, H. M. "An Analysis of the Legal Basis of the Practice of Instructional Supervisors in Selected State Statutes," a paper presented at the annual meeting of the American Educational Research Association, New Orleans, 1984.

Hazi, H. M. "Who Are Instructional Supervisors Any Way? A Case of Identity Claimed or Lost through Certification Regulations," a paper presented at the annual meeting of the American Educational Research Association, Chicago, 1985a.

Hazi, H. M. 1985b. "Co-Rechting West Virginia Public Schools," *Educational Leadership*, 42(6):75–78.

Hazi, H. M. 1986a. "The Third Wave: Competency Tests for Administrators," working paper, order no. EI 85-1. Denver, CO: Educational Commission of the States.

Hazi, H. M. "Toward a Definition of Standard of Care: Educational Malpractice Revisited," a paper presented at the annual meeting of the American Educational Research Association, San Francisco, 1986b.

Hazi, H. M. "Teacher Evaluation Incognito: Madeline Hunter and School Reform," a paper presented at the annual meeting of the American Educational Research Association, Washington, DC, 1987.

Hazi, H. M. 1988. "Instructional Improvement in the Courts: Lessons for Supervisors," *WVASCD Journal* (Spring):25–31.

Hazi, H. M. 1989a. "Teachers and the Recht Decision: A West Virginia Case Study of School Reform. A Technical Report," ERIC Document Reproduction Service No. ED 318 597. Morgantown, WV: West Virginia University.

Hazi, H. M. 1989b. "Measurement versus Judgment: The Case of *Sweeney v. Turlington*," *Journal of Curriculum and Supervision*, 4(3):211–229.

Hazi, H. M. 1992. "Discovering and Releasing the Voices of Authority in Legal-Educational Inquiry," in *Informing Educational Policy and Practice through Interpretive Inquiry*, N. Haggerson and A. Bowman, eds., Lancaster, PA: Technomic Publishing Co., Inc., pp. 251–266.

Hazi, H. M. and N. B. Garman. 1988. "Legalizing Scientism through Teacher Evaluation," *Journal of Personnel Evaluation in Education*, 2(1):7–18.

Hazi, H. M., C. Johnston and M. Hoepfl. "Supervisors and School Reform: A Case Study in Grievances," a presentation at the annual meeting of the American Educational Research Association, Boston, 1990.

Hunter, M. 1988. "Effecting a Reconciliation between Supervision and Evaluation—A Reply to Popham," *Journal of Personnel Evaluation in Education*, 1(3):275–279.

Nolte, N. C. 1984. "Empirical Research on Education Law Issues: A Model," in *School Law Update: Preventive School Law*, T. N. Jones and D. P. Semer, eds., Topeka, KS: National Organization on Legal Problems of Education.

Pajak, E. 1989. "Identification of Supervisory Proficiencies Project," Athens, GA: University of Georgia.

1990. "Pension Law Excludes Teachers, Lawyer Says," *The Charleston Gazette* (June 30):9A.

Rubin, L. 1982. "External Influences on Supervision: Seasonal Winds and Prevailing Climate," in *Supervision of Teaching*, T. J. Sergiovanni, ed., Alexandria, VA: Association for Supervision and Curriculum Development, pp. 170–179.

Scott, D. "Democratic Leadership," unpublished doctoral thesis, University of Maryland, 1954.

Southern Regional Education Board (SREB). 1990. *Preliminary Report: Teacher Evaluation Programs in SREB States*. Atlanta: Southern Regional Education Board.

Spears, H. 1953. *Improving the Supervision of Instruction*. New York: Prentice-Hall, Inc.

1933. *Supplement to the West Virginia Code of 1932*. Charlottesville, VA: The Michie Company, Law Publishers.

Tanner, D. and L. Tanner. 1987. *Supervision in Education: Problems and Practice*. New York: Macmillan.

Van Til, W. 1965. "In a Climate of Change," in ASCD's *Role of Supervisor and Curriculum Director in a Climate of Change*. Washington, DC: Association for Supervision and Curriculum Development, pp. 7–29.

1949. *The West Virginia Code of 1949*. Charlottesville, VA: The Michie Company, Law Publishers.

II

THE OBSERVATION CYCLE AS METHODOLOGY AND CONTEXT FOR COACHING

In this next section of the book are four chapters focusing upon the methodology of clinical supervision and the context that it provides for coaching. It opens with an analysis of competency development, continues with a thorough description of the observation cycle, moves to discussion of the communication skills that are essential to effective coaching, and concludes with an examination of clinical supervision in practice.

Snyder's opening chapter links the goals of school restructuring to the functions of training and coaching. Focusing on the ways that professional development activity provides and/or develops the cohesive force within the organization for making necessary changes, she addresses, in turn, the changes occurring at the levels of the team or department, the school, the district office, and the staff development office. In the second section of the chapter, after a brief discussion of adult learning, she presents the six core dimensions of, and the rationale for, a competency development model that is designed to enhance adult learning and problem-solving processes.

With the stage thus set for thinking about the structure within which supervisory competencies can be put to work, Krajewski then describes the observation cycle as a methodology for coaching and problem solving. He opens with a brief discussion of the attitudes the supervisor and the teacher should bring into the process, and then discusses rapport as an integral, essential ingredient. The bulk of the chapter is devoted to descriptions of the five stages of the cycle.

In a chapter loaded with practical suggestions about how coaches can communicate effectively, Swarzman first offers a set of basic assumptions and then proposes that certain behaviors can help one to become a "winning coach." She identifies and develops three themes that are found

75

in the success literature: positively focused images, positively focused body language, and positively focused statements and questions. She concludes with strong advocacy of persistence as the ultimate key to successful coaching.

The section concludes with a chapter by Pavan, whose focus is upon a diagnostic tool that has been developed to identify current levels of practice in clinical supervision. She opens with material comparing several different models of clinical supervision, including one of her own: the Goldhammer model in five stages, the Cogan model in eight phases, the Acheson-Gall model in three stages, and the Pavan model with five elements. Four of the Pavan elements are analogous to elements in the other models, but the element of reflection is derived from the work of Schon.

Then, following a useful discussion of features and elements, Pavan introduces a questionnaire that can be used to identify clinical supervision practices by administrators, supervisors, and teachers. Information from research studies using that questionnaire is then provided, and the possibilities for using it in coordination with staff development are noted.

6

Competency Development: Linking Restructuring Goals to Training and Coaching

Preparing for a new schooling age requires that all professional role groups develop new knowledge bases, skills, and orientations to work. Great schools and school districts will be sorted out in the next several decades, and at the heart of each success story will exist a greater capacity to think and act collectively in responding to changing needs and conditions. Most certainly, restructuring schools for the transformation of learning patterns for all children will succeed to the extent that educators become a community of learners and skilled problem solvers as they respond to client needs.

The best school districts thrive today due to the emphasis placed on staff development programs and the funds allocated for their enhancement. This chapter seeks to address the challenges of developing competence among all role groups in a school district, both professional and nonprofessional, in ways that influence school and district performance. The concept of professional development has grown over the last three decades from a once-in-a-while event for teachers, to a continuous series of varied learning opportunities for all role groups.

Restructuring efforts that transform the workplace of schools and school districts necessarily will emphasize two dimensions: (1) new job-specific knowledge and skill bases, and (2) new conceptual frames and tools for productive partnerships. As a consequence, a shift is likely to occur in the purpose for professional development programs, moving from the segmentation of functions to integration; from compliance orientations to problem solving and invention; and from deficiency reduction to capacity building. The existence of a common language of work and common processes for decision making will enhance both future staff development programs and organizational

77

productivity. A culture of risk taking, piloting, success, and pride are additional cultural features that are likely to influence professional development and its effects on the workplace.

As new staff development programs are designed for schools and districts in transition, emphasis will be placed on enhancing basic job performance, as well as on developing groups of competent and autonomous professional thinkers, problem solvers, decision makers, and producers. More attention will be given to programs that nurture professional maturity, helping all role groups to move from dependency to autonomy as decision makers; beyond compliance to empowerment; from reaction to proaction; from the application of prescribed behaviors to shared problem solving and the creation of multiple strategies; and from role isolation to role interdependence.

This chapter addresses the issue of professional development for all role groups, of the sort that enhances organizational performance and outcomes, for this provides the backdrop for productive supervision and coaching activity. Attention in the first part of the chapter, "Restructuring and Retooling," is given to the organizational restructuring context for professional development. The second part of the chapter, "Competency Development and the Training Function," provides a conceptual model and set of strategies for designing programs for professional competency development. It is within the context of professional development and program or product creation that coaching assumes its most powerful function.

RESTRUCTURING AND RETOOLING

Schools and school districts in transition require new knowledge bases, conceptual schemas, and problem-solving capacities. In those districts that are clear about new directions and outcomes, the function of staff development becomes a major enabling force to success. So strong is the relationship between goal-driven professional development and organizational productivity that the two functions are likely to emerge as dominant strategies in future reform efforts.

All role groups will require greater capacities to work together interdependently as client needs are addressed. Restructuring for success requires that all groups work with conceptual schemas for forming synergies, what Kanter (1983) refers to as the new powerful organizational tool of the 1990s. In synergies, members from numerous role groups and institutions meet to address a particular problem in common, making use of multiple orientations in the problem-solving process.

Equally important to schooling transformation is an understanding of the dynamic of the system as a whole (a school or school district) in changing or altering the effects from any part of the system. Major attention to the system and its work traditions will play an increasingly important role in planning; continuing to alter parts of the system will never create responsive organizations in the whole. Only when the system and its structures and processes are addressed as a unit is there hope that coaching and other development strategies will influence work and learning patterns and produce qualitatively different outcomes within a school and district.

Consequently, there is likely to be a shift in the purpose of professional development activity, progressing from the segmentation of functions by schools and district departments, to the integration of overall orientations, beliefs, values, and practices. Given a collective vision or direction for restructuring, development activity of a wide variety provides a cohesive force within an institution for an age that also requires increasing specialization. We can predict that a school or district will become productive to the degree that all role groups learn (1) to work more productively with and among each other, (2) to enhance the system's potential to alter traditional practices, and (3) to influence learning outcomes. Teachers need to address the learning problems they face within their teams, making use of a variety of human resources. Schools need to solve learning challenges schoolwide, while making use of their own human resources, and tapping into those from the district, community, state, and professional organizations. District service units will focus more on meeting school-based needs, linking human resources together across the district to solve client problems. Hence, all role groups are likely to shift their work patterns considerably as they explore and invent new ways to be more responsive to client needs.

A major management and supervisory strategy for maturing a professional staff is empowerment, which for any role group represents the opportunity to solve problems or address challenges and to invent new programs and systems. Empowerment, then, is a management strategy for restructuring where the problems and challenges of transforming conditions for working and learning are addressed by all levels of the system. Certain organizational conditions exist that serve as enabling mechanisms for empowerment. Shared visions of greatness and specific goals of the organization provide direction for development and thus for empowerment activity. A productive organizational culture of pride nurtures, expects, and rewards risk taking, small starts, piloting, and turning old practices upside-down. High management and supervisory expectations stimulate workers as opportunity is provided for learning and developing within synergistic structures. A consequence is that synergy emerges from adults working together to solve problems and becomes a driving energy source and force for transforming learning conditions and outcomes, schoolwide and districtwide.

New Skills for Supervisory Functions

Pajak (1989) conducted a study for ASCD to determine supervisory proficiencies across role groups: team/department leader, principal, supervisor, director, assistant superintendent, and superintendent. His extensive review of the education literature, combined with reactions from those who now hold those roles, provide clarity about the proficiencies that seem to cross role groups and facilitate successful outcomes. The twelve proficiences include: community relations, staff development, planning and change, communication, curriculum development and implementation, instructional program improvement, service to teachers, observation and conferencing, problem solving and decision making, research and program evaluation, motivating and organizing, and personal development. In Chapter 17, Pajak and Carr elaborate on the study.

These job dimensions in themselves are likely to become the focus for professional development and coaching activity for those who perform supervisory functions, and enlarge the scope of job skills needed for exemplary performance. In the next several pages we will examine the changes that are likely to occur at various levels of school district organization as a result of restructuring efforts, which have implications for training and coaching activity. There will continue to be an emphasis placed on training and coaching teachers in skills for effective instruction; however, the menu for coaching is likely to extend to all role groups and focus upon a wide range of job-specific skills and those required for shared decision making.

Team/Department Development

One level of supervision is found in teams or departments at the school site. As a team or department moves from compliance to a problem-solving orientation, greater professional maturity evolves and more autonomy is achieved. The overarching professional challenge for a school team or department is constantly to create more favorable learning conditions for a particular group of students. Productive teams now set "stretch" goals for addressing major learning problems, and then develop comprehensive plans for addressing needs using a wide variety of strategies. Team members find that new skills are required for collaborative goal setting and action planning, and for designing comprehensive team/department plans (Snyder, 1988). Also important to the productive efforts of permanent teams are many group problem-solving techniques, along with skills for conducting productive group meetings. Additional tools also are important for organizing and facilitating task forces whose members are students, parents, and community groups, and which plan, monitor, and assess outcomes. Managing team development, of the sort that restructures the work of teaching and learning and its effects, necessitates new orientations, knowledge bases, structures, and skills for partnerships. Learning the skills of bargaining and negotiating for new opportunities, resources, access to information, and specialized services is likely to sort out the most productive teams and departments in the future.

Out of an increasingly complex and dynamic work context, different forms of training and coaching will be needed for teams and departments to develop greater capacities to communicate in groups and to solve problems. If new teaching skills and techniques are required, skills workshops are designed, with follow-up coaching to aid in the transfer of skills. If more generic work-oriented problems are to be solved, or if new programs need to be designed, coaching provides data bases for changing or modifying work patterns. In sum, coaching facilitates data-based problem solving for altering work effects, providing a tool for restructuring, and as such, plays a vital role in the team's development. Coaching becomes a major development feature in the work culture of productive and inventive teams and departments as the future is created.

School Development

Another level of supervision is at the school site. Developing great schools requires a schoolwide problem-solving orientation, moving beyond the limitations of compliance. In restructuring schools, new orientations are required for collaborative forms of envisioning, planning, and problem solving (Snyder, 1988). The management and supervisory focus shifts from individual teaching patterns to the conditions for learning and working within and across permanent work group structures. Consequently teachers, principals, and supervisors need skills for organizing, launching, and managing partnership efforts within teams, service units, and client populations. One principal in a particularly dynamic school district observed that someone in the district (professional) seemed to be teaching someone else something all the time, with role groups learning with and from each other continuously. In view of the research on productive schools, there appears to be a dynamic relationship between numerous collaborative efforts, group empowerment to solve problems, and increases in student success patterns.

A school is viewed here as a living, growing system that progresses through natural growth cycles in its development, as evidenced for example in the Managing Productive Schools (MPS) model of school work cultures (Snyder and Anderson, 1986). The research base for productive work cultures draws from over 500 studies of successful organizations found in business, industry, social agencies, and schools, and reinforces the concept that productive systems are goal-driven and developmental as they strive for new capacities to influence productivity and services (Snyder and Anderson, 1986, 1990). The school work culture model delineates four clusters of shared work (organizational planning, staff development, program development, and school assessment) and provides a conceptual schema and practical framework for managing and supervising restructuring efforts. Ten dimensions of productive work cultures include the following shared functions:

- schoolwide goal setting

- work organization (structures)
- performance planning and management
- staff development and training
- coaching/clinical supervision
- work group development
- quality control
- instructional program development
- resource management
- schoolwide assessment

The MPS work culture construct recently has been validated as a cohesive force in school development, a construct that turns upside-down professional's work patterns within and across units in productive educational enterprises (Parkinson, 1990).

Managing productive school work cultures requires that supervisors shift from providing professional answers, while controlling for certain teaching behaviors, to stimulating professional inquiry and structuring networks where control focuses on development and on new products and services and their effects. In coaching, the supervisory challenge is to empower groups of teachers to gather classroom teaching and learning data and make use of knowledge and information bases to solve school-specific/team-specific learning challenges. Teachers, principals, and supervisors forming partnerships will, if given opportunities, stimulate new kinds of working, learning, product development, and coaching patterns to enhance adult learning and productivity. A work culture of development and success, schoolwide, provides the fertile ground for empowerment, which becomes the energy source for learning that is necessary for driving productive systems.

Principals report that empowering teachers happens gradually and naturally over time as competence is developed and enhanced within the organization. To launch an era of shared decision making (the foundation of productive work cultures), principals report that selected groups of teachers are invited initially to solve a few schoolwide problems. Eventually teachers themselves ask permission to work on a particular task. In time, when teachers come to understand that they are the shapers of the school's future, principals report that groups of teachers want, not to ask permission, but to discuss the outcomes of their efforts to solve a problem. Gradually teachers begin reaching across units within their own school to work with others facing similar problems, or to address a need schoolwide. Networks and partnerships are born as professionals seek solutions to the challenges of school learning.

Eventually several school faculties decide to address problems they face in common, such as the transition years between school levels (sixth grade, ninth grade), dropout prevention programs, student tutoring programs, and buddy systems. Staff development programs also begin to emerge from school partnership efforts as they examine common goals and development needs. Task forces of teachers from across several schools plan, coordinate, seek funding and expertise, and evaluate staff development programs for achieving common purposes. Synergistic groups of teachers, principals, supervisors, and directors over time develop partnership capacities to tackle some of the old nagging schooling problems, as well as emerging challenges.

District Office Development

Many central office supervisors now are abandoning the practice of coaching individual teachers, where they have sought to serve as part of the teacher support system. Instead, there is greater emphasis on "managing" the support system by developing teachers and others for many leadership functions, including coaching. Training and coaching activities naturally follow attempts to develop new programs or skills and become part of an enhancement strategy.

Simultaneous with Pajak's research project to determine supervisory proficiencies, Snyder and Giella (1988) developed a new conceptualization of central office supervisors and directors as "managers of programs and services": Managing Productive Programs (MPP). An adaptation of the MPS programs for school leaders and principals, MPP sought to enable supervisors and directors to work with differing school agendas more effectively, to enhance the school district's ecology by managing interdependence, and to increase the effects of their own programs and services on school performance. The new definition of the district office staff functions centers on ten management competencies that fall within four clusters of job tasks: district/department/program planning, staff development, program/services development, and program/department assessment. The ten job competencies include the following:

- district and department goal setting

- work organization structures
- performance planning and management
- staff development design and training
- clinical supervision design and training
- work group and leader development
- instruction system or service program design and management
- resource development and management
- quality control
- achievement and productivity assessment

The MPP ten competencies (drawn from the research literature of management, business, social agencies, and schooling) overlap the Pajak proficiencies (drawn from the education literature) with considerable consistency. In a recent study of the effects of MPP training on district supervisory performance, the MPP model was validated as providing useful job dimensions for supervisors and directors in all departments with a district in transition (Fitzgerald, 1991). Consequently, a management orientation to central office roles provides a cohesiveness for the district that has been lacking, and a framework for district planning and development, as well as for professional enhancement.

Districts in transition find that staff development is fast becoming the centerpiece of professional activity, with every role group involved in teaching, learning, and coaching. The central office directors and supervisors in the Pasco County School District in Florida (instruction, media, personnel, finance, data processing, and special services) recently were asked to what extent they now were engaged in training others. Their average job allocation currently given to training others is 80 percent, an almost unbelievable allotment of time and energy. Training activity centers around new technologies for processing, communicating, and accessing information, as well as processes to facilitate shared decision making in teams, task forces, networks, and partnerships. Every service unit in the district seems to be in the staff development business.

The Changing Staff Development Office

Given the expansion of the staff development function into the work culture of every major service unit in a district and its schools, the functions of a staff development department change considerably.

Many shifts are occurring: (1) from training all teachers in a district, to training teacher trainers; (2) from designing all training programs, to consulting with many units on the design of local programs; (3) from providing the same training for all, to making available a wide variety of training options; (4) from being the training support system, to managing the support system; and (5) from funding all training programs, to offering competitive grants for staff development programs within schools and district units. Coaching likewise shifts from a focus upon teachers alone, to a development strategy within all role groups. Consequently, the staff development office is finding it increasingly impossible to provide actual training and coaching for all, and instead is inventing more powerful forms to manage the support structure for staff development services throughout the district.

Summary

In this section a linkage has been identified between the restructuring thrust within schools and districts and the need for all role groups to become engaged in professional inquiry and growth through a variety of approaches to staff development, training, and coaching. By becoming coinvolved, the energy system of schools and of districts are stimulated to respond in more powerful ways to meet challenges. Consequently, professional development and coaching are fast becoming the expectation of all role groups in a school system, not just teachers. Given that all roles will become increasingly engaged in their own learning and teaching, another challenge is emerging: to design professional growth programs that enable differing role groups to address emerging schooling challenges with confidence and skill. Within a context where invention thrives, the design of professional development programs create new opportunities.

COMPETENCY DEVELOPMENT AND THE TRAINING FUNCTION

The knowledge base of adult learning processes, approaches, and structures provides helpful guidelines for planning professional development programs. In this section, adult learning is discussed from differing orientations to provide a comprehensive view of influence variables on learning in the work place. Building upon several principles of adult learning, a structure for planning workshops is provided to link training with organizational and/or program goals, and to coaching activity.

Adult Learning

Adults learn in a variety of ways, and most effectively in the pursuit of a goal or challenge. Assumptions about adult learning have changed in recent years, influenced to a great extent by the work of Malcolm Knowles (1980), who has discussed the ideas of pedagogy and andragogy. The term synergogy, a third concept, was coined by Mouton and Blake (1984) and enlarged by Snyder and Anderson (1988). All three views are appropriate guides to staff development in differing contexts, and provide planners with varying orientations to competency development.

Within a *pedagogical approach* to staff development it is assumed that there exists a need to acquire certain knowledge and/or to learn certain skills. Training programs are designed around identified concepts, and the trainer develops within the learner a dependence upon the new knowledge while dispensing information, and then controlling for certain qualities in performance. Professionals who are entering a career, learning new skills, or learning the parameters of a new job, may benefit from training within a pedagogical framework. The training and management tasks are to inform adult learners, and then to control for certain professional or work-related effects.

An *andragogical approach* to adult learning makes different assumptions, and more often is appropriate for professional development. It is assumed that there exists a need to know certain information, knowledge, or skills in order to solve specific job-related problems. Staff development programs, from an andragogical perspective, are designed to provide knowledge and skills for resolving job-specific challenges. The trainer's role is to facilitate individual problem solving by sharing multiple sources of knowledge, facilitating inquiry, and controlling for problems being solved on-the-job. One might expect that novice professionals would prefer a pedagogical approach to an andragogical approach for learning basic skills. However, Ramos (1987) found that student teachers in their undergraduate preparation program prefer the problem-solving approach of andragogy to the information dispensement of pedagogy. An andragogical approach to training and coaching tends to nurture greater independence of the adult learner to both the knowledge base and the trainer, than does the pedagogical approach.

The most promising approach to adult learning is built upon the foundation of andragogy and focuses on groups of adults solving problems: *synergogy*. Research on cooperative learning (Johnson et al., 1981; Slavin, 1990) and on adult learning (Brookfield, 1986) suggests that people learn better when working with colleagues to solve real job-related problems. A synergogical approach assumes that workers need to solve common problems or address challenges together with colleagues, which enhances learning and subsequent performance. The trainer's role is to develop interdependence among learners by accessing multiple resources, facilitating problem-solving networks, and then controlling the effects of group solutions to problems. Given the favorable effects of collaboration on school learning, and of cooperative learning on student performance, this latter view of adult learning shows great promise for developing adult performance in schools and school districts.

The Competency Development Model

Organization-wide approaches to training and coaching are enabling dimensions in a system's development. In productive schools and districts there exists a dynamic relationship between goals, workshops, and follow-up coaching activity. In the model in Figure 6.1, consider the relationship between organizational goals, a skills workshop, and coaching activity (Snyder, 1988). (A) *Organizational goals and expectations* drive the selection of a particular workshop and provide a context for developing new knowledge and skill bases; (B) *workshops* are designed around a competency development model and are organized to enable professionals to acquire new skills that relate in some way to organizational goals; and (C) a *coaching structure* enhances the transfer of new skills and orientations to the job.

Now let us consider a set of guidelines for planning workshops that focus on the six core dimensions and rationale for the competency development model. Professionals are more likely to engage in workshop and follow-up activity to the extent that the content is perceived to help solve job problems, that engagement is valued by management, and

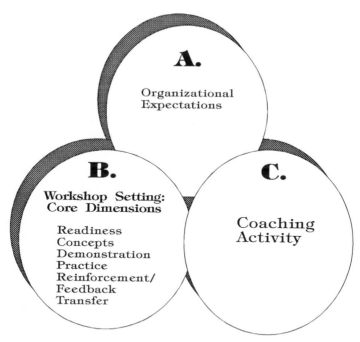

Figure 6.1 *Competency Development Model.*

that provisions are made for the transfer of skills to the job. The six core dimensions function in a distinct and interdependent fashion to enhance the problem solving and adult learning processes.

Inherent in most organizational goals are areas for professional growth. Organizational goals guide planners in the selection of knowledge bases and skills to learn. Professional development can be addressed through university course work, through conferences and seminars, through training programs, through visiting programs or schools, or from reading professional literature. Professionals also develop new understandings and skills by working with others to design and pilot new programs or to solve problems.

In this section, attention is given to planned development in a workshop context. It is assumed that the kinds of workshops addressed are based on goals that grow out of an analysis of organizational priorities, and focus on enabling workers to enhance their goal-related capacities. Consequently, workshop goals link to the organization's current emphasis and provide an enabling structure to enhance performance.

Dimensions of the workshop design for facilitating synergistic professional development follow.

Core Dimension One: Introduction/Readiness (Rationale for the Workshop)

People tend to be motivated to accomplish their own goals, whether consciously or not. Theories of worker motivation have identified many influence factors that stimulate people productivity in the workplace. Affiliation with others tends to create a synergistic environment (Mayo, 1933; Purkey and Smith, 1982). Achievement, reinforcement, and recognition (Sergiovanni and Carver, 1973, 1975), job goals (House, 1971, 1973), and opportunity with responsibility for invention (Kanter, 1983) all tend to stimulate productive behaviors for the organization while bringing satisfaction to the worker. In addition, both personal and organizational expectations tend to influence on-the-job performance (Vroom, 1964; Odiorne, 1979). A person's perception of a task's capacity to help her/him solve a job problem greatly influences the motivation to engage in such tasks or activities.

Without a need to know, little is likely to occur in workshops. An area of cognitive dissonance within a job, when stimulated, enhances learning. Individuals tend to respond in one of several ways to a dissonant state, either to ignore the problem situation or to address the problem and seek a state of resolution (consonance) (Festinger, 1957). A workshop can be organized to facilitate the process of moving from cognitive dissonance to consonance, with the trainer managing the thinking and problem-solving processes. The trainer's challenge is to create a need to know, and show the probability that the acquisition of certain knowledge and skills will help to resolve a job problem or challenge.

The training function in the *readiness stage* is to stimulate the dissonance-to-consonance process in a variety of ways: by providing information about workshop activities; by engaging groups to identify both strengths and challenges (as they relate to the workshop focus); by engaging participants in a simulation that highlights the problem and creates a need to know; by appealing to interests in new professional opportunities; by recognizing the exemplary performance of other units or individuals; and by communicating high expectations for enhancing overall worker performance. Hence, in the readiness stage of the workshop, attention is focused on job performance, and interest is stimulated in acquiring new concepts and skills.

Core Dimension Two: Concepts (Altering Perceptions)

Scholars have long sought to understand more clearly the factors that stimulate cognition. Early psychologists identified insight as a means by which new concepts were developed. Lewin (1936) identified forces within one's perceptual field as a major variable to insight acquisition. Festinger (1957) described the insight gaining process as basically a problem-solving process that resolves dissonance. Later, scholars such as Bigge (1971) and Rokeach (1968) suggested that learning results from a cluster of psychological forces that include insight, new knowledge, beliefs, attitudes, and behaviors.

The purpose of the *concept stage* in a workshop is to provide new knowledge or information that is likely to stimulate fresh ways of thinking about a given set of problems. New information functions either as a dissonant factor or as a driving force in the consonance-seeking process. On the basis of new knowledge or information and orientations or perspectives, people are likely to engage in activities that facilitate new skill development. Inherent in the concepts must exist a promise for enhancing performance or solving a problem.

The trainer's role is to provide both a research and a scholarship base for that which is being taught and learned (a rationale for new approaches), and to do so in ways that actively engage the learner's thinking process. A major challenge in the concept stage is to plan for knowledge acquisition in ways that enable the learner to become actively engaged in thinking about the problem, and understanding intellectually the ways in which new concepts and models hold promise. If dissonance is to be resolved well, learners need to be challenged intellectually, respond to questions, share examples, ask questions, and in general, discuss new concepts from their job perspectives.

Core Dimension Three: Demonstration (Modeling as a Reinforcer)

The work of Bandura (1969) on behavior modification provides a rationale for offering "good" models of the new skill to be learned. He contends that vicarious processes (demonstrations) are as powerful a behavior shaper as is direct experience. A good model provides an example, first for consideration, and then for copying. Imitation, observation, identification, copying, and role-playing are all effective forms of demonstrating that which is to be learned.

In the *demonstration stage* of the workshop, a good model is provided of how the concepts can be operationalized into performance on the job. Participants observe a demonstration (e.g., a live simulation, a videotape example) and record specific observed behaviors and their effects. Later, the observational notes become the basis for discussion of and reflection upon the example observed. As the learner observes a successful example, the cognitive construct is further stimulated to question, to challenge, to probe, and to reflect on personal experiences. A successful demonstration reinforces the importance of the concepts being taught, and provides a vicarious experience for solving a problem. Discussion following a demonstration further enhances reflection, insight acquisition, and a state of consonance. The demonstration stage is the first direct attempt to modify a professional behavior.

Core Dimension Four: Practice (Trying New Behaviors)

Psychologists have long agreed that practicing a new skill is fundamental to its acquisition. Skinner (1969) and Luthans and Kreitner (1975) have demonstrated that new behaviors are a function of their being taught, learned, reinforced when successful, and maintained when repeated successfully over time.

The trainer's task in the *practice stage* of the workshop is to structure a practice activity that outlines essential performance elements and expectations. Participants need to practice new skills in a safe and controlled environment prior to trying the skill on the job. The practice activity further stimulates the consonance building process with attention given to new behaviors and their capacity to solve the job problem at hand. To ensure that participants function at high levels of inquiry, the practice task will require groups, rather than individuals, to solve a job problem using the new skill(s), for it engages thinking along with behaviors. As group members practice a new skill, they simultaneously discuss the new and old patterns, further stimulating new competency acquisition. The practice experience is perhaps the critical dimension of the workshop for acquiring new skills. Without practice, concepts demonstrated are likely to influence thinking alone, and not penetrate performance patterns.

Core Dimension Five: Feedback (Information on Practice Effects)

Bloom's (1976) theory of school learning and later studies on his instruction variables, verifies the important function of feedback and correctives to the learning process (Lysakowski and Walberg, 1981). The provision of feedback enables the learner to know quickly which new practice behaviors are appropriate, and which need to be modified. The *feedback stage* of the workshop further nurtures the development of desired behaviors (competency development) and helps to eliminate those that are undesired. Moreover, feedback on the initial practice of a new set of behaviors reinforces correct patterns and stimulates the learner to perceive that success will eventually result from on-the-job use of those behaviors.

At the first trial of a behavior, immediate feedback tends to strengthen understanding of a concept or practice, and prevents the learner from repetitions of unproductive behaviors. Consequently, feedback provides an immediate reinforcer of the desired behaviors during training that will be practiced on the job. Reinforcement tends to stimulate new insights. The practice and feedback stages often are the most important stages for altering behaviors and refining new skills.

An additional function of reinforcement and feedback during training relates to the observer. A vicarious practice experience is created during training by organizing peer feedback and reinforcement, in addition to trainer feedback. By assuming the role of observer, with the task of giving specific behavioral feedback, the trainee is provided with an additional opportunity to learn about the concept and about skills through modeling. Further, as the peer provides verbal feedback, the trainee is provided with an additional opportunity for a successful experience with the concepts taught, and the competency development process is further enhanced.

Core Dimension Six: Transfer (Getting Ready for On-the-Job Practice)

The function of transfer in the workshop is to review major dimensions of the skills learned and to discuss the nature of an on-the-job practice activity. Sharing reflections facilitates consonance about the problem addressed. Metacognition also can be stimulated by asking individuals or groups to share, or to draw symbols of "what we now know about meeting the challenge." By evaluating the workshop and providing feedback to the trainer on its effect, the participant further is engaged in thinking about that which was taught and learned and its potential for solving a job-related problem. Plans are made for following up practice and for peer coaching, ensuring that new skills become integrated into the performance repertoire.

The power of workshops alone to alter job behaviors is quite limited (Joyce and Showers, 1980). The function of the *transfer stage* of the workshop is to ensure that goals are established for on-the-job practice of skills and to provide for follow-up coaching experiences. Personal practice goals are likely to direct performance, while coaching will reinforce and ensure competency development. Specifically, coaching increases the likelihood of certain behaviors becoming incorporated into a person's skill repertoire.

Follow-up can take many forms, but each should be designed to focus on the reinforcement of skills taught in the workshop. Monthly seminars help participants to problem solve together and to report successful experiences with implementation. Problem sharing and reporting opportunities tend to reinforce desired behaviors, to stimulate thinking, and to provide a sense of shared learning. On-the-job observation of a specific competency-related event provides an additional opportunity for feedback and correctives. If peer observation is a planned event, the opportunities for vicarious learning are extended. Whether opportunities are provided for group discussion or on-the-job observation and feedback, the focus for implementation is the plan. Hence, the competency development process continues after the workshop, with feedback to reinforce desirable behaviors.

Coaching in the form of the five-stage observation cycle holds great promise for helping professionals to turn their thinking upside-down (necessary for restructuring an organization) and to develop better patterns over time. When colleagues share in the training and follow-up coaching, collective thinking is refined continuously. Data bases and knowledge bases are used by professionals as they think collectively and at higher levels, and make more informed decisions about the future.

Summary of Workshop Dimensions

Workshops that link with organizational priorities have the greatest potential for influencing work patterns over time. To begin the workshop, the readiness stage engages the learner in events that are designed to focus attention on specific job challenges, creating a need to know. The concept stage provides the research base and conceptual models and theories for better or alternative ways to solve the specific set of job challenges, and engages the learner in rethinking the nature of the problem and potential solutions. In the demonstration stage a good example of the concepts operationalized (on the job) provides the first model of new skills and orientations. The practice stage provides a structured engagement activity for groups (preferably) to sample the new job behaviors, further stimulating the thinking process. During the feedback stage, effects of the practice activity are observed and shared by peers, providing an additional vicarious experience with the new behaviors, and reinforcement and correctives are offered by the trainers as well. In the transfer stage, the essential ideas and skills are reviewed, and participants engage in reflection and also in evaluation of the workshop, focusing on the potential for meeting new job demands. In addition, practice and coaching expectations and plans are shared for integrating the new skills into job performance. Coaching activity that follows an organizational goal-based workshop has great potential for enhancing and/or altering performance patterns. When used together, goals, workshops designed to enhance competencies, and coaching activity are powerful strategies for reshaping performance.

CONCLUSIONS

In preparing for a new schooling age, all role groups will become increasingly involved, both in their own professional development, and in designing development programs for others. Moving to an era of shared decision making at all levels stimulates the need for more powerful tools for group problem solving, planning, decision making, and conducting group meetings. In addition, more emphasis will be placed on skills required to make productive use of new technologies, and for developing response patterns to the learners in America's schools. All role groups will find themselves increasingly involved in the learning and inventing business, and in providing forms of training and coaching for others.

The six-stage competency development model provides a practical set of guidelines for planners, setting training within the context of organizational priorities. The model provides planning guidelines that can be viewed as both linear and curvilinear approaches to adult learning in workshops and institutes. Training that is synergogical in orientation provides the context for group problem solving about job-related problems, and stimulates the thinking processes for engaged learners. Coaching activity, within the context of organizational goals and workshop objectives, flourishes because of organizational expectations and the coaching conditions for competency development over time. Developing new professional capacities is the foundation and condition for restructuring and transforming schooling outcomes. Planning for professional training and coaching will link dreams to new realities.

REFERENCES

Bandura, A. 1969. *Principles of Behavior Modification*. New York: Holt, Rinehart and Winston.

Bigge, M. L. 1971. *Learning Theories for Teachers*. New York: Harper and Row.

Bloom, B. S. 1976. *Human Characteristics and School Learning*. New York: McGraw Hill Book Co.

Brookfield, S. 1986. *Understanding and Facilitating Adult Learning*. San Francisco: Jossey-Bass.

Festinger, L. 1957. *A Theory of Cognitive Dissonance*. Stanford, CA: Stanford University Press.

Fitzgerald, J. 1991. "Management Practices: A Case Study of District Level Supervisors and Directors of Curriculum and Instruction in One School District," doctoral dissertation at the University of South Florida, Tampa.

House, R. J. 1971. "A Path Goal Theory of Leader Effectiveness," *Administrative Science Quarterly*, 16(September):321–338. Reprinted in Scott and Cummings. 1973. *Reading in Organizational Behavior and Human Performance*. Homewood, IL: Richard D. Irwin.

Johnson, D. W., G. Maruyama, R. Johnson, D. Nelson and L. Skon. 1981. "Effects of Cooperative, Competitive, and Individualistic Goal Structures on Achievement: A Meta-Analysis," *Psychological Bulletin*, 89:47–62.

Joyce, B. and B. Showers. 1980. "Improving In-Service Training: The Messages of Research," *Educational Leadership*, 37(February):379.

Kanter, R. M. 1983. *The Change Masters*. New York: Simon and Schuster.

Knowles, M. 1980. *The Modern Practice of Adult Education: From Pedagogy to Andragogy, 2nd Ed*. New York: Cambridge Books: The Adult Education.

Lewin, K. 1936. *Principles of Topological Psychology*. New York: McGraw Hill Book Co.

Luthans, F. and R. Kreitner. 1975. *Organizational Behavior Modification*. Glenview, IL: Scott, Foresman.

Lysakowski, R. and H. J. Walberg. 1981. "Classroom Reinforcement in Relation to Learning: A Quantitative Analysis," *Journal of Educational Research*, 75:69–77.

Mayo, E. 1933. *The Human Problems of an Industrial Civilization*. New York: Macmillan.

Mouton, J. S. and R. R. Blake. 1984. *Synergogy: A New Strategy for Education, Training and Development*. San Francisco: Jossey-Bass.

Odiorne, G. S. 1979. *MBO II: A System of Managerial Leadership in the 80's*. Belmont, CA: Fearon Pitman.

Pajak, E. 1989. "Identification of Supervisory Proficiencies Project," sponsored by ASCD, Athens, GA: University of Georgia.

Parkinson, A. 1990. "An Examination of the Reliability and the Factor Structure of the School Work Culture Profile," doctoral dissertation at the University of South Florida, Tampa.

Purkey, S. C. and M. S. Smith. 1982. "Effective Schools: A Review," paper presented to a conference on Implications of Research for Teaching, National Institute of Education, Warrenton, VA, February 25–27, 1982.

Ramos, I. 1987. "Relationship between the Educational Orientation and the Perceived or Preferred Leadership Behavior of University Supervisors and Interns," doctoral dissertation at the University of South Florida, Tampa.

Rokeach, M. 1968. *Beliefs, Attitudes and Values*. San Francisco: Jossey-Bass.

Sergiovanni, T. J. and F. D. Carver. 1973. *The New School Executive: A Theory of Administration*. New York: Dodd, Mead and Co.

Skinner, B. F. 1969. *Contingencies of Reinforcement*. New York: Appleton-Century Crofts.

Slavin, R. E. 1990. *Cooperative Learning: Theory, Research and Practice*. Englewood Cliffs, NJ: Prentice Hall.

Snyder, K. J. 1988. *Competency Training for Managing Productive Schools*. San Diego: Harcourt, Brace and Jovanovich.

Snyder, K. J. and R. H. Anderson. 1986. *Managing Productive Schools: Toward an Ecology*. San Diego: Harcourt, Brace and Jovanovich.

The Observation Cycle: A Methodology for Coaching and Problem Solving

INTRODUCTION

Clinical supervision effectiveness requires more than strict adherence to the observation cycle presented in this chapter. The observation cycle is the "process" of clinical supervision, the acting out, if you will, of the clinical supervision model. Integral to the model are concepts and assumptions that form its foundation; without these any model becomes mechanical and attains neither the efficiency nor the outcomes for which it was intended. In this chapter, I will limit my discussion to several of the assumptions basic to the success of the observation cycle. These assumptions deal with both the supervisor and the supervisor's relationship with teachers. The supervisor must:

- display an attitude of confidence in the role of supervisor
- cultivate a positive attitude in teachers
- develop a constructive rapport with the teacher which is nonthreatening and beneficial to both

SUPERVISOR ATTITUDE

For supervisors to be successful in improving instruction, they must become proficient in working with others. Such proficiency is only possible if the supervisor first feels comfortable in the supervisory role. A positive attitude toward supervision begins with knowing and understanding one's self. Capable and effective people grow because they feel good about themselves in various relationships; accept new ideas/challenges; and involve themselves in a confident, yet flexible manner. Capable people set realistic, professional goals that enable them to harness their energy and seek assistance when needed: a formula that encourages self-fulfillment and success.

A positive, enthusiastic attitude is infectious; in other words, positiveness is catching. Clinical supervision insists that the supervisor model the positive interaction behaviors expected of teachers. Therefore, it is essential that the supervisor first have a strong self image, project that image to colleagues and significant others, and expect the same of teachers in all their teaching efforts.

The supervisor must harbor a professional attitude, academic supervisory competence, and self-confidence; these traits must be evidenced in all actions. A teacher who perceives these traits in the supervisor is more likely to respond positively toward the support and assistance provided. Supervisors also learn to recognize the importance of time for themselves to provide the technical skills and competence required to achieve job goals. Capable and effective people come to realize that if they don't protect some "self time" they won't be able to call on the "reserve" needed for significant tasks.

TEACHER ATTITUDE

Since clinical supervision is a reciprocal process, teacher self-esteem is as important as supervisor self-esteem. Therefore, if the teacher lacks confidence and self-acceptance, the supervisor must diagnose these weaknesses and stimulate the development of more effective personal qualities. Only when the teacher is working at an acceptable level of self-esteem can the process of clinical supervision be fully utilized to address the quality of instruction.

There are several approaches the supervisor can incorporate to motivate teacher self-esteem. Using praise, accepting differences, and encouraging self-growth are among the common sense methods. Of course, any approach will fail if the supervisor lacks sincerity and conviction. The supervisor must convey authentic projections of self that display understanding of and respect for the teacher.

While the descriptions are easily applicable for teachers working with students, the following five considerations may assist the *supervisor* in building a sincere and productive professional relationship with the teacher:

(1) Know yourself. The ability to understand one's self helps one to relate more realistically to others. By objectively reflecting upon feelings from previous personal experience, one can get a more accurate idea of what others are dealing with in similar situations, remembering always to trust your own judgment.

(2) Ask others. The supervisor should stress the importance of collegial assistance in the process of knowing self. Peer coaching can be a wonderful assistance tool, and in the long run, advice from others should be stored and used.

(3) Accept yourself. Competence and preparedness contribute most significantly towards self-acceptance. A person who is accepting of self has an appreciation for human dignity and is aware of the worth of others. Praise yourself occasionally, especially when it's deserved. Continue to seek encouragement from others and yourself as you need it.

(4) Respect yourself. Supervisors need to help teachers become successful in professional growth and development. Self-acceptance of strengths and weaknesses can help one to gain respect for the uniqueness and individuality of others. Teachers need to be reminded that to receive respect from students, they must first show respect to students. Respecting students becomes easier when teachers first respect themselves. If you don't respect yourself, how can others respect you? If you like yourself, the chances are that you'll like and respect others.

(5) Respect others. An individual must develop a strong belief in the worth of other human beings; only then can two individuals work toward a common goal. The ability to respect others is contingent on the four previous steps concerning oneself. Strength and success in working with others in supervision depends upon the relationship the supervisor has with them. Showing respect for them is key.

RAPPORT

A positive, harmonious relationship between people is the essence of rapport. Clinical supervision pioneers Morris Cogan and Robert Goldhammer spoke sparingly of the term "rapport," relegating it to a minor role in the clinical supervision theory and process. Indeed, both apparently thought that rapport, once established at the beginning of the observation cycle, would then last throughout the process and presumably throughout other interactions between the supervisor and respective teachers with whom it was established. Their assumptions, I feel, were too limited. Once rapport is established, it must be encouraged to grow. It must be nurtured.

Rapport is both prerequisite and integral to the entire clinical supervision process. Once established, rapport requires continuing emphasis. Rapport nurturance, therefore, is central to clinical supervision. The rapport nurturance process in clinical supervision requires a knowledge base of motivation, instructional theory, and adult psychology. Motivation and adult psychology foundations can be addressed, in part, by the positive self-attitude concepts presented in the previous paragraphs. The instructional theory foundation can be addressed through a substantial knowledge base in observational systems, together with a knowledge base of analysis of teaching. Rapport nurturance depends on the supervisor setting the tone for an environment of collegiality dedicated to improvement of teaching and student learning. Displaying an interest in understanding of teachers is the beginning. Displaying competencies within the observation cycle and the use of human relations skills throughout is an essential step. Most important is that both the supervisor and teacher know and accept their respective individual and interactive roles in student learning and growth through instructional improvement.

THE MODEL

The observation cycle model delineated in this chapter is derived from the Goldhammer clinical supervision model. For more than two decades, I have used this model in supervising teachers in kindergarten through graduate school. The model encompasses five stages: (1) preobservation, (2) observation, (3) analysis and strategy, (4) the conference, and (5) the post-conference analysis. Integral to each stage is the emphasis on rapport. As noted earlier, rapport is the glue that holds the clinical supervision process together (see Figure 7.1).

The model is essentially the same as Goldhammer's except for the deliberate emphasis on rapport throughout the cycle.

R	Pre-observation
A	
P	Observation
P	Analysis and Strategy
O	
R	Conference
T	Post-conference analysis

Figure 7.1 *Observation Cycle Model.*

Pre-Observation

Objectives

- continue/strengthen rapport
- establish teacher instructional needs and goals
- present cycle format
- share teacher/supervisor expectancies

Procedure

The pre-observation conference represents the first step in clinical supervision. It is important to remember, however, that an effective supervisor has already established contact and begun to build rapport with the teacher. Therefore, the supervisor should be entering the pre-observation conference with a general idea of the teacher's attitudes about self and others and also an historical relationship, on which the present meeting builds.

One major objective of the pre-observation conference should be to reestablish communication, which works toward improving rapport. Pre-observation represents an excellent opportunity to improve teacher confidence and build mutual respect. Initially the meeting should allow the teacher and supervisor to simply renew their communication and their familiarity with each other's interactive patterns. Next, the supervisor should work to reduce teacher apprehension while at the same time increase teacher confidence in preparing the lesson to be offered.

It is important that the pre-observation remains positive and un-complicated so that the teacher feels comfortable and secure.

A second objective of pre-observation is to elicit areas for instructional concern or areas of improvement. Both members should agree to focus upon a limited number of teaching skills that the teacher and supervisor feel will better assist instruction. The most important points to remember when identifying areas of improvement are:

(1) The number of emphasized areas should be manageable. If the observation process is to be successful, goals must remain within reason. Therefore, whenever possible, it is best in each observation cycle to limit the number of areas selected for observation and coaching. Certainly a supervisor who focuses on one or two skill areas will gain a more thorough idea of the teacher's competencies and needs than a supervisor who attempts to address ten or more areas. In addition, a teacher who has been targeted for a number of areas of instructional improvement is likely to feel overwhelmed or inadequate. Most teachers accept their need for assistance in one or two skill areas, but it is unlikely they would be receptive to many more.

(2) The scope of an emphasized area should be realistic and specific. Supervision must focus improvement of instruction in a positive and supportive manner. Therefore, the supervisor and teacher should use the clinical supervision process as a means to address specific skills that will assist in pupil learning. Both supervisor and teacher must realize that progress in improvement is a step-by-step procedure. The supervisor and the teacher should use the process to improve one or two specified skills with a scope small enough so that improvement can be measured over a short period of time. The key to success is to keep one's goals manageable so that improvement can occur.

(3) The skill areas emphasized should be determined to the greatest extent by the teacher. If a teacher has a particular concern about an aspect of the teaching lesson to be observed, chances are it may be more well founded than the supervisor's concerns, especially in the beginning stages of their collaborative work. To facilitate rapport, supervisors should be willing to defer their own concerns if the teacher has deeper concerns. Therefore, it is mainly the teacher who initially sets the stage for supervision during the pre-observation meeting.

Another pre-observation objective is to determine the terms or conditions for the entire observation cycle process. Once again it is important that the teacher play an integral role in establishing these terms. The quality and authenticity of the lesson will depend in part on the comfort of the teacher. Therefore, the teacher and supervisor must decide on observation ground rules that best meet established goals and consider observation techniques that are the least disruptive to the lesson. Some details to be worked out in the pre-observation meeting include:

- time, length, focus, and place of observation
- methods for recording observed lesson
- supervisor participation in lesson, if any
- other "ground rules" (e.g., where to be seated)

Good intentions on the part of the supervisor are necessary but not sufficient. How the supervisor begins the pre-observation is critical in determining the outcome of the entire observation cycle. One important point to consider is the teacher's sense of active involvement. Pitfalls can be avoided as the teacher becomes engaged in the process. Analyze the supervisor's behavior in Example One.

Example One

Supervisor: OK, let's get the show on the road. What can I do for you today?

Teacher: Well, ah! I might need you to focus a little bit on my questioning techniques. I'd like to get greater class participation.

Supervisor: You know what I would do? I would just call on the kids randomly. It always worked for me! Anyhow, I'll do an objective analysis and we'll look at how many times you question.

In this example, the supervisor's approach and choice of words are somewhat condescending to the teacher and indicate that the supervisor knows best; in other words, you need help and I'm the one to give it to you. In addition, the direct suggestion made by the supervisor essentially removes the teacher's sense of involvement. The teacher will feel compelled to use the supervisor's ideas during the lesson for fear of an unfavorable evaluation, even if this is not the intention of the supervisor. The most probable result is to create teacher dependency or worse yet, resentment. Read and react to Example Two, comparing the supervisor's behavior with that observed in Example One.

Example Two

Supervisor: Hi Gina, is everything set for your lesson?

Teacher: Yes, I think so.

Supervisor: Is there anything specific you'd like me to look for in the observation?

Teacher: Well, I would like to get greater participation when I'm questioning.

Supervisor: OK, do you think a Flanders analysis might be helpful?

Teacher: Well, perhaps, but maybe you could just watch my actual technique instead of just counting the number of times I question.

Supervisor: Good idea. This seems like a good place to begin. I'll pay close attention to your technique, and also chart the number and types of questions you ask. Is that agreeable to you?

Teacher: Yes, sounds good.

In Example Two, the supervisor is facilitating/advising instead of controlling. Such an approach brings the teacher into the improvement process. Not only is it more desirable for the teacher, it also assists the supervisor by providing a more accurate picture of the teacher's needs. In Example Two, the supervisor uses teacher input to better facilitate the observation. In Example One, the supervisor merely devised suggestions independent of possible valuable teacher input.

Observation

Objective

- carry out a lesson observation as agreed upon in the pre-observation plan.

Procedure

Observation in the classroom is the next step in carrying out the plan of action decided upon in pre-observation. During the classroom observation, the supervisor collects lesson data requested by the teacher in a manner agreed to by both supervisor and teacher. Observing is both a science and an art, and there are various technologies available for gathering data: formats within which to classify behaviors, maps to show classroom traffic patterns, and methods to measure the kinds or quantities of interactions. Thus, choosing what to observe – the student responses, teacher-student interactions, teacher questions and reinforcement, lesson pacing, teacher centeredness and body language, student interactions, and social climate – how to observe – video, audio, interaction analysis, typescripts, coding via systematic observation systems – and when to observe – linking behaviors and data variables, selecting sequences and interaction patterns – are all keys to the observation process and therefore the success of the remaining components of the observation cycle.

However data are collected, they should be gathered as objectively as possible, to supervisor expertise. On the other hand, any technique is only as good as the person using it. Information garnered from using objective techniques has to be considered as simply a part (albeit an integral part) of the total teaching actions.

Objective data should, when analyzed, provide as clear and accurate a picture as possible of those areas of focus that were agreed upon in pre-observation. A supervisor must acquire skills for data collection. When I supervise teachers, I prefer using videotape in classroom observation with a combination of one or several objective analysis instruments. For example, I might use self-developed variations of Flanders Interaction Analysis, At Task, or the Teacher Question Inventory either individually or in some combination. By using combinations, the obtained data complement each other and help provide a clearer, more objective picture. In conferences, then, teachers can see both written and visual playback data on classroom action. Such feedback can be powerful and effective when used well by a competent supervisor.

Analysis and Strategy

Objectives

* reconstruct/organize/condense data on agreed-upon foci
* identify patterns in data
* determine significance of patterns; arrange in order of importance
* return to data to see if there is more to be learned
* develop a structured plan for the conference

Procedure

Analysis and strategy are the heart of the observation cycle. The analysis and strategy stage is geared to developing the most productive conference possible. To allow data to remain fresh, analysis should be carried out as soon as possible after observation, and never longer than several days.

Making sense of data collected and then arranging the data into a manageable form for both supervisor and teacher to understand and use is an important process in teacher improvement. Identifying and reorganizing data is complex, involving behavior patterns, their cumulative effect on pupil learning, and the significance of teacher uniqueness filtered through sensory, cognitive, and expressive screens. Due to the necessity of thinking of strategy while performing analysis, I believe it is necessary to keep both as one stage of the observation cycle, rather than separating them.

Systematic observation instruments enhance data reconstruction. The clearer the lesson picture, the greater the possibility of providing usable data to analyze the teaching. Data pattern significance can be determined by referring to teacher goals and student demonstrated or inferred experiences. Given all the data that must be reviewed, strategy must be effected as the supervisor begins to determine which patterns are more significant than the others.

When determining which patterns to discuss in the conference, I suggest that the supervisor arrange patterns in some hierarchical fashion. Some patterns are more prominent, and some more consequential either by frequency or by the way they affect students. To determine pattern significance, the supervisor could ask such questions as: Have observable patterns been repeated enough to be of concern? Are they consistent (in either being there or omitted if they should be there) throughout the lesson? Might they occur in other lessons? What value do they have?

Answers to some of these questions become evident in observation instrument data. Teacher Question Inventory data, for example, would provide the number of times the teacher asked a recall, comprehension, analysis, or opinion question during the lesson. Coupled with creative use of other objective instrumentation and videotaping, one could extract data indicating when each type question was asked, to whom it was addressed, what type of interaction pattern occurred, and which students were involved in what way. Determining pattern hierarchy becomes much easier with such objective data. And supervisor concerns regarding treatability become more readily answerable for strategy planning.

A structured plan for the conference must be developed. Once the time of the conference has been established, the supervisor might want to pay some attention to such important logistic and temporal details as:

- Conference length—length will vary with individual needs. The most important thing to keep in mind is that the conference should cover a manageable amount of material in an adequate amount of time.
- Distractions—take every precaution to avoid distractions during the conference.
- Participant comfort—consider ambience, appropriate lighting and seating, as well as proximity to the teacher's classroom.

Strategy is effective planning for the conference, incorporating decisions relating to means and ends, setting goals to look at short- and long-range planning, and providing data analysis for instructional improvement purposes. Like observation, strategy is both a science and an art and has no prescriptive balance of these two ingredients. Strategy is a complex technique that results from and is enhanced by the total of one's professional and personal cultural experiences. Strategy involves skills of analysis, synthesis, and comprehension. It also involves intuition, boldness, and taking chances within reason. In short, when one skillfully considers supervisory implications of selecting issues and developing a plan for the conference based on significant salient data, one is building an effective strategy.

Conference

Objectives

- provide lesson feedback on pre-agreed issues
- determine short- and long-range instructional improvement plans
- provide basis for additional instructional improvement goals
- provide an analysis of observation cycle

Procedure

The conference might be considered the most critical stage of the observation cycle. If a supervisor is unable to effectively share observations and ideas during the conference, all previous efforts will be wasted. Effective supervisor communication skills are necessary during this stage if meaningful instructional improvement is to occur.

The first conference goal is to provide lesson feedback to the teacher on specific focus issues agreed upon by supervisor and teacher during the pre-observation. To this point, the cycle has been focused and the conference should maintain that focus. The supervisor must, by keeping the instructional improvement goal in constant view, communicate objective feedback to the teacher as effectively and interactively as possible. The format of the feedback need not be ritual, but rather designed to meet teacher needs.

All efforts of the observation cycle should lead to instructional improvement. While the conference format may vary, each conference should contain (1) review of pre-observation agreements, (2) review of observation procedures, (3) review of data in relation to lesson objectives and observation focus, (4) analysis of data, to include strengths and improvements needed, and (5) plan of action to include roles of teacher and supervisor in the plan, as well as resources needed to implement the plan. Thus a crucial goal should be to determine a short- and long-range action plan.

This plan of action is the basis for an individualized supervision program for the teacher. Subsequent observation cycles or portions thereof are reflective of this plan. The short-range plan, for example, may replace or reinforce the next pre-observation meeting. Perhaps the plan may call for elimination of several pre-observation meetings, with emphasis on observation/analysis/feedback on foci determined in the short-range plan. The key to the improvement plan is the working relationship between supervisor and teacher, and the responsibility for an effective working relationship remains that of the supervisor.

The long-range plan depends, in part, on the effectiveness of the observation cycle. Thus an important contributing portion of the conference is the post-conference analysis by supervisor and teacher of what has transpired in the cycle, how both feel about each other's role effectiveness, and how the supervisor's role can be improved for future interactions with the teacher.

Post-Conference Analysis

Objectives

- assess the teacher's and supervisor's goals
- evaluate the worth of the conference to the teacher
- hold self-reflective sessions

Procedure

The post-conference analysis serves as the conscience of the clinical supervision process. It is a self-improvement strategy that provides a foundation for assessing supervision productivity. It is a time when the supervisor's performance is examined with the same vigor, professionalism, and practices used previously with the teacher. The teacher and supervisor interpret the cycle data, examine relevant effects on consequences of supervision techniques, and consider modification of supervisor's practices to better meet the teacher's and supervisor's needs and future actions.

The importance of this step cannot be overstated. The process of engaging in systematic self-evaluation and drawing conclusions based on factual information rather than inferential judgments will enhance the supervisor's professionalism.

CONCLUSION

This chapter has investigated and stressed core methods within the observation cycle, emphasizing the importance of developing trust/rapport between supervisors and teachers. Methodology must be wed with context, especially in supervision that deals with teacher coaching and instructional development. While objectives must be delineated for each stage of the observation cycle, procedures within respective stages must be implemented creatively with each teacher. Supervisors must develop a knowledge base of observation cycle foundations and acquire and sharpen skills in implementing the methodology.

Communication and Coaching

OVERVIEW: COMMUNICATING FOR RESULTS

Communication in the technological world of today has meant an exciting series of new breakthroughs as witnessed by the power of remote satellites, the speed of FAX machines, and the convenience of a cellular phone. Each emphasizes the human urge to send messages to one another.

The more traditional, less glamorous approach to communication has involved people-to-people, eye-to-eye interaction. Sending messages through this well-established line of communication has meant the success or downfall of marriages, leaders, parent-child relationships, athletic coaches, and counseling methods, to name a few. In this volume, the link has been made between the supervision process and the art of coaching. Joyce and Showers (1982) made the link between training in education and training in athletics, while contemplating the dilemma of how to transfer skills learned and practiced in workshops and training courses to the realities of the classroom. In support of Showers' and Joyce's work, the business of training often leaves a void between the transfer of knowledge and skills from the learning setting to the work setting. This void seems to occur even when people deem the skills to be valuable. Adapting the athletic coaching model to educational training, whereby learning continues at the work site through guided follow-up supervision, was an idea that was readily accepted as viable in education settings. Hasenstab (1989) furthers the coaching analogy to include theatre, dance, music, and art, while reminding his readers that all great professionals are coached. Typically, the better the professional the greater the coach.

The term "coaching" implies a specific set of learned skills that when used together in certain patterns derive specific results. It has been rumored that the legendary coach of the University of Alabama, Bear Bryant, sent his scouts to film the feet, arms, and body movements of the best players in the NFL in the belief that if his players could match the patterns of the best, they could reproduce similar results. Bestselling authors Peters and Waterman (1982) and Robbins (1986) researched successful companies and individuals in search of existing commonalities that would give clues to others about how to repeat the same behaviors to produce the same results. The driving force for Robbins' findings, as stated in his workshop, as well as in his books, tapes and T.V. appearances, is *success leaves clues*.

The challenge is to communicate the clues for success in order to repeat the patterns that achieve desired results. The focus for this chapter is to pinpoint a set of skills identifying how to communicate effectively as a coach, by proposing a set of specific generic beliefs and skills for effective communication.

COMMUNICATION AND COACHING: FOUR BASIC ASSUMPTIONS

The following four assumptions about communication and the coaching role should be kept firmly in mind.

The Best Teachers or Administrators May Not Always Be the Best Coaches

In order to be a superstar coach in the NFL, it is not a prerequisite to have been in the Super Bowl as a quarterback or to have held any other position for that matter. What is key remains in the realm of how to communicate the winning behaviors and attitudes needed to make a winning season. The same formula exists in education. The best teachers or administrators may not always be the best coaches. Their ability to translate their success into repeatable patterns may, in fact, be limited by their success. In many areas, repeated success leads to a comfortable position where one becomes so unconsciously skilled (on automatic pilot) that the obvious is often overlooked. What appears obvious to a skilled practitioner may be a major "Aha!" or insight to someone learning, refining, or growing. Take, for example, a desire to learn to cook or bake a special recipe, which is often met by frustration due to incomplete data to accomplish the task. A request made to the chef or talented cook might receive the following information: "Oh, that's so easy, I know you can do it—all you have to do is. . . ." The "all you have to do . . ." may leave out some very major or minor steps necessary to meet with similar success in completion of the recipe.

This example does not mean to imply that a successful teacher, principal, athlete, pilot, or singer may not be a successful coach, but it does suggest that it takes more than personal success to coach others.

People Do Not Take Action or Change Simply Because Someone Else Tells Them to Change

People change or respond to suggestions, requests, or commands of others only if they perceive an opportunity for pleasure or avoidance of pain (Robbins, 1986).

The Carl Rogers era of psychology led disciples to utilize paraphrasing and reflective listening, sometimes called active listening, to allow individuals to come to their own conclusions about how, when, where, and why to make changes. As a counselor in training during the early 1970s, I was exposed to the "know thyself" experience-based learning. All answers were to come from within ourselves and from our willingness to change. External direction was provided only through parroting, paraphrasing, and other names tagged to these verbal strategies for counseling. People were expected to set their own expectations.

Unlike nondirective counselors and clinicians, coaches take more liberties as encouragers and leaders who share and deliver a common mission or vision, which is based upon the organization for whom they are employed. If the commitment to an expected goal is lacking, the coach has but a limited amount of time and resources to wait for a player to get his/her act together on the field, a musician to land an engagement, or a ballet dancer to be asked to join a touring company. The verbal skills of nondirective counseling, which allow the supervisee to control the direction and time of change, have also not been utilized in the worlds of entertainment, sports, and business because they are not cost or time effective in producing results. If children are to be considered our most valuable resources, then administrators and teachers as caregivers for children need more than the time-honored models of nondirective supervision in order to accomplish a "winning season."

If the analogy to coaches in other areas holds true, the educator's coach will need to orchestrate the vision and skills deemed necessary for success, utilizing communication strategies that are more directly guided and engaging, yet packaged in a manner that supports the second assumption.

The Primary Responsibility of the Coach Lies in Creating an Environment That Produces a Satisfied Customer

If this assumption is true, then individuals or groups being coached are the coach's secondary clients. The primary clients are, therefore, the fans in sports, the audience in entertainment, the consumer in sales, and the students in education. Keeping these clients satisfied is a major responsibility for the coach. Increasing losses in ticket sales can cost a coach his/her position. Education, as does a losing football team, finds itself the subject of much criticism and cries for overhaul because the consumers (business, industry, parents) are not pleased with the results of the products (students). Students also live the role of the consumer. Well-documented statistics are in abundance showing unwilling, dissatisfied customers in numerous instances.

When Teachers Are Coached to Winning Seasons, Everyone Is a Winner

Being a successful coach in athletics implies winners and losers. There is only one first place, one second place, and one third place position in competitive sports. When teachers guide their students to successful seasons, however, then everyone benefits—kids, parents, the community, and employers. Learning has no limit on the number of winners permitted.

If it is not a prerequisite to be a master performer in your field, if it is understood that people change because they want to change not because someone tells them to change, if they keep student success as the primary target in a coaching strategy, and if it is clear that winning experiences are available to all in the learning process, then anyone who is in education is eligible to be an educator's coach. In fact, Joyce and Showers (1982) included administrators, curriculum supervisors, college professors, teachers, and peers in their eligibility list for who could enter into the process of coaching. Levels of mastery and expertise for the coach were not defined.

BECOMING A WINNING COACH

Given the conviction that any role group can coach or be coached, the ultimate question still remains—how does one become a winning coach? What are the specific generic behaviors attributed to coaching? The contributions of experts to the success literature (how individuals positively influence themselves and others to achieve success) are used to formulate this chapter's content.

Three themes, all relating to how we communicate with ourselves and others, were found to be consistently present in the success literature. They fall into the following three categories:

(1) Positively focused images relate to how our personal mindset directs the quality of our communication skills.

(2) Positively focused body language, which defines how we control our physiology, maximizes the message we want to communicate.

(3) Positively focused statements and questions chart the direction of the verbal message we communicate.

POSITIVELY FOCUSED IMAGES

Kehoe (1987), Robbins (1986), Schwartz (1987), and Bandler and Grinder (1979) all examined the question "What distinguishes people who succeed from people who fail?" These authors joined a growing number of experts in the belief that the answer lies within our minds. Human beings have control over their own states and circumstances.

People who have attained levels of success follow a consistent path to optimize results (Robbins, 1986). An individual in the role of coach can utilize mind power information to maximize his/her own performance as well as to produce positive results in others. The challenge for the coach is how to engage others to produce and then reproduce the desired result.

Four strategies to channel the power of the mind utilizing positively focused images are consistently described in the success oriented literature. These strategies include insertion, visioning, visualization, and modeling.

Insertion

"What we do in life is determined by how we communicate to ourselves" (Robbins, 1986, p. 22). Positively focused images inserted into our minds produce what we want our minds to know and do. David Schwartz in the *Magic of Thinking BIG* (1987), describes the process like this:

> We do not think in words and phrases. We think only in pictures and/or images. Words are the raw materials of thought. When spoken or read, that amazing instrument, the mind automatically converts words and phrases into mind pictures. . . . If someone tells you "Jim bought a new split-level" you see one picture. But if you're told, "Jim bought a new ranch house" you see still another picture. The mind pictures we see are modified by the kinds of words we use to name things and describe things. (p. 55)

The study of neuro-linguistic programming (Bandler and Grinder, 1979; Robbins, 1986) extends the knowledge of the power of negative messages to the functions of the brain and its ability to orchestrate a person's defeat or failure. This is clarified by attempting the following exercise:

> Please stop reading this text for thirty seconds and *don't think of the color blue*.

Now that you've completed the exercise you're aware that in order not to think of the color blue, you first conjured up an image of blue that either appeared as a color, as a series of letters spelling the word "blue," as an item with the color blue, or as any combination of the three. The images we create determine how we act. For example:

> When you believe something is impossible, your mind goes to work for you to prove why. But when you believe, really believe, something can be done, your mind goes to work for you and helps you find ways to do it. Believing something can be done paves the way for creative solutions. (Schwartz, 1987, p. 69)

Positively focused images can be produced simply by inserting positively phrased messages and positive pictures in the mind. In the section later discussing visualization, we deal with how to maximize the possibilities of positive pictures. Our focus in this section will be to concentrate on what we say and hear in our minds.

Words combined into phrases and sentences inserted in our minds can be a first step in creating new or better results. Successful people specialize in pulling positive thoughts into their memory bank (Schwartz, 1987). For example, an athletic coach desiring a winning season needs to think like a winner. A positive message sometimes called self-talk might be, "I have the confidence to lead my team to great accomplishments."

> Big Thinkers are specialists in creating positive forward-looking optimistic pictures in their own minds and in the minds of others. To think big we must use words and phrases which produce big, positive mental images. (Schwartz, 1987, p. 55)

Tonality is also a critical dimension of producing positive images in the brain. Try this exercise briefly and see/hear what happens. Repeat the following words five times in a monotone, disbelieving voice: "I have the confidence and ability to guide others to achieve success."

Now repeat the same words to yourself using a positive rhythm or tonality that expresses excitement and belief as if it were actually true. You may have noticed that the second time brought you more energy, more positive images of confidence and a sense that the statement is true.

Try the same exercise using another message to the brain, "I feel happy and healthy!" Note the results by comparing the differences in how you said each statement using the two different tones or rhythms. Words alone cannot sustain positively focused images, but words and appropriately congruent sounds (tonality) can deliver the desired images.

The obvious question is, what does all this mean for me as a coach? The message self-inserted in the coach's mind may determine the successful outcome of the coaching experience. It can limit or empower the level of expectation communicated to the one(s) being coached. For example, a teacher's coach who conjures up an image by inserting "This is going to be a tough one, I'll be lucky to get him/her to even agree to participate in this process," may have limited results compared to the coach who inserts, "This is going to be a challenge to get the best results so the students in the classroom who deserve the best get the best."

Kehoe's work summarizes this section with the belief that we will always remain where we are unless we change our thinking.

Your mind creates your reality. You can choose to accept this or not. You can be conscious of it, and get your mind working for you or you can ignore it, and allow it to work in ways that will hinder and hold you back. But your mind will always, and forever be creating your reality. (Kehoe, 1987, p. 23)

Visioning

Insertion combined with visioning increases the likelihood of achieving a winning season, because a vision stretches the possibilities inserted in the mind.

If we consider day to day schooling experience, much of it has been at the "ho-hum," routine level, where work is individually focused and follows a pattern of read the text, answer the questions, and take the test. The ho-hum syndrome persists even though low student motivation is a major obstacle to success for administrators and teachers, who face increasing droputs and major disciplinary problems throughout all grade levels. Teachers often take their problems, personal boredom, and even burnout to the teachers' lounge for consultation and reinforcement. There the potential for positively focused images is quickly replaced by the wear and tear of negatively focused images transmitted to the mind.

Visioning acts as a strategy to overcome apathy, burnout, and acceptance of mediocrity by shifting images from what is to what can be. "Great accomplishments are always preceded by great visions" (Barker, 1990, p. 9).

What does vision mean to those in the role of coach? If "our visions of the future are the most powerful motivators for human change" (Barker, 1990, p. 8), then visioning becomes a powerful strategy for guiding, leading, and inspiring great leaps of advancement in others. If successful people share a positive and profound vision of their own future (Barker, 1990), then perhaps successful teachers also share a profound vision for the future of their students.

If one accepts the designation of coach, one must ask if it is good enough to embrace a vision stating "If I make a difference in the life of one child, then I will have succeeded." Perhaps the reader has children or grandchildren, or plans to have children. Would you be satisfied if your child was one of the twenty-nine out of thirty children excluded from the umbrella of influence?

Visions that are powerful and profound stretch beyond the limits of current reality. Coaches should take positions that lead educators to embrace energetic, worthwhile visions such as Snyder notes in an earlier chapter: "Every student a winner, every day."

Barker (1990) outlines four essential characteristics that comprise good vision:

(1) A good vision is leadership initiated. For our purposes the coach can lead in stating the vision, share in its development, or undertake the task or implementation through coaching.

(2) A good vision is shared with all members and supported by the team who will carry out the vision to provide understanding and direction.

(3) A good vision is *comprehensive* and detailed and is never expressed in numbers or increased profitability. The numbers are only a consequence of the defined vision.

(4) A good vision is positive and inspiring and challenges everyone to *stretch* their images and skills.

The model portraying a coach as a mover, shaker, challenger of ideas and people, encourager, and an inspirer can be multiplied in significance through insertion of Joel Barker's message that: "Vision without action is merely a dream. Action without vision is just passing time. Vision with action can change the world" (Barker, 1990, p. 7).

Visualization

Visualization is the third strategy utilized to empower positive images to produce positive action. Visualization is using our minds to see ourselves in situations that create a time of success in order to prepare to do it again, and to create new images of actions yet to be undertaken that we desire to successfully achieve.

Visualizations can range from the simple insertion of the image of self-confidence in a particular situation, all the way to imagining that students engaged in learning are animated and motivated to learn more and more. A coach might visualize a scene whereby one's own coaching behaviors positively influenced an individual or group to embrace the "team" vision with vigor and zeal. Visualization possibilities are limitless. Visualizations are intended to put people in a resourceful state that empowers the individual to take the "types and qualities of actions" that create desired outcomes (Robbins, 1986). General steps to visualization include:

(1) First pose empowering questions. What vision would provide me with the greatest satisfaction?

(2) Visualize your positively focused images as if they were actually happening at the moment.

(3) Visualize what you desire, being careful not to be limited by current reality.

(4) Visualize the action/scene at least once a day, noting that repetition increases the clarity and likelihood of implementation (Kehoe, 1987 and Robbins, 1986).

Specific steps to visualizing include tapping into our visual, auditory, and kinesthetic senses to consciously direct the mind's action. Paying close attention to the mind's film clips can allow us to call up the images as we would a document on a computer screen. Note the details of the visualizations in this manner: Are you in the picture or out of the picture? Is it in color or black and white? Is it dark or bright? Is the picture moving or is the action still? Is it close or far away? Are there words or sounds — loud or soft? Do you have warm sensations or distant feelings?

Once the images have been carefully noted, it is possible to adjust or fine tune the image to achieve optimum results. Try calling up a desired visual that provided a splendid moment in your life or a compelling vision for the future. Reframe and refine the image by making it smaller or larger, bringing it closer or pulling it further away, adjusting for brightness or darkness, adding positive sounds or words, stepping in the scene to live it, or stepping out to observe what's happening. Our minds have the ability to reframe the future by adjusting the images inserted into them.

Modeling

Insertion, visioning, and visualizations are personal actions that require mental aerobics to prepare to take appropriate action. Modeling is the fourth strategy noted in the success literature for achieving desired outcomes. Modeling actually involves positively focused visualizations of how others whom we respect behave in specified situations. If we buy into Robbins' adage, "success leaves clues," then the key is to study those who succeed—for people are our greatest resource.

I learned this lesson as a beginning teacher in my first assignment in the Chicago Public Schools inner city. My classroom was on the first floor of one of the three sixteen-story housing projects that were built around a concrete playground and formed a "U" shape bordered by a railroad track. The teacher librarian named Bettie Wilkes shared the other half of the first floor for her classes. Mrs. Wilkes became my self-appointed coach in the days when mentors were only assigned during student teaching.

After eating the federally supported lunch, my students would go out on the playground to spend the remainder of their lunch time. At least once or twice a week, youth gangs would come down to the playground and terrorize the young ones. Bettie Wilkes would step outside, pull her shoulders back and announce in a voice of authority that the gangs were to leave the grounds and leave these children alone. Each time these young men towering over Bettie Wilkes would retreat, stating, "yes ma'am."

I was always asking myself, how does she do it? Was it because she was black? The answer had to be no, because at that time all of the other teachers were black except for me, and they didn't set foot out of their classrooms to remedy this terror. Was it because she was bigger, meaner, or more important than the rest of us? The answer again had to be negative because she was moderate in height and weight and was firm, not mean. Finally, I came to the conclusion that she acted like she knew what she was doing and they believed her!

One day it finally happened. Lunch time arrived, Bettie Wilkes was not there, and the gangs arrived to prey on the younger children. Being twenty-two, white, and very inexperienced, I debated about moving from my desk and instead buried myself in the paperwork. When the noise and cries began to escalate, the call to action no longer could be suppressed, and I headed toward the door. Suddenly, I stopped and inserted Bettie Wilkes in my mind. With her image as a guide, I drew back my shoulders, strengthened my walk, adjusted my head and walked out on the grounds reproducing her words and tonality for the offenders. In my mind's image, I looked, sounded, and moved like Bettie Wilkes, and to my great surprise and relief, I produced the same results. By modeling the model, I was able to overcome my fear of rejection and helplessness and gained the strength to champion my students. That moment was a turning point in my career.

Modeling can help individuals, groups, and organizations achieve excellence. We have the ability to model either ourselves, when we can draw upon past successful experiences, or others who appear to have achieved the results we desire. A key element in coaching in any field is to identify those who model excellence, and to coach others in the actions and attitudes needed to reproduce that success. Anthony Robbins has spent his career studying and researching the belief systems of people who model excellence in their fields. Robbins (1986) identified seven beliefs that have empowered people to do more, take greater action, and produce greater results. If we want coaches who model excellence as well as coach for excellence in education, then perhaps these belief systems will also empower coaching interactions. We will examine six of these beliefs.

(1) "Everything happens for a reason and a purpose, and it serves us . . . all successful people have the uncanny ability to focus on what is possible in a situation, what positive results could come from it. No matter how much negative feedback they get from their environment they think in terms of possibilities" (p. 75). They insert options for handling obstacles.

(2) "There is no such thing as failure, there are only results" (p. 77). The famous story about Thomas Edison illustrates this second belief. After he had tried thousands of times to perfect the light bulb, he was questioned about his failures and encouraged to give up. He is said to have answered, "I didn't fail, I just discovered that I need to find another way to invent the electric light bulb." He learned from his experience that he needed to discover a different set of actions to produce the result intended.

With that belief system as a model, just imagine how educators could achieve success with students, if we were willing to analyze the results and try 9,999 times until we succeeded.

"Winners, leaders and masters . . . all understand that if you try something and do not get the result you want it's simply feedback" (Robbins, 1986, p. 78). To utilize the strategies discussed thus far, the process may work like this: insertion of a positive message about what was learned will in turn achieve a positively focused image about what was learned; this will lead one to refocus on the vision, and then to utilize visualization procedures to reframe one's own or other's possibilities.

(3) "Whatever happens, take responsibility" (p. 79). If every event has a learned lesson, then by taking responsibility one is forced to examine how to improve for the next time. Two "feedforward" questions to produce this belief within us are: "How can we get better results next time?" and "What actions would lead us closer to our goals?"

(4) "People are your greatest resource" (p. 80). Peters and Waterman, authors of *In Search of Excellence*, observe that companies that succeed treat people with dignity and respect. The school restructuring movement is a good example of the education power base coming to a realization that all parties in the education process need to be partners to achieve excellence. The challenging task for the coach is to use insertion to retain the belief that people are our greatest resource even when dealing with resistant "players."

(5) "Work is play" (p. 82). Work is exciting and fun to many of us who find opportunities to learn and explore new and creative ways to do things. A coach who discovers what people like about "free time" can guide them to add those strategies to the workplace, thus providing a more enriched work world. (Remember that students are the ultimate beneficiary of such beliefs turned into action.)

(6) "There's no abiding success without commitment" (p. 83). Robbins describes how the great golfer Tom Watson was not considered as a hot golf prospect at Stanford. He surprised everyone including his coach because of the *commitment* that he had to practice more than any of this teammates. In our Suncoast Area Teacher Training Program at University of South Florida, we encourage, cajole, and model "D.W.I.T.ism"—whereby each student inserts, visualizes, and visions words and options to "Do Whatever It Takes" to succeed with their own students. Their commitment to do whatever it takes has given our students a reputation for being sought after by numerous principals who share in their belief.

In summary, modeling can provide a pathway to creating "massive success" by consistently modeling specific beliefs and actions to produce similar results in a shorter learning time (Robbins, 1986).

POSITIVELY FOCUSED BODY LANGUAGE

Even though preparation of the mind is critical to the coaching process, all of the mental aerobics may be for naught unless the message is delivered appropriately. We learn from advertising research that 78 percent of the message sent is visual, 13 percent of the message is the tonality used, and 9 percent of the message relates to the words delivered (Hasenstab and Wilson, 1989). Once again the coach can be coached, and can teach others to send a congruent message that connects the positively focused images with positively focused body language. Physiological adjustment becomes as important as mental attitude adjustments.

The physiological state of the coach that is visually identified by those receiving the message will be examined in two areas: posture and facial movement.

Posture

Modeling energy, action, and enthusiasm during the process of interaction provides congruency between the messages we want to send and those that we actually send. A message of openness can be sent more congruently if along with posture, we avoid distancing ourselves from our audience by use of table or desk. Behaviors to avoid include:

(1) Closed arms may signal distance, an attempt to hide something, or a feeling of discomfort.

(2) Swinging feet may communicate impatience or nervousness.

(3) Slumping in the chair may communicate boredom, lack of confidence, or disinterest.

Behaviors to *wear* to produce an interested, energetic approach include:

(1) Shoulders back signals confidence.

(2) Feet and shoulders should face the one(s) being coached.

(3) Holding your head up with a slight tilt to the left or right to be shifted appropriately during the coaching conference shows interest.

(4) Open arms utilizing gestures that are congruent with our words show energy, interest, and excitement in the process.

(5) Lean in to show interest and lean back to allow for think time for response.

Facial Movement

Many people learn to gain information about what's on another person's mind by reading their expressions. The eyes and the mouth can be utilized to send a positive message about the quality of the interaction expected. The better we use our face, the more apt we are to attract interest in our vision and develop a pleasant rapport.

Eye contact opens the channels for communication. In our culture, we expect good direct eye contact, yet many people lose the opportunity to establish rapport by glancing at their watches, the ceiling, or the floor. If we're coaching a small group, focus on one person at a time, holding the eye contact for five to eight seconds (PDS, Inc. trainers manual, 1990). Keeping eyes wide open while presenting or receiving information conveys interest and enthusiasm.

Our sincere smiles can be utilized to encourage participation and creativity and to send messages of support. A smile should fit the sender. Inserting a positively focused image in the mind about the person can help our lips form a genuine smile. Congruence with the content of the topic is an indicator of how to utilize our eyes and mouth.

Just as the ballet dancer learns the appropriate movements to produce an arabesque and the tennis player the moves of a backhand swing, so can coaches learn the specific nonverbal behaviors that can facilitate a positively focused coaching session. The same nonverbal behaviors required to produce positive interaction between the coach and those coached are similar to those for teachers to students, principals to teachers, and teachers to parents. Good coaching skills are good people skills.

POSITIVELY FOCUSED STATEMENTS AND QUESTIONS

"It's one thing to be an opera critic and entirely another to train the opera singer" (Hasenstab, 1989). Theatre critics have been known to champion the careers of some and crush the careers of others through their "sideline" evaluations of a performance. Athletes often fear the wrath of fans as Broadway actors fear the morning reviews. Rapport between critic and performer often remains dependent on the analysis of the critic and/or the "thick skin" of the performer. On the other hand, rapport between the player and the coach is an essential element to communicating for success.

A supportive and trusting relationship between adult learners and trainers (coaches) is created best: (1) when there is mutual respect between adults, (2) when there is involvement in realistic challenges, and (3) when there is a compelling reason to be involved, in other words, "what's in it for me?" (PDS, 1990). Appropriate positively focused body language skills combined with positively focused questions and statements send a congruent message from the coach to the individual or group which conveys the feeling, "I value and respect you as a professional and as a person."

The counseling literature and excellent verbal skills training programs, such as Project T.E.A.C.H. (Hasenstab, 1989), are well equipped to define the utility skills for building trusting and supportive relationships. This section will examine positively focused statements and questions designed to create an expectation for dreaming of what can be—thinking beyond current reality. The two categories of positively focused statements presented here are those utterances that are empowering and those that are exploring in nature.

Empowering

Questions are verbalizations utilized to elicit information from others. Questions can be open or closed, depending on whether or not they are meant to elicit a wide or a narrow range of responses. Empowering questions help stretch the imagination, causing people to think *big*, think of possibilities, imagine potential, and dream without limits. All of us can share stories about what happens when people begin to ask themselves empowering questions. As an example, the name Walt Disney is immediately associated with taking imagination and turning it into reality.

Empowering questions insert empowering words in the mind, resulting in empowering thoughts and images. Examples of words that stretch the imagination are: success, benefits, impact, maximum, excellence, great, prestigious, unlimited, possibilities, influence, motivation, and inspiration.

Examples of empowering questions for coaches of teachers are:

- If you had a championship winning class, what would it be like?
- What are the greatest goals you have for your students?
- What would your students be doing, seeing, feeling, if you had created a masterpiece classroom?
- How would we know if we positively influenced our students' lives?
- What would students be saying, doing, feeling, if what occurred in our schools had a positive impact on their lives?
- What significant difference would you like to contribute to your students/school? For what compelling purpose?
- What is the value of going for a winning season?
- How would students be performing if "every student a winner, every day" was actually happening?
- What would you hope to accomplish for the students in your classroom if you had the power to make the decisions regarding curriculum and resources?
- What models do you have that have achieved great strides or accomplishments in your field?
- What has been powerful, productive, or positive about your accomplishments in your work?

Empowering statements are positively focused to encourage the person to insert possibilities rather than resist the challenge presented by potential change. Our mind, which Kehoe (1987) refers to as the great trickster, often impedes the empowering process of visioning, visualizing, and modeling by inserting statements such as "This is ridiculous . . . ," "This will never work . . . ," and "yeah, but. . . ." Empowering statements help maintain the "can do" focus with positively focused information and encouragement.

Examples of empowering statements are:

- You're beginning to challenge your mind.
- Those ideas help us see possibilities.
- Thinking about such models provides us with a vision of what can be.
- Examine other benefits that would inspire you to continue.
- Take that thought further.
- Think more about the potential of your impact.
- Consider what the customer (student) can do for you.

In summary, empowering questions insert empowering words in the mind to challenge the status quo in an attempt to "go for the gold." Empowering statements serve the purpose of directing the moves of the mind to consider endless possibilities about how great potential can be "tapped" into action.

Exploring

Visions or empowering dreams can escape the realm of reality unless a game plan is devised to create a strategy for implementation. Vision without action is an idea before its time; yet, vision with action is not a guarantee for success. All great or small dreams are ridden with obstacles emanating from endless sources such as economics, time, rules and regulations, organizations, and/or human resistances. Since every great idea has its share of obstacles, the challenge to succeed lies in our ability to turn obstacles into options.

Exploring questions and statements are words used to pique the mind to pursue options, alternatives, strengths, and possibilities, as opposed to limiting statements that inhibit the power to generate viable strategies. Rarely is there one best way to do anything. That is certainly an accepted premise in education.

Exploring questions assists the coach in involving the player(s) in formulating and maintaining the game plan through option seeking and brainstorming for possibilities. Similar to empowering questions, exploring questions are used to elicit a wide range of ideas.

Exploring statements are gentle or powerful reminders that solutions are limited only by what the mind perceives as possible. Since there is no shortage of obstacles, exploring statements act as information givers or as encouragement to continue to pursue the limitless possibilities that are awaiting our discovery.

Formerly in our daily work lives, whenever any of our staff was faced with a major or minor problem (and at a university we have our share), the first reaction was to say, "this will never work" or "this can't be done this way." Now we coach each other with exploring questions and statements. We insert and say, "What are our options?" (an exploring question) or "Let's pursue our options for a positive solution" (an exploring statement that encourages a positive focus). This triggers a problem-solving model toward action rather than a problem-producing syndrome of inaction.

Examples of exploring equations include:

- How can we do this better?
- What are our options?
- What resources can we use to create new success?
- What strategies can help us achieve our goals?
- How do we divide up the chunks for an action plan?
- What can be done to maximize the possibilities?
- How can I (the coach) best help you to pursue your strengths?
- What are the areas where you'd like to improve?
- What are some other ways to get at it?

Examples of exploring statements are:

- Keep considering your options.
- Focus on your strengths.
- Think about areas for improvement.
- That's a good option-seeking strategy.

In summary, exploring questions and statements allow the coach to guide and engage the individual(s) to formulate game plans that target specific action(s) with an eye on reaching the goal.

PERSISTENCE

The old adage "repetition is the mother of skill" holds true in our coaching model. Many people have an enormous desire to reach a goal, yet they are thwarted due to inaction. The statement, "I want to be the best teacher (coach or principal) possible" is only a verbal exercise unless accompanied by action. Action might include: indicating a willingness to be coached, reading research for best practices, attending conferences, viewing demonstrations, implementing new ideas, joining a network of "players" energized through positive action, finding models to insert for visioning, and visualizing and/or inserting positively focused messages with consistency and regularity.

Many people go beyond the stage of desire to engage in action. But when there are obstacles, there is a tendency to retreat behind what are camouflaged as legitimate reasons: too busy, a supervisor standing in the way, no resources, budget cuts, fear of being the only one, not enough pats on the back. These can'ts, won'ts, and don'ts can turn what started out to be a successful season into a series of losses.

Persistence leads to the ultimate win. Persistence wins the gold, cashes the check, and gets the diploma. Persistence is the ability to generate options when the obstacles tumble along our paths. Persistence is an outcome of the positively focused messages sent to our brain. Persistence gets the job done, the article written, the failing student to act like a winner, and the product on the market. Persistence also puts the smile on one's face and keeps the vision alive. Persistence is an essential element of a successful coaching relationship.

> Nothing in this world can take the place of persistence. Talent will not; nothing is more common than unsuccessful men with talent. Genius will not; unrewarded genius is almost a proverb. Education will not; the world is full of educated derelicts. Persistence and determination alone are omnipotent. The slogan "press on" has solved and always will solve the problems of the human race. (Calvin Coolidge)

CONCLUSION

This chapter has suggested strategies for the purpose of strengthening the role of an educator's coach. It requires great expectations for oneself and others to go for that winning season. A game plan with minimal expectations gets minimal results.

The task for a coach who desires to elicit maximum results is an uphill challenge. At a recent accreditation renewal of a secondary school, I was reminded of the need for quality coaching to embrace schools and communities. When a parent was asked about the quality of instruction in her child's school, she responded, "There are sorry teachers and there are good teachers." All of the parents and evaluators in this fact-finding meeting nodded their heads in agreement. Instead of an attempt to challenge the statement, both parents and educators shared a willingness to tolerate mediocrity as a fact of life. I repeatedly asked myself, "Why are we willing to accept less than the best for children when we demand so much more from athletes, performers, and leaders?"

The supervisor as coach can take an active and proactive role in charting a positive future — a winning season — if a game plan is used that challenges the status quo. Insertion of empowering ideas in the mind, daring to dream of visions of what can be, and adapting models that help us visualize the best practices in action are some essential elements of a successful game plan.

A final word of encouragement to all coaches: *live with vision and persist with passion!*

REFERENCES

Bandler, R. and J. Grinder. 1979. *Frogs into Princes: Neurolinguistic Programming.* Moab, UT: Real People Press.

Barker, J. 1990. *The Power of Vision. Discovering the Future Series.* Burnsville, MN: Charthouse International Learning Corporation.

Hasenstab, J. 1989. *Project T.E.A.C.H. Teacher Effectiveness in Classroom Handling.* Emerson, NJ: Performance Learning Systems, Inc.

Hasenstab, J. and C. C. Wilson. 1989. *Training the Teacher as a Champion.* Nevada City, CA: Performance Learning Systems, Inc.

Joyce, B. and B. Showers. 1982. "The Coaching of Teaching," *Educational Leadership*, 40(October):4–10.

Joyce, B. and B. Showers. 1983. *Power in Staff Development through Research in Training.* Alexandria, VA: Association for Supervision and Development.

Kehoe, J. 1987. *Mind Power.* Toronto: Zoetic, Inc.

Peters, T. J. and R. H. Waterman, Jr. 1982. *In Search of Excellence: Lessons from America's Best-Run Companies.* New York: Harper and Row.

Robbins, A. 1986. *Unlimited Power.* New York: Simon and Schuster, Inc.

Schwartz, D. 1987. *The Magic of Thinking Big.* New York: Simon and Schuster, Inc.

1990. *Team Building.* Clearwater, FL: Productivity Development Systems, Inc.

Timmerman, T. 1975. *Growing Up Alive.* Amherst, MA: Mandala Press.

9

Examining Clinical Supervision Practice

During the past decade, attempts have been made by many school districts to implement variations of clinical supervision. Reports on these programs have been difficult to interpret because no standards have yet been devised for clinical supervision practice. However, a diagnostic tool has been developed for examining current levels of CS practice, which may serve as a set of standards to determine degrees of implementation. Use of this tool enables practitioners to review present practices and to determine readiness for increasing the level of use. Frameworks for scoring provide data on individual practices, total usage, and conceptual and sequential elements. This information places CS in the practitioner's control, providing a standard and thus empowering many to address local challenges. In what follows, CS is briefly described and then the instrument and its development are presented, followed by a research perspective on current levels of the institutionalization of clinical supervision.

ELEMENTS AND CONCEPTS

To recapitulate for the reader, CS was developed during the 1960s from the pioneering work of Morris Cogan, Robert Goldhammer, Robert Anderson, and others at the Harvard Graduate School of Education. The cycle or pattern of supervision that evolved from groups of faculty members, student teachers, graduate students, and classroom teachers interacting in various training programs at Harvard resulted in two major models of clinical supervision. These two models, which in fact are very similar, were described in the volume

135

by Goldhammer, originally published in 1969 and issued in a second edition by Anderson and Krajewski in 1980, and in Cogan's 1973 volume.

Acheson and Gall (1980) developed a third model, designed to train supervisors in clinical supervisory skills and promote its practice. Goldhammer's five stages, Cogan's eight phases and Acheson and Gall's three stages are presented in Table 9.1 along with a different model for the 1990s (Pavan) which revises the terminology. The elements in this 1990s model are not essentially different, but the names are meant to stress the idea of Instructional Improvement through Inquiry (III). The model recognizes that CS in the 1990s is often a peer inquiry process conducted by mentor teachers, lead teachers, or instructional coaches as often as (or possibly more frequently than) principals.

In the Pavan model, the names for the first four elements—plan, observe, analyze, and feedback—are taken directly from the previous works on clinical supervision.

The last element—reflect—is clearly derived from the writing of Schon. Reflection is the part of the CS process that is usually the most neglected, and by so doing, supervisors lose an excellent opportunity for enhancing their own professional growth. Supervisors need to reflect on their supervision in exactly the same way that they expect teachers to reflect on their teachings using the elements: plan, observe, analyze, feedback, and reflection. For supervisors, the process might be called Supervisory Improvement through Inquiry (SII). The elements for a teacher cycle would look like a clinical supervision cycle:

- Plan—proposed lesson is reviewed by the teacher and the observer(s), and a specific focus for the observation is jointly determined.
- Observe—observer collects objective data in the classroom related to the purpose previously determined.
- Analyze—observer reviews and interprets collected data in relation to the plan, pedagogical theory, and research.
- Feedback—all collected data and analysis are shared with teacher so lesson dynamics are understood and future plans may be made.
- Reflect—there is individual or joint examination of all elements in the cycle, with analysis of the supervisor's role.

The elements of clinical supervision detail only a bare bones outline of the procedural aspect of clinical supervision. Without an under-

Table 9.1. The Process of Clinical Supervision.

Goldhammer (Stages)	Cogan (Phases)	Acheson and Gall (Phases)	Pavan (Elements)
Pre-observation conference	Establish relationship Planning with teacher Planning the observation	Planning	Plan
Observation	Observation	Classroom observation	Observe
Analysis and strategy	Analysis session Planning conference strategy		Analyze
Supervisory conference	Conference Renewed planning	Feedback Conference	Feedback
Post-conference analysis			Reflect
Robert Goldhammer, *Clinical Supervision.* New York: Holt, Rinehart & Winston, 1969. Goldhammer, Anderson, Krajewski. Revised ed. 1980.	Morris L. Cogan, *Clinical Supervision.* Boston: Houghton-Mifflin Co., 1973.	Keith Acheson & Meredith Gall *Techniques in the Clinical Supervision of Teachers.* New York: Longman, 1980.	Barbara Pavan Instructional Improvement through Inquiry

standing of the concepts of clinical supervision, the supervisor could well use the process in a mechanical, lock-step fashion. Clinical supervision at its best is a collaborative process whereby teacher and observer work together for instructional improvement. The collegial emphasis should be noted in the concepts that Anderson (1986) synthesized after an extensive review of the literature. An abbreviated version of the concepts follows.

- *Systematic inquiry* — clinical supervision is a direct and deliberate systematic inquiry into classroom instruction conducted in a spirit of hypothesis development and testing.
- *Improvement of the teaching/learning process* — clinical supervision has the intended outcomes of improving the teaching/learning process through modified teacher behavior.
- *Planned supervision objectives* — planned supervision objectives are developed collaboratively from the teacher's personal growth objectives, the intended outcomes of the curriculum, and the school and/or system's annual goals.
- *Objective data* — supervisor determines a method for classroom data collection in order to create a record of the lesson as bias-free as possible.
- *Pattern analysis* — the data are analyzed and organized by the supervisor to illustrate patterns of behavior that have been discussed in the pre-observation conference, related behaviors that are meaningful to the teacher and pertinent to the teacher's objectives, or critical incidents. Following data analysis, the supervisor develops a strategy to construct the most productive possible conference.
- *Flexible methodology* — although the familiar sequence of clinical supervision consists of five stages: (1) pre-observation conference (plan), (2) observation (observe), (3) analysis and strategy (analyze), (4) supervision conference (feedback), and (5) post-conference analysis (reflect), the stages are malleable and may be adapted for specific situations. For example, a pre-observation conference may not always be necessary if a prior sequence has already set the stage and/or identified questions to be further explored.
- *Role delineation* — the supervisor and teacher operate as intellectual equals as they collaborate to reach mutually acceptable

objectives. However, they have different roles and responsibilities. The supervisor is responsible for planning the direction and objectives of the clinical supervision cycle and developing and maintaining a nurturing, collaborative relationship. The teacher is the owner of the pedagogical questions being examined as well as expert in the immediate classroom situation with expertise relating to the students and their prior curriculum experiences. The teacher must become an active collaborator and must accept responsibility for, and make a commitment to, his/her own professional growth.

If peer clinical supervision is taking place, its success depends upon one of the peers assuming the role and responsibilities of the supervisor.

- *Trained clinical supervisors* – clinical supervisors need training not only in clinical supervision, but also in such related areas as learning theory, instructional methodology, research on effective teaching and schools, communication skills, and organizational change. Skills need to be developed in contract building, observing, data collecting, analysis of teaching through data analysis, designing conference and supervision program strategies, and self-analysis.
- *Productive tension within a nurturing climate* – although the clinical supervisor has the responsibility to initiate the nurturing, collaborative relationship with each individual teacher, the school (and in fact the district as a whole) needs to establish a nurturing, supportive atmosphere. The examination and change of professional behavior coupled with the change to a new teacher/supervisor relationship can produce tension. Tension is a necessary precursor to change. Because cycles of clinical supervision imply long-term commitment to the improvement of instruction, the productive tension fosters continuous professional growth.

ANALYZING CURRENT CLINICAL SUPERVISION PRACTICE

The questionnaire described here was originally developed by Snyder, Johnson, and MacPhail-Wilcox (1982) for use in a study entitled

The Implementation of Clinical Supervision. The questionnaire sought to obtain a description of the clinical supervision practiced by administrators, supervisors, and some teachers after they had received training in clinical supervision from the authors. The questionnaire had been piloted on a dozen groups throughout the country and had a Cronbach Alpha reliability coefficient of 0.80433.

Pavan revised the questionnaire to identify clinical supervision practices by administrators, supervisors, and teachers without biasing answers toward clinical supervision, this was done by removing the words "clinical supervision" and inserting "supervision process" or "observation." The revised questionnaire was analyzed for content validity by twelve members of the Council of Professors of Instructional Supervision (COPIS).[1] The revised questionnaire was then pilot-tested by Pavan on three different groups: sixty-two teachers and administrators in the Montgomery County Intermediate Unit, twelve principals in a Lancaster-Lebanon workshop, and twenty-nine members of a Temple University supervision class. Following the check for content validity by the COPIS members and the three pilot studies, Pavan again revised the questionnaire by removing some items and revising and restructuring others for the purposes of clarity. See Table 9.2 for the final version.

A Statistical Package for the Social Sciences (SPSS) administered on the data from Scott's (1990) study yielded a Cronbach Alpha reliability coefficient of .886. This value indicates good internal consistency for the revised questionnaire. The Snyder-Pavan questionnaire consists of thirty-four statements related to supervision. Statements 1 through 28 are scored on a five-point scale: always, often, occasionally, seldom, and never. Because the Ohio State Leadership Behavior Description Questionnaire (LBDQ-XII) was to be used in conjunction with the first administration of the supervision practices questionnaire, those descriptors were selected for the scale. The LBDQ is a list of items, each of which describes a specific supervisory behavior. Respondents are to indicate how frequently the leader engages in the behavior described by each item (Stodgill and Coons, 1957).

[1]Robert J. Alfonso, Robert H. Anderson, David W. Champagne, Noreen Garman, Carl D. Glickman, Charles Guditus, Robert J. Krajewski, Barbara N. Pavan, Charles Reavis, G. Bradley Seager, Karolyn J. Snyder, and Cheryl Granade Sullivan.

Table 9.2. Snyder-Pavan Clinical Supervision Practices Questionnaire.

	Always	Often	Occasionally	Seldom	Never
DRAW A CIRCLE around the response that is most representative of your school situation.					
1. Classroom observation is based on the idea that supervision is used to "coach" teachers.	A	B	C	D	E
2. Conferences are held within 24 hours of the classroom observation.	A	B	C	D	E
3. Classroom observation is a part of a formal annual plan designed to improve instruction.	A	B	C	D	E
4. Classroom observation is used to help the teacher become more effective.	A	B	C	D	E
5. Classroom observation is used only to evaluate teachers.	A	B	C	D	E
6. Prior to each observation, teachers and observers agree that the data to be collected will be relevant to the teacher's concerns.	A	B	C	D	E
7. Teachers have little input into the decisions about what will be observed during the supervision process.	A	B	C	D	E
8. Observations are conducted when the administrator believes they are needed.	A	B	C	D	E
9. Before classes are observed, the teacher and observer agree upon the specifics of what will be observed in the class.	A	B	C	D	E
10. Teachers do not know how the observer decided what data to collect during an observation.	A	B	C	D	E
11. Teachers know what behaviors to expect of the observer during the classroom observation.	A	B	C	D	E
12. When teachers are observed, the teacher's lesson objectives are the focus for data collection.	A	B	C	D	E
13. Teachers instruct according to a specific model of good instruction.	A	B	C	D	E
14. Good instructional standards have been defined by the administrator.	A	B	C	D	E
15. The post-observation conference includes specific plans for future instruction.	A	B	C	D	E

(continued)

141

Table 9.2. (continued).

	Always	Often	Occasionally	Seldom	Never
16. The observer and teacher discuss "patterns" or "trends" clearly evident in the data during the post-observation conference.	A	B	C	D	E
17. Observers tell teachers what was good or bad without showing data.	A	B	C	D	E
18. During the post-observation conference, teachers will see data that indicate what did or did not work well.	A	B	C	D	E
19. Classroom observation helps teachers to become more effective.	A	B	C	D	E
20. During an observation, it is obvious to the teacher that the observer's behavior is pre-planned.	A	B	C	D	E
21. The observer devises a plan for the post-observation conference.	A	B	C	D	E
22. The observer spends adequate time analyzing the classroom data collected before the post-observation conference is held.	A	B	C	D	E
23. The teacher and the observer work together productively toward the improvement of instruction.	A	B	C	D	E
24. Administrators meet to discuss the improvement of the supervision process.	A	B	C	D	E
25. Administrators and teachers meet to discuss supervision.	A	B	C	D	E
26. Central office personnel are involved in the classroom observation process.	A	B	C	D	E
27. The observers critique their own professional behavior in some systematic manner.	A	B	C	D	E
28. The post-observation conference is video or audio taped so the conferencing process can be analyzed.	A	B	C	D	E

Table 9.2 (continued).

CIRCLE *all appropriate responses.*

29. Classroom observations are conducted by:

    a. principal
    b. central office administrator
    c. supervisor
    d. teacher
    e. (other) _____

30. Data gathered during the observation are analyzed within the framework of

    a. the teacher's lesson objectives
    b. the school's annual goals
    c. a formal teaching model
    d. the teacher's concerns
    e. the observer's perceptions of deficiency needs
    f. the teacher's annual goals
    g. (other) _____

31. During the observation data are collected by

    a. personal note taking
    b. systematic note taking
    c. using district form
    d. audio tapes
    e. video tapes
    f. check lists
    g. graphs and tallies
    h. none of the above
    i. (other) _____

32. Each tenured teacher is observed _____ time(s) per year.

33. Each non-tenured teacher is observed _____ time(s) per year.

34. What do you call the observation/supervision process in your school(s)? _____

143

The majority of the items are to be scored five through one for always through never, respectively. However, seven of the items—5, 7, 8, 10, 13, 14, and 17—have a negative connotation for clinical supervision, so they are to be scored in reverse with "never" being five and "always" being one. The questionnaire also contains three items—29, 30, and 31—which provide the respondent the opportunity to select multiple answers. Each possible answer has an assigned value, although the maximum value for any one of the three items is five. The final three items on the questionnaire are write-in answers.

The total score for each respondent is obtained by totaling the responses of items 1 to 31. The number represents the degree of usage of clinical supervision practices. Individual item analysis will reveal which practices are in most frequent usage. See Table 9.3 for scoring guide.

The data obtained from the questionnaire are analyzed with descriptive statistics. Usage categories have been established as a percentage of the possible score for the questionnaire, which represent the use of clinical supervision. Categories of use as established are found in Table 9.4.

These other frameworks have been devised for data analysis using the Snyder-Pavan Supervision Practice Questionnaire (SPQ). While the item analysis will reveal specific practices and their degree of usage, the various elements in clinical supervision may be determined by looking at question clusters. These elements are purpose, plan, observe, analyze, feedback, and reflect, which were earlier related to the clinical supervision literature. Table 9.5 indicates the questions related to each element.

L. Anderson (1986) synthesized the concepts underlying clinical supervision and analyzed the questionnaire to determine which items related to the various concepts. Table 9.6 shows his analysis.

To obtain an understanding of a person's readiness to use clinical supervision, the instrument may be used with revised directions. The directions for this purpose would read, "Draw a circle around the response that is most representative of what you would like to happen in your school situation."

RESEARCH

Five separate studies have been conducted in Pennsylvania utilizing the Snyder-Pavan Supervision Practices Questionnaire. The studies

Table 9.3. *Snyder-Pavan Clinical Supervision Practices Questionnaire Scoring Guide.*

	Always	Often	Occasionally	Seldom	Never
	A	B	C	D	E
Items 1, 2, 3, 4	5	4	3	2	1
6, 9, 11, 12					
15, 16, 18, 19					
20, 21, 22, 23					
24, 25, 26, 27, 28					
Items 5, 7, 8, 10	1	2	3	4	5
13, 14, 17					

29. Classroom observations are conducted by:

a. principal	1		d. teacher		
b. central office administrator	1		e. (other) _____		3
c. supervisor	2				

30. Data gathered during the observation are analyzed within the framework of

a. the teacher's lesson objectives		3	
b. the school's annual goals		2	
c. a formal teaching model		1	
d. the teacher's concerns		5	
e. the observer's perceptions of deficiency needs		1	
f. the teacher's annual goals		4	
g. (other) _____			

31. During the observation data are collected by

a. personal note taking	1	f. check lists	2
b. systematic note taking	4	g. graphs and tallies	4
c. using district form	0	h. none of the above	0
d. audio tapes	4	i. (other) _____	
e. video tapes	5		

Points for each question (29-31) are to be added for each item circled. No question may receive more than 5 points.

145

Table 9.4. Categories of Use: Snyder-Pavan Clinical
Supervision Practices Questionnaire.

Scott's Total Score and Range		Anderson's Item Range	Label	Category of Use
31 × 5 = 155	125–155	4.5–5.0	Always	Very high
31 × 4 = 124	94–124	3.5–4.49	Often	High
31 × 3 = 93	63–93	2.5–3.49	Occas.	Moderate
31 × 2 = 62	32–62	1.5–2.49	Seldom	Low
31 × 1 = 31	0–31	0–1.49	Never	Very low

Table 9.5. Instructional Improvement through Inquiry.

Pavan Elements	Question Cluster	Range
Purpose	1, 3, 4, 5,* 19	5–25
Plan	6, 7,* 9, 10,* 11	5–25
Observe	8,* 12, 13,* 14,* 20, 26, 29, 31	8–40
Analyze	21, 22, 30	3–15
Feedback	2, 15, 16, 17,* 18, 23	6–30
Reflect	24, 25, 27, 28	4–20
Total		31–155

*Reverse scoring.

146

Table 9.6. The Concepts of Clinical Supervision and
Their Respective Question Clusters.

Concept	Question Cluster	Range
Systematic inquiry	1, 8*	2–10
Improvement of the teaching/learning process	3, 4, 19	3–15
Planned supervision objectives	6, 7,* 10*	3–15
Objective data	12, 17,* 18, 31	4–20
Pattern analysis	13,* 16, 22, 30	4–20
Flexible methodology	2, 9, 15, 20, 21, 27	6–30
Role delineation	11, 14,* 26, 29	4–20
Trained clinical supervisors	24, 28	2–10
Productive tension within a nurturing climate	5,* 23, 25	3–15
Total		31–155

*Reverse scoring, L. Anderson (1986).

were conducted over different time periods with different populations and different variables. As a group, these studies document quite well the rather moderate usage of clinical supervision in the state.

The data for Bennett's (1990) study were collected in the spring of 1983 by Sarah Moore Larch. The assumption that there is a relationship between the usage of clinical supervision practices by elementary principals and their leadership behaviors was tested. The perceptions of school district superintendents, elementary principals, and elementary school teachers were analyzed to determine the extent to which elementary principals who employ clinical supervision practices demonstrate the leadership behaviors on the LBDQ-12.[2] A statewide random sample excluding Philadelphia and Pittsburgh yielded 623 responses.

[2]The LBDQ (Stogdill and Coons, 1957) is a list of items each of which describes a specific supervisory behavior. Each respondent is to indicate how frequently the leader engages in the behavior described by each item.

In his spring 1984 survey, L. Anderson (1986) received responses from 179 elementary principals in the six-county area surrounding Philadelphia. Supervision in elementary schools in districts of different sizes and varying socioeconomic characteristics was examined to determine the use of clinical supervision and the nine concepts of clinical supervision that Anderson had synthesized.

Holodick (1988) interviewed principals in the spring of 1986 and had them complete the CSQ. The major purpose of this study was to discover whether elementary school principals utilizing clinical supervision as a technique within the total scope of supervision modified their clinical supervisory practices after they implemented the process. The subjects of this study were seven practicing elementary school principals from three northeastern Pennsylvania school districts. These three school districts were the only districts in a three-county area that had a districtwide clinical supervision program implemented for at least three years.

Jamula (1990) compiled data on over 4,000 students, 321 teachers, and twelve principals in the spring of 1988 in an urban school district. She studied the relationships between the degree of usage of clinical supervision by the principals and student achievement, SES, school size, staff development of teachers and principals, and principal experience and gender.

Scott (1990) received replies from 231 principals to his fall 1988 survey in south central Pennsylvania. He compared the degree of use of clinical supervision of principals in elementary, middle/junior high, and senior high schools. Other variables included gender, school district size, expenditure per pupil, and administrative experience and training.

An item analysis of items 1–28 for four of these studies is presented in Table 9.7. Very few differences are noted among the items, with each study showing responses in the same range. In fact, only Holodick's data differ from that of the other groups; he reports higher levels of usage of clinical supervision where an expectation exists for teachers to use a specific instructional model. Holodick had sought out districts that used clinical supervision. However, he found that the model being used was that of Madeline Hunter, not the clinical supervision model of Goldhammer. The uniform responses across the state probably reflect the influence of Hunter and her trainers in this state. Even the Pennsylvania State Department of Education has endorsed the Hunter model and provided extensive funding for training.

Table 9.7. Comparison of Items 1–28.

	Year of Survey	Bennett Study 1983	Anderson Study 1984	Holodick Study 1986	Scott Study 1988
1.	Classroom observation is based on the idea that supervision is used to "coach" teachers.	Often 3.82	Occas. 3.42	Often 4.14	Often 4.21
2.	Conferences are held within 24 hours of the classroom observation.	Often 3.79	Often 3.84	Often 4.0	Often 3.97
3.	Classroom observation is part of a formal annual plan designed to improve instruction.	Always 4.61	Always 4.72	Always 4.71	Always 4.64
4.	Classroom observation is used to help teacher become more effective.	Always 4.61	Always 4.65	Always 4.71	Always 4.69
*5.	Classroom observation is used only to evaluate teachers.	Occas. 3.40	Occas. 3.37	Occas. 3.14	Occas. 3.51
6.	Prior to each observation, teachers and observers agree that the data to be collected will be relevant to the teacher's concerns.	Occas. 3.27	Occas. 3.22	Occas. 3.26	Occas. 3.22
*7.	Teachers have little input into the decisions about what will be observed during the supervision process.	Occas. 3.10	Occas. 3.37	Occas. 3.57	Occas. 3.33
*8.	Observations are conducted when the administrator believes they are needed.	Occas. 3.10	Occas. 2.58	Occas. 3.42	Occas. 2.72
9.	Before classes are observed, the teacher and observer agree upon the specifics of what will be observed in the class.	Occas. 2.87	Occas. 3.16	Occas. 3.42	Occas. 3.07
*10.	Teachers do not know how the observer decided what data to collect during an observation.	Seldom 3.69	Seldom 3.90	Seldom 4.00	Seldom 3.72
11.	Teachers know what behaviors to expect of the observer during the classroom observation.	Often 4.40	Often 4.35	Always 4.71	Often 4.40
12.	When teachers are observed, the teacher's lesson objectives are the focus for data collection.	Often 3.99	Often 4.15	Often 4.42	Often 4.09
*13.	Teachers instruct according to a specific model of good instruction.	Often 2.36	Often 2.36	Always 1.42	Often 2.22

(continued)

Table 9.7. (continued).

Year of Survey	Bennett Study 1983	Anderson Study 1984	Holodick Study 1986	Scott Study 1988
*14. Good instructional standards have been defined by the administrator.	Often 2.08	Often 1.80	Always 1.41	Often 1.85
15. The post-observation conference includes specific plans for future instruction.	Often 3.99	Often 4.02	Often 4.0	Often 4.14
16. The observer and teacher discuss "patterns" or "trends" clearly evident in the data during the post-observation conference.	Often 3.92	Often 4.08	Often 4.14	Often 4.09
*17. Observers tell teachers what was good or bad without showing data.	Seldom 3.90	Seldom 4.02	Seldom 4.42	Seldom 3.86
18. During the post-observation conference, teachers will see data that indicate what did or did not work well.	Often 4.15	Often 4.23	Often 4.42	Often 4.09
19. Classroom observation helps teachers to become more effective.	Often 3.99	Often 4.06	Often 4.0	Often 4.11
20. During an observation, it is obvious to the teacher that the observer's behavior is pre-planned.	Occas. 3.07	Occas. 3.49	Often 3.71	Occas. 3.46
21. The observer devises a plan for the post-observation conference.	Often 4.08	Often 4.27	Often 4.28	Often 4.27
22. The observer spends adequate time analyzing the classroom data collected before the post-observation conference is held.	Often 4.07	Often 4.34	Always 4.85	Often 4.23
23. The teacher and the observer work together productively toward the improvement of instruction.	Often 4.33	Often 4.28	Often 4.28	Often 4.33
24. Administrators meet to discuss the improvement of the supervision process.	Often 3.62	Often 3.70	Often 3.71	Often 3.74
25. Administrators and teachers meet to discuss supervision.	Occas. 3.16	Occas. 3.34	Occas. 3.14	Occas. 3.32

150

Table 9.7. (continued).

Year of Survey	Bennett Study 1983	Anderson Study 1984	Holodick Study 1986	Scott Study 1988
26. Central office personnel are involved in the classroom observation process.	Occas. 2.52	Occas. 2.75	Occas. 3.00	Occas. 2.88
27. The observers critique their own professional behavior in some systematic manner.	Occas. 3.06	Occas. 3.10	Occas. 3.42	Occas. 3.23
28. The post-observation conference is video or audio taped so the conferencing process can be analyzed.	Never 1.24	Never 1.27	Seldom 1.85	Seldom 1.50

*Reversed scored statement.

The total mean scores for clinical supervision rise by a few points for each survey from 1983 to 1988, but all the scores hover around the mid-point of "often" from 107.17 to 116.16. In the four studies with the type of analysis as shown on Table 9.7, over 80 percent of the respondents' total scores are in the "often" range. This indicates that the most common response to each supervisory practice was "often." Note that the publication dates are much different from the actual survey dates. All studies were based on elementary principals except Scott's, whose total mean score for them was 118.29. He found that the lower the school level, the greater the usage of clinical supervision, although the differences were not significant.

Analysis of the data by the concept framework has been performed by Anderson and Bennett, with very similar results. Both groups reported very high usage of the concept, teaching/learning improvement. Over 50 percent of the respondents in each group noted high usage of planned supervision objectives, objective data, pattern analysis, and productive tension within a maturing climate. The need for role delineation and trained clinical supervisors was rated low by over 50 percent of each group.

All studies except the one by Jamula found that female elementary principals used clinical supervision practices to a greater degree than their male counterparts. Jamula's school district had provided extensive training in a particular model of supervision, which probably resulted in the scores being clustered together.

Both Anderson and Scott found a greater usage of clinical supervision practices in larger school districts. While Anderson found per pupil expenditure positively related to usage, Scott did not. Scott found no relationship between administrative experience or supervisory training and the clinical supervision usage, while Jamula found a tendency for teachers to indicate that the least experienced principals used more clinical supervision practices than the more experienced administrators.

The common finding that teachers rate their principals less favorably than principals rate themselves was collaborated by both Bennett and Jamula. Teachers reported that principals who had high usage of leadership behaviors also had high usage of clinical supervision practices (Bennett).

As noted in an earlier clinical supervision review by Pavan (1985), it does not seem possible to demonstrate a relationship between clinical supervision and student achievement. Jamula's study of twelve principals has not yielded any statistical relationship.

CONCLUSIONS

Five research studies have been conducted in the state of Pennsylvania using the Snyder-Pavan Supervision Practices Questionnaire (SPQ). The results have been surprisingly similar, which may be due to the influence of a strong state department of education. Comparison with data collected in other states using the SPQ needs to be made.

As the instrument has wider usage, refinements might be made. No changes were contemplated until these five studies were completed, but the response descriptors might be clarified. While the response descriptors for the CSQ have had much use for instruments of this type, one wonders how respondents decide if a given practice should be rated often, occasionally, or seldom. Might the usage of percentages be more helpful than the words? For example, instead of or along with "always," use 100%; often, 75%; occasionally, 50%; seldom, 25%; and never, 0% as more precise response points.

The instrument provides a tool for diagnosing the level of clinical supervision usage in a school or a school district. Data from the instrument would enable the practitioner to determine if further training is needed or desired. Because several analytic frameworks have been devised and results have been indicated, comparisons have been made possible. The intent here is not to prescribe the total usage of clinical supervision, but to enable the practitioner to have baseline data as to present usage. This seems consistent with the assumptions of clinical supervision in which collaborative decisions are made after interpretation of objective data.

Many school districts are encouraging teachers to observe each other's teaching as a way to increase the amount of supervision, with the expectation that this will lead to instructional improvement. As has happened so often in the past, teachers are being told to be peer supervisors or peer coaches, but are given little training or guidelines as to how to proceed. The clinical supervision model described here provides a framework to be used by teachers during the coaching process. The SPQ could be used to assess teachers' readiness for clinical supervision prior to staff training in the process. In addition, administrators and supervisors in the district who have been responsible for the supervisory function could be surveyed. The very act of responding to the SPQ brings the elements and concepts to the consciousness of the respondent. Such heightened awareness may enhance motivation for this type of staff development. Completion of the SPQ after training and practice in the schools will indicate progress in the implementation process. In order to remove the discomfort experienced by teachers and administrators as they coach teachers, a structure is needed. Clinical supervision, with its emphasis on collaboration and feedback of nonjudgmental data, provides such a structure.

REFERENCES

Acheson, K. A. and M. D. Gall. 1980. *Techniques in the Clinical Supervision of Teachers: Preservice and Inservice Applications.* New York: Longman, Inc.

Anderson, L. A. 1986. "Clinical Supervision Concepts and Implementation of Elementary Principals," Ed.D. dissertation, Temple University.

Bennett, G. T. 1990. "Clinical Supervision Practices and the Leadership Behaviors of Elementary Principals as Reported by the Principals, Their Superintendents and Teachers," Ed.D. dissertation, Temple University.

Cogan, M. L. 1973. *Clinical Supervision.* Boston: Houghton Mifflin.

Goldhammer, R. 1969. *Clinical Supervision.* New York: Holt, Rinehart and Winston.

Goldhammer, R., R. H. Anderson and R. J. Krajewski. 1980. *Clinical Supervision: Special Methods for the Supervision of Teachers, Second Edition.* New York: Holt, Rinehart and Winston.

Holodick, N. A. 1988. "Clinical Supervision Practices as Reported by Elementary School Principals," Ed.D. dissertation, Temple University.

Jamula, M. 1990. "The Relationship between Student Achievement and the Degree to Which Principals Use Clinical Supervision," Ed.D. dissertation, Temple University.

Pavan, B. N. 1980. "Clinical Supervision: Some Signs of Progress," *Texas Tech Journal of Education*, 7:241–251.

Pavan, B. N. 1985. *Clinical Supervision: Research in Schools Utilizing Comparative Measures*. ERIC, ED 255 516.

Pavan, B. N. 1987. *Hunter's Clinical Supervision and Instructional Models: Research in Schools Utilizing Comparative Measures*. ERIC, ED 273 606.

Scott, J. W. 1990. "Comparison of Clinical Supervision Practices as Implemented by Elementary, Middle/Junior High, and High School Principals," Ed.D. dissertation, Temple University.

Snyder, K. J., W. L. Johnson and B. MacPhail-Wilcox. 1982. *The Implementation of Clinical Supervision*. ERIC, ED 213 666.

Stogdill, R. M. and A. E. Coons, eds. 1957. *Leader Behavior: Its Description and Measurement*. Columbus, OH: Bureau of Business Research, Ohio State University.

III

CONTINGENCY VARIATIONS TO COACHING

The notion of "landscapes" of clinical supervision becomes clearer as the chapters in this section on variations unfold. That supervision must necessarily take the unique circumstances of each situation into account is the main theme in the opening chapter. Uses of coaching methodology in preservice teacher education are explained in the following chapter. A third, examining metacognitive training models, is followed by a chapter on "technical" coaching. The section concludes with commentary on how coaching facilitates professional problem solving, exemplified in the joint effort of a school system and a university seeking to restructure an elementary school with teaching teams.

In the Anderson chapter, for which "different strokes" establishes a theme, there is a section on leader behaviors within which is included the classic depiction by Hersey and Blanchard of situational leadership along the axes of task behavior and directive behavior. Worker maturity and levels of experience are examined as concepts to be taken into account as appropriate supervisory behavior is determined.

Hatch, drawing upon his experience in developing a model (CITE) for coaching in an undergraduate teacher preparation program, looks at ways that teacher training has changed in this century. Linking coaching with transfer of training, he then describes and illustrates his five-phase model: coaching and teaching, team observation, peer and formative coaching, collegiality, and professional development. He concludes that the fourteen key factors for success in major change projects as identified by Miles must be addressed and supported if models such as CITE are to be successful.

Fitzgerald's chapter, linking cognition and metacognition with the coaching of teachers, also presents a model of the author's invention. An opening section investigates operational models of transfer of training, the next examines the dimensions of coaching and metacognition (of which clinical supervision and peer coaching are major subsets), and the third and final section develops the metacognitive coaching model.

In Chapter 13 Nielsen defines technical coaching, one of the three forms of coaching in Garmston's schema, and seeks to give the term an expanded and more concrete meaning. Her purpose is to provide guidelines for implementing technical coaching, present an example drawn from a Reading Training Project, and discuss implications for practitioners. Her descriptions of the five stages of the coaching observation cycle offer a useful additional perspective on the cycle. Among her conclusions are that training in procedures and process, as well as content, is essential, and that careful and thorough training in the technology of coaching is essential to its successful implementation.

Finally in this section, Bahner describes coaching as a problem-solving process in the context of a summer inservice training program, and then describes how the processes within such a program can be used during the regular school year. Propounding that team organization facilitates efforts to improve teaching, he assumes that, in his hypothetical illustration, the school system had decided to restructure by having teaching teams throughout the school. The immediate task was to provide inservice training, and a university was invited to offer a four-week program for that purpose. The design of the program is then explained, as is the implementation. There follows a section on "the classroom environment" within which some basic questions are noted. A similar section on student assessment follows, after which are offered comments on adaptations for the regular school year.

Contingency Supervision:
Basic Concepts

DIFFERENT STROKES

The need for teachers to deal with students in ways appropriate to
their unique educational histories and capabilities is almost universally
accepted. "Different strokes for different folks" is a colloquial expression for the truism that human beings must necessarily be treated in a
variety of ways because there is infinite variation in the makeup and the
predispositions of any given population. Usually in education that expression is used to remind teachers of the importance of understanding,
and then responding to, the uniqueness of each student in a group or a
class. In this chapter we reinforce the concept that supervisors, and
others who seek to assist teachers to be proficient in their classrooms,
must similarly understand, and then respond to, the uniqueness that
each teacher represents.

In the educational literature that develops this concept various terms
or labels are used, including "contingency supervision," "situational
leadership," "developmental supervision," "differentiated supervision,"
and "individualized supervision." Contingency seems to be the adjective most often used, however, and it therefore seemed an appropriate
choice for the title of this chapter.

Of the many things that a supervisor does to help Teacher A (who is
unique among all teachers in the world) to perform more effectively in
the classroom, those hands-on services for which we use the term clinical supervision will (at least potentially) have the strongest impact. It
is within the cycle of conferring, observing, and providing feedback
that the most tailor-made supervisory approaches will develop. We
therefore perceive that the ideas that follow in this chapter are of cen-

tral importance to an understanding of clinical supervision's land-scapes. Conversely, it is when they are connected to clinical super-vision that the ideas embodied in contingency supervision become most meaningful.

In every population of teachers there can be, and almost always is, a considerable range or variance with respect to such factors as personal maturity, general intelligence, professional skill and awareness, role maturity, role motivation, command of information and knowledge, psychological and social orientation, biases and prejudices, creativity and imagination, and dozens of other characteristics (many overlap-ping) that have some bearing upon their performance and their morale. Furthermore, the environments within which teachers work are very different from each other, for a variety of reasons (e.g., neighborhood makeup and history, physical plant and surroundings, outside pres-sures, internal politics, leadership styles of principals and other ad-ministrators, and the personnel mix). What may be appropriate as a supervisory approach for Teacher A in Context X therefore will proba-bly be inappropriate if applied exactly to any other teacher in whatever context.

LEADER BEHAVIORS

Over more than half a century, marked by a veritable explosion of research and commentary since the early 1980s, scholars and analysts have been seeking to define effective leadership and to identify nur-turant contexts within which front-line workers can be helped to become maximally productive while enjoying commensurate high morale. Although aimed primarily at the worlds of business and indus-try, the widely circulated literatures of effective management, leader-ship styles and behaviors, worker performance, worker involvement in decision making, work culture, worker development, worker empow-erment, and goal attainment have had a very great impact upon the ways that educators approach their tasks.

Of particular relevance to educational supervisors is the focus within this extensive literature on the situational variables, or contingencies, that must be taken into account and then acted upon by those who manage an enterprise. Well known within education, in part because publications and videotapes elaborating it have been produced by

ASCD and other organizations, is a proposition set forth by Hersey and Blanchard in 1977, and subsequently polished and refined by various other writers. The Hersey and Blanchard model states basically that directive behaviors and supportive behaviors should be modulated to fit the relative maturity of the individual(s) with whom one is working. An adaptation of the Hersey and Blanchard model is presented in Figure 10.1.

What Figure 10.1 seeks to present is a relatively simple and easy-to-follow approach to dealing with teachers, who may in each case fall into one of four categories along the professional skills continuum. In brief, it identifies, on the North-South axis, relationship behavior (for which a subtitle "supportive behavior" was inserted), and on the East-West axis it identified task behavior (for which a subtitle "directive behavior" was inserted). There are four quadrants rather arbitrarily provided. In the lower right quadrant, the leader is heavily engaged in planning, organizing, and controlling (high task), and there is low con-

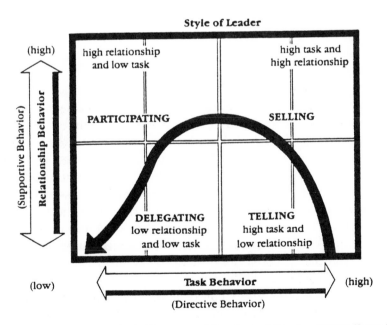

Paul Hersey/Kenneth H. Blanchard, *Management of Organizational Behavior: Utilizing Human Resources*, 5e, © 1988, p. 287. Adapted by permission of Prentice-Hall, Englewood Cliffs, New Jersey.

Figure 10.1 *Adaptation of Hersey and Blanchard Model.*

cern for impact upon interpersonal relationships. Hersey and Blanchard labeled the appropriate behavior of the leader/supervisor in this quadrant as *telling* behavior. ("This is what you must do.")

In the upper right quadrant, which calls for *selling* behavior, the leader/supervisor is concerned with both task clarification and relationship maintenance. ("These ideas or practices are potentially useful.")

Moving to the left side, the upper quadrant reflects high concern for the relationship and for shared process, and relatively low concern for organizing and controlling the task. The label, *participating*, reflects leader behavior that assigns the major responsibility for task structure to the worker and implies more of a partnership. ("What ideas do you have?")

In the lower left quadrant, the assumption is that the worker is fully capable of planning, organizing, and controlling the task, and therefore the supervisor is sufficiently comfortable with that assumption and with the supervisor-worker relationship so that *delegation* of the responsibility to the worker seems to be warranted. ("Go ahead, use your own ideas.")

As can be seen, the arrow in Figure 10.1 travels a nonlinear continuum that reflects an assumption of progressively greater maturity on the part of the worker (teacher). In a simpler depiction of the continuum for our purposes in this chapter, Figure 10.2 suggests that the least mature teachers (in Box 1) can best be approached by the supervisor who uses a *teaching* model; the next most mature teachers (in Box 2) can best be approached in what amounts to a *counseling* mode; teachers who are even more mature (in Box 3) are in effect invited to solve the problem in *partnership* with the supervisor; and finally, the most mature teachers (Box 4) through *delegation* have an opportunity for job enlargement and/or enrichment.

In Figure 10.3 we further simplify by placing the continuum on a straight line, with M1 (maturity level 1) and M4 (maturity level 4) at the extreme ends. In what follows, for convenience we will use the labels M1, M2, M3, and M4 as descriptive of teachers whose behaviors and needs correspond to the conceptional model in each case. One could easily argue that four maturity levels are either too many or not enough, just as one could easily argue that the progression of supervisory behaviors from "tell" to "sell" to "participate" to "delegate" is not necessarily linear or perfect. It is also probable that few teachers can

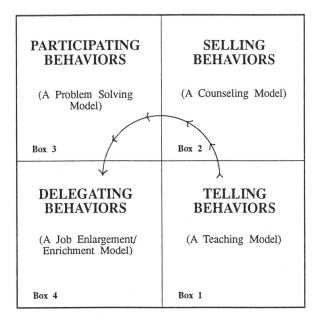

Figure 10.2 *A Contingency Approach to Coaching Teachers – Guidelines for Supervisory Behavior.*

be accurately classified as 100 percent M1, or 100 percent M4 (or M2 or M3), since every person will possess a range of skills, understanding, and attitudes. Persons we choose to label as M3 (or whatever) will invariably have some strengths associated with a higher category and/or limitations that fall within a lower category. All the same, the model can be used to support some procedural and other suggestions, with the supervisor presumably aware that the categorical labels are only an approximation of reality.

In workshop situations and in discussions of the contingency approach with experienced supervisors, lists have been generated to

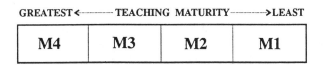

Figure 10.3 *Levels of Teaching Maturity.*

describe some probable characteristics and tendencies of teachers who appear to fall within each of the four categories.

People in the lowest maturity level (M1) are perceived to lack self-esteem; lack self-confidence; not be self-directed; lack motivation and/or knowledge; tend to make excuses; have a generally negative orientation; not be explorers or seekers (to be closed); tend not to share or participate; lack enthusiasm; have less sense of responsibility; be defensive; and lack experience.

Persons in the M2 maturity level are perceived to be sellable and/or approachable; have a degree of knowledge, but hesitant to share; be fairly satisfied with the status quo; be preoccupied with the mundane; feel that they are spread too thin; be apathetic about new ideas; and tend not to participate with zeal.

Persons in the M3 quadrant are perceived to be willing to give a yes response to new challenges; be open to change; recognize that they need direction; respond to assistance; make good partners in change processes; find satisfaction in their work; and be "M4's in the rough" (not yet recognized or developed as leaders).

In the highest maturity level (M4), persons are perceived to have a very positive orientation; be enthusiastic; be self-directed; be knowledgeable, capable, creative; be eager to share; initiate and complete tasks; seek challenge; be eager to improve; be goal-oriented; make good leaders; search for new ways and new knowledge; and go beyond basic responsibilities.

Many readers might elect to edit these descriptions in various ways, and groups of supervisors and teachers probably should be encouraged to develop their own descriptions. The important point is that supervisors may need to become aware of and sensitive to the various attitudes, behaviors, and signals that they encounter when dealing with teachers at various maturity levels.

An article by Newstrom and Lengnick-Hall (1991), although addressed to trainers in the business world rather than to clinical supervisors, advocates a contingency model. The model contrasts, they say, with the inappropriate pedagogical model, which views the learner as a passive recipient of knowledge, and with the andragogical model, which makes some assumptions about adult learning that in their view have not been sufficiently examined. The contingency approach, they argue, is more likely "to stimulate human resource professionals to reflect on their own guiding paradigms and improve them when appropriate" (p. 45). Instead of being homologous adult learners who require a uniform and singular approach to training and development, such professionals are a heterogeneous group requiring different approaches, depending on individual differences across ten important dimensions or characteristics. These dimensions include:

(1) *Instrumentality* — the degree of concern for immediate applicability of a concept or skill

(2) *Skepticism* — the extent of a questioning attitude and demand for evidence

(3) *Resistance to change* — the extent of fear about moving to the unknown

(4) *Attention span* — the ability to maintain focus

(5) *Expectations level* — the quality and quantity required

(6) *Dominant needs* — the range of intrinsic and extrinsic needs

(7) *Absorption level* — the pace at which he/she expects and can accept new information

(8) *Topical interest* — the extent of personal job-relevant interest in the topic

(9) *Self-confidence* — the view of self, and extent of need for high or low levels of feedback, reinforcement, and success

(10) *Locus of control* — the extent of perception that he/she can implement the training with or without organizational support [1]

Newstrom and Lengnick-Hall propose that groups and individuals can be assessed or surveyed on these ten dimensions, for example by arranging them on seven-point Likert scales, after which a profile could help in the design of a training (or, for our purposes in this volume, clinical supervision) program.

MATURITY AS A CONCEPT

Although the four-quadrant and M1-2-3-4 schemes for thinking about worker (teacher) maturity are potentially useful, they may also be somewhat simplistic if not at times misleading. Glickman, one of the authors in this volume, has adopted the term "developmental supervision" in examining how supervisors can/should respond to the vari-

[1] Adapted from Newstrom, J. W. and M. L. Lengnick-Hall, "One Size Does Not Fit All," *Training & Development*. Copyright June 1991, the American Society for Training and Development.

ability in teacher background and needs. First presented in an ASCD booklet (Glickman, 1981) and in 1985 elaborated in an excellent textbook (Glickman, 1989), developmental supervision is based in large measure upon the proposition that teachers operate at different levels of professional development, that they need to be supervised in different ways, and that the long-range goal is to help them to grow toward progressively higher levels of thought.

A recent article (Glickman and Gordon, 1987) sought further to clarify the propositions underlying the process. In brief, the supervisor's first task is to diagnose the level at which the teacher (or group) is functioning; the second (tactical phase) is to match as far as possible the supervisory approach to the teacher's level of abstraction; and the third (strategic phase) is to utilize various means for increasing the level of teacher abstraction and self-direction. Glickman asserts that developmental supervision is not a contingency or situational theory, and he rejects the idea of labeling teachers into fixed categories or utilizing arbitrary, prescriptive actions. He devotes special attention to the cognitive development of a teacher or group.

The maturity focus for contingency supervision provides a powerful conceptual guide for responding to teachers in ways that stimulate cognitive, affective, and performance growth.

One way of looking at worker maturity is described by Tindal and Doyle (1987), who note that eleven factors need to be considered when assessing the extent to which a training session should be dominated by the trainers or by the trainees. These factors are: maturity level of participants, their motivation level, the level of difficulty of the subject matter or material, the nature of the training material (e.g., technological orientation), whether the activity is task oriented or process oriented, the nature and extent of the trainer's repertoire, the availability and adequacy of resources, the physical environment, the time perspective in which results are expected, and the clarity of goals. With respect to maturity level, they suggest that there are three degrees of distinction: independent-dependent, active-passive, and behavioral flexibility. They note that trainers must be especially sensitive to whether or not participants appear able to function in groups.

This latter observation is especially critical, as is noted both directly and indirectly in many of the other chapters in this volume, since self-containment is a declining work pattern and the most productive teachers of the future will be those who can work well together. Supervisors will be spending much of their energy providing training/staff development toward that eventuality.

Stallings (1987) also notes the importance of delivering staff development services and programs to teachers in ways that respond to their differing levels or stages of professional maturity. Of interest is that she separates teachers into three categories—novice, maturing and growing, and mature professional—each with a different focus and each requiring a different staff development approach. She indicates that novices are cognitively different from mature teachers, in that they process information in the classroom based upon what they can handle. The novice needs survival skills, and learns best through a direct approach in staff development.

Maturing teachers, on the other hand, learn best in a collaborative approach, through support groups, and peer observations of classroom interactions and levels of questioning are welcome. Their focus is upon the classroom environment and instructional strategies.

The most mature teachers are more innovative, are interested in developing new strategies of curriculum, and function well in a non-directive mode as teachers of teachers. Stallings notes, as do Glickman and others, that teachers may move from stage to stage depending upon the skill or strategy in question.

LEVELS OF EXPERIENCE

Another way to differentiate teachers is to identify the extent of their preparation and experience. Given the ups and downs in the teacher supply over several decades, there are (and probably will continue to be) substantial numbers of teachers who were employed under emergency or other conditions and who have previously received very little if any preparation for teaching at the college/university level. While some critics of university-provided course work in education may see little harm in the employment of such persons, it seems obvious to many educators that teachers need at least some grounding in human development, in social and philosophic foundations, in measurement, in teaching materials and methods, in classroom management, and in other dimensions of schooling in order to understand and pursue their teaching role with reasonable skill and confidence.

Since the great majority of teachers who have not had such preparation are placed in self-contained classrooms with limited opportunity for learning from colleagues, most of the professional skill and insight they acquire is hard-earned, and some of it, alas, may not be appropriate. Although there are certainly some in this group who perform very well and perhaps even excel, supervisors should know who they are and pay careful attention to conceptual and other help that may be needed.

In recent years, beginning teachers with teacher-education backgrounds, usually although not always in their early twenties, have arrived at the school with fewer deficiencies in their general preparation than did beginners a decade or more ago. For the most part, they have a keen awareness of the complexities of teaching and the need for continuous and intensive assistance. They tend to welcome supervision and to respond to it with appreciation. Most are well aware of the developmental process they must undergo, and many pursue part-time graduate work and other growth opportunities voluntarily, or at least in good spirit, in recognition of that fact.

Another group of teachers consists of those who have had several years of apparently successful experience (as attested by renewed contracts and/or tenured status) and whose professional repertoires are beginning to take shape. Some of these may still be struggling or are perhaps in a probationary status that reduces their self-assurance, but most are achieving a degree of self-confidence and their attitudes toward supervision and the need for supervisory intervention may in some cases be cooling down.

It is hard to know when the word "veteran" can be appropriately used, but for our purposes it may be sufficient to suggest that teachers with more than five or six years of successful experience are veterans, with relatively fixed professional repertoires and a sense of security about those repertoires that makes the prospect of changes, especially significant changes, generally less than welcome.

We think it is mostly unfair, however, to consider such veterans as rigid and habit-ridden. It is true that some teachers with decade(s) of experience get into a terrible rut and lose the "spark" and enthusiasm that once may have characterized their work. However, what is probably much more true is that fine-tuning continues throughout their careers, a mature perspective develops, and while ostensibly unchanging these people remain learners of their craft. It could be a serious mistake to read their relative stability as a sign of professional decay or ossification.

SUMMARY

Teachers are best served by supervisors, within the context of examining classroom performance, when their uniqueness is taken fully into account. Well-informed awareness of each teacher's personal characteristics and tendencies, professional skills already mastered, extent and quality of prior experience, personal drive and motivation, ability and willingness to expand one's repertoire, and overall professional maturity will make it more possible for the supervisor to facilitate and influence that teacher's continuing growth. With a nod to Newstrom and Lengnick-Hall, who used the phrase for the title of their article from which we borrowed some good suggestions, "One Size Does Not Fit All."

REFERENCES

Glickman, C. D. 1981. *Developmental Supervision: Alternative Practices for Helping Teachers Improve Instruction*. Alexandria, VA: Association for Supervision and Curriculum Development.

Glickman, C. D. 1989. *Supervision of Instruction: A Developmental Approach, Second Edition*. Needham Heights, MA: Allyn and Bacon.

Glickman, C. D. and S. P. Gordon. 1987. "Clarifying Developmental Supervision: Supervision in Context," *Educational Leadership*, 41(8):64–68.

Hersey, P. and K. H. Blanchard. 1988. *Management of Organizational Behavior: Utilizing Human Resources, Fifth Edition*. Englewood Cliffs, NJ: Prentice-Hall.

Newstrom, J. W. and M. L. Lengnick-Hall. 1991. "One Size Does Not Fit All," *Training and Development Journal*, 45(June):43–48.

Snyder, K. J. and R. H. Anderson. 1986. *Managing Productive Schools: Toward an Ecology*. San Diego: Harcourt, Brace and Jovanovich.

Stallings, J. 1987. "Professional Development and Teacher Supervision: What Works and What Doesn't," presentation at California State University, Dominquez Hills, CA, May 6. See also: "What Students Should Learn in Schools: An Issue for Staff Development," *NASSP Bulletin*, 71(April):67–76.

Tindal, C. R. and P. Doyle. 1987. "Trainers or Trainees—Who Dominates?" *Training and Development Journal*, 41(May):64–77.

11

Early Encounters: Coaching in Teacher Education

The supervision of teachers can be highly varied, ranging from satisfying and productive to threatening and dehumanizing (Garland, 1982). Blumberg (1980, p. 5) found that " . . . much of what occurs in the name of supervision in the schools (the transactions that take place between supervisor and teacher) constitutes a waste of time, as teachers see it. In many instances, the best evaluation that teachers give of their supervision is that it is not harmful." Such teacher attitudes towards supervision are not a product of misguided thinking but unfortunately stem from malfunctioning, poor, or nonexistent supervision in the schools. It would appear to make sense that early encounters with clinical supervision, in the form of its installation in teacher preparation programs, would eventually alter the poor attitudes of teachers toward supervision, and more importantly, supply schools with a more capable, better prepared pool of teacher trainees to push school improvement to new heights.

It has been well established that clinical supervision in its many forms is an excellent strategy for enhancing the transfer of training (Joyce and Showers, 1982; Snyder, 1982; Siedentop, 1981). The purpose of this chapter is to explore and conceptualize a mode for integrating the well-documented positive features of clinical supervision and peer coaching into the teacher preparation program. The relevant literature of teacher training, clinical supervision in transfer of training, and initial efforts at the integration of clinical supervision, peer coaching, and collegiality in teacher preparation will be examined.

TEACHER PREPARATION

In the twentieth century, teacher training has undergone several changes. The advent of compulsory schooling and mass enrollment in secondary schools in the first half of the century brought about changes that were largely ignored by universities and colleges (Conant, 1963). It wasn't until the Soviet Union's successful launch of the Sputnik space satellite in 1955 that government and higher education began to turn their full attention to public schools and to reform in the preparation of teachers.

The criticism of schools and teachers engendered by Sputnik and the perception of "falling behind" the Soviets resulted in massive federal spending on education (Garland, 1982). Schools of education used new resources to enact reforms in the training of teachers. One major reform that was adopted by some teacher preparation institutions was Competency-Based Teacher Education (CBTE) (Garland, 1982). CBTE gained popularity as state legislatures became concerned about the results of expenditures by school districts. This concern led to what became known as the accountability movement.

Competency-based teacher education was so ill-defined that critics arose to challenge the notion of competence (Garland, 1982). In the late 1960s, about the same time that the CBTE movement was gaining momentum, a movement to increase clinical experiences in teacher training began to take hold. In tune with the old Deweyan notion of "the teacher as apprentice," supporters of clinical experiences believed that teachers would best be trained by trying out their notions of teaching in a real school setting (Garland, 1982). Colleges of education responded by increasing the number and length of field experiences in their education degree program (Galambos, 1985).

Elliott (1978, p. 2) suggests four reasons for the increased emphasis on field experiences in teacher education:

(1) The field setting is an integral part of a great many competency-based teacher education programs that have been widely initiated in schools of education in recent years.

(2) There is a growing demand from practitioners that they become more involved in the process of teacher preparation; it is their position that the translation of theory into practice is best accomplished in the setting in which they operate.

(3) When some dissatisfaction exists with the performance of students in educational institutions, as at present, alternative forms of functioning in all areas related to the institution are usually sought out as a means of redress for the grievances, whether founded or unfounded.

(4) In this time of lower enrollments, many schools of education are seizing this period of lessened teaching demands on faculty to experiment with and implement more time-consuming programs and interfacing activities with other agencies in the field of education.

Increased field experiences require increased supervision of teacher trainees. Unfortunately, in the late 1960s and early 1970s most schools of education did not respond with unique supervisory processes. Griffin (1983) points out that teacher trainees perceive their student teaching experiences as the most relevant aspect of their degree program, and they judge the evaluations made by classroom supervising teachers as more relevant than university supervisors' evaluations. As supervision of field experiences increased, opportunities for university supervisors to impact student teachers were squandered by the perpetuation of the old techniques and strategies. Instead of assisting and coaching practice teachers, university supervisors were mainly fulfilling a supporting or evaluating role. Meanwhile, clinical supervision was emerging and gaining popularity in the area of inservice training.

COACHING AND THE TRANSFER OF TRAINING

Clinical supervision and peer coaching are now well established as staff development techniques aimed at enhancing the transfer of inservice training for teachers (Joyce and Showers, 1982; Snyder, 1982; MacPhail-Wilcox, 1982). Use of clinical supervision appears to lead to desirable and specified behavioral changes in teachers (MacPhail-Wilcox, 1982), and school improvement has been linked to clinical supervision (Snyder, 1982). All of these successful outcomes have resulted from efforts related to coaching.

In addition to stimulating instructional improvement in teachers, clinical supervision in its various forms appears to increase motivation and improve attitudes and morale of teachers (Ellis et al., 1979). Staff development models in which teachers share in the decision-making process are by far the most successful models (Mohlman et al., 1982). Transfer of training using coaching guarantees teachers a stake in their own professional development and allows professionally mature individuals a role in the implementation of the training.

In sum, coaching has met with success in many instances in short-term inservice training of professional teachers. Additionally, there exists great potential for improved motivation, attitude, and morale in coached teachers. Based on the evidence from the inservice staff development research cited above, this writer believes that coaching's potential for training pre-service teachers appears to be significant.

COACHING IN TEACHER EDUCATION

Forms of coaching and collegiality are beginning to appear in the preparation of teachers. One of the earliest models to be developed was for physical education students at Ohio State University (Siedentop, 1981). In this case applied behavior analysis is mixed with the observation cycle to improve physical education student teacher teaching behavior by: (1) agreeing on a set of teacher behaviors (or competencies) that the researchers wish to have student teachers demonstrate, (2) designing a highly reliable and valid system for observing the frequency and degree of utilization of these behaviors, (3) observing significant behavior change as a result of the observation/feedback intervention, (4) utilizing all three members of the student teaching triad in both the observation and feedback systems, (5) packaging material to support or encourage use of the observed behaviors, and (6) insuring maintenance of behavior change through continuous feedback and follow-up programming (Siedentop, 1981).

Another experimental model of note is the Wynn model conceived and created at Florida Southern College (Wynn, 1986). The Wynn model was developed to enhance the transfer of training of elementary student teachers. As part of the seminar course taken concurrently with full-time student teaching, students in the experimental group were encouraged to choose their own instructional goals and supervise each other in a peer coaching arrangement. The members of the experimental group scored significantly higher on the observational instrument, designed to measure the transfer of training, than those in the control group (Wynn, 1986).

The Siedentop (1981) and Wynn (1986) models are successful instances of coaching in the preparation of teachers. One of the most promising developments in collegiality is Grimmett's (in press) concept of collegial teams of student teachers. Teams of fifteen students are split into groups of five. Each group of five is assigned one university supervisor and two mentor classroom teachers. The five students are assigned to the same school and are partly responsible for the development of their fellow students. Assigning only two teachers to the five students implies that students will never incorporate a 100 percent teaching load. However Grimmett defends the need for less than 100 percent teaching loads for student teachers by exposing the fallacy of typical teacher preparation programs that expect student teachers to teach full time and learn about teaching at the same time. The collegial team allows student teachers the opportunity to observe exemplary teaching, develop their own teaching skills, and reflect intelligently on their own teaching performances. In effect, the collegial team arrangement is meant to provide a culture in which student teachers are exposed to the perspectives and habits of collegiality.

All three models of teacher training discussed above represent creative attempts at fostering meaningful development in teacher trainees. In the next section a fourth model is proposed that combines the best features of the paradigms examined above with extensive, continuing, comprehensive cycles of coaching and collegial encounters from entry into teacher preparation until completion of career.

COACHING IN TEACHER EDUCATION MODEL (CITE)

Coaching's record of success in transfer of training and potential as a supervisory system, coupled with the need for improved teacher training, served as a catalyst for the development of the Coaching in Teacher Education model. The CITE model as developed by this author has five distinct phases that encompass the totality of teacher development, from introduction into the teacher training institution to follow-up inservice programs for teachers in the field. The five phases include: Coaching and Teaching, Team Observation, Peer and Formative Coaching, Collegiality, and Professional Development (see Figure 11.1). What follows is a description of the conceptual model, which remains to be implemented in practice.

Phase One—Coaching and Teaching

The first phase of the CITE model is a *coaching and teaching* course that is added to the standard teacher preparation program. The coaching and teaching course focuses on effective teaching research, and on

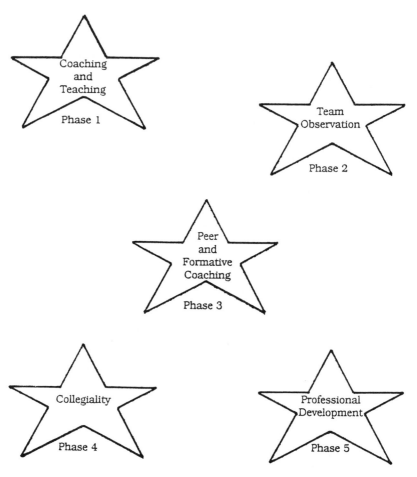

Figure II.1 The Coaching in Teacher Education Model (CITE).

exploration of the technology of coaching. As the novice education ma-
jors are exposed to the rich teacher effectiveness literature, they will
also become immersed in the five-stage observation cycle of clinical
supervision.

The content of the course includes the basic skills of clinical supervision and the effective teacher behaviors known from research. To
achieve acquisition of these skills, videotaped examples of exemplary
teaching, along with tapes on the clinical supervision observation cycle, are examined. Students are encouraged to practice the various
stages of the observation cycle using noneducation examples, such as

supervising a friend changing a tire on a car, or supervising a family member baking a new recipe. These first tentative forays into the technology of clinical supervision lay the groundwork for examining examples of instruction.

The importance of acquiring the clinical supervision knowledge base goes beyond the simple acquisition of a new skill for aspiring teachers. Research indicates that clinical supervision can be a motivating influence for those who are involved in it (Ellis et al., 1979). It is vital that the novice teacher begin teaching within a culture in which formative supervision is an expected norm, not an unwanted intrusion. By intertwining the clinical supervision knowledge base with effective teacher research in a required course, teacher trainees are exposed to two vital school work culture expectations. The assumptions are that one is expected to aspire to be the best teacher possible, and that help in improving teaching skills can be provided in a systematic and logical manner.

Phase Two—Team Observation

Phase two of the CITE model occurs during the semester that the education major enrolls in the pre-internship field experience. Most education programs require a part-time field experience that precedes the semester-long full-time student teaching component of the program (Galambos, 1985). Generally, programs that include a pre-internship require a concurrent seminar course in which students and university supervisors share experiences and hone teaching skills necessary for the classroom. The classroom experiences and subsequent seminar sessions are where phase two, *team observation*, is initiated.

During the pre-internship and the accompanying seminar, the students are encouraged to sharpen their observation skills, particularly the data-gathering and analysis portion of the observation cycle. The pre-internship affords the students an opportunity to observe exemplary teaching and to practice the observation cycle. It is suggested that the classroom teachers who serve as models for the student teachers exhibit excellent teaching and classroom management skills, and understand the relevant effective teacher research in the literature.

Phase two is also an appropriate time to introduce the concept of collaboration. Students are organized in groups of three or four persons to observe and discuss a teaching episode. The collaborative effort exposes team members to unique viewpoints and forces them to consider a variety of teacher behaviors and options. Coming to grips with questions such as, "What is excellent teaching?" and "How do we know when excellent teaching has occurred?" will stimulate professional understanding.

Phase Three—Peer and Formative Coaching

At the end of the teacher training program, students are expected to complete a capstone experience of full-time student teaching. This full-time internship provides the forum for the third phase of the CITE model, *peer and formative coaching*. By the time teacher trainees reach the student teaching term they have completed the majority of their degree coursework, including professional education courses. The internship term usually consists of full-time student teaching in a public or approved private school, plus a once-a-week seminar.

Immersion into the culture of the classroom on a full-time basis represents the biggest challenge for prospective teachers. It is with this in mind that the CITE model introduces peer coaching to extend the practice of collaboration and to partly transfer the responsibility of supervision to the student teachers. With the clinical supervision and effective teaching knowledge bases in hand, student teachers can begin to interact professionally by observing each other's teaching and offering suggestions for improving practice.

Formative supervision is also provided by the university supervisor and the supervising classroom teacher. Coaching in the form of the observation cycle is continued throughout the student teaching term. Continual observation and feedback is structured to maintain a professional focus during the internship. This is in contrast to typical practice (Griffin et al., 1983).

Peer coaching teams are established in a number of ways. The simplest teaming arrangement would be to match all interns assigned to one school. However, not all schools are large enough (or lucky enough) to have more than one intern per semester. Logic dictates that geography in terms of proximity be a determining factor in establishing peer coaching teams. Another important factor is matching subject matter interns at the secondary level, although differing subject matter interns can be teamed if the teacher training institution prefers an arrangement of this type. No matter what the teaming strategy, collaboration is essential.

So far, only the training of the students in colleges of education has been addressed in the CITE model. However, it is appropriate to address the issue of professional development for classroom teachers and university supervisors involved in teacher preparation. Both key roles can have a profound influence on the success of student teachers (Feiman-Nemser and Buchmann, 1989; Jelinek, 1986), but only if the supervision they provide is helpful and valuable (Yates, 1981; Blank and Heathington, 1987). It is imperative that all participants in the coaching process, including university supervisors and classroom teachers, receive proper training in clinical supervision to insure continuity and consistency in the supervision of the student teachers during the most important aspect of their teacher training program.

Phase Four—Collegiality

Phase four of the CITE model is *collegiality*, or the creation of a culture that is comprised of four components (Little, 1981, pp. 12–13):

(1) Teachers engage in frequent, continuous, and increasingly concrete and precise talk about teaching practice, thereby developing a shared language adequate to relate to the complexity of teaching.
(2) Teachers and administrators frequently observe each other teaching, and provide each other with useful evaluations of their teaching. Shared observation and feedback provides referents for the shared language of teaching.
(3) Teachers and administrators plan, design, research, evaluate, and prepare teaching materials together.
(4) Teachers and administrators teach each other the practice of teaching.

Collegiality is beneficial to teachers in a number of ways. They obtain instructional range, depth, and flexibility from working together (Little, 1987). In addition, teachers derive influence among their ranks, and respect from others—such as administrators, pupils, and parents—through collegial work conditions (Little, 1987).

In the CITE model, collegiality begins when the recent graduate of the college of education embarks on her/his first teaching position. As a requirement of the probationary period of the beginning teacher's career, collegial groups of first year teachers and their matched mentor teachers continue to practice peer coaching. The collegial groups serve as a support group as well as a supervisory team charged with improving the teaching competencies of the novice teachers.

Many states are moving to a beginning teacher program, such as those in Florida and Virginia, requiring new teachers to demonstrate basic teaching competencies. Ostensibly these programs are designed to provide formative assistance to new teachers. Collegial teams provide a support structure for the supervisory dimension of the beginning teacher program. At one of the most crucial junctures in a teacher's career, coaching through collegiality can be a significant factor in motivating and sustaining novice teachers in their acquisition of basic competence.

Although the CITE model calls for administratively arranged collegiality—what Grimmett and Crehan (in press) term contrived collaboration—the framework for novice teacher collegiality is established not only for professional development, but also as a support group. Beginning teachers who have experienced the first three phases of the CITE model experience forms of collegiality, and discover for themselves the intrinsic values of colleagueship. Motivation on their part to continue working with others, in pursuit of professional excellence, enhances administrative attempts to facilitate collegiality among the teaching staff, and thereby reduces or eliminates the contrived nature of the administratively arranged collegiality.

Phase Five—Professional Development

A primary concern of principals as instructional leaders is the continued growth and development of their staff. Teachers are forced into self-renewal efforts by most state boards of education via the teacher certificate renewal requirements. Most states allow districts to initiate staff development programs that can be used to count towards recertification of the teaching staff. Since teachers are required to participate in most development programs, it is sensible to devise programs that are useful and motivating. Research from the staff development knowledge base indicates that coaching can be helpful in the transfer of training in at least five ways (Showers, 1985, pp. 45–46). Teachers who have been coached:

(1) Generally practice new strategies more frequently and develop

greater skill in the actual moves of a new teaching strategy than do teachers who have experienced identical initial training

(2) Use the new strategies more appropriately in terms of their own instructional objectives and the theories of specific models of teaching

(3) Exhibit greater long-term retention of knowledge about the skill with strategies in which they have been coached and, as a group, increase the appropriateness of using new teaching models over time

(4) Are much more likely than uncoached teachers to teach the new strategies to their students, ensuring that students understand the purpose of the strategy and the behaviors expected of them when using the strategy

(5) Exhibit clearer cognitions with regard to the purposes and uses of the new strategies, as revealed through interviews, lesson plans, and classroom performance than do uncoached teachers

Teachers are adult learners, and as adults they appear to pass through distinct development stages (Krupp, 1987). An educator who is entering the second half of his/her career has special personal needs that can be addressed through professional development programs (Krupp, 1987). Coaching, mentoring, and collegiality are three ways that mature, talented teachers can be given a chance to meet their personal and professional needs and affect school improvement and staff development. In the CITE model, coaching, mentoring, and collegiality will enhance efforts in school improvement, and provide experienced, talented teachers an opportunity to meet their developmental needs.

The CITE model must be supported by administrators, professors, parents, teachers, and legislatures to be successful. Miles (1986) has identified fourteen key factors for success over three distinct phases of major change projects:

(1) Initiation
   (a) Linked to high-profile need
   (b) Clear model of implementation
   (c) One or more strong advocates
   (d) Active initiation
(2) Implementation
   (a) Coordination

(b) Shared control

(c) Pressure and support

(d) Ongoing technical assistance

(e) Early rewards for teachers

(3) Institutionalization

(a) Embedding

(b) Links to instruction

(c) Widespread use

(d) Removal of competing priorities

(e) Continuing assistance

As stated at the beginning of this chapter, the CITE model is a conceptualization for a new process in teacher preparation. However, for a college of education/school district(s) partnership willing to undertake initiation, implementation, and institutionalization of this concept, the fourteen areas reported by Miles (1986) would have to be addressed and supported. It is believed here that the challenge of improving teacher training and the future of schooling make the effort worthwhile.

Recent research indicates that coaching and teacher education are natural partners. The powerful, exciting combination of the two in the CITE model provides educators with an opportunity to utilize the collaborative, supervisory expertise of coaching without disrupting the institutionalized teacher education program now in place at most teacher preparation institutions. The time has come for changes in the way we prepare teachers, and coaching as described in the CITE model can become the catalyst necessary to make the changes successful.

REFERENCES

Blank, M. A. and B. S. Heathington. 1987. "The Supervisory Process: A Consistent Approach to Help Student Teachers Improve," *Teacher Educator*, 22(4):2–14.

Blumberg, A. 1980. *Supervisors and Teachers: A Private Cold War, 2nd Ed.* Berkeley, CA: McCutchan.

Conant, J. B. 1963. *The Education of American Teachers*. New York: McGraw-Hill Book Co.

Elliott, P. G. 1978. *Field Experiences in Preservice Teacher Education*, Bibliographies on Educational Topics No. 9. Washington, DC: ERIC Clearinghouse on Teacher Education.

Ellis, E. C., J. T. Smith and W. H. Abbott. 1979. "Peer Observation: A Means for Supervisory Acceptance," *Educational Leadership*, 36(6):423–426.

Feiman-Nemser, S. and M. Buchmann. 1989. "Describing Teacher Education: A Framework and Illustrative Findings from a Longitudinal Study of Six Students," *The Elementary School Journal*, 89(3):365–377.

Galambos, E. C. 1985. *Teacher Preparation: The Anatomy of a College Degree*. Atlanta: Southern Regional Education Board.

Garland, C. 1982. *Guiding Clinical Experiences in Teacher Education*. New York: Longman.

Goldhammer, R., R. H. Anderson and R. J. Krajewski. 1980. *Clinical Supervision: Special Methods for the Supervision of Teachers, 2nd Ed.* New York: Holt, Rinehart and Winston.

Griffin, G., S. Barnes, R. Hughes, S. O'Neal, M. Defino, S. Edwards and H. Hukill. 1983. *Clinical Preservice Teacher Education: Final Report of a Descriptive Study*. Austin: Research in Teacher Education Program, R&D Center for Teacher Education, University of Texas.

Grimmett, P. P. (In press.) "Teacher Planning, Collegiality, and the Education of Teachers: A Developmental Integration of Research-Validated Knowledge with Practice," in *Advances in Teacher Education, Vol. 4*, L. G. Katz and J. D. Raths, eds., Norwood, NJ: Ablex, pp. 50–81.

Grimmett, P. P. and E. P. Crehan. (In press.) "The Nature of Collegiality in Teacher Development: The Case of Clinical Supervision," in *Teacher Development and Educational Change*, M. G. Fullan and A. Hargreaves, eds., Philadelphia: Falmer Press.

Jelinek, C. A. 1986. "Stress and the Pre-Service Teacher," *Teacher Educator*, 22(1):2–8.

Joyce, B. and B. Showers. 1982. "The Coaching of Teaching," *Educational Leadership*, 40(1):4–10.

Krupp, J.-A. 1987. "Understanding and Motivating Personnel in the Second Half of Life," *Journal of Education*, 169(1):20–44.

Little, J. W. "The Power of Organizational Setting: School Norms and Staff Development," paper presented at the annual meeting of the AERA, Los Angeles, CA, 1981.

Little, J. W. 1987. "Teachers as Colleagues," in *Educators' Handbook: A Research Perspective*, V. R. Koehler, ed., New York: Longman, pp. 491–518.

MacPhail-Wilcox, B. 1982. "Review of Clinical Supervision Research," *Wingspan*, 1(1):5–6.

Miles, M. "Research Findings on the Stages of School Improvement," Conference on Planned Change, The Ontario Institute for Studies in Education, 1986.

Mohlman, G., J. Kierstad and M. Gundlach. 1982. "A Research-Based Inservice Model for Secondary Teachers," *Educational Leadership*, 40(1):16–18.

Showers, B. 1985. "Teachers Coaching Teachers," *Educational Leadership*, 42(7): 43–48.

Siedentop, D. 1981. "The Ohio State University Supervision Research Program Summary Report," *Journal of Teaching in Physical Education*, 1(Spring):30–38.

Snyder, Karolyn J. 1982. "Clinical Supervision: A Coaching Technology," in *Texas ASCD Monograph: Improving Classroom Practice through Supervision*, R. H. Anderson, ed., Dallas: Texas Association for Supervision & Curriculum Development, pp. 34–44.

Wynn, M. J. 1986. "Student Teacher Transfer of Training to the Classroom: Effects of an Experimental Model," Ed.D. dissertation, University of South Florida.

Yates, J. W. 1981. "Student Teaching in England: Results of a Recent Survey," *Journal of Teacher Education*, 32(5):44–46.

12

Cognition and Metacognition in Coaching Teachers

The conscious integration of coaching and metacognition creates a powerful cognitive tool that affects how we think about our teaching behavior. Metacognitive thinking, the thinking about one's thinking, can be helpful when coaching with a colleague. When we examine the elements of training programs, and the "observation cycle" (Goldhammer et al., 1980), we can conclude that coaching equates to a "mini" training. Coaching uses the elements ascribed to effective training.

The process of training and coaching, complete with its metacognitive underpinnings, allows us to expand that which is known, and to explore that which is unknown. Coaching, through interaction, aids metacognition and enables the teacher to function more effectively as an independent learner. Gavelek (1985) says that the promise of metacognition is that it addresses the problem of generalization of performance across settings. Metacognition represents a self-correcting system and identifies one who has learned to learn. This self-mirroring effect provides the indirect meta knowledge that enables one to behave proactively and influence the input, which in turn influences one's activity. The transfer or generalization of knowledge to use across different settings is enabling "to the extent that the individuals know what and know how they know . . ." (p. 129).

This chapter is organized into three sections: (1) an investigation of operational models of transfer of training, (2) the dimensions of coaching and metacognition, and (3) a metacognitive coaching model. This metacognitive coaching model can affect, positively, the transfer of theory into practice. The challenge for the coach or supervisor is to stimulate the cognitive and metacognitive processes of both themselves and the teacher toward an ultimate "executive control."

Figure 12.1, a comparative chart of various training and coaching models, illustrates the parallel features of these models and establishes an organizational framework for the first half of the chapter. An outline of each scholar's ideas will be presented. Each outline will emphasize the main features of each stage for a specific model in order that the stages may be compared easily.

METACOGNITIVE TRAINING MODELS

This section will investigate transfer of training, metacognition, and reflection, and will demonstrate that training and coaching are akin. Each model to be presented in this section represents what Costa (1984) refers to as a *before*, *during*, and *after* of metacognition. That is, when we ask students to actively focus on "what's going on" at each stage of a model, they are applying metacognitive practice (Costa and Marzano, 1987).

The argument that training and coaching are actually the same process is illustrated by Figure 12.1. The Goldhammer et al. (1980) clinical supervision and coaching model, and the Little (1985) skilled pairs model may be seen as a format for discussion about what has occurred. They also become a foundation for examining each of the other training models. For example, the pre-observation conference is a readiness stage, where, according to Bransford (1979), a person searches for prior knowledge of an event in an attempt to give advanced organization to an event. The observation stage involves an acquisition of information during an event, which forms conceptual understanding about the event. Analysis of the evidence allows the observer to reorganize and classify the concepts of the observation into an understandable sequence, which may then be demonstrated or modeled. The conference stage of interaction is a communication between the observer and the teacher, which may include a tentative suggestion for refinement to the teacher. The post-observation conference is an additional opportunity for more generalized feedback about the process. This stage contributes to the transfer of the suggested refinement through a valuing of the teacher's opinion. This provides the teacher with a sense of ownership and an understanding of "what's in it" for him/her.

Model	Purpose	Stage 1	Stage 2	Stage 3	Stage 4	Stage 5	Stage 6
Bransford	A transfer model which assumes metacognition in its final phase	Concept Identification	Concept Formation		Practice		Transfer
Joyce & Showers	A training model which stresses "executive control"		Theory & Examples	Model & Demonstration	Practice	Feedback	Coaching
Snyder	A training model providing self-awareness	Readiness	Concepts	Demonstration	Practice	Feedback & Reinforcement	Transfer
Meichenbaum & Cameron	A medical training model designed to utilize internal self-talk at each of its four stages	Conceptualization	Acquisition		Rehearsal	Application	Follow-through
Little	A coaching model to foster "skilled pairs"	Focus	Hard Evidence		Interaction	Predictability & Reciprocity	
Costa & Garmston	"Cognitive coaching" model moves teacher toward self-regulation	Creating Teacher Trust	Facilitating Teacher Learning				Teacher Autonomy
Goldhammer	A formal clinical-supervision and coaching model	Pre-Observation Conference	Observation	Data Analysis	Conference	Post-Observation Conference	

Figure 12.1 A Comparative Chart of Metacognitive Training and Coaching Models.

185

The improvement of instruction is the ultimate aim of supervision, and efforts to do so support the notion that teachers want to be more proficient. Joyce and Showers (1980) note that teachers can be taught new skills and can be helped in fine tuning classroom skills, but there is a need to help teachers to transfer skills to the classroom. Showers (1984) suggests that much training has disappeared at the point we most care about, the interaction between the teacher and the student. Transfer of training is the end result of coaching. Teachers engage in coaching to help themselves internalize a particular teaching behavior.

Transfer of training is the ability to know how to use the knowledge gained in training in a practical setting. Dansereau and Brooks (1984), suggest that transfer occurs when an individual's prior "how to" knowledge influences the acquisition of a new skill.

Reflection

Practitioners often use the terms "reflection" and "metacognition" interchangeably, but they are separate cognitive functions. Reflection is a practice of remembering a past action, or projecting what might happen in a future situation. Cruickshank and Applegate (1981) consider reflective teaching a form of simulation that provides opportunities for teachers to consider past teaching experiences with the intention of improving subsequent practice. Reflection "encourages teachers to be students of teaching" (p. 553). They also suggest that reflective teaching can be effective during directed discussion of a classroom observation.

For the purposes of coaching, reflection and metacognition are independent concepts, and interweave with one another. Reflection provides the material with which metacognition works. Reflection provides the fabric, and metacognition, the loom.

Van Manen (1977) identifies three levels of reflective behavior in teaching. The first, *technical*, is concerned with the effectiveness of strategies used to achieve set aims. The second, *interpretive*, focuses on goals, the reason for their establishment, and how they were achieved. The goals in this case are referred to as being fluid. The third, *critical*, examines the ethical and moral platform from which goals were set, and how this bias affects choices about curriculum and instruction. At the critical level, reflection delves into the metacognitive by developing an understanding of ways of knowing, and facilitates what is known through reflection (p. 33).

Metacognition

The metacognitive process, active throughout training and coaching, is the "hinge" for transfer of skills. Metacognition plays a key function in training, and therefore in coaching. Flavell (1976), and Flavell and Wellman (1977) developed the theoretical notion of metacognition, referring to an awareness of one's cognitive processes, products, and self-regulation. Wong (1985) indicates that metacognitive theory has had great impact on the design of current instructional studies. Wong also identifies "informed training," where trainees are given the rationale of the strategy to be learned, as a tool to help teachers to see the relationship between strategy use and increased learning. "Self-control training" (Wong, 1985) instructs trainees in the "executive control" functions of planning, checking, monitoring, and overseeing the activities assigned. The idea is to learn "how" to learn.

Brown et al. (1983) claim that self-control training induces the same awareness as informed training. Self-control training may lead to more general effects than may be expected from providing information on specific strategies.

Flavell and Wellman (1977) provide a classification scheme concerned with meta-memory (your memory of how you know). They describe a "person category" as dealing with the individual's knowledge about his/her own memory limitations and capacities, and also his/her ability to monitor personal experiences. "Task variables" involve an awareness that task demands influence memory performance. "Strategy variables" refer to an individual's knowledge of his/her storage and retrieval strategies.

Costa and Marzano (1987) indicate that teaching students to be alert to the cognitive processes embedded in written and spoken language helps them to become aware of their own language and thought (p. 33). Marzano et al. (1988) define metacognition as "a dimension of thinking that involves knowledge and control of self and knowledge and control of process" (p. 144). Metacognition is an understanding of how to achieve an end using an organized cognitive plan.

Transfer

Bransford's (1979) model of transfer (Figure 12.1) provides four concepts of transfer of training that illustrate how people internalize the use of a skill with the aid of metacognition. The four phases are (1) concept identification, (2) concept formation, (3) practice, and (4) transfer.

"Concept identification" represents a readiness decision. Is the information new, or does an organization of prior knowledge (schemata) exist? If prior knowledge is found, how can one use it to provide for the integration of new data?

In the second phase, called "concept formation," the individual has no prior knowledge of the concept, and existing general knowledge must be sorted to build a structure on which to hang the new concept. Mayer (1975) suggests that activation of appropriate current knowledge clarifies new information. Ausubel (1968) called this clarified information an "advanced organizer."

Practice for developing "schemata" is the third phase. Schemata are organizations of prior knowledge that act as a hook on which the brain hangs new information that is appropriate to the topic at hand. Mayer (1975) suggests that by activating appropriate prior knowledge, which both clarifies and is clarified by new information, one is able to transfer more tasks into use. Some methods of practice better facilitate remembering. For example, practice using examples from a variety of situations is more effective than practice using examples from limited situations.

In the fourth phase of his approach, Bransford discusses the benefits of personal metacognition on transfer:

> The ability to plan and evaluate our own learning strategies seems to be a hallmark of intelligent activity. From this perspective, intelligence involves the development of skills for utilizing and modifying previously existing knowledge, rather than the possession of some fixed capacity. (p. 244)

"Learning to learn" requires the abilities of self-regulation to allow transfer of learning. The "metacognitive process" is the understanding of one's "how to" knowledge. Active and efficient learners know the value of analyzing experiences, which aids in the process of knowledge application. Knowing what strategies to use to solve a problem is a valuable skill.

Joyce and Showers (1982) indicate that an "executive control" factor or a "meta-understanding" about how a training model works should be included during instruction. They suggest that it is a "self talk" method of figuring how teaching skills or techniques can be fitted into an instructional repertoire and adapted to students. The need to emphasize the highest possible skill level to forecast success increases the odds that successful transfer will take place (p. 9).

The Joyce and Showers Training Model (1982)

Joyce and Showers (1982) provide a five-stage model, which includes a coaching application as its final step. Joyce and Showers indicate those elements of training that allow an individual to utilize and demonstrate effective utility with a new skill or information. They suggest that a meta-understanding about how the training model works should be included in training. They maintain that it is valuable to analyze experiences that will help people to learn to use knowledge when it is needed. "Self talk" is a method suggested as a way of figuring out how skills or techniques can be fitted into an instructional repertoire and adapted to students.

- Stage one presents theory and defines the technique. Concept attributes are described with examples and rationale for its use.
- Stage two demonstrates the techniques using clear visual and auditory examples and nonexamples.
- Stage three practices, safely, the strategy under simulated conditions.
- Stage four provides structured and unstructured feedback. This involves a system of observing behaviors, collecting data, and receiving feedback. During a practice cycle, an observer gives response to behavior through a "playing back" of events.
- Stage five coaches for the application of the strategy. The coaching element of the training process involves helping teachers to analyze classroom behaviors, and to develop plans in anticipation of the use of new or other specific skills.

Bransford's theoretical transfer model closely parallels the Joyce and Showers (1982) practical training model.

Snyder's Competency Development Model (1988)

Snyder (1988) presents an adult learning model in six stages. The six dimensions of the model are (1) readiness, (2) concept definition, (3) demonstration, (4) practice, (5) feedback, and (6) transfer. The Snyder model (1988, p. 154) builds on the Joyce and Showers (1982) model, with the very important dimension of "readiness" as a first stage of training, and "transfer" as the final step of training.

The Snyder model assumes organized workshop goals and follow-up coaching. In the first stage, readiness activities include rationale for a concept; trainee diagnosis of personal awareness of the concept; anticipated development of the concept; and projected training outcomes and uses. This readiness dimension gives the participant a reason to learn this concept, which includes a projection of "what's in it for me." This can be interpreted as an early metacognitive stage where the participant is assessing personal needs and setting personal goals for training. Goals are monitored in future readiness dialogues found in the Snyder model.

The second, third, fourth, and fifth stages of concept presentation, modeling and demonstration, practice, feedback and reinforcement, respectively, are parallel to the Joyce and Showers (1982) model, with the understanding that the coaching dimension is used in the feedback and reinforcement stage.

The sixth stage of the Snyder model is called "transfer." This stage formalizes the Joyce and Showers (1982) suggestion that transfer be forecast throughout training. Trainees not only project how they might use a technique in the classroom, but each discusses successes and failures with that technique at a follow-up session.

Stress Inoculation Training (1983)

Meichenbaum and Cameron (1983) practice metacognition at each stage of a stress reduction training model (Figure 12.1). This model proved successful with patients in a medical setting. Client training in a self-regulatory process increases the probability that the client will activate and integrate coping responses. An internal dialogue in which one provides "self talk" about what one thinks and believes about thought and action is emphasized throughout the training.

The phases of training used by Meichenbaum and Cameron (1983) are "conceptualization," "acquisition and rehearsal," and "application and follow through." Meichenbaum and Cameron imply direct coaching in their "follow through" section. Their work is conducive to an application of coaching and metacognition in a real setting.

Conceptualization

The personal data gathering or needs assessment step represents a readiness phase where the trainee grasps training needs. It is a problem-solving focus, which trains clients to independently analyze and specify what is required to produce a direct response to each situation. This metacognitive exercise forecasts skill needs and emphasizes self-control. Both Bransford (1979) and Snyder (1988) advocate this step in a training process.

Acquisition and Rehearsal

This stage promotes the presentation and integration of a specific skill, or strategy, which represents an attempt to change one's cognitive structures. This is most likely to occur by discovering through practice which "old" cognitive structures are adaptive. The metacognitive process fits into each stage of the training model. During the presentation of definition, theory, demonstration, and modeling, participants introspectively evaluate and share past images and experiences with their partners and in small groups. These reflective discussions about what one did, how one did it, and how one knew to do it, represent an extension of the metacognitive process from a personal level to a partnership level and then to a group level.

Application

In a practice-feedback cycle, participants are encouraged to monitor themselves through activities while maintaining consideration for their original direction. The self-checking action of this practice allows reinforcement of both the metacognitive elements and the skill elements.

Follow Through

This phase emphasizes practice in real situations where gradual risk taking is encouraged. In this stage, the metacognitive process is focused on training, particularly when the coaching dimension is added. The coach assists in the construction of future strategies, aids recovery from a failed situation, and reinforces a sense of self-efficacy. Meichenbaum and Cameron (1983) support the collaborative notion that an individual can discuss past situations to obtain more information and clarify what is known about oneself. The model provides for the metacognitive elements of "informed training" and "self-control training." This allows each participant to consciously revisit and reprocess information in relation to past images and actions. Each person is able to share a reciprocal experience from another's point of view. Each partnership is encouraged to share its reflective evaluation of the training.

Summary

The "informed" aspect of training is an application of learned concepts in a real situation. This gives the trainee a rationale and a goal. To plan, monitor, check, and evaluate one's ongoing performance encourages self-regulation and a process of learning to learn. The consensus seems to be that these strategies are conducive to the skill-transfer process. Active and efficient learners know what they need to do in order to master information. Bransford (1979) emphasizes that the ability to use metacognitive strategies to improve one's own learning is a sign of intelligent activity, and that intelligence involves the development of skills for using and modifying already held knowledge.

DIMENSIONS OF METACOGNITIVE COACHING

This section explores coaching processes, first taking the reader through Little's (1985) "skillful pairs" model, and then applying the Little model to the observation cycle of clinical supervision (Goldhammer et al., 1980). This will give the reader a sense of the similarities between the two. Next, "cognitive coaching" (Costa and Garmston, 1986) is presented to set the stage for a metacognitive coaching model. The cognitive coaching concept pulls together all the aspects of training, coaching, and metacognition.

Clinical Supervision

The term "clinical supervision" refers, here, to a nonevaluative model that uses the five steps indicated by Goldhammer, Anderson, and Krajewski (1980). The observation cycle becomes the "tool" for individuals seeking to help each other. Clinical supervision, according to Snyder and Anderson (1986), is a technology for improving instruction by representing a direct intervention into the instructional process. It is a systematic process requiring a flexible methodology and a strong working relationship, maintained by mutual trust. This approach generates a productive tension, so coaches must be well versed in positive verbal and nonverbal skills in order to be successful.

Coaching

Showers (1984) defines coaching as ". . . a process in which education professionals assist each other in negotiating the distance between acquiring new skills or teaching strategies and applying them skillfully and effectively for instruction" (p. 48). Supporters of the "coaching of teaching" suggest that the coach can become the guide who leads the teacher through the transfer task. Coaching has been found to be essential for skill transfer (Joyce and Showers, 1982; Showers, 1981; Showers, 1984; Cook, 1982; Baker, 1983). "Coaching is the agent that has the power to transform teaching into a facilitating function in the student mastery process" (Snyder and Anderson, 1986, p. 451).

Coaching parallels the whole training sequence, and can also parallel specific parts of that sequence. Reflection allows a pair of individuals to mutually consider and discuss the activity observed, and to elicit intent to facilitate further teaching practice. Coaching encourages the development of a self-regulatory process, which becomes an internal metacognitive dialogue where, like Hamlet, one discusses the appropriateness of one action over another.

Peer Coaching

Who better to coach than a trusted colleague who has experienced similar training, and who experiences the same classroom problems and rewards? "Teachers should coach each other . . . the logistics involved in a continuous growing and learning process favor peer coaches" (Showers, 1985, p. 45). Collaboration helps to organize information and make contingency plans for future eventualities. Coaching with a colleague, in a professionally trusting situation, prompts the introspective reflection about how one works. This process allows the teacher and coach to recognize positive elements in their teaching which may have eluded them in the past. Little (1982) suggests that working together in paired groups produces "professional talk." She indicates that professional growth ensues when teachers engage in frequent, continuous, concrete, and precise talk about teaching practice. Through such talk, they build a shared language appropriate to the complexity of teaching and capable of distinguishing one practice and its virtues from another (p. 331).

Little (1985, pp. 34–35) has developed the shared language concept into a methodology of how "skillful pairs" (see Figure 12.1) operate to better understand and refine teaching. Skillful pairs have:

(1) Focus on one or two key questions, issues, situations, or problems, and address them with depth, persistence, imagination, and good humor

(2) Hard evidence recorded as a basis for generating questions, drawing conclusions, and pursuing alternatives; pairs work together to invent or select observation methods that suit their purposes

(3) Interaction in lively discussions, engaging a pair in making the conference a vehicle for joint work on teaching and an opportunity to improve their ability to learn from one another

(4) Predictability in topic and critical method, providing trust building by reliance on that which is known

(5) Reciprocity as a vehicle for building trust by acknowledging and referring to one another's knowledge and skill, and by talking to each other in ways that preserve individual dignity

Cognitive Coaching

Costa and Garmston (1986, p. 39), define "cognitive coaching" as "the supervisor's application of a set of strategies designed to enhance the teacher's perceptions, decisions and intellectual functions." They suggest that an understanding of the teacher's inner thought processes is "prerequisite to improving overt instructional behaviors which will . . . produce greater student learning." Costa and Garmston suggest that teachers use the intellectual, metacognitive processes of goal setting, monitoring, evaluation, and modification, drawing on their skills repertoire. A superior teacher knows how and when to do this.

The supervision process facilitates the rearrangement of teacher thoughts to change overt teaching behaviors. According to Costa and

Garmston, the cognitive practice of selecting appropriate strategies for coaching is driven by three goals: (1) creating and managing trust, (2) facilitating teacher learning, and (3) developing teacher autonomy. Trust is created with the skillful selection of appropriate rapport-building skills (observational, verbal, and nonverbal) that allow teachers to gain access to their own inner resources. Learning is nurtured with the professional pair, formulating clear images of desired classroom outcomes. These outcomes preserve the positive intentions of the teacher's present behaviors, and map out strategies of more effective teacher behaviors. The supervisor should draw on a repertoire of collegial skills to facilitate this exchange. Finally, teacher autonomy is achieved as the teacher becomes more self-regulating, and displays the ability to establish goals, monitor, evaluate, and modify (Costa and Garmston, 1986).

"Cognitive coaching" is an intellectual process engaged in by the supervisor to coach the teacher toward a more confident, self-regulatory action. The resulting effects serve to increase teacher self-esteem, knowledge of available teaching strategies, and self-governance.

A METACOGNITIVE COACHING MODEL

The similarities of the clinical supervision "observation cycle," Little's skillful pairs (1985), Costa and Garmston's (1986) cognitive coaching, Bransford's (1979) transfer model, the training models of Joyce and Showers (1982) and of Snyder (1988), and the Meichenbaum and Cameron (1983) training model create common ground for a metacognitive coaching approach. Through a merging of models, along with the "Johari window" (Luft, 1970), teachers and coaches can gain an appropriate method to practice and view clinical supervision. The elements of coaching and metacognition facilitate the ultimate transfer of behavior from the theoretical to the practical.

The clinical supervision model is used by a teacher and coach as a form of "training" to achieve transfer of skill and knowledge. Personal and paired reflections regarding what one has done in specific teaching situations, and how one has selected particular strategies while teaching, provide the subjects for discussion. Personal discussion regarding how one knows about what one has done is the essence of metacognition. Paired discussion can be considered an extension of a metacognitive process as teachers indicate that they identify with other teachers' descriptions of mutual experiences. Shared experiences allow isolated teachers to justify, confirm, or plan to change past actions, while working in a "safe environment."

Skillful paired discussion can act as a "metacognitive switch," which cues one into metacognitive self talk while simultaneously pursuing the first discussion. A paired dialogue may trigger something new and start an internal discourse toward understanding a new idea or concept. Both parties to a discussion extend within themselves a monologue prompted by the external discussion. Spurred by an "extended metacognitive" discussion, the Johari window helps us see and learn from that part of ourselves that has been hidden. We can deliberately tap previously unavailable resources for solving problems.

In the Johari window [Figure 12.2(a)] each of the four cells represents "a different combination of what the teacher knows or does not know about his or her teaching as contrasted with what the coach knows or does not know about that teacher's teaching" (Sergiovanni and Starratt, 1983, p. 306). The first quadrant, "what both know," represents what the teacher and the coach both know about the teacher's instructional behaviors. The second quadrant (labeled "Hidden") represents what the teacher knows, but the supervisor (or coach) does not. The third quadrant, what the supervisor knows but the teacher does not, represents aspects of the teacher's behavior of which he/she is not aware. The fourth quadrant represents aspects of teaching of which neither the teacher nor the supervisor is aware. This quadrant represents the potential for the teacher and the supervisor to acquire new information about the process of teaching. It is the job of both supervisor and teacher to expand quadrant one.

The metacognitive coaching model (Fitzgerald, 1986) was constructed from a metacognitive training model designed to utilize what is known about training, coaching, metacognition, and transfer in order to ensure more effective results from training. This training would benefit instruction in the classroom, and ultimately the students' learning. The coaching model analyzes the observation cycle in terms of training, coaching, and metacognition. The concept is presented from the perspectives of the teacher and the coach.

Using the Johari window as a frame of reference [Figure 12.2(b)–(d)] the first four stages of the observation cycle are represented by stages

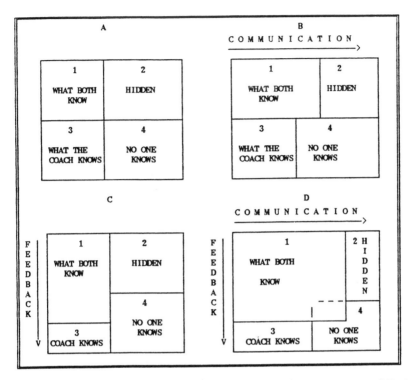

Figure 12.2 The Johari Window for Skillful Pairs Utilizes Communication and Feedback (adapted from Thomas J. Sergiovanni, Handbook for Effective Department Leadership: Concepts and Practices in Today's Secondary Schools, *Second Edition. Copyright © 1984 by Allyn and Bacon. Reprinted with permission).*

of the Johari process, and the fifth stage takes an holistic look at the process. Metacognition and the extended metacognition of the paired discussion will be discussed through the five stages. The coach's task is to cause the teacher to carry on two discussions—internal and external. The coach must set a trusting tone so that the teacher will accept the challenge and gradually reveal the internal discussion. The teacher, in monitoring the discussion, will already be reestablishing goals and directions.

Stage One: Focus

The pre-observation conference gives the teacher and the coach the opportunity to establish rapport and the agenda for the "ob cycle." Using recall-level self-questioning, (i.e., "What have I done in the past that I want to investigate?") the teacher begins a self-questioning cycle that outlines what will be revealed or not revealed. Higher-level self-questions such as "How have I done this?" and "Why have I done it this way?" lead to "How does what I do relate to information that others have?" "If it does relate, how do I want to change what I do?" This establishes what is known for the teacher. The process is similar to the readiness stage of training proposed by Bransford (1979), Meichen-baum and Cameron (1983), and Snyder (1988). The process attempts to draw out prior knowledge and understanding from both parties, and establish a participation rationale for both (e.g., "What's in it for me?").

For the coach, the focus stage helps to provide a safe climate to address overt questions similar to those the teacher asked. The coach, through higher-order questions, helps the teacher to focus on an approach to what the teacher wants to investigate. The questions establish what the coach knows. The coach is also self-questioning about how best to combine what is known about the topic with what the teacher wants to improve. An added dimension is the coach's revealed identification with the teacher's situation and needs. Recall allows the coach to self-question and monitor personal teaching practices.

The discussion between the two colleagues establishes the "extended metacognitive" format, as each provides for the other: (a) "informed training" and (b) an "executive control."

Stage Two: Evidence

The data-gathering phase allows a sample of behavior to be systematically collected. The evidence stage encourages the teacher to observe an ongoing awareness of a personal decision-making process (executive control) and the selection of words and actions in response to the classroom situation. Due to an observer's presence in the classroom, the metacognitive "switch" is turned on, and the teacher self-monitors the process in progress ("What am I doing as I am doing it?" and "How am I doing it?"). The parallel training application is a "readiness stage" where the teacher and coach collect data to ascertain the teacher's needs.

The coach is not only collecting information, but is also observing adjustments in the pre-conference plan. The coach is metacognitively monitoring self-behavior and making appropriate personal adjustments. Subjectively, the coach identifies with the teacher's situation and reviews his/her own classroom experiences. The coach's self questions are comparative in nature (e.g., "How do I do what is being practiced?" or "Would I have done this in another way?"). From the Johari window perspective, the observation stage provides further opportunity for attaining information about what the other knows.

Stage Three: Analysis

The playback step of the cycle is a search for a commonality of behaviors that form patterns to be used in discussion and critique. Due to the metacognitive elaboration of the previous two stages, the "snap shot" may have been perceived differently by each participant. The process of analysis plays back, for teacher and coach, what was being considered at specific points in time, and attempts to have the partner help make sense out of the actions.

For the teacher, metacognition is the "tool" of analysis. The challenge is to arrange and rearrange the data to illuminate the question established in the "focus" stage, and to identify patterns of behavior around that question. The interpretive and applicative self questions of "How do all of these behaviors fit together?" and "Why didn't that work?" and "What should I have done here?" link actions with past knowledge of one's behavior to knowledge about effective behavior. From the training perspective, at a readiness level, this stage represents a decision-making process. The teacher now knows what improvement is needed.

The coach, too, is involved in a self-talk process bringing together the data, existing research, and personal experience. Snyder and Anderson (1986) state that the analysis stage challenges the intellectual and professional skill of the observer more than do other stages (p. 456). The coach is also involved in a self-analysis through identification with the teacher and past experiences. The coach is self-questioning (planning) about the most appropriate approach to the discussion for the post-observation conference. The coach might be making judgmental self-enquiries about types of appropriate questions or paraphrases to use in order to elicit redirection from the teacher. Each participant has expanded the "what each knows" about the observation. The process should have created alternatives stemming from the "unknown" realm.

Stage Four: Interaction

Through communication and feedback, the post-observation conference expands the information about what is known by both the coach and the teacher. The coach's role is to reinforce appropriate behavior and elicit from the teacher a personal critique to be developed into a plan of action. The coach carefully probes and challenges the teacher to consider other options and alternatives. This puts the teacher into a metacognitive reassessment, and allows the teacher to restructure a plan for instruction. The plan gives direction to the teacher while the coach considers personal future actions. The teacher's conclusions from analysis should motivate the coach to reexplore what was learned from the teacher's classroom performance. This interaction is an example of an "extended metacognitive" practice. An internal metacognitive debriefing will probably continue after the conference, particularly if a new commitment has been made which both must consider. For the teacher, many new "how" questions are in order. The training application for this stage relates to theory and concept acquisition, and to the practice-feedback cycle. Further coaching interventions will reinforce the practice-feedback stage as the teacher begins to internalize new skills.

Stage Five: Reciprocity

Process analysis gives the participants a "macro" view of the whole observation cycle. An assessment of behavior through the extended metacognitive process calls for both the teacher and coach to move through the cycle in retrospect, as armchair quarterbacks who question the effectiveness of their past procedures. The overt remonitoring ("How have we done this?") gives rise to further covert reflections and self questions such as: "Has my contribution been effective?" "Was I critical?" "Was I receptive?" "Did I synthesize?" and "How can I improve this exercise?" The importance of this stage is more than critique and feedback. The process allows the individuals to delve deeper using "self talk" as a vehicle toward a more complete understanding of the whole experience. The exercise establishes a deeper self-confidence in the process through a mutual critique. The transfer of training is represented holistically by coaching. The metacognitive dimension is reinforced in the reciprocity stage as a reflection about the process. This gives rise to a positive need for continued growth and development.

SUMMARY

The ability to "learn to learn" requires the encouragement of self-regulation that allows transfer to many new and novel learning situations. Active and efficient learners know what they need to do in order to understand and gain mastery of information. The clinical supervision process, used as a vehicle for teachers to coach themselves, makes it easier for the teacher to consciously use knowledge when it is needed in the classroom.

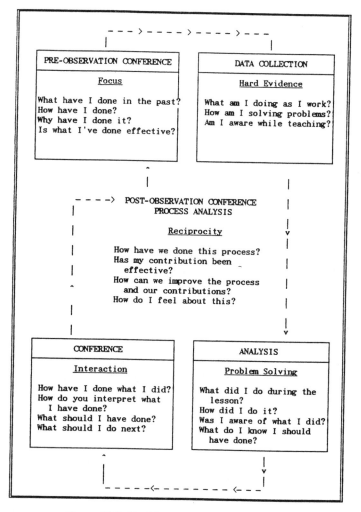

Figure 12.3 The Metacognitive Coaching Model.

Metacognition is the unconscious or conscious catalyst that allows the training models presented in the first section of this chapter to be effective. Metacognitive practice for both coach and teacher creates a complexity of simultaneous internal and external discourse, which challenges both coach and teacher to move to higher cognitive levels. Finally, in the metacognitive coaching model (Figure 12.3), we see that metacognition provides a vital component of the coaching process. The internal discussion about how one knows about what one has done is the key to transfer of training in coaching.

REFERENCES

Ausubel, D. P. 1963. *The Psychology of Meaningful Verbal Learning.* New York: Grune and Stratton.

Ausubel, D. P. 1968. *Educational Psychology: A Cognitive View.* New York: Holt, Rinehart and Winston.

Baker, R. G. 1983. "The Contribution of Coaching to Transfer of Training: An Extension Study," doctoral dissertation, University of Oregon.

Bransford, J. D. 1979. *Human Cognition: Learning, Understanding and Remembering.* Belmont, CA: Wadsworth Publishing Company.

Brown, A. L., J. D. Bransford, R. A. Ferrara and J. C. Campione. 1983. "Learning, Remembering, and Understanding," in *Handbook of Child Psychology, 3rd Edition,* P. H. Mussen, ed., New York: Wiley, Vol. 3, pp. 77–166.

Cook, G. E. "Teachers As Learners: Approaches to Professional Education," a paper presented at the annual meeting of the National Council of the Teachers of English, NCTE, Minneapolis, April, 1982.

Costa, A. L. 1984. "Mediating the Metacognitive," *Educational Leadership,* 42(3):57–62.

Costa, A. L. and R. Garmston. 1986. "The Art of Cognitive Coaching: Supervision for Intelligent Teaching," *Wingspan,* 3(1):38–43.

Costa, A. L. and R. J. Marzano. 1987. "Teaching the Language of Thinking," *Educational Leadership,* 45(2):29–33.

Cruickshank, D. R. and J. H. Applegate. 1981. "Reflective Teaching as a Strategy for Teacher Growth," *Educational Leadership,* 38:553–554.

Dansereau, D. and L. W. Brooks. 1984. *Transfer of Learning from One Setting to Another.* ERIC 248 653.

Fitzgerald, J. H. 1986. "Metacognitive Aspects of Clinical Supervision," *Wingspan,* 3(1):43–46.

Fitzgerald, J. H. 1989. "Metacognition in Clinical Supervision," *The Canadian School Executive,* 8(9):13–16.

Flavell, J. H. 1976. "Metacognitive Aspects of Problem Solving," in *The Nature of Intelligence,* L. B. Resnick, ed., Hillsdale, NJ: Lawrence Erlbaum Associates, pp. 231–235.

Flavell, J. H. and H. M. Wellman. 1977. "Metamemory," in *Perspectives on the Development of Memory and Cognition*, R. V. Kail and J. W. Hagen, eds., Hillsdale, NJ: Erlbaum, pp. 3–33.

Gavelek, J. R. and T. Raphael. 1985. "Metacognitive Instruction and Questioning," in *Metacognitive Cognition and Human Performance*, D. L. Forest-Pressley, G. E. MacKinnon and T. M. Waller, eds., Orlando: Academic Press.

Goldhammer, R., R. H. Anderson and R. J. Krajewski. 1980. *Clinical Supervision: Special Methods for the Supervision of Teachers*. New York: Holt Rinehart and Winston.

Joyce, B. and B. Showers. 1980. "Improving Inservice Training: The Messages of Research," *Educational Leadership*, 39(5):379–385.

Joyce, B. and B. Showers. 1982. "The Coaching of Teaching," *Educational Leadership*, 40(1):4–8, 10.

Joyce, B. and B. Showers. 1983. *Power in Staff Development through Research on Training*. Alexandria, VA: ASCD.

Levine, M. 1975. *Hypothesis Testing: A Cognitive Theory of Learning*. Hillsdale, NJ: Lawrence Erlbaum Associates.

Little, J. W. 1982. "Norms of Collegiality and Experimentation: Workplace Conditions of School Success," *The American Education Research Journal*, 19(3):325–340.

Little, J. W. 1985. "Teachers as Teacher Advisors: The Delicacy of Collegial Leadership," *Educational Leadership*, 43(3):34–46.

Luft, J. 1970. "The Johari Window: A Graphic Model of Awareness in Interpersonal Relations," *Group Process: An Introduction to Group Dynamics*. Palo Alto: Mayfield Publishing Company, pp. 11–20.

Marzano, R. J., R. S. Brandt, C. S. Hughes, B. F. Jones, B. Z. Presseisen, S. C. Rankin and C. Suhor. 1988. *Dimensions of Thinking: A Framework for Curriculum and Instruction*. Alexandria, VA: ASCD.

Mayer, R. E. 1975. "Information Processing Variables in Learning to Solve Problems," *Review of Educational Research*, 45:525–541.

Meichenbaum, D. and R. Cameron. 1983. "Stress Inoculation Training," in *Stress Reduction and Prevention*, D. Meichenbaum and M. Jaremco, eds., New York: Plenin Press.

Sergiovanni, T. and R. Starratt. 1983. *Supervision: Human Perspectives, Third Edition*. New York: McGraw-Hill.

Showers, B. 1982. "Transfer of Training: The Contribution of Coaching," a paper presented at the University of Oregon Doctoral Seminar, University of Oregon, Eugene. ERIC Document 231 035.

Showers, B. 1984. "Peer Coaching: A Strategy for Facilitating Transfer of Training," Center for Educational Policy and Management, College of Education, University of Oregon. ERIC Document ED27189.

Showers, B. 1985. "Teachers Coaching Teaching," *Educational Leadership*, 42(7):43–48.

Snyder, K. J. 1988. *Competency Training for Managing Productive Schools*. New York: Harcourt, Brace and Jovanovich.

Snyder, K. J. and R. H. Anderson. 1986. *Managing Productive Schools: Toward an Ecology*. Orlando: Academic Press.

Van Manen, M. 1977. "Linking Ways of Knowing with Ways of Being Practical," *Curriculum Inquiry*, 6(3):205–228.

Wellman, H. M. 1985. "The Origins of Metacognition," in *Metacognition, Cognition and Human Performance, Volume 2*, G. E. MacKinnon and T. G. Waller, eds., Orlando: Academic Press, pp. 1–31.

Wong, B. Y. L. 1985. "Self Questioning Instructional Research: A Review," *Review of Educational Research*, 55(2):227–268.

Yussen, S. R. 1985. "The Role of Metacognition in Contemporary Theories of Cognitive Development," in *Metacognition, Cognition and Human Performance, Volume 2*, D. L. Forrest-Pressley, G. E. MacKinnon and T. G. Weller, eds., Orlando: Academic Press, pp. 253–284.

Technical Coaching: Equipping Professionals with Basic and Emerging Tools for Enhancing Performance

Imagine Sherlock Holmes sitting in front of his *fin de siècle* coal fire at 221 B Baker Street, London, saying in triumph to his companion, "Elementary, my dear Watson!" Now transpose the pair to the late twentieth century and follow his brilliant (as always) deduction based on the following propositions:

- Public interest in and demand for quality education continues to be great (e.g., Carnegie Task Force, 1986; Holmes Group, 1986; National Commission on Excellence in Education, 1983).
- Research has established a growing body of "best practices" on pedagogical approaches and how to prepare teachers to use those approaches.
- Supervision can provide the link between state-of-the-art instruction in a specific field and actual classroom practice.
- Inservice training can increase the probability that teachers will use the new knowledge and skills in the classroom.
- Teachers can use new knowledge and skills to improve the instruction of students in the classroom.
- Student achievement will be increased if students receive optimal instruction.

Ergo, a major responsibility of the educational community is to prepare teachers to use the best practices in their field to have a positive impact on student academic achievement.

The linkages among educational research, teacher training, changed classroom practice, and increased student achievement are growing steadily stronger. Bloom (1980), in his description of new directions in educational research, clearly classifies teaching as a variable that can be altered through appropriate inservice education to effect significant positive change in student achievement. However, some of the links in the improvement chain (e.g., between teacher training and resulting changed classroom teaching behaviors) are not yet as strongly forged as they need to be. A major challenge is to determine how to maximize the benefits of training to change teachers' classroom behaviors in ways supported by research on effective instructional practices (Sparks, 1983).

TECHNICAL COACHING DEFINED

One inservice training model, based on the work of Joyce and Showers (1982), appears to have great promise for assisting teachers not only to learn new content but also to incorporate that new learning into their classroom teaching repertoire. In this procedure, the theoretical basis and rationale for the new teaching method is first studied. Then the strategy is demonstrated numerous times by persons who are relatively expert in the strategy. Following the demonstration, participants practice the strategy under protected conditions (e.g., structured skills practice during the training session) and receive feedback on their performance. These three components enable most teachers to use a new strategy fluidly and appropriately. However, to ensure transfer of the skill to the classroom, a fourth training element, coaching, is suggested as an essential part of the training process.

Coaching may be defined as the "provision of on-site, personal support and technical assistance for teachers" (Baker and Showers, 1984, p. 1). The underlying metaphor of an athletic coach suggests that change in individuals can be brought about through close supervision by an expert in the field. The coach operates according to a clearly understood game plan that can be modified as game conditions change. Furthermore, the coach works closely with players, observing their performance, providing feedback, demonstrating techniques, and monitoring progress. In the Joyce and Showers conception, coaching is characterized by a collegial analysis of teaching in a problem-solving mode through an observation and feedback cycle.

Coaching facilitates transfer by serving five functions. First, coaching provides companionship, or interaction with another individual, during the difficult process of changing teaching behavior. Secondly, coaching provides the learner with technical feedback about successes and areas for improvement. Coaching also fosters analysis of application, or determination of when to use the strategy and what consequently will be achieved. Determining how to adapt the strategy to meet the needs of particular students in a specific teaching situation is also an outcome. Finally, coaching facilitates transfer by providing support during the many but necessary trials with a new strategy (Joyce and Showers, 1982).

Garmston (1987) uses the term "technical coaching" to describe the form of coaching developed by Joyce and Showers. The other forms of coaching in his schema are collegial and challenge coaching. Technical coaching is built on the premise that teachers will improve teaching performance if they are provided with objective data in a supportive climate. Its major goals are to accomplish transfer of training, establish a common vocabulary to talk about teaching activities, and increase collegiality and professional dialogue. Observers engage in several cycles in which they check for the presence and quality of prescribed teaching behaviors. Coaching skills emphasized include observation and data collection related to specific teaching methodology, feedback, reinforcement, and conferencing.

While Garmston's delineation of technical coaching augments the model developed by Joyce and Showers, both descriptions are more conceptual than concrete. To move towards a set of procedures that can be adapted and implemented in schools, Snyder (1981) has defined coaching operationally in terms of the clinical supervision model (Cogan, 1973; Goldhammer, Anderson, and Krajewski, 1980). While supervision has historically served an inspection or evaluation function, she suggests that in the form of coaching technology, clinical supervision can "assist teachers in acquiring proficiency in facilitating student mastery of knowledge and skills" (p. 521). The clinical supervision cycle consists of the following five stages: pre-observation conference, observation, analysis and strategy sessions, conference, and post-observation critique. Within the coaching process, the coaches adhere to guiding principles including building and maintaining the self-esteem of the teacher being coached, giving behavioral feedback, seeking cooperation from the teacher, and coaching for learning. Snyder, in collaboration with Anderson (Snyder and Anderson, 1986), has developed a coaching technology that integrates concepts from clinical supervision, business management, and effective teaching and schooling.

The purpose of this chapter is to develop this expanded definition of technical coaching by providing guidelines for implementing technical coaching, presenting an example of technical coaching, and discussing implications for practitioners. Technical coaching is a promising approach to empowering teachers to address the varied learning challenges they face each day in their classes.

A DESCRIPTION OF TECHNICAL COACHING

Each of the five stages of the coaching observation cycle has its own purpose, activities, and key concerns. An understanding of these elements can guide the development of specific procedures to be used as schools and districts implement technical coaching. The description that follows is synthesized from the writings of Snyder and Anderson (Snyder, 1988; Snyder and Anderson, 1986) and the application of their work in a major staff development project (Nielsen, 1988).

Snyder and Anderson (1986, p. 460) strongly recommend that two- or three-member coaching teams be used rather than one-on-one interaction with the teacher. They cite several reasons why a team of observers is more effective than a single person. First, the depth and breadth of data collection and analysis are greater when several persons contribute their individual perspectives. Additionally, team members benefit from the group analysis process at least as much as does the individual teacher. In a personal conversation, Anderson (May 3, 1986) recalled that Cogan commented that teachers preferred to be evaluated by a group of people rather than by an individual, a phenomenon not unlike the difference between being tried by a jury rather than by a judge. Anderson further drew on the literature of group dynamics, noting that interaction among three or more people was found to be especially evocative of productive thought. An observation team lessens the interpersonal tension that may exist between two people, ensures that in-depth analysis does occur, and establishes a form of quality control in the observation cycle. Finally, Anderson commented that a team of observers involves a different physical configuration than the single principal who normally conducts summative evaluations, visually signaling that the coaching process is not the same as evaluation.

The *pre-observation conference* allows for building rapport between the coaches and the teacher and for the establishment of a "contract" or focus for the coaching cycle. Coaches obtain information about the teacher's intentions for the lesson and establish any ground rules about the conduct of the observation. Adequate time should be provided in initial cycles for the pre-observation conference, although less time might be required after a positive working relationship has been established. Especially in later observation cycles, the conference serves as a link with past sessions and redirects attention on unresolved issues. In some cases, the conference can be devoted to a rehearsal or practice for the actual lesson to be observed. Prior to the observation, the observers should agree on data collection techniques and procedures each will follow.

In the second stage, *observation and data collection* occurs as agreed in the pre-observation conference. Data collection must be systematic and the means of collection should fit the goals of the coaching cycle. Either standardized or specialized observation forms may be selected or constructed. During the observation, the task of the observers is to collect rather than to analyze data. Because events in the classroom occur so rapidly, the observer must be alert and active throughout the observation period. The length of observation will vary according to its purpose, but observations of approximately twenty minutes in length usually generate adequate data for a coaching cycle. Observers should exert care so that their presence is minimally distracting to students. External data-gathering means, including audio and video taping, may provide additional valuable information to be used in subsequent stages.

The *analysis and strategy session* is the intellectual epicenter of the coaching process. At the end of the session, the observers should be able to verbalize what worked in the observed lesson and why it worked, what did not work and why, and what next steps should be taken by the teacher to promote professional growth. To achieve these ends, observers first array and share their data without making judgments about the teacher's performance. After the classroom events have been reconstructed, coaches interpret the data, looking for patterns and themes in the teacher's behavior. To this end, they consider research and theory, personal experiences, and general knowledge about the classroom situation. After the analysis is completed, the observers plan the strategy session, including which issues to address, how to open the conference, who will take the lead, and what recommendations will be made. During the analysis and strategy session, the observer team must attend to its own dynamics to ensure that the session will be productive. Also, adequate time needs to be provided for the session (e.g., approximately an hour) because the process is quite time-consuming.

If the analysis and strategy session is the intellectual center of the observation cycle, the *feedback conference* is its heart. While cognitive processes govern the former, communication skills are critical in the latter. Conferencing skills include setting a positive tone, requesting additional information, asking open-ended questions, checking perceptions, and agreeing on future actions. Purposes of the conference include the following: providing feedback based on the observation and related to the contract issues; reinforcing the teacher's effective behaviors and general sense of professional self-worth; stimulating higher-level thinking about critical teaching issues; providing didactic help to the teacher, if needed; assisting the teacher in relating data analysis and reflective thinking to self-improvement; and developing incentives for continuing professional self-analysis.

The final stage of the observation cycle, the *post-conference analysis*, is actually a metacognitive activity in which the persons involved in the coaching session reflect on the effectiveness of the process. The post-session critique is to the coaching process what the superego is to the functioning of personality: it provides an assessment of whether the coaching is productive and indicates any necessary modifications for future sessions. Topics that may be discussed in this stage include observation team techniques, implicit assumptions that were made, values, emotional variables, and technical and process goals.

TECHNICAL COACHING: AN EXAMPLE

While the educational community has a vested interest in enhancing the quality of schooling, operationalizing successful improvement efforts is of particular concern to school districts. In an era of scarce resources and increasing demands, district decision makers need substantial data to inform the setting of priorities among competing programs and the establishment of policy for staff development. One large school district attempted systematically to gather information that would assist in determining the direction district inservice training efforts should take (Nielsen, 1988).

The instructional program in this school district included two closely related alternative elementary programs for intermediate students who either were not achieving academically or were demonstrating non-adaptive characteristics. The curriculum in the alternative program emphasized acquisition of basic skills in reading, language arts, and mathematics, and gave teachers considerable flexibility to motivate students and to meet their individual needs.

The development of the Reading Training Project occurred in response to the program supervisor's assessment that teachers needed training to increase their effectiveness in teaching reading comprehension. A development team composed of the reading supervisor, a university reading consultant, and the supervisor of staff development identified the content and design and created all materials used in the project. The project included design and delivery of training, follow-up in the form of technical coaching, and extensive program evaluation.

In spring 1986 the development team identified both research-based content and training process. The core content of the Reading Training Project consisted of seven reading comprehension instructional strategies: the directed reading activity, comprehension skill lesson, story grammar and story mapping, the ReQuest[1] procedure, pre-reading guided reading, question-answer relationships, and directed reading-thinking activities. These strategies were selected from state-of-the-art literature on reading comprehension. They were intended to offer an eclectic set of reading instructional techniques to teachers working with students in the elementary alternative program. Two of the strategies, the directed reading activity and the comprehension skill lesson, corresponded to the district's traditional basic reading program; the other five strategies offered more variety to teachers in their attempts to meet the needs of special students.

The design used in the inservice training component was based on the Joyce and Showers model. Individual modules prepared for each of the seven reading comprehension strategies included the purpose and overview, an operational definition, a positive model, coached practice, and an opportunity to practice in the work setting. Materials for each module included frameworks, observation forms, videotaped

---

[1]ReQuest is a procedure for improving reading comprehension skills by requiring students to formulate questions and then take turns asking and answering each others' questions (see A. V. Manzo description in *Journal of Reading*, 1969, 13:123–126).

demonstration, practice directions, supplementary resources, review sheets, and cue cards. The total training program was assessed by an objective pre-/post-test. Principles of effective instruction were reviewed and incorporated into the frameworks for each of the strategies.

After the second training program, follow-up in the form of four technical coaching sessions was conducted over a five-month period. Each teacher was coached on the use of the reading strategies by a pair of coaches who followed the five stages of the clinical supervision model. Through the coaching, teachers were provided technical feedback on their delivery of the reading strategies. The directed reading activity and the comprehension skill lesson were each the basis of at least one coaching cycle. Other sessions focused on the reading strategies of interest to the teacher.

All teachers in the alternative program were invited to participate in the forty-hour training program. The forty teachers who completed the training successfully were placed in two groups according to predetermined criteria. One group was then randomly selected to receive technical coaching as a follow-up to training.

Pairs of coaches were identified to work with each teacher during the follow-up. Coaches were either elementary curriculum supervisors or school-based specialists who were trained in both the reading comprehension content and in coaching technology. Coaches received an average of eighteen hours of training.

A multitude of program evaluation activities occurred before, during, and after the Reading Training Project was implemented. Findings included the following:

(1) The Reading Training Project was successful in providing training in reading comprehension strategies to teachers, which they subsequently used as a regular part of their instructional program.

(2) Teachers used the reading strategies during the time they were coached on an almost daily basis and continued to use the strategies with considerable frequency a year after project completion.

(3) Following the technical coaching follow-up, all teachers used the strategies appropriately. Sixty percent of them used the strategies in a routine manner, either as specified in the frameworks or modified to be more effective for students.

(4) Immediately following training, teachers were concerned about how strategy use affected them personally. After coaching, per-

sonal concerns had been reduced, and teachers were focused on the impact of the strategies on student learning.

(5) After coaching, teachers delivered the key strategies (directed reading activity and comprehension skill lesson) at an acceptable level of effectiveness, although room for improvement was still evident.

(6) Teachers responded in a consistently positive manner to the project and expressed the belief that it had considerable long-term value in their teaching.

(7) Teachers rated coaching as very effective and cited the teachers' opportunity to receive specific feedback about teaching, team communication, the motivation to practice, and enhanced teacher self-esteem and confidence. Most participants said that coaching was an experience they would like to have again.

(8) Coaches felt that as a result of project participation, they refined their own skills, had the opportunity to interact with colleagues, and saw teachers presenting many excellent reading lessons. All coaches said they would elect to coach again given the same opportunity.

IMPLICATIONS FOR SCHOOLS

To forge successfully the chain of logic that opened this chapter, technical coaching must be included as a critical link. Technical coaching maximizes the likelihood that teachers will actually incorporate new learnings into their active teaching repertoire. Staff developers cognizant of this relationship need to develop the procedures and process for technical coaching with at least as much attention as they give to the training content itself. Indeed, both the inservice training and the technical coaching design should be developed in tandem.

If coaching is to be implemented effectively, coaches must be carefully and thoroughly trained in its technology. The design for coaching training should follow the same model as other effective training: theoretical background and rationale, positive model, safe practice, and ample on-the-job follow-up. The content of coaching training must include the stages of the observation cycle, data collection methods, and communication skills. Subsequently, each time technical coaching is applied to a new training program, the process should be reviewed and adapted to match the specific content.

Although the example presented in this chapter reported a district-wide training program, technical coaching holds particular promise for school-based staff development. Peers working with one another provide a powerful option that facilitates growth from the two vantages of giving and receiving coaching. Several considerations impact the potential for the success of technical peer coaching efforts. The administrators at the school have to be knowledgeable and supportive of coaching, sanctioning the process and making resources available to allow it to occur. The time factor is as critical at the school site as it is at the district level, and time is a resource that administrators can help supply. Also, the work culture of the school has to be strong enough for teachers to be willing to work with one another in a trusting, collegial atmosphere. Using only volunteers for coaching would be an important first step in implementing a peer coaching program.

As reported in the Reading Training Project, when technical coaching is included as an element in a staff development program, participants benefit cognitively, affectively, and behaviorally. Teachers increased their knowledge of the content, reacted positively both to the training and to the coaching, and, in fact, changed their teaching behaviors in a positive direction. Even with all the support that this project offered, however, teachers did not achieve an optimal level of performance overall.

Change is indeed an arduous process, and reinforcement of change efforts must continue over time. Continued, intense work is required to assist teachers in reaching the level of instructional delivery that would most likely result in increased student learning. Technical coaching is a valuable tool to support teachers as they strive towards this end.

REFERENCES

Anderson, R. Personal communication with Lore Nielsen, May 3, 1986, re Morris Cogan.

Baker, R. G. and B. Showers. "The Effects of a Coaching Strategy on Teachers' Transfer of Training to Classroom Practice: A Six Month Follow-Up Study," paper presented at the annual meeting of the American Educational Research Association, New Orleans, Louisiana, 1984.

Bloom, B. S. 1980. "The New Direction in Educational Research: Alterable Variables," *Phi Delta Kappan*, 61:382–385.

Carnegie Task Force. 1986. *A Nation Prepared: Teachers for the 21st Century*. Hyattsville, MD: Carnegie Forum on Education and the Economy.

Cogan, M. L. 1973. *Clinical Supervision*. Boston: Houghton Mifflin.

Garmston, R. J. 1987. "How Administrators Support Peer Coaching," *Educational Leadership*, 44(5):18–26.

Goldhammer, R., R. H. Anderson and R. J. Krajewski. 1980. *Clinical Supervision: Special Methods for the Supervision of Teachers, 2nd Edition*. New York: Holt, Rinehart and Winston.

Holmes Group. 1986. *Tomorrow's Teachers*. East Lansing, Michigan: Holmes Group.

Joyce, B. R. and B. Showers. 1982. "The Coaching of Teaching," *Educational Leadership*, 40(1):4–10.

Joyce, B. R. and B. Showers. 1984. "Transfer of Training: The Contributions of 'Coaching,' " in *Alternative Perspectives on School Improvement*, D. Hopkins and M. Wideen, eds., London: Falmer Press.

National Commission on Excellence in Education. 1983. *A Nation at Risk: The Imperative for Educational Reform*. Washington, DC: U.S. Department of Education.

Nielsen, L. A. "Coaching Teachers in Reading: Transfer from Training to Practice," unpublished doctoral dissertation, University of South Florida, Tampa, Florida, 1988.

Snyder, K. J. 1981. "Clinical Supervision in the 1980's," *Educational Leadership*, 38(April):521–524.

Snyder, K. J. 1988. *Competency Training for Managing Productive Schools*. San Diego, CA: Harcourt, Brace and Jovanovich.

Snyder, K. J. and R. H. Anderson. 1986. *Managing Productive Schools: Toward an Ecology*. Orlando, FL: Academic Press.

Sparks, G. M. 1983. "Synthesis of Research on Staff Development for Effective Teaching," *Educational Leadership*, 41(3):65–72.

JOHN M. BAHNER

14

Professional Problem Solving: Coaching for Restructuring the Work Environment of Classrooms

In Chapter 1, Anderson describes how clinical supervision became a "value added" concept as it emerged from a supervisor training technique to a comprehensive process of improving most aspects of the learning environment.

Early in its history, the developers of clinical supervision made modifications to provide users with a powerful problem-solving process incorporating ideas from a wide variety of professionals. Key elements were generating operational solutions and then implementing the most promising using a monitoring process that fine-tuned them for future use.

It is neither efficient nor wise to isolate the teaching act as the primary focus of coaching. The entire learning environment is the appropriate context of coaching processes. Widespread change and continuous improvement processes can be institutionalized when coaching is used as the vehicle of information exchange as well as the vehicle for implementing new techniques of classroom management and instruction.

This chapter will first describe coaching as a problem-solving process in the context of a summer inservice training program. The description of the summer program derives from the so-called Harvard-Lexington Summer Program of the 1960s, and numerous variants thereof, as it evolved during the following twenty-five years in more than fifty places throughout the world. The chapter then describes the same process as it might be used during the regular school year. In both instances, the goal is to assist in restructuring the work environment of the classroom. However, the reader will have little trouble—especially after internalizing the contents of other

217

chapters in this book—seeing its applicability to less complex problems.

A SCHOOL SYSTEM AND UNIVERSITY SUMMER INSERVICE PROGRAM

One of the underlying assumptions of peer coaching is that teachers have much to offer each other as they strive to improve. Just as talented principals and supervisors have insight into good teaching and understanding of how to develop it, so too do teachers. All who agree with these statements should therefore see the advantages of organizing teachers into teams to carry out their professional responsibilities.

This section assumes that a school system has decided to restructure an elementary school by having teaching teams throughout the school. The narrative is based on a composite of thirty years' experience rather than a single event.

Using teaching teams is only illustrative. The problem to be solved could be creating a magnet school within a school, or doing away with departments—or Carnegie units—in a high school. The principles described throughout this chapter can be used to solve whatever problem is posed as faculties work to restructure classroom environments.

The Task

Because no school in this hypothetical system had teaching teams and there was only a modicum of personalized instruction, the immediate task was an inservice function. The school administration desired to create an environment within which each team would work with a multi-aged group of students and provide them with a nongraded, highly individualized educational program.

The restructuring philosophy included provisions that each team could make any decisions (including those involving staff hiring, expenditures, and schedules) that did not affect or involve other teams. Similarly, the school could make its own decisions about all matters that did not directly affect other schools. (Of course, all schools had to abide by state and local regulations or go through normal channels to receive exceptions.)

The staff members of the central office and the aforementioned elementary school asked a nearby teacher training institution to assist them in planning and conducting a four-week session designed to instill understanding of new roles and provide practice, with coaching, of new behaviors that the restructuring entailed.

As is true with elementary and secondary school students, good adult learning dictates that new knowledge be applied as soon as possible in real but nonthreatening environments, while receiving the counsel of helpful observers. Summertime provides an excellent opportunity to create these favorable conditions for school people.

The Design

Participants in the summer program were divided into teams of five persons: four teachers and an administrator/supervisor. It was decided up-front that rank was left at the door: these were peer groups. For approximately eight hours a day throughout the four weeks, the teams assembled in the school that was to be restructured. After three days of orientation and introduction to new ideas, the next sixteen days (during which pupils were present during the morning hours) had a common pattern. There were four phases of about two hours each: planning, teaching, observing, and conducting post-observation sessions, and receiving theoretical input.

The faculty of this summer inservice session included a teaching team leader who worked with team members during the planning and teaching phases, and an observation team leader who worked with team members throughout the observation cycle. Both types of faculty leaders were experienced in teaming and/or coaching, and had been recruited from university doctoral students or other school systems.

Additional faculty members were university professors and outside consultants who augmented the typical coaching process by presenting theoretical input sessions, typically in the form of lectures or demonstrations. Two or three of the professors were resident throughout the four weeks because of their scholarly interest in, and the contributions they could make to, the entire four weeks. These professors joined participants in team planning meetings and observation cycles as resource persons. Other presenters for the theoretical input sessions were brought in on an ad hoc basis.

A teams coordinator, analogous to a principal, chaired daily faculty meetings to resolve problems affecting two or more teams as well as to engender a sharing of information regarding team successes and situations wherein teams were not yet successful.

Students aged seven to twelve, recruited from the local geographic area for an "enrichment" summer experience, came to school from 8:30 A.M. until noon. They were divided into groups of twenty, without regard to learning ability or current achievement levels, but with each group having a three-year chronological age span. The children worked with the same group of teachers during each of the sixteen days.

The essence of the design was to use a wide variety of educators from the school system and the university to deal with curriculum issues, generate a plethora of possible classroom environments and instructional techniques, and try out the most promising of them in real situations with students. Coaching was used in the planning, teaching, and observation phases because of the power it has to enhance the understanding and performance of all involved.

The Implementation

University and school system designers of the summer inservice program wanted the four weeks to be a continuous problem-solving venture for the participants. While they received help from the faculty in the form of information and modeling, decisions were made by the teams.

Planning

During the first week, one of the early "theoretical input" sessions stimulated discussions in each team regarding the artificiality of extant subject matter boundaries. In part because the restructuring philosophy made them feel untethered to tradition, each team decided to intertwine content areas to the greatest extent possible. They also identified several critical education goals that transcended their current curriculum areas. Some selected critical thinking, others chose to emphasize life-long learning attitudes and skills, and still others elected to interject into their sixteen days of teaching the concept of having their students assume increasing responsibility for their own education.

Specific learning objectives for these goals needed to be generated. Each team also selected learning objectives in more traditional subject areas as they got to know their students' capabilities. Brainstorming techniques were employed to obtain uninhibited responses while generating objectives and possible learning activities. A division of labor occurred as each team member assumed responsibility for preparing a detailed lesson plan for a portion of their deliberations.

Coaching principles were used in reviewing the respective members' plans. Experience over the past thirty years has shown that discussions among team members at this planning stage always enhance the members' understanding of the curriculum. Most teachers are more oriented toward activities than toward learning objectives of individual students. It is a major function of the coaching process in the planning stage to help teachers focus on desired student achievements while simultaneously considering the nuances of the curriculum and optional instructional activities. In the case of this illustrative summer inservice program, the result was a true team plan, one-fifth of which was executed by each team member while the lesson was observed by the others.

The Classroom Environment

Coaching is advocated by a number of scholars and practitioners. Accordingly, a number of "systems" have evolved as prescriptions of what to do. Most of these concentrate solely on what the teacher says and does during the observation. The teams believed these functions were important and took steps to record relevant data in the manner adequately described elsewhere in this book. However, they knew their instructional environments consisted of more than teacher behavior. Thus, the team took cognizance of the role of coaching in concomitant factors requiring the team's attention during the observation. They determined that they needed to collect data regarding the adequacy of the plan.

For example, does our hindsight agree with our foresight that the activities were appropriate for the type of achievement expected of the students? Is the mode of instruction (e.g., lecture, discussion) appropriate for the intended purpose? To illustrate, if the purpose was to inform or to motivate, then lecturing may be an appropriate mode of instruction. If the purpose was something else, then the team should probably generate one or more constructive alternatives for future use in similar situations. Is there feedback within the classroom that causes or should cause the teacher to:

- modify plans
- reinforce a point
- support a student
- change the physical conditions (lights, seating arrangements, temperature, etc.)
- group the students differently
- provide different instructional aids

What evidence is there that each student is achieving or is failing to achieve what is expected? What teaching behaviors should be reinforced by citing evidence that they were effective? What data are there that a teaching behavior is ineffective, and what constructive alternative can we offer?

The observing team members organized themselves to collect data necessary to answer the above questions. Of course, the teacher being observed often requested that feedback be provided regarding specified areas, and data were assembled to satisfy such requests.

Another important goal of the coaching process is to assist each teacher in becoming more adept in analyzing her/his own classroom instruction. Earlier chapters have discussed the observation cycle, including the feedback conference with the teacher who was observed. Suffice for now to reiterate the necessity for some "think time" between the observation and this conference to enable all parties concerned to analyze what went on. As notes were compared in post-observation sessions of the summer program, the level of discussion reflected each person's considered thoughts based in large measure on data and not merely on fleeting impressions.

Personal mannerisms and other idiosyncracies of teachers were certainly part of the picture, but the teams were determined not to spend too much time on relatively minor trivia. Rather, they wanted to concentrate their thoughts on the broad aspects of the total classroom environment, which they were now perceiving in a totally different light. Improving teacher behavior was important, but they deemed it to be a subordinate factor in the context of the entire educational setting.

Student Assessment

Just as several witnesses to the same event do not have identical perceptions, teachers often do not assess students in the same manner. This is to be expected when the student is viewed at different times by different teachers. It is also true when teams view students simultaneously or when they evaluate a common student product such as a written assignment.

Rather than bemoaning differences of opinion, the teams were asked to value this diversity. Students and teachers alike should grow as they discuss varying perceptions of student achievement. The coaching process provides an important opportunity for teachers to hold these discussions and to see that future plans and events are based on these assessments.

In one form or another, all teams considered the "bottom line" of student assessment to be whether or not: (1) the student has the information (knowledge) expected of an educated person, and (2) the student can perform those increasingly complex tasks expected of an educated person. If the answer is "yes" to both conditions, then they knew they need go no further in assessing students. But if the answer to either of those conditions is "no," then they recognized that student assessment must take on added dimensions.

(1) How much of the expected knowledge does the student now possess?

(2) How many of the desired tasks can the student now perform?

(3) How did the student get to where he or she is at present (i.e., how did the student learn)?

(4) What are the student's next steps to insure he/she is making progress toward the two major goals?

There are a multitude of benefits if team members have had an opportunity to discuss the qualities of an educated person—or at least of the ideal student who leaves their school. This seldom happens in the real world. Yet, most teachers have an idea, perhaps unarticulated, of what they want a student to achieve. When asked about a specific trait of a given student, almost all teachers will have an answer, even if the accuracy of their answer is debatable.

Only in the past decade have most teachers been exposed to the concept that they have a responsibility for knowing the learning styles of each student under various learning conditions. Fortunately, an increasing number of teachers can now talk confidently about the learning styles of individual students, although records of such assessments are seldom to be found.

Because of their predisposition to think and talk about learning activities rather than learning outcomes, many teachers fail to use the knowledge described in the preceding two paragraphs to begin formulating plans for the immediate future. To their credit, talented teachers intuitively, if not deliberately, take such knowledge into account as they work with students in the classroom.

If the coaching process is focused primarily on the teaching act, then student assessment considerations are usually neglected. In many school districts, emphasis on student achievement has been given a black eye because it usually refers to standardized tests, comparisons of schools and teachers, treating students as factory products, and other dysfunctional if not unsavory practices.

On the other hand, it is legitimate to target student achievement as an important aspect of the coaching process, if the team also accepts responsibility for analyzing those conditions that contribute to learning and doing what they can to improve those conditions. Equally important is for the team to discuss means by which they all can motivate students and provide them with processes to accept increasing responsibility for their own learning.

Another theoretical input session in the summer inservice stimulated discussion among team members regarding the concepts of summative and formative evaluation. Assessment of student achievement is summative because it measures the end goal. This fact need not dictate that assessment procedures all be paper and pencil tests. The coaching teams discussed a variety of ways in which students could demonstrate achievement. Many of these ways were innovative and tentative. The coaching teams accepted a collective responsibility to determine the adequacy of these alternatives as they observed them being used.

The coaching teams did not neglect discussion of the formative aspects of evaluation. To what extent were the students engaged in what was planned for them? To what extent was the learning environment appropriate for each student? Discussions of these and similar questions demonstrated the desire of the teams to improve all conditions directly related to student achievement.

Follow-up discussions of these questions led to defining next steps for individual students, for the class as a whole, and for the teacher. These discussions, as is true of most discussions among practitioners, culminated in the formulation of action plans.

ADAPTATIONS FOR THE REGULAR SCHOOL YEAR

Coaching for restructuring the work environment of the classroom is not limited to summer programs or to school year practice with teaching teams. Without repeating all the detail presented previously, this section will describe briefly how the process can be used by ad hoc coaching teams during the regular school year.

The setting is Fernandez High School, Bordertown, U.S.A.

The Task

Jose Roosevelt Jones is a social studies teacher who, along with many of his colleagues, is dismayed at the 43 percent dropout rate in the school. The teachers attribute at least part of the cause to the traditional nature of the school itself. Jose has volunteered to be a guinea pig in a major restructuring of his classroom: what is being taught, how it is taught, and how students are assessed.

The Design

Jose has asked for a coaching team composed of an assistant principal, a teacher from his social studies department, a teacher from the Washington High Social Studies department, and a teacher from the Fernandez High English department. They have agreed to meet for two hours of planning every two weeks for the next two months and to conduct observation cycles for at least one period of Jose's teaching on alternate weeks during the same period.

The Implementation

As was true in the summer inservice program described above, the planning sessions of Jose's coaching team were devoted to:

- goals describing an educated person who leaves Fernandez High

- potential learning objectives and learning activities to accomplish those goals
- a variety of ways students could gradually take more responsibility for their own learning
- techniques other than oral questioning and paper and pencil tests for ascertaining student achievement

Subsequent to those planning sessions, Jose did most of the work to prepare lesson plans, following which the coaching team offered constructive, positive criticism. All members felt the end results were team plans that Jose would implement.

Every other week, Jose's coaching team conducted an observation cycle. They emphasized the adequacy of the plan in their deliberations. Watching Jose try new instructional techniques, they got caught up in the spirit of nonconformity. They became extremely creative in generating activities, which the students helped to define and during which the students designed many of their assessment criteria.

Student interest in the class increased noticeably and attendance actually improved. Students knew what they were supposed to learn and usually had a good reason for why they wanted to learn it.

Jose and all members of his coaching team increased their professional repertoire of ideas from two- to ten-fold. At the end of the two month period no one claimed that Mecca had been reached, but all were satisfied that the coaching process was a vehicle they could recommend to their colleagues as providing more opportunities for growth than any other program in which they have been involved.

CONCLUSION

The emphasis of this chapter is on the total classroom environment. There is little doubt among educators that the single most important element of the learning environment is the classroom teacher. The caveat of this chapter is that professional improvement using coaching should not be limited to the didactic component of teaching, but rather should be directed to all aspects of teachers as creators of the educational environment.

All phases of the coaching process have a professional development component. Teachers who engage in the process talk about it as one of the most important elements in their professional lives. When conducted in a professional, positive, nonthreatening manner, teachers are appreciative and teacher unions are supportive. Central office personnel find coaching to be far more effective than most of their other inservice activities. University professors find they have a new medium of communication in a setting that provides an immediate opportunity for application—and which most find to be a welcome alternative to campus classrooms.

One should not expect the coaching process to be the total source of professional development, although it might well be the most satisfying. As teachers are involved in the coaching process, they will identify additional areas in which they need further help. As teachers ask for assistance in these deficient areas, the coaching team should contribute suggestions regarding sources of help. These might range from demonstrations by a teacher in the building, to visiting in classrooms throughout the area, to interaction with consultants, to formal classes at a nearby university.

Coaching is not a panacea. It has the strength of being an exceptionally powerful tool to enhance the learning environment. It has a limitation in that it requires significant amounts of time, which must take the place of some other activity currently being conducted by busy teachers, administrators, and professors.

Training for coaching as described in this chapter is more comprehensive than training for coaching that concentrates on what the teacher says and does during an isolated observation. There are very few school faculties who will be successful if they venture into this type of coaching without benefit of knowledgeable and experienced assistance in the processes described.

IV

PEER COACHING STRUCTURES

Of the offshoots or corollary mechanisms related to clinical supervision, peer coaching is one of the most powerful and most viable. In this section, six chapters probe the possibilities for mutual assistance that exist in classrooms, in school districts, in supervisory and administrative contexts, in the university environment, and in noneducation settings.

Hosack-Curlin, drawing upon her own research study, describes a specific effort by teachers, in pairs, to improve their implementation of new programs through coaching each other in ob cycles. She notes that opportunities for positive professional interactions, through coaching, not only benefitted the individuals but created a positive, contagious spirit within the school of helping and encouraging others.

Giella and Stanfill, administrators in a particularly dynamic school system, review the events that led to the development of a peer coaching system in their district. They then report on staff development efforts in which peer coaches were trained, and then describe the rationale for a clinical supervision approach to assessment. Theirs is a story that should be of much interest to school district leaders looking for ways to invigorate their school programs.

In Chapter 17, Pajak and Carr report the findings from a study that focused on outstanding mentor teachers and peer coaches, with particular attention to verifying the importance of the twelve dimensions of supervisory practice that were identified in a larger study sponsored earlier by the Association for Supervision and Curriculum Development. Among their conclusions was that many of the responsibilities and functions of mentor teachers and peer coaches fall within the realm of supervision. To the extent that the specialized functions of meeting the supervisory needs of individual teachers can be provided by mentors and peer coaches, principals and central office supervisors will be able to concentrate on other program-related functions.

Hunt provides two chapters in this section, both derived in part from his personal experience with peer coaching. Chapter 18 includes a description of how the clinical supervision cycle came to be used not only with principals in districts where he served as superintendent, but also by principals who conducted ob cycles on his behavior in school board meetings. In Chapter 20, he reports the values of using the ob cycle in military flight training, in sales work, and in sailing. From these examples he refers to some noteworthy consistencies: the role of the expert as observer, the candor of the conference, and the internalization of the process.

Ways in which faculty members at the university level engaged in, and profited from, peer coaching activities are reviewed in Chapter 19 by Skoog. Although the effects of the experience he reports were not sufficiently documented, he concludes that the peer observation model "can be a powerful and effective component of staff development programs in institutions where pedagogical cultures exist that value and support teaching and its improvement." This conclusion, well worth emphasizing, would seem to be one of the most important ideas in this volume.

15

Peer Coaching among Teachers

Although public scrutiny and lively debate about the failings of schools is hardly new, the current atmosphere of renewed interest in improving instruction and teacher training opportunities is an important development. Since public interest may wane as unexpectedly as it began, it is necessary that those in positions of leadership act quickly, decisively, and intelligently to improve staff development programs for teachers currently in service (Sergiovanni and Moore, 1989).

THE MULTIPLE EFFECTS OF PEER COACHING

Though we now have a research base on effective teaching, systematic inquiry into effective delivery systems for training teachers about this data is neoteric. Joyce and Showers (1982) surveyed the staff development literature and identified five elements that are necessary for maximizing adult learning: (1) presentation of theory, (2) skills modeling/demonstration, (3) practice in simulated situations, (4) structured feedback/support, and (5) coaching. They concluded that the coaching component, which is built upon a collaborative relationship between observer and teacher, significantly increases classroom utilization of newly acquired skills following inservice training.

The applications of coaching are many: as a follow-up to inservice, to refine teaching practice, to deepen collegiality, to increase professional dialogue, and to encourage teacher reflection about the instructional process. Coaching helps to make schools more effective not only through enhancing implementation of new instructional skills, but also through encouraging a more collaborative school culture. In one recent

231

study, teachers in a traditional setting reported that they spent approximately two minutes per day discussing work, but in schools where peer coaching was conducted the amount of teacher talk was greatly increased (Garmston, 1987).

Coaching has been used effectively with preservice, beginning, and experienced teachers (Russell and Spafford, 1986; Schultze, 1984; Showers, 1984; Wynn, 1986) and has been used in conjunction with a pyramid training model—one group of trained teachers training other teachers (Servatius and Young, 1985; Showers, 1984; Sparks, 1983).

As personnel limitations preclude having district-level supervisors or school-based administrators in classrooms as often as needed—and seldom are the actual inservice trainers available to follow the teachers back to their workplace—some have recommended the implementation of peer supervision, also called "peer coaching" (Alfonso and Goldsberry, 1982; Joyce and Showers, 1983; Russell and Spafford, 1986). Classroom teachers are trained to function as "coaches" for one another. Peer coaching directly addresses five dimensions of school culture: collegiality, experimentation, support, utilization of the knowledge of effective teaching, and honest and open communication.

A review of the current research on peer coaching suggests it is a viable means to provide ongoing supervision, decrease teacher isolation, and encourage greater collaboration within schools.

KEY IDEAS AND FINDINGS ABOUT PEER COACHING

- Teachers who collected behavioral data and who shared that data in meaningful ways during reciprocal peer coaching were less anxious when observed by a peer rather than an administrator or supervisor, preferred self-selection of partners, and made changes in their teaching behavior as a result of coaching (Clarke, 1986).
- Department chairpersons demonstrated successful mastery of clinical supervision skills when coaching teachers within their departments (Cook, 1985).
- College professors spent more time planning for classes, used a greater variety of instructional techniques, reflected more about the impact of their teaching on student learning, and felt greater confidence and excitement about teaching responsibilities following peer coaching (Garmston, 1989).

- Teachers initially resistant to an innovation were more positive following participation in self-help teams that monitored classroom implementation of new skills (Hertz-Lazarowitz and Sharan, 1982).
- Teachers who used a clinical supervision model of peer coaching following inservice training implemented new techniques more proficiently and developed more positive attitudes towards collaboration than teachers only observed by peers (Hosack-Curlin, 1988).
- The amount of time spent in direct-instruction in reading comprehension tripled following peer coaching (Kurth, 1984).
- A pyramid training/coaching model proved highly successful; however, it was necessary to rotate teacher trainers each year to eliminate their being perceived as "an arm of administration" by other teachers (Little and Guilkey-Amado, 1986).
- Teachers scored significantly higher on variables associated with planning, instruction, evaluation, and self-evaluation following peer coaching (Phelps, 1986).
- Teachers who received skills training and coaching successfully trained and coached another group of teachers the following year (Showers, 1984).
- Teachers who participated in peer observations following inservice training demonstrated greater implementation of new techniques and more camaraderie than teachers who received no follow-up or were coached by the trainer (Sparks, 1986).
- Peer coaching cannot be successful unless teachers are provided with more time for developing rapport and engaging in meaningful problem solving, are reassured that data collected in a coaching setting will not be used for evaluation, and feel less competitive toward one another (Wade, 1985).
- Beginning teachers rated experienced teachers who coached them as highly competent and peer coaching as very necessary. In a follow-up study, experienced teachers demonstrated successful use of conferencing skills in coaching other experienced teachers (Wilburn, 1986).
- Intern teachers whose teaching was videotaped and used as the focus for peer coaching at weekly group sessions demonstrated higher scores on overall teaching performance than interns that received traditional supervision. Interns who had received peer

coaching expressed positive attitudes about the experience (Wynn, 1986).

CLINICAL SUPERVISION: A STRUCTURE FOR PEER COACHING

Although several studies of coaching have been conducted, there has been little mention of the actual methodology utilized in coaching. Clinical supervision can provide a framework for coaching based upon "hands-on, in-classroom, face-to-face supervisor/teacher interactions" (Goldhammer et al., 1980). Its major tenets are collaborative decision making between teacher and supervisor, mutual problem solving, collegial relationships, and nonevaluative/nonjudgmental feedback. Denham (1977) has called clinical supervision a "potential tool for real instructional improvement."

The observation cycle within clinical supervision, as defined by Goldhammer et al. (1980), begins with a pre-observation conference between the supervisor (or team of teacher colleagues) and teacher to establish rapport, discuss students and classroom environment, plan for the lesson, and define the purposes of the observation. Following the pre-observation conference, the lesson is observed. Anecdotal records of verbal interactions, observation schedules, audio or video recordings, and other data-gathering devices are used as appropriate and with the agreement of the observed teacher. Following the observation, the observer analyzes the data collected and plans how the data can best be shared with the teacher. The teacher and supervisor then meet for a post-observation conference to discuss the data that were gathered and to plan the next lesson (thus beginning a new cycle). An important part of the post-observation conference is a critique of the completed cycle.

The "observation cycle" appears to provide a practical methodology for the coaching of teachers. Coaches and teachers can use the observation cycle to supplement inservice training. For example, specific skills learned in a workshop setting could be the focus of the coaching cycle.

The remainder of this chapter describes two peer coaching projects. In the first, the coaching observation cycle was used as a supplement to writing process inservice training in a large urban school district (Hosack-Curlin, 1988); in the second, to supplement the teaching of newly learned math and science skills in a school-based project. The first study sought to investigate whether adding a coaching component utilizing clinical supervision would increase teacher implementation of the writing process teaching model and create more positive teacher attitudes towards writing. The effects of this coaching are contrasted with the effects of simple peer observation and support.

UTILIZING PEER COACHING IN A SCHOOL SITUATION

The first study sought to bridge the gap between the research on coaching and that on clinical supervision, and to investigate whether a structured model of peer coaching was more helpful than peer observations alone in encouraging teachers to transfer new strategies from a workshop setting into classroom use.

Reported here is the methodology used for peer coaching, and the effects of that coaching on teacher implementation of new instructional techniques following inservice. The clinical supervision observation cycle (see Figure 15.1) provided the model for structuring or formalizing peer coaching, and a writing process approach was selected to compare transfer of new skills by elementary language arts teachers.

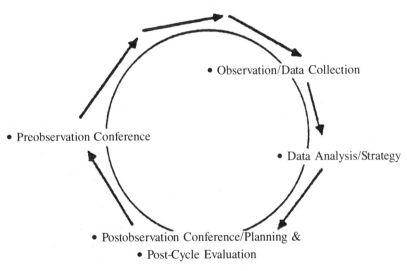

Figure 15.1 *Clinical Supervision Observation Cycle.*

Descriptive statistics, analysis of variance, and chi square tests were used to measure teacher implementation of writing process strategies and teacher concerns about the new teaching model during one school year. Process data were gathered to investigate fidelity to the clinical supervision coaching model and teacher attitude and interaction.

During the first semester, twelve volunteer teacher pairs from different elementary schools attended writing process inservice. Following the inservice, the pairs were randomly assigned to treatment or comparison groups. Those in the treatment group received two full days of training in clinical supervision. The comparison group was expected to observe a partner and to provide helpful feedback. During the second semester, teachers in both treatment and comparison groups alternated between coaching or being observed during writing instruction weekly for twelve weeks. To ensure that treatment group teachers used the observation cycle, conference audiotapes and a checklist were collected weekly.

It became important to encourage teachers in their attempts with the new writing process and coaching strategies. Teachers in both groups were expected to record regularly in a journal their thoughts and experiences with coaching. The journals were collected, read, and returned with written comments monthly. In addition, classrooms were visited and phone calls made to each teacher team.

Data were analyzed and reported for three areas: implementation, attitudes and concerns, and the coaching process.

Implementation

Implementation was measured using the Levels of Use of the Innovation (LoU) (Hall et al., 1975), and Innovation Configuration (Hall and Loucks, 1978) instruments. Pre- and post-LoU scores obtained from analysis of interview data were summarized. Based upon these scores all teachers were identified at one of eight levels: (0) nonuse, (1) orientation, (2) preparation, (3) mechanical use, (4a) routine use, (4b) refinement, (5) integration, or (6) renewal.

Frequencies of teachers at each level were graphed illustrating the change process which occurred between the beginning and the end of the school year (see Figure 15.2). When comparing the two groups, efficient and refined use of writing process instruction occurred more often in the treatment group.

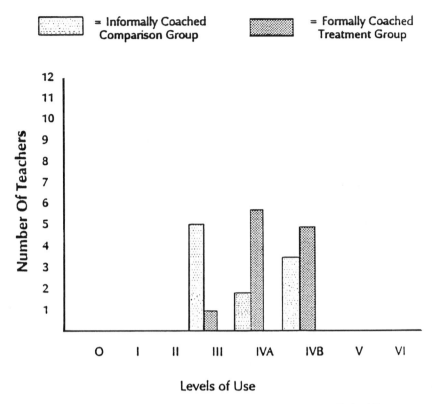

Figure 15.2 *Teachers' Overall Level of Use of Writing Process at End of Treatment Period.*

At the end of the study, 50 percent of the comparison group teachers functioned at level 3, "mechanical use." These teachers planned and prepared for students in a disjointed day-by-day manner. In contrast, only 8 percent of the treatment group teachers functioned at that level while 92 percent operated at a "stable," "routine" level or above following treatment. Treatment group teachers were more efficient and well-organized than comparison group teachers in their use of the writing program.

To determine the significance of the relationship between levels of use and group membership, data were compared using the Chi Square Test of Independence (see Table 15.1). The chi square value $\times 2 = 5.683$, ($p = .058$) just failed to reach the established statistical level of significance.

Table 15.1. Overall Level of Use: Chi Square Test.

Group	Level Categories			
	III	IVA	IVB	Total
Formally coached	1	6	5	12
Treatment	(4)	(25)	(21)	(50)
Informally coached	6	2	4	12
Comparison	(25)	(8)	(17)	(50)

$N = 24$; $X^{2(2)} = 5.683$; $p = .058$.

A configuration checklist containing thirteen components of a writing process classroom was created. Pre- and post-treatment scores were derived for teachers through the use of interviews, observation, and document analysis. Teachers were assigned a score of 1–5 on each of the thirteen writing process components. Scores of 1 or 2 indicated little or no use of the writing process strategies; scores of 3 represented satisfactory implementation; ratings of 4 or 5 indicated advanced and sophisticated implementation of the concepts and techniques per component. Obtained scores were summarized in group frequencies.

Although not statistically significant, results suggested differences in the quality of implementation of treatment and comparison group teachers. Teachers in both groups demonstrated great gains in the areas of publishing student writing in a variety of ways, presenting a variety of kinds of writing assignments, and evaluating student writing. However, treatment group teachers made large gains and exceeded comparison group teachers on almost all components, most notably publishing student writing frequently, conferencing with students, and implementing peer conferencing (see Figure 15.3).

This is even more interesting in light of the fact that the treatment group began the study with more scores of 1 and 2 than the comparison group. At the conclusion of the study, they received a greater number of scores of 4 and 5 on ten of the thirteen components. The higher scores suggested that teachers who received training in clinical supervision implemented the new strategies more proficiently.

Teacher Concerns and Attitudes

Concerns and attitudes about implementation of the writing process model were measured using the Stages of Concern (SoC) questionnaire

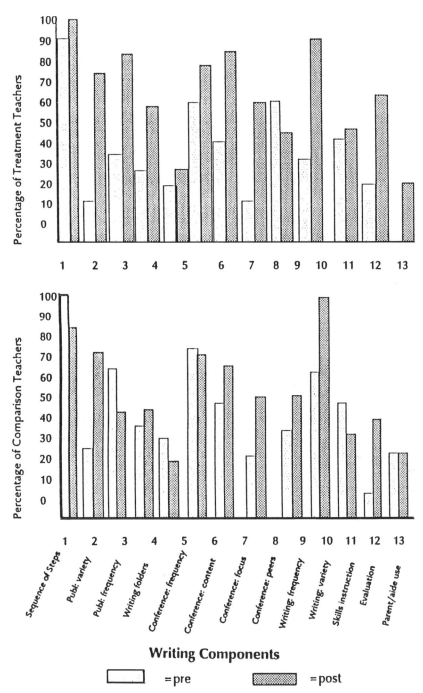

Figure 15.3 *Percentage of Treatment and Comparison Teachers Exhibiting Satisfactory Implementation of Writing Process: Pre- and Post-Treatment.*

(Hall and Loucks, 1987). Pre- and post-treatment mean raw scores were converted into percentiles to create a profile showing changes in intensity of concern with regard to the new writing program. Scores were categorized into seven stages progressing from nonuse to teacher concerns about obtaining information and managing materials and schedules, to the impact of the new program upon them and their students, and finally to concerns about modifying and sharing the innovation with their colleagues. A profile of pre- and post-treatment frequencies of these concerns (Figure 15.4), illustrates that the treatment group received higher scores on stage 5, collaboration, and stage 6, refocus, than comparison group teachers. This would indicate that treatment group teachers were actively using the innovation, sharing it with their partners, and modifying it to fit the needs of their students. The comparison group profile changed little, however, demonstrating a relative lack of growth or expansion with regard to implementation.

The Coaching Process

To better understand why the majority of treatment group teachers became more proficient in the use of the new writing program, process data were examined. Audiotape transcripts revealed that treatment teachers were able to successfully use the clinical supervision model in peer coaching.

These teachers successfully planned for and then collected data that were used in helping their partners to understand their impact on students. They were comfortable working with their partners as they implemented the writing program and engaged actively as partners in planning for and reflecting upon their individual and joint experiences during observation cycles.

Journal entries from both groups revealed enthusiasm with the process of coaching, even in view of the problem of "too little time." Both groups reported more willingness to "risk" using a new strategy with a colleague than they would have in a traditional observation by an administrator.

The development and success of treatment teachers attest to the importance of providing structured, collegial support following inservice. The collaboration in observation conferences provided an environment rich for enhancing metacognition.

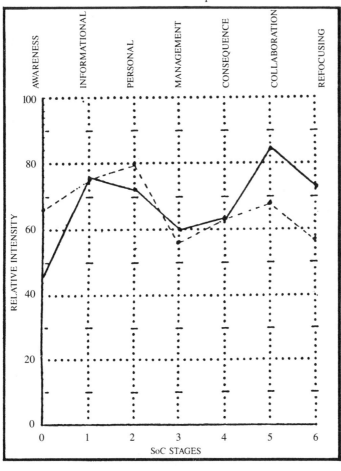

Formally Coached
Treatment Group

- - - - - = Pre-treatment

_____ = Post-treatment

Figure 15.4 *Profiles of Stages of Concern (SoC)/Percentile Scores on "Relative Intensity" Axis Indicates Group Mean for Each Stage (0–6) Listed on Horizontal (Top) Axis.*

Informally Coached
Comparison Group

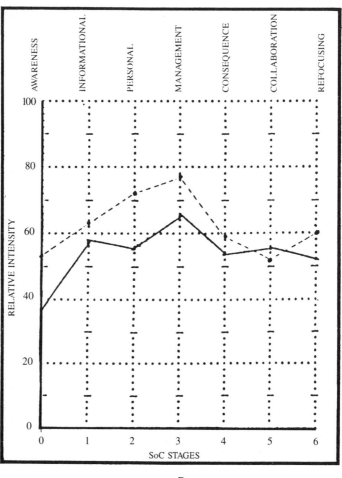

- - - - - = Pre-treatment

_____ = Post-treatment

Figure 15.4 (continued) *Profiles of Stages of Concern (SoC)/Percentile Scores on "Relative Intensity" Axis Indicates Group Mean for Each Stage (0–6) Listed on Horizontal (Top) Axis.*

ORGANIZING FOR SCHOOLWIDE PEER COACHING

Encouraged by the findings from this districtwide inter-school study, a similar school-based peer coaching project was coordinated in an elementary school.

Much groundwork had been laid to implement peer coaching in the school district. Two classroom teachers in each school had been selected and trained previously as "collegial coaches." These teachers were provided with many hours of specialized training in effective classroom practice, communication skills, and coaching strategies. Together with the two enthusiastic teacher coaches and me (an assistant principal), an action plan for the implementation of peer coaching was created with teachers of science and math.

We met after school three times to discuss the concepts and training strategies we felt were of importance in preparing teachers to begin coaching one another. We then presented an orientation to the entire faculty describing the peer coaching project. Teachers were encouraged to sign up for coaching if interested. Twenty-two teachers indicated an interest.

Training responsibilities were shared by the three of us. Two two-hour training sessions were held after school. Training activities were based upon an adult learning model that included readiness activities, theory presentation, modeling, and role-playing with feedback. The ASCD videotape series "Opening Doors: An Introduction to Peer Coaching" and "Another Pair of Eyes" and selected written materials were the major components of the training sessions. Teachers were invited to select math or science skills training given during that year as the focus for their coaching.

The first session began with activities designed to get teachers better acquainted with the research and theory about peer coaching and with one another. Models of good communication were discussed, and the clinical supervision cycle was introduced using a "peer coaching checklist" that outlined the steps in the observation cycle. The "Another Pair of Eyes" videotapes were used to demonstrate different means of observing teaching and gathering information; the "Opening Doors" videotape, to simulate a coaching cycle with participants role-playing the parts of the teachers, coaches, and observers.

In preparation for the next training session, participants were asked to select a partner, complete one pre-observation conference and classroom observation, and to read articles provided about research on coaching. Each participant kept a journal to record reactions to the written articles and observation cycles. In order to demonstrate administrative support of the coaching process and to relieve the pressures of lack of time reported by teachers in the first study, a full-day substitute teacher was hired with local grant funds to release teachers to conduct a half-hour classroom observation. In addition, the names of the teacher coaches were publicized in the school newsletter, and the collegial coach trainers and I monitored participants' progress informally between sessions.

The second session was scheduled for three weeks later in order to give each coaching team time to plan and complete a classroom observation. At the beginning of the second session, teachers completed the feedback portion of their observation cycle and planned for the second cycle, in which they would exchange roles.

In the large group, we discussed teacher reactions to the first cycle and to the written material. Participants reported that they had no problems with the coaching and were very enthusiastic about establishing professional dialogue with a colleague.

In the session, trainers shared additional information about different means of data gathering, and the participants were divided into small groups to discuss and create data collection techniques that they felt would be helpful in observing for specific purposes related to math and science teaching. These techniques were then shared with the large group. Following this meeting, partners were to complete three more cycles for a total of four by the end of the school year.

Following the training sessions, sign-up sheets for substitute coverage were posted and evaluation forms were distributed. The collegial coaches kept in contact with each coaching team in order to assist them as needed. After participants finished the fourth observation cycle, they submitted their completed post-tests, inservice evaluations, and journals to me in order to receive ten hours of inservice credit.

Although six participants did not complete all four coaching cycles, the journal responses of those that completed the entire series reflected teacher enthusiasm. I have summarized their comments below:

- 70 percent felt comfortable being observed.
- 60 percent learned from and enjoyed watching a colleague teach.
- 40 percent found the data collected were helpful.

- 40 percent would like to continue next year.
- 35 percent enjoyed the professional discussion. ("It feels so professional to be using the lingo we used in college!")
- 35 percent enjoyed sharing teaching ideas.
- 35 percent felt observations by a peer were more "realistic" than those done by administrators.
- 35 percent were able to help a peer through observing.
- 20 percent believed they had gained competence in coaching through practice.
- 20 percent enjoyed receiving positive reinforcement from their coach.
- 20 percent felt coaching was fun.
- 10 percent reported that their students were interested in the coaching process of their teachers.

Pleased with the positive feedback, we have planned to initiate peer coaching again for all interested teachers as well as all beginning teachers and their supervising peer teachers.

I had expected the provision of substitute time to be popular with the teachers. Interestingly, very few of them took advantage of having substitute coverage provided to do their observations. When asked, several indicated that it was easier to do coaching activities during their planning periods than to plan for substitutes for one half hour. This was surprising and points out that peer coaching need not necessarily involve extra expense.

Several teachers suggested that a period longer than the twelve weeks of this project was needed to complete the two training sessions and four cycles required. Therefore, next time we will begin the training and the cycles early in the school year. Additional information is needed on how administrative support for coaching could be provided more helpfully. Hopefully, these changes will encourage all teachers to complete the coaching project.

CONCLUSIONS

Too often, it has been assumed that teachers who "learned the content" taught during inservice would be able to integrate new strategies into their classroom repertoires. This has seldom been the case. Instead, in most instances, teachers have found that the task of introducing new techniques into their classrooms is not an easy one. Smooth routines are often disrupted and student reactions to newly introduced change have not been positive at first. Students may feel insecure with the new expectations and unfamiliar "rules" of the game. Coaching serves a valuable purpose, to support and assist teachers in their classrooms as they attempt to adapt the newly learned strategies into daily, routine use.

Peer coaching empowers teachers to transcend the isolation often typical of schools. Many school systems are allocating human and financial resources to accommodate peer coaching practice, but more attention needs to be given to developing different means for combining peer coaching with traditional supervision. Different staffing models such as team teaching may facilitate peer coaching.

As supervisors, administrators, trainers, and professors, the importance of providing support to teachers during the transition period following training in new skills needs to be an important consideration in how we conduct staff development and allocate human resources, funding, and instruction time. It is imperative that we provide for classroom support and inservice follow-up if new teaching techniques are to have an opportunity to germinate and grow in a safe climate until they are ready to stand on their own merits. If we don't, the incorporation of innovative and effective classroom strategies will continue to be laborious and ineffectual.

The role of the principal in recognizing the potential that peer coaching provides for enhancing the professional growth of teachers and for creating a climate that makes it a norm in schools is crucial. Based upon a survey conducted in four hundred secondary schools, Huddle (1985) observed that (1) classroom observations are done infrequently if at all, (2) supervision can be helpful but many teachers feel it is not, and (3) teachers rated supervision by administrators as less helpful than that provided by department heads or peers. Huddle concludes that peer coaching can provide for regular, ongoing supervision that improves instructional practice and decreases teacher isolation. In addition, he suggests that principals are able to encourage peer coaching and orchestrate its use by providing training and scheduling that facilitates peer observation and conferencing.

For peer coaching to be effective, the school administrator must demonstrate that coaching is valued by providing resources (e.g., a budget for substitutes and training), arranging for inservice credits, establishing coaching teams, clarifying the difference between evaluation and coaching, and encouraging teachers to take risks in order to grow in their teaching. In addition, using peer coaching to supplement inservices planned to achieve school or team goals; publicizing coaching activities at meetings with teachers, parents, and the community; asking teacher-coaches to share at faculty meetings; writing them personal notes; asking them informally about their coaching; and providing publicity for peer coaching in school and district newsletters are many important ways that administrators can let teachers know their commitment to peer coaching is noticed and appreciated.

While demonstrating a personal commitment, it is important that the administrators understand that as with anything else, teacher ownership of the peer coaching program is necessary. If teachers have not been involved in the goal-setting, planning, and implementation, the process will meet with resistance. Providing for an ongoing process of teacher input and participation through surveys, discussions, and support groups is imperative.

My experience with peer coaching has convinced me that the clinical supervision observation cycle is a practical tool for classroom teachers to use in their coaching, and that peer coaching is a valuable means of encouraging professional development and dialogue within a school. The opportunities created for positive and professional interactions among the faculty members through coaching have helped to make our school climate one in which teachers feel safe to share and to risk and to grow. That spirit of helping and encouraging others is contagious and serves to make our school a better one for all who work and learn together there.

REFERENCES

Alfonso, R. and L. Goldsberry. 1982. "Colleagueship in Supervision," in *Supervision of Teaching*, T. J. Sergiovanni, ed., Alexandria, VA: Association for Supervision and Curriculum Development, pp. 90–107.

Clarke, C. 1986. *Peer Clinical Supervision: A Collegial Approach.* ERIC Document Reproduction Service No. ED 276 696.

Cook, G. E. 1985. "Teachers Helping Teachers. A Training Program in Peer Supervision," paper presented at a meeting of the Association of Teacher Educators, Las Vegas, Nevada, February, 1985. ERIC Document No. ED 258 956.

Denham, A. 1977. "Clinical Supervision: What We Need to Know about Its Potential for Improving Instruction," *Contemporary Education*, 49(1):33–37.

Garmston, R. 1987. "How Administrators Support Peer Coaching," *Educational Leadership*, 44(5):18–26.

Garmston, R. 1989. "Peer Coaching and Professors' Instructional Thought," *Wingspan*, 5:14–16.

Goldhammer, R., R. H. Anderson and R. Krajewski. 1980. *Clinical Supervision: Special Methods for the Supervision of Teachers, Second Edition*. New York: Holt, Rinehart and Winston.

Hall, G. E. and S. L. Loucks. 1987. *Innovation Configurations: Analyzing the Adaptations of Innovations*. Austin, TX: University of Texas.

Hall, G. E., S. L. Loucks, W. L. Rutherford and B. W. Newlove. 1975. "Levels of Use of the Innovation: A Framework for Analyzing Innovation Adoption," *Journal of Teacher Education*, 26:52–56.

Hertz-Lazarowitz, R. and S. Sharan. 1982. "Effects on an Instruction Change Program in Teacher Behavior, Attitudes and Perceptions," *Journal of Applied Behavioral Science*, 18:185–201.

Hosack-Curlin, K. 1988. "Using Peer Coaching to Improve the Implementation of a Writing Process Approach to Writing: A Clinical Supervision Model," University Microfilms No. 8819359.

Huddle, G. 1985. "Teacher Evaluation—How Important for Effective Schools? Eight Messages from Research," *NASSP Bulletin*, 69:58–63.

Joyce, B. R. and B. Showers. 1982. "The Coaching of Teaching," *Educational Leadership*, 40(1):4–9.

Joyce, B. R. and B. Showers. 1983. *Power in Staff Development through Research on Teaching*. Alexandria, VA: Association for Supervision and Curriculum Development.

Kurth, R. J. 1984. "Training Peer Teachers to Improve Comprehension Instruction," paper presented at the meeting of the American Educational Research Association, Chicago, Illinois, March, 1984. ERIC Document No. ED 256 733.

Little, J. W. and J. Guilkey-Amado. 1986. *Expanding Professional Collaboration in Schools. Can Districts Organize Leadership by Teachers?* San Francisco: Far West Laboratory for Research Development.

Phelps, M. S. and J. Wright. "Peer Coaching: A Staff Development Strategy for Rural Teachers," paper presented at the National Conference of the States of Inservice Education, Nashville, Tennessee, November, 1986.

Russell, T. L. and C. Spafford. "Teachers as Reflective Practitioners in Peer Clinical Supervision," paper presented at the meeting of the American Educational Research Association, San Francisco, California, April, 1986.

Schultze, C. 1984. "The Effect of Coaching on Vertical Transfer of a Teaching Model," *Dissertation Abstracts International*, 45(04A):817.

Servatius, J. D. and S. E. Young. 1985. "Implementing the Coaching of Teaching," *Educational Leadership*, 42(April):50–53.

Showers, B. 1984. "Peer Coaching: A Strategy for Facilitating Transfer of Training," Center for Educational Policy and Management Report.

Sparks, G. M. 1983. "Synthesis of Research on Staff Development for Effective Teaching," *Educational Leadership*, 41(November):65–72.

Sparks, G. M. 1986. "The Effectiveness of Alternative Training Activities in Changing Teaching Practices," *American Educational Journal*, 23(2):217–225.

Wade, R. K. 1984–1985. "What Makes a Difference in Inservice Teacher Education? A Meta-Analysis of Research," *Educational Leadership*, 42(December/January): 48–54.

Wilburn, K. T. 1986. "Collegial Coaching: A Challenge for Inservice Clinical Supervision," *Wingspan*, 3(1):47–51.

Wynn, M. J. 1986. "Student Teaching Transfer of Training to the Classroom: Effects of an Experimental Model," *Wingspan*, 3(1):54–58.

MARY GIELLA
MYNDALL STANFILL

16

Institutionalizing Peer Coaching in School Districts

A system of peer coaching has been developed in Pasco County, Florida that enables teachers to work together to solve performance and schooling challenges. In this chapter, we discuss the beliefs and values about peer coaching and the development of a districtwide system. The relationship between the coaching system and assessment system is discussed, as is the selection of the clinical supervision approach to coaching. Finally, suggestions are made for planning and implementing a districtwide peer coaching system.

EVENTS THAT LED TO THE DEVELOPMENT OF A PEER COACHING SYSTEM

The findings of a Rand comparative study parallel the Pasco experience. In the early 1970s, Rand, under the sponsorship of the United States Office of Education (USOE), completed a four-year, two-phase study of federally funded programs designed to introduce and spread innovative practices in public schools. The study, often referred to as the Change Agent Study, was concerned about the way the many Great Society education reforms seemed to fall short of their goals. One main reason why the reform efforts seem to fall short is that planners seriously underestimate teacher-training needs. Even the best educational practices are unlikely to succeed in the hands of inadequately trained or unmotivated teachers.

It was found that program or project strategies that foster staff learning and change, and which are combined with staff training and support activities, do in fact improve implementation, promote student

251

gains, foster teacher change, and enhance the continuation of the project or program. In other words, the training and support variables account for a great portion of program success.

The Rand study determined that skill-specific training alone influenced student gains and program implementation for only a short period of time. By itself, this training does not support staff learning and teacher change over time. The learning involved is often mechanistic and does not allow teachers to assimilate new techniques and procedures. However, staff support activities can reinforce the contribution of staff training and can promote teacher change. Such activities can aid teachers in understanding and applying complex instructional strategies.

Another finding was that the professional development needs of experienced teachers are different from those of new teachers. After several years in the classroom, teachers want to explore new areas and take more responsibility for their professional growth.

In summary, the Rand study proposed a change from the quick-fix workshop. Instead, the study emphasized learning for professionals as part of an ongoing program within an organizational context.

The following concepts represent a view of staff development that is one of the most important aspects of the Rand study. There were a number of findings:

(1) Teachers often represent the best clinical expertise available.
(2) For teachers, the learning task is more like problem solving than like mastering proven procedures.
(3) Involving classroom teachers in identifying problems and solutions is valuable.
(4) Professional learning is a long-term, nonlinear process.
(5) Staff development is part of the program-building process in schools.

The Pasco County experience is consistent with the findings of the Rand study. The development of programs, schools, and school districts is based upon principles of organizational development. The Rand study findings coincide with the beliefs and values upon which peer coaching and development in Pasco County are based.

Over the years, beginning in approximately 1980, there were various timely events or trends that coaxed the process along: (1) the school restructuring movement; (2) requirements announced by the Florida Department of Education in the area of personnel assessment; (3) teachers' desire for more professional growth opportunities; and (4) the Pasco School Board's request of the superintendent and district administrator for more accountability. All of these factors assisted in the process of instituting a peer coaching system. However, awareness of and belief in the Rand study findings pointed the direction toward a coaching system.

THE DESIGN AND IMPLEMENTATION OF AN ASSESSMENT SYSTEM INVOLVING PEER COACHING

Two initiatives from the Florida legislature and the Florida Department of Education helped to shape the circumstances from which the Pasco County peer coaching system evolved. In the early 1980s all Florida school districts were required to develop a Human Resource Management Development plan for the recruitment, selection, certification, training, assessment, and compensation of all school-based administrators (*Management Training Act*, 1979, Florida Statutes 231.095; State Board of Education Rule 6A-4.0082). In the latter part of the decade, the state legislature and the Department of Education established new statewide requirements for teacher assessment.

In response to a request in 1982 by the school board for increased performance accountability of administrators, a group of principals, district directors, and supervisors had already been working on the development of a new administrative assessment system when the HRMD plan requirement was introduced. It was (and still is) the belief of the superintendent and the administrators on the committee that a good assessment system should clearly define the district's performance expectations of the personnel being assessed. These same performance expectations should then become the basis on which administrative personnel would be recruited, selected, trained, assessed, and compensated. Consensus on these beliefs led the assessment committee to expand its membership and the scope of its work to address new state guidelines for HRMD (*Guidelines for School District Management Training Programs: Training, Selection, Appointing, Assessing, Certifying, Compensating Educational Managers for Excellence*, FCEM, 1986). The assessment and compensation sections were those first addressed in the development of the district's Human Resource Management Development plan.

The new administrator assessment system incorporated performance-based evaluation by a supervisor, career coaching, individual goal setting related to district goals and school/department goals, and job performance coaching. The task force focused on a professional development approach to assist each administrator to improve and stretch performance, rather than on an inspection system which tends to have a depressing effect on risk-taking behaviors necessary to strong and effective leaders. Both district-level and school-based administrators agreed that the competencies being assessed with the new instruments and the individual goal-setting activities were appropriate. Only the work context in which the individual operates would be considered differently. The assessment system with its strong coaching elements became the driving force for the development of the five other sections of the district's Human Resource Management Development plan.

As soon as the new assessment system was approved by the school board, the staff development director and selected members of the assessment task force began designing a process to train all their peers in the use of the new assessment. The staff development plan sought to follow an adult learning model. Teams of administrators were identified to lead their peers through the entire assessment cycle, with guided practice at appropriate intervals. All participants had opportunities to practice writing professional objectives, and objectives related to district and school or departmental goals, with feedback and coaching provided by the peer trainers. They also observed videotaped examples of coaching conferences and then practiced such a conference with their fellow trainees. Further support for developing an understanding of the new assessment system was provided for an entire year as all administrators worked through the process on a "dry run" trial basis. The year of practice was as important for the assessors as for the assessees, because the coaching/conferencing role was new for everyone.

After the trial year and the first year of actual implementation, the Research and Evaluation Department began a systematic evaluation of the entire HRMD plan. The evaluations focused on one section of the plan each year, followed by refinements and revisions of the section being reviewed. Modifications to the assessment section were made by reconvening selected members of the original assessment task force.

The team studied the results of the evaluation, examined the directions and the results of administrative staff development since the assessment system was designed, and related the information from both sources to current goals and projected plans for district development.

In 1990 the coaching and assessment model remains the same, with emphasis on setting individual professional and school/departmental objectives within the context of a coaching-conferencing cycle with a supervising administrator. What has changed are the competency areas of job performance for principals. It is important that as job performance expectations change, based on new knowledge and training, the process by which the performance is assessed changes to reflect the new expectations. They are now focused on the ten competencies of the Snyder/Anderson Managing Productive Schools training program, which has been the core of administrative staff development for the past six years (Snyder and Anderson, 1986). Among the ten job tasks for principals are individual staff performance goal setting, coaching, and assessment.

During the same period of the early 1980s, when the Human Resource Management Development plan was developing for district and school-based administrators, staff development for teachers was also changing. A new system for the continuous professional development of instructional personnel created a natural foundation for the peer coaching model to emerge. Through the cooperative efforts of the Staff Development Department and Performance Learning Systems, Inc., ninety-five teacher leaders were trained to become trainers of their peers in the Performance Learning System programs: T.E.A.C.H., P.R.I.D.E., and Learning Channels. These same teacher-trainers now have trained almost 2,000 of their fellow teachers and administrators within the district and several have had opportunities to train teachers in adjoining counties. The concept of using peer trainers has been widely accepted and has proven to be a most successful model for districtwide staff development.

In 1986 the Florida legislature made changes (Florida Statutes, Section 231.29) that are intended to bring higher levels of consistency to the major operational components of teacher assessment systems across the state (State of Florida, Department of Education, *A Guide for Designing Teacher Assessment Systems*, Tallahassee, Florida, May, 1987, p. 3). All school districts were directed to examine their current teacher assessment systems and either to revise their systems or develop entirely new systems to meet the new legal requirements. Pasco County took this opportunity to develop an entirely different process for developing instructional skills and assessing teacher performance.

A committee of teachers, principals, and district-level administrators was organized to design a new instructional assessment system for the district. The group first spent several months examining model assessment systems currently in use in various parts of the country. Although none seemed to be the exact model for meeting Pasco County needs, the exercise was valuable because it provided new knowledge for committee members. Best practices were gleaned from several of the assessment models and incorporated into the Pasco County model.

After reviewing the assessment systems, noting the success of the HRMD Performance Management System developed for administrators, considering the wide acceptance of the peer training model established with the PLS staff development, and observing the positive experiences of peer teaching in the Florida Beginning Teacher Program, the Teacher Assessment Committee reached consensus on a clinical supervision model for the new assessment system. It was also determined that a Human Resource Development plan for teachers was needed to systematize the procedure for the recruitment, selection, orientation, certification, training, and assessment of instructional personnel in the district. Task forces were appointed to design a Human Resource Teacher Development plan (HRTD) that would parallel the Human Resource Management Development plan (HRMD).

The work of the Teacher Assessment System Committee formed the foundation for the other sections of the HRTD Plan. The following purposes of assessment were established by the committee.

This assessment system is designed to help members of the instructional and administrative staff to:

(1) Improve the quality of instruction
(2) Promote the growth and development of the individual and the organization
(3) Link the individual's job-related objectives to the current goals of the organization
(4) Permit discussion of actual job performance relative to the established expectations and establish methods for continuous improvement
(5) Emphasize self-assessment and individual development that will

lead to motivation for improvement and acceptance of the fairness of the system by members of the instructional staff

(6) Provide support and direction for staff members for both short-term improvement and long-term professional development

(7) Effectively utilize sound educational principles based on contemporary research when assessing performance

Subcommittees were assigned to design various sections of the assessment system. One group developed the six areas of Essential Teacher Competencies and Behavioral Indicators, which formed the assessment criteria. Another subcommittee designed the assessment process and described the procedure's format and timelines to be followed. Assessment forms for all phases of the system were designed by another subcommittee as were all the data collection procedures, and the instrument and forms were designed by a fourth group. The task that was most essential to the success of the new assessment system was that of training assessors and assessees in all phases of the system. A staff development committee created a unique and very effective plan for managing the huge task of training all administrative and instructional personnel.

TRAINING PEER COACHES

The staff developmental plan involved selecting and training collegial coach trainers, who would then provide thirty hours of training for two collegial coaches from every school in the new assessment system. The school-based collegial coaches would train their colleagues over the next year in the process and procedures. All administrators who supervise instructional personnel were also trained in the new coaching and assesment system. Administrators had already received training in Florida Performance Management System Observer Training, Clinical Supervision, and Coaching Teachers Towards Higher Levels of Effectiveness (Performance Learning Systems). The staff development program was designed to span two full years, with a week of intensive training for the collegial coaches each year prior to the beginning of school. Observation techniques, data collection procedures, and coaching/conferencing skills were emphasized in all training.

The implementation of the new assessment system was phased in over the two years of staff development. In the first year, while all instructional personnel were being introduced to the new system by their principals and peer coaches, the individual goal-setting dimension was viewed as practice only and was not included in the annual summative evaluations. In the second year, principals and peer coaches worked through the entire clinical supervision cycle with selected teacher volunteers who served as models in the assessment process. Care was taken to select only those volunteers who were sure to be successful examples of the clinical supervision process. As teachers observed the positive interactions between colleagues involved in the peer coaching process, many came forward and asked to be included, while others began to lessen their suspicions regarding the perceived threats related to peer observation and feedback. The full implementation of the new assessment system will begin in the third year.

The Research and Evaluation Department has already begun the evaluation of the new system. Although it is too soon to consider evaluating the assessment system itself, the Director of Staff Development was most anxious to obtain feedback on the effectiveness of the training model. An evaluation of the training program by the Research and Evaluation Department confirmed that the collegial coach trainers and the school-based collegial coaches provided effective training for their colleagues. With a few minor adjustments, this model has become the vehicle for districtwide training for coaching assessment and other areas of staff development.

RATIONALE FOR A CLINICAL SUPERVISION APPROACH TO ASSESSMENT

Clinical supervision systems are described as having the highest level of complexity of the various types of assessment systems by the authors of *A Guide for Designing Teacher Assessment Systems* (Florida Department of Education, 1987, p. 1–3). The very elements of the clinical supervision systems that add to its complexity made it attractive to the assessment system developers: "In addition to collecting and analyzing performance data, this type of system includes working with teachers to develop professional development plans that are to further improve performance" (Florida Department of Education, 1987). The coaching/conferencing and planning dimensions to this system add purpose, opportunities for professional growth, and a foundation for collaborative decisions that can directly affect the improvement of instruction in the classroom.

The timeline (Figure 16.1) outlines the planning, development/formative, and summative components of the Pasco County Teacher Assessment System. Its design involves cooperation and collaboration between teachers and administrators, which is the heart of shared decision making in the school. The conferencing, observing, conferencing/coaching cycles bring teachers and principals together in personal-professional interactions for the common purpose of improving instruction. The model provides a coaching basis rather than a threatening,

I.	PLANNING	
	Schoolwide comprehensive plan development	March–May
	Unit goal setting (grade, department, or team)	April–May
	Teacher self-assessment	April–May
	Teacher sets individual objectives with assistance from collegial coach.	May
II.	DEVELOPMENT/FORMATIVE	
	Teacher and administrator meet to discuss professional development plan.	May–September
	Units work together to accomplish unit goal.	August–March
	Teacher works toward the accomplishment of individual objectives.	August–March
	Teacher will participate in staff development as indicated.	August–March
	Collegial coach/peer teacher works with teacher upon request.	August–March
	Unit leader develops portfolio.	August–March
	Teacher develops portfolio.	August–March
III.	SUMMATIVE	
	Administrator will observe teacher (clinical cycles utilized).	August–March
	Teacher and administrator will meet to share data that have been collected, analyze data, and draw conclusions; a summative evaluation form will be completed and signed.	February–March
	Administrator and unit leader will meet to share data and review portfolio; analyze data and draw conclusions; make decisions on new planning directions.	April–May

Figure 16.1 Teacher Assessment Timeline.

judging approach. The very term coaching implies strengthening and developing skills to win.

In addition to promoting the collaborative interactions between teachers and administrators, the clinical supervision model provides opportunities for peer coaching and cooperative planning between teachers. Not only does this element of the model enhance the spirit of professional collaboration among colleagues, it also breaks down walls of isolation in the classroom that have depressed the teaching experience for too long. Through peer coaching opportunities, teachers with talent and leadership abilities can be recognized and tapped for new roles within the school as staffing developments occur.

Another reason the clinical supervision model was attractive to Pasco teachers and administrators was that it provides a way of identifying staff development needs within a school and in the district. As the school, teaching units, and individuals set goals and objectives for stretching beyond present conditions, the needs for new knowledge, skills and instructional strategies, and methodology begin to surface. Meaningful staff development that relates directly to the school's and the individual's improvement can be provided. The "hit-or-miss" inservice model of the past gives way to new, focused professional growth opportunities.

And lastly, teachers chose the clinical supervision model because it is goal focused. The professional literature on successful organizations and successful people indicates that both are goal driven. The district model for planning is based on collaborative goal setting. The Pasco County Teacher Assessment System provides opportunities for the school, the team, and individuals to set goals and objectives that are interrelated and connect directly to the improvement of the school and the school district. The conferencing and coaching are directed toward supporting and asserting successful goal accomplishment at every level. Pasco administrators, like the teachers, developed an appraisal system that is based on a conferencing-coaching model with a focus on goal setting. The Pasco Performance Management System is a management tool designed to help employees perform better. Whereas the past assessment process suggested a once-a-year evaluation in which a supervisor let employees know where they stood, the Performance Management System requires a sequence of activities that stress ongoing supervisor-employee relationships. The process is designed to:

(1) Link the employee's job-related objectives to the current goals of the organization

(2) Lead to the establishment of performance expectations for the employee based on the requirements of the job and the employee's experience and education

(3) Permit honest discussions of actual job performance, relative to established expectations, and methods for continuing improvement

(4) Emphasize self-assessment and individual development, which will lead to greater motivation for improvement and greater acceptance of the fairness of the system by employees

(5) Emphasize both short-term improvement and long-term development of employees in their current jobs

(6) Reward individuals for meeting or exceeding performance expectations

Examination of the Performance Management System activities and timeline (Figure 16.2) reveals opportunities for an administrator and the immediate supervisor to focus on mutual concerns that lead to school improvements. A team relationship develops between the supervisor and the administrator as they work together to solve school problems.

The conferencing/coaching cycles of this appraisal system provide opportunities for administrators to influence the direction and the strategies for their own professional growth. Staff development needs are determined during coaching/conferencing sessions, where the administrator and supervisor set objectives for appropriate experience, research, and training. The system also allows the administrator to provide his/her own evidence of competency development through portfolios and/or projects. The method of providing this evidence is a collaborative decision of the supervisor-coach and the administrator.

In Pasco County all district-level and school-based administrators are engaged in their own performance appraisals through a clinical supervision process. Their experiences have provided a positive model for the teachers to follow. Because the two assessment systems are providing parallel experiences in conferencing and coaching of colleagues, peer relationships, mentorships, and cooperative staff devel-

STEP 1.	Preparation of individual for objective setting and career counseling session	June–July
	(A) Individual completes Part I, Item A. (MIS 365) and all of Part II (MIS 366)	
	(B) Individual completes Individual Objectives form (MIS 364)	
	(C) Supervisor completes Part III (MIS 366)	
STEP 2.	Individual and supervisor meet for the career development session	July–August
	(A) The individual and the supervisor discuss and complete the Individual Ojectives form (MIS 364)	
	(B) Both discuss Part I, Item A (MIS 365) and complete it	
	(C) Both discuss Part I, Items B and C (MIS 365) and complete it	
	(D) Both discuss Part II (MIS 366)	
STEP 3.	Individual and supervisor meet for mid-year performance review	December–January
	(A) Both review Part I (MIS 365)	
	(B) Both review (MIS 364)	
	(C) Both agree on mid-year changes, corrections, if necessary	
STEP 4.	Prior to performance assessment	March
	(A) Individual reviews Individual Objectives form (MIS 364)	
	(B) Individual completes Performance Evaluation form (MIS 367)	
	(C) Supervisor reviews Individual Objectives form (MIS 364)	
	(D) Supervisor reviews Performance Evaluation form (MIS 367)	
STEP 5.	Individual and supervisor meet for year-end performance review	April–May
	(A) Both review the attainment of established objectives	
	(B) Supervisor communicates performance evaluation results	
	(C) The Performance Evaluation form (MIS 367) is completed	
STEP 6.	Beginning of cycle	June–July

Figure 16.2 Performance Management System Activity Timeline.

opment have been encouraged. The district perception of performance appraisal is shifting from "Gotcha!" to a supportive, developmental mode where winning is the goal for all educational personnel and the students in their schools.

SCHOOL DISTRICT IMPLEMENTATION OF A PEER COACHING SYSTEM

A productive coaching system is based on an open exchange among peers. It promotes a sense of professional camaraderie where individual growth is at the core. Therefore, a school district must have a readiness level to support such a system.

The leaders of the district must have a commitment to the development of people, who are recognized as the most important resource. Their learning, experimenting, and exploring must be encouraged. The school board, the superintendent, and the principals must provide opportunities under safe and positive conditions. Unless such a culture exists, peer coaching could be considered another ploy of administrators to annoy teachers and each other.

The teacher staff development opportunities provided should be based on the school needs identified by teachers and on the adult learning mode. The "dog and pony show" of the outside consultant or specialist is not the model of choice. Staff development is an outgrowth of the problem-solving needs determined by the entire teaching staff. The staff development learning design is based on the core dimensions of readiness, concepts, demonstration, practice, feedback/reinforcement, and transfer (Snyder, 1988).

As teachers become accustomed to working out problems with one another and planning training sessions related to the problem to be solved, they would be close to the comfort level it takes to invite a peer coach into their classroom. Teachers must feel and believe they are empowered to plan and solve problems together. The leadership of the district must enable teachers to serve as leaders, developers, participators, explorers, and creators. They should be encouraged to spread their wings and gain learning experiences by visiting other schools and school districts and by attending and participating in state and national committees and conferences.

With the richness of experiences gained by working with one another, planning staff development, solving problems, visiting each others' schools, and participating in conferences, teachers should be tapped to serve on district committees that are collaboratively planning the instructional programs. Joining feeder schools' planning and work sessions is another example of utilizing their experience. Such opportunities should be supported by the means and resources to implement plans and programs.

These opportunities, along with a district's spirit of continuous growth and change, would create an environment of risk, adventure, and learning. All school personnel would learn that the old saying "If it ain't broke—don't fix it" can apply to a living, changing organization. This spirit, coupled with opportunities for socialization, recreation, and just plain fun, enables everyone to feel like a learner as well as a teacher. An administrator has observed that, "In the Pasco County School District, everyone is teaching someone something all the time." By this he meant that teachers and administrators feel like a community of learners.

With this orientation, there is a success expectation and an opportunity for growth and change. When handed a difficult assignment, a person in the Pasco district tends to say, "what an opportunity!" There is a belief that a problem is something to be solved together.

All of this adds up to trust of one another. The culture says people are important in this school district. They have the opportunity to grow and develop. They can plan and work towards goals together. In such an environment, peer coaching or clinical supervision can become a reality, because it will be built on trust and become part of the growth experience.

REFERENCES

Dillon-Peterson, B. 1981. *Staff Development Organization Development*. Alexandria, VA: Association for Supervision and Curriculum Development.

1987. *A Guide for Designing Teacher Assessment Systems*. Tallahassee, FL: State of Florida, Department of Education.

1989. *Human Resource Management Development Plan, Revised*. Land O'Lakes, FL: District School Board of Pasco County.

1988. *Human Resource Teacher Development Plan*. Land O'Lakes, FL: District School Board of Pasco County.

1979. *Management Training Act.* Tallahassee, FL: State of Florida, Florida School Laws, Statute 231.095, State Board of Education Rules, 6A-4.0082.

Milbrey, W. M. and D. D. Marsh. 1973. "Staff Development and School Change," *Teachers College Record*, 30(1).

Snyder, K. J. 1988. *Competency Training for Managing Productive Schools.* Orlando, FL: Harcourt, Brace and Jovanovich.

Snyder, K. J. and R. H. Anderson. 1986. *Managing Productive Schools: Toward an Ecology.* Orlando, FL: Harcourt, Brace and Jovanovich.

EDWARD PAJAK
LETITIA CARR

17

Supervisory Proficiencies for Mentor Teachers and Peer Coaches

BACKGROUND FOR A STUDY

Peer assistance to teachers is being implemented across the United States as school districts seek new ways to help teachers improve their instruction and develop professionally. A major reason for the popularity of peer assistance is that traditional staff development has been found lacking. Training teachers in large groups, for example, does not fully meet the needs of new teachers (Compton, 1979) and is only moderately successful with experienced teachers (Wade, 1984–85). Further, administrative responsibilities often prevent principals and central office supervisors from providing individual assistance to teachers, so teachers' needs for induction, support, and feedback sometimes go unmet (Lyman and Morehead, 1987). In recent years, peer assistance has been recognized as an effective way of helping teachers improve their instruction while also relieving over-burdened administrators and providing an avenue for experienced teachers to seek new challenges (Lyman and Morehead, 1987).

The notion of teachers providing assistance to other teachers is well established in the supervision literature. Older and more experienced teachers, Alfonso (1977) notes, informally instruct beginning teachers about proper behavior and expectations. He suggests that a formalized program of peer supervision may help teachers gain a greater sense of professional autonomy. Neagley and Evans (1980) view peer supervision as occurring spontaneously when teachers share materials, strategies, and innovations with each other, as well as when teachers observe one another's classrooms. Direct peer assistance, delivered through the

267

clinical supervision cycle, has been recommended by a number of authors (e.g., Alfonso and Goldsberry, 1982; Oliva, 1984; Glickman, 1985).

Mentoring and peer coaching are two concepts that have emerged quite recently in the peer supervision literature. Mentoring programs for the induction of new teachers are being implemented in many districts and states in hopes of increasing retention rates among beginning teachers (Huling-Austin, 1988). Peer coaching is being tested as a means of reducing teacher isolation and providing interpersonal support for teachers (Joyce and Showers, 1982). Mentor teachers are actively involved in developing and facilitating opportunities for the professional growth of their proteges (Benningfield et al., 1984; Taylor, 1986). Peer coaches facilitate professional growth in others, but are usually also themselves involved as participants in ongoing staff development programs (Sparks, 1986; Kwiat, 1988).

Research on mentoring and peer coaching is largely exploratory, and the findings are at best tentative. Most research on mentoring has focused on the outcomes for the new teacher (Fagan and Walter, 1982; Huling-Austin and Murphy, 1987; Huling-Austin, 1988). Research on peer coaching has centered on outcomes such as achievement of instructional goals, transfer of training, student learning, and the development of collegiality among teachers (Sparks and Bruder, 1987; Munro and Elliot, 1987; Showers, 1984). Beyond training in the techniques of clinical supervision, little is known about the knowledge, attitudes, and skills that are needed by mentor teachers and peer coaches as they go about providing support to their colleagues.

This chapter reports findings from a study that focused on outstanding mentor teachers and peer coaches (Carr, 1990). The study was part of a more comprehensive project that was sponsored by ASCD, the purpose of which was to identify and verify knowledge, attitudes, and skills that have strongest support for representing highly effective supervisory practice in education (Pajak, 1989). The broader study involved a review of research literature and supervision textbooks, and resulted in the identification of twelve general dimensions of effective supervisory practice. The purpose of the study reported here was to verify the importance of the twelve dimensions of supervisory practice with a national sample of mentor teachers and peer coaches who have a reputation for providing outstanding leadership in their districts.

IDENTIFYING EFFECTIVE PRACTICE: A STUDY

Identifying the Knowledge, Attitudes, and Skills

An extensive review of research and supervision textbook literature was conducted by a research team consisting of nine doctoral students in the Department of Curriculum and Supervision at the University of Georgia. The review focused on a variety of leadership positions in education that involve supervisory responsibilities, including superintendents, associate and assistant superintendents, district-level generalists and specialists, principals (high school, middle/junior high, and elementary), assistant principals, school-based supervisors, team leaders, department chairs, peer coaches, and mentor teachers. This search yielded hundreds of research documents, reviews of research, research-based articles and reports, and papers presented at meetings of professional associations, as well as supervision textbooks.

Identifying Dimensions of Practice

The documents generated by the search were read and specific statements of knowledge, attitudes, and skills associated with effective supervisory practice were copied onto index cards. The team of doctoral students and a Project Advisory Committee comprised of the supervision faculty in the Department of Curriculum and Supervision discussed and sorted the knowledge, attitudes, and skills derived from the literature into categories. Statements that were closely related or duplicates were combined into single statements. Those that related to traditionally administrative functions, such as finance, facilities, discipline, and personnel evaluation were removed from consideration. As a rule of thumb, a knowledge, attitude, or skill had to be cited in at least two references in order to be included. Statements were then grouped into categories on the basis of content. Eventually, twelve categories of supervisory practice emerged. These are as follows:

(1) *Community relations*—establishing and maintaining open and productive relations between the school and its community

(2) *Staff development* – developing and facilitating meaningful opportunities for professional growth

(3) *Planning and change* – initiating and implementing collaboratively developed strategies for continuous improvement

(4) *Communication* – ensuring open and clear communication among individuals and groups throughout the organization

(5) *Curriculum* – coordinating and integrating the process of curriculum development and implementation

(6) *Instructional program* – supporting and coordinating efforts to improve the instructional program

(7) *Service to teachers* – providing materials, resources, and assistance to support teaching and learning

(8) *Observation and conferencing* – providing feedback to teachers based on classroom observation

(9) *Problem solving and decision making* – using a variety of strategies to clarify and analyze problems and to make decisions

(10) *Research and program evaluation* – encouraging experimentation and assessing outcomes

(11) *Motivating and organizing* – helping people to develop a shared vision and achieve collective aims

(12) *Personal development* – recognizing and reflecting upon one's personal and professional beliefs, abilities, and actions

Participants and Their Selection

Members of six professional organizations assisted with the identification of a national sample of mentors and peer coaches who helped to verify the importance of the twelve dimensions of supervisory practice. Members of the Council of Professors of Instructional Supervision, the Supervision Network of ASCD, the Instructional Supervision Special Interest Group of the American Educational Research Association, presidents and executive secretaries of ASCD affiliates, and exemplary teachers identified by the National Educational Association and the American Federation of Teachers were asked to nominate outstanding instructional leaders, including mentor teachers and peer coaches. A total of 108 mentor teachers and peer coaches were thus nominated.

Questionnaires

A questionnaire based on the twelve dimensions of supervisory practice was constructed and mailed to the sample of 108 mentor teachers and peer coaches who had been nominated as outstanding instructional leaders. These participants were instructed to indicate the extent to which they agreed or disagreed that the dimension is important to their job as it *currently is* and to their job as it *should be*. The participants were asked to circle one of four possible responses for each item on the questionnaire: SA = Strongly Agree, A = Agree, D = Disagree, and SD = Strongly Disagree. They were also asked if they would be willing to respond later to a second survey.

A second survey was developed, comprised of statements that described the specific knowledge, attitudes, and skills that are associated in the literature with each dimension of supervisory practice. Some 335 distinct statements were identified in total. Participants in the second survey were asked to indicate the extent of their agreement that the knowledge, attitudes, and skills listed were relevant to the effective enactment of their job.

Questions Asked

The following questions are among those we hoped the responses of the mentor teachers and peer coaches would help us answer:

(1) How do outstanding mentor teachers and peer coaches view the importance of the twelve dimensions to their jobs as they currently exist?

(2) How do outstanding mentor teachers and peer coaches view the importance of the twelve dimensions to their jobs as they ideally should be?

(3) Do the perceptions of outstanding mentor teachers and peer coaches differ with respect to the importance of the twelve dimensions as they currently exist versus as they should be?

(4) Which knowledge, attitudes, and skills associated with the twelve dimensions of supervisory practice do outstanding mentor teachers and peer coaches view as most relevant to their jobs?

Results

Seventy-five mentor teachers and peer coaches responded to the first survey, reflecting a response rate slightly better than 69 percent. More than three-fourths of the mentor teachers and peer coaches who responded were female. As a group, mentors tended to have more years experience in the classroom and were more often employed at the elementary level than were peer coaches. The latter tended to have from one to five years of experience and more often taught in the middle or high school grades.

Figure 17.1 illustrates that mentor teachers ($n = 61$) strongly agreed that all twelve dimensions were important to their job, both as it *currently is* and as it *should be*. The difference in perception between the real and the ideal job for mentor teachers was statistically significant for all twelve dimensions ($p < .01$). This may suggest that the mentor teachers who were surveyed would like to expand their supervisory responsibilities, if given the opportunity.

Peer coaches ($n = 14$) similarly viewed all twelve dimensions as important to their job, both as it *currently is* and as it *should be* (see Figure 17.2). The small number of peer coaches in the sample makes comparisons extremely tentative, but it is interesting to note that the only statistically significant difference between the real and ideal perceptions of the job of peer coach was for the dimension of research and program evaluation. Apparently, except for research and program evaluation, peer coaches see less need to expand their supervisory duties.

Again, while recognizing that the small number of peer coaches in the sample makes the results of comparisons tenuous, it is interesting to note that peer coaches viewed the dimensions of staff development, planning and change, communication, and personal development as significantly more important to their job as it currently is than did mentor teachers ($p < .01$). Peer coaches also perceived planning and change and personal development to be significantly more important to their job as it *should be* ($p < .01$). The findings suggest that the positions of mentor teacher and peer coach may differ in the emphasis placed on these particular dimensions.

While both mentor teachers and peer coaches strongly agreed that all twelve dimensions were important to their jobs as they *should be*, a ranking of the dimensions by mean scores suggests that six of the dimensions were viewed as somewhat more important than the others.

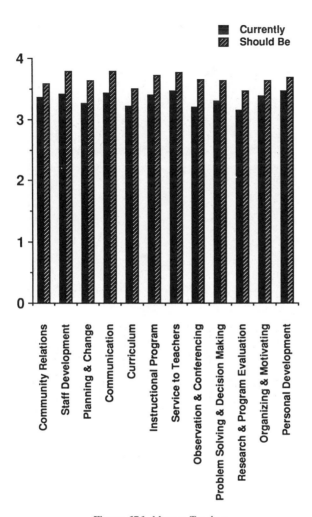

Figure 17.1 *Mentor Teacher.*

These are staff development, communication, service to teachers, observation and conferencing, personal development, and instructional program. This finding seems entirely consistent with the classroom and interpersonal focus of mentors and peer coaches.

A second survey was mailed to fifty mentor teachers and twelve peer coaches who had indicated on the first survey a willingness to participate further. Because 335 statements of knowledge, attitudes, and skills had been identified, three versions of the instrument were developed,

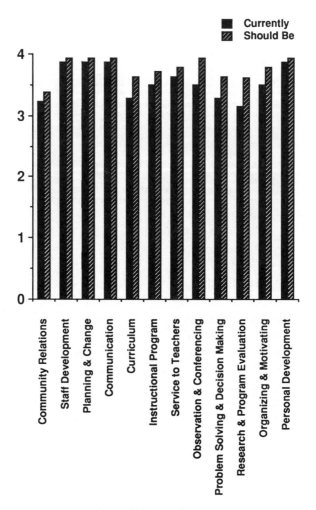

Figure 17.2 Peer Coaching.

each comprised of approximately 112 items. The respondents indicated the extent to which they agreed or disagreed that statements of knowledge, attitudes, and skills derived from the literature were relevant to the effective performance of their positions.

Thirty-five mentor teachers and nine peer coaches completed and returned these surveys. While this represents a response rate of 71 percent, the small number of respondents ($n = 44$) and the fact that three separate versions of the second survey were used, suggests that strong caution should be exercised in generalizing the findings to other populations. Keeping this admonition in mind, the knowledge, attitudes, and skills for which strongest agreement was obtained are discussed below for the six dimensions of supervisory practice that received the highest mean score ratings from mentor teachers and peer coaches. References to supporting literature are included.

TEACHING – SIX MAJOR DIMENSIONS

Staff Development

According to the findings from our second survey, mentors and peer coaches strongly agreed that knowledge of teacher and adult development was relevant to their jobs, along with knowledge of the specific needs and interests of the teachers with whom they worked. The respondents also endorsed the beliefs that teachers want to improve their instruction and that teachers should participate in decisions concerning their own professional growth. They also expressed personal commitment to ongoing professional development that is based on actual needs instead of the latest educational fads. The mentors and peer coaches surveyed were sensitive to individual differences and to the diverse and changing needs of the staff, and believed that teachers are generally capable of making desirable changes in their teaching. They preferred to orient their efforts toward the development of strengths rather than the remediation of weaknesses.

Mentors and peer coaches believed that the development of support networks was helpful for reinforcing staff development efforts. Implementing staff development efforts, encouraging teachers to reflect on their teaching, and orienting and inducting teachers to new situations were viewed as important skills (Krupp, 1987). Mentors and peer coaches strongly agreed that identifying strengths and needs of colleagues, assisting in developing professional growth plans (Hawk, 1986–1987), introducing new ideas and information at appropriate times, and providing technical assistance and practice opportunities were relevant to the effective performance of their jobs.

Communication

Ensuring open and clear communication among individuals and groups throughout the school is essential for both mentor teachers and peer coaches (Egan, 1985; Sultana and Leung, 1986; Kwiat, 1988). The mentors and peer coaches whom we surveyed expressed the belief that it is important to be open and approachable (Godley et al., 1986–1987), to encourage mutual trust, to be collegial and committed to open channels of communication (Showers, 1984), and to be accepting of diverse viewpoints. Specific skills considered especially relevant by mentor teachers and peer coaches included writing clearly and concisely (Wagner, 1985), listening attentively (Fagan and Walter, 1982; Odell, 1986), speaking clearly, using and interpreting nonverbal behavior, and creating opportunities for professional dialogue.

Observation and Conferencing

Providing feedback to teachers based on classroom observation is a key function of mentor teachers and peer coaches. Most peer coaches use the clinical model of supervision (Ellis et al., 1979; McFaul and Cooper, 1983). According to their responses to the second survey, mentors and peer coaches believe that it is important to be knowledgeable about effective teaching strategies and methods, lesson design, and classroom management techniques (Taylor, 1986; Odell, 1986). Information related to learning theory, to a variety of supervisory models, and to the difference between supervision and evaluation is highly relevant to the effective performance of mentors and peer coaches.

Key attitudes supported by mentors and peer coaches included valuing collegial relationships with teachers, supporting experimentation by teachers through a nonthreatening atmosphere, a commitment to development of individual teaching styles, and recognizing that a variety of supervisory approaches is needed. The ability to establish mutual trust and respect was also viewed as very relevant by both groups. Skills such as identifying teachers' concerns about instruction, translating teachers' concerns into observable behavior, using pertinent conferencing techniques and a variety of observation techniques (Johnston and James, 1986; Clarke and Richardson, 1986), along with providing teachers with opportunities for practice and comparison were also endorsed by mentor teachers and peer coaches.

Service to Teachers

Providing materials, resources, and assistance to colleagues in support of teaching and learning are important functions of mentor teachers and peer coaches. Knowledge of a variety of instructional techniques and strategies was perceived as highly relevant to the effective performance of both positions (Howey, 1988; Winger and Desrochers, 1989), as well as knowledge of classroom management techniques (Showers, 1984; Taylor, 1986), and optimal environments for learning.

Attitudes viewed as relevant to effective performance included a willingness to share resources (Godley et al., 1986–1987), a belief in the worth of individuals, and a commitment to work with other teachers as colleagues. Being supportive toward teachers and protective of instructional time were also considered highly relevant. Identifying, locating, evaluating, and selecting resources and learning materials were viewed as important skills by mentors and peer coaches (Sultana and Leung, 1986; Huling-Austin and Murphy, 1987), along with responding to teachers' psychological needs and providing opportunities for teachers to help each other.

Instructional Program

Mentors and peer coaches are very involved in supporting and coordinating efforts to improve the instructional program. A knowledge of instructional methods, strategies, and techniques was viewed as essential to this dimension of their jobs (Taylor, 1987; Sparks and Bruder, 1987). An awareness of research on effective instruction, teaching and learning styles, instructional theory, and instructional materials, resources, and improvement processes was also perceived as important by mentors and peer coaches.

Key attitudes supported by both groups were a willingness to be personally involved in improvement efforts and a commitment to supporting others' involvement in those efforts (Huffman and Leak, 1986). Attitudes characterized by a commitment to a high-quality instruction and instructional improvement, and an openness to new ideas and practices were also viewed as vital. The demonstration of instructional strategies and methods (Taylor, 1987), and engaging teachers in dialogue about instruction (Irvine, 1985) were identified as key skills by mentors and peer coaches. In addition to planning for instructional improvement, mentors and peer coaches perceived that supporting development of individual teaching styles, managing instructional programs, assisting teachers in evaluating instructional effectiveness, promoting instruction by establishing supportive routines, and removing obstacles were relevant skills for successful job performance.

Personal Development

Mentors and peer coaches recognize and reflect upon their personal and professional beliefs, abilities, and actions. Statements of knowledge, attitudes, and skills in this dimension were overwhelmingly endorsed as relevant to the effective performance of the job of mentors and peer coaches. Being self-directed, modeling ethical behavior, and participating in professional meetings were perceived as most important, according to mean ratings by mentor teachers and peer coaches.

The results of the second survey also indicated that mentors and peer coaches strongly agree that a knowledge of one's self and one's own theory of education, as well as knowledge of how self-image influences what happens in situations, are important. In addition, the possession of a broad range of experiences, a knowledge of one's own philosophy of schooling, and knowledge of how one's personal history influences current behavior are vital.

Mentors and peer coaches believe that it is important to respect the dignity of the classroom teacher, to possess a positive view of self, to accept individual differences, and to view supervision as a means to enhancing teaching. Along with a commitment to ethical principles and a professional orientation (Showers, 1984), they report that it is also essential to have a sense of humor. Other key attitudes include being reflective on issues of practice, a willingness to exert leadership, feeling secure in uncertain situations, and questioning established understandings, routines, and practices.

Recognizing when to lead and when to follow, staying current with professional literature (Benningfield et al., 1984), practicing continuous self-improvement for professional growth (Munro and Elliot, 1987), and identifying what can and cannot be realistically accomplished are essential skills, according to the mentors and peer coaches whom we surveyed. Other skills strongly agreed upon as relevant to effectiveness were accepting responsibility (Kwiat, 1988), behaving in a manner that projects credibility, using power and authority wisely, and serving as a role model for others (Gehrke and Kay, 1984). Mentors and peer coaches also believed that they should draw on intuition to inform practice and employ self-preservation skills.

DISCUSSION

Mentor teachers and peer coaches viewed all twelve of the dimensions of supervisory practice as important to their jobs. Mentor teachers, in fact, reported that the twelve dimensions should be more important to their jobs than is currently the case. Staff development, communication, service to teachers, observation and conferencing, instructional program, and personal development are the six dimensions that seem to be most relevant to the effective performance of both positions.

These findings suggest that many of the responsibilities of mentor teachers and peer coaches, as well as the elements of their jobs that contribute to effectiveness, fall within the realm of supervision. It may be that the emergence of these positions in recent years reflects a trend toward specialization of supervisory functions. That is to say, while mentors and peer coaches look after the supervisory needs of individual classroom teachers, principals and central office supervisors will be able to direct their efforts to schoolwide and districtwide needs including curriculum, problem solving and decision making, planning and change, research and program evaluation, organizing and motivating, and community relations. Such specialization of function may improve the overall delivery of supervisory services to teachers.

As peer assistance programs are implemented by school districts and states, these dimensions and the knowledge, attitudes, and skills that they comprise may be useful for planning training programs for mentor teachers and peer coaches, as well as for defining job responsibilities. Colleges and universities might also use these dimensions to guide the content and directions of their preparation programs. Finally, mentor teachers and peer coaches may use them for assessing and planning their own professional development.

REFERENCES

Alfonso, R. J. 1977. "Will Peer Supervision Work?" *Educational Leadership*, 34(8): 594–601.

Alfonso, R. J. and L. Goldsberry. 1982. "Colleagueship in Supervision," in *Supervision in Teaching*, T. J. Sergiovanni, ed., Alexandria, VA: Association for Supervision and Curriculum Development, pp. 90–107.

Benningfield, M., T. Brooks, D. E. Kapel, J. Liedke, S. Mour and B. L. Whitford. 1984. *A Proposal to Establish Demonstration Schools and the Identification, Training and Utilization of Master/Mentor and Master Teacher: A Joint School District and University of Louisville Project.* ERIC Document Reproduction Service No. ED 241 465. Louisville, KY: Louisville University.

Carr, L. "The Importance of Twelve Dimensions of Supervisory Practice Derived from Educational Literature as Perceived by Selected Mentor Teachers and Peer Coaches," unpublished doctoral dissertation, University of Georgia, 1990.

Clarke, C. and J. A. Richardson. "Peer Clinical Supervision: A Collegial Approach," paper presented at the Annual Conference of the National Council of States on Inservice Education, Nashville, TN, November, 1986.

Compton, R. S. 1979. "The Beginning High School Teacher . . . Apprentice or Professional?" *American Secondary Education*, 9(3):23–29.

Egan, J. B. 1985. "A Descriptive Study of Classroom Teachers' Mentor-Protege Roles and Relationships," doctoral dissertation, Syracuse University, *Dissertation Abstracts International*, 47:1696A.

Ellis, E. C., J. T. Smith and W. H. Abbott, Jr. 1979. "Peer Observation: A Means of Supervisory Acceptance," *Educational Leadership*, 36(March):423–426.

Fagan, M. M. and G. Walter. 1982. "Mentoring among Teachers," *Journal of Educational Research*, 76(2):113–117.

Gehrke, N. and R. R. Kay. 1984. "The Socialization of Beginning Teachers through Mentor-Protege Relationships," *Journal of Teacher Education*, 35(3):21–24.

Glickman, C. D. 1985. *Supervision of Instruction: A Developmental Approach.* Boston: Allyn and Bacon, Inc.

Godley, L. B., D. R. Wilson and B. J. Klug. 1986–1987. "The Teacher Consultant Role: Impact on the Profession," *Action in Teacher Education*, 8(4):65–73.

Hawk, P. 1986–1987. "Beginning Teacher Programs: Benefits for the Experienced Educator," *Action in Teacher Education*, 8(4):59–63.

Howey, K.. 1988. "Mentor-Teachers as Inquiring Professionals," *Theory into Practice*, 27(3):209–213.

Huffman, G. and S. Leak. 1986. "Beginning Teachers' Perceptions of Mentors," *Journal of Teacher Education*, 37(1):22–25.

Huling-Austin, L. "A Synthesis of Research on Teacher Induction Programs and Practices," paper presented at the annual meeting of the American Educational Research Association, New Orleans, LA, April, 1988.

Huling-Austin, L. and S. C. Murphy. 1987. *Assessing the Impact of Teacher Induction Programs: Implications for Program Development.* ERIC Document Reproduction Number ED 283 779. Austin, TX: University of Texas.

Irvine, J. J. 1985. "The Master Teacher as Mentor: Role Perceptions of Beginning and Master Teachers," *Education*, 106(2):123–130.

Johnston, J. M. and T. L. James. "Leadership and Cooperation through Mentoring: Rethinking Roles in Teacher Education," paper presented at the Association of Teacher Education Summer Workshop, Flagstaff, AZ, 1986.

Joyce, B. R. and B. Showers. 1982. "The Coaching of Teaching," *Educational Leadership*, 40(1):7–10.

Krupp, J. A. 1987. "Mentor and Protege Perceptions of Mentoring Relationships in an Elementary and Secondary School," *International Journal of Mentoring*, 1(1):35–40.

Kwiat, J. "A Peer Coaching Model for Teachers of Limited English Proficient Students," a paper presented at the annual meeting of the American Educational Research Association, New Orleans, LA, April, 1988.

Lyman, L. and M. Morehead. 1987. "Peer Coaching: Strategies and Concerns," *Thrust*, 17(3):8–9.

McFaul, S. A. and J. M. Cooper. 1983. "Peer Clinical Supervision in an Urban Elementary School," *Journal of Teacher Education*, 34(5):34–38.

Munro, P. and J. Elliott. 1987. "Instructional Growth through Peer Coaching," *Journal of Staff Development*, 8(1):25–28.

Neagley, R. L. and N. D. Evans. 1980. *Handbook for Effective Supervision of Instruction, Third Edition*. Englewood Cliffs, NJ: Prentice Hall.

Odell, S. J. 1986. "Induction Support of New Teachers: A Functional Approach," *Journal of Teacher Education*, 37(1):26–29.

Pajak, E. 1989. "Identification of Supervisory Proficiencies Project," final report, University of Georgia. Alexandria, VA: Association for Supervision and Curriculum Development.

Showers, B. 1984. "Peer Coaching: A Strategy for Facilitating Transfer of Training," a Center for Educational Policy and Management R & D Report. Eugene, OR: University of Oregon Center for Educational Policy and Management.

Sparks, G. M. 1986. "The Effectiveness of Alternative Training Activities in Changing Teaching Practices," *American Educational Research Journal*, 23(2):217–225.

Sparks, G. M. and S. Bruder. 1987. "Before and After Peer Coaching," *Educational Leadership*, 45(3):54–57.

Sultana, Q. and E. Leung. "Evaluation of Resource Teachers: Kentucky Beginning Teacher Internship Program," paper presented at the annual meeting of Mid-South Educational Research Association, Memphis, TN, November, 1986.

Taylor, S. E. 1986. "Mentors: Who Are They and What Are They Doing?" *Thrust*, 15(6):39–41.

Taylor, S. E. 1987. "The California Mentor Teacher Program: A Preliminary Evaluation of One District's Program," *International Journal of Mentoring*, 1(1):27–34.

Wade, R. K. 1984–1985. "What Makes a Difference in Inservice Teacher Education?: A Meta-Analysis of Research," *Educational Leadership*, 42(4):48–54.

Wagner, L. 1985. "Ambiguities and Possibilities in California's Mentor Teacher Program," *Educational Leadership*, 43(3):23–29.

Winger, M. and C. Desrochers. 1989. "Designing a Districtwide Peer Coaching Program," *Thrust*, 18(5):48–50.

JOHN J. HUNT

18

Peer Coaching for Supervisors and Administrators

AN INVIGORATING OUTLOOK

Because of its potential, a serious investigation of the application of the clinical supervision "ob cycle" within an administrative organization ought first to begin with a few words about the supervision of administrators by administrators. Researchers, corporate CEO's, administrators, and many other leaders, both United States and foreign, attest eloquently and frequently to the proven reality that administrators who perceive the supervisory role as an "invigorative" opportunity experience greater career success — greater, that is, than administrators who perceive the supervisory role as a "preventative" necessity.

The difference is important, and an overly broad example can help to illustrate it. The difference between an invigorative and preventative outlook toward supervision is very much like the difference between the perceptions of the loving parents of a teenager and the perceptions of a prison guard. Both want to avoid having bad things happen to their respective wards, but they have very different motivations. The parents want the youth to grow, develop, and reach his/her potential. At the same time, the parents are wary of the difficulties that a teenager can face while transiting the shoals of inexperience.

Hence, the parents view the parenting role as an opportunity to invigorate the youngster. They are wary at all times, however, of the hazards around which the youngster must be steered. Much of the usual parent-adolescent conflict derives from the youngster's desire to move ahead, into more of adulthood, faster than the parents perceive to be appropriate.

The prison guard, on the other hand, wants to prevent his wards from "trying" anything. He is wary at all times of the hazards into which his wards might conspire to drag him. Hence, the guard rightly perceives the need to routinize absolutely every aspect of his wards' existence, the slightest deviation being easily recognized and "corrected." Much of the conflict among prison philosophies derives from the inherent conflict between the certainties of uniformity and the rehabilitative growth prospects of individuality.

MANAGEMENT LINKAGES

Researchers into organizational triumphs and disasters consistently cite the successes as deriving from management supervision that stimulates growth, while the organizational failures derive from management supervision that insists upon precise and pervasive uniformity. The morale-siphoning feature of the supervision of management consists of the fallacy—both arrogant and dangerous—that one can climb up by assuring conformity below. In fact, one rides up in an organization on the wave of creativity from below. The ob cycle, therefore, has a purpose. Through its careful use with subordinates, a supervisor can teach and legitimize organizational creativity, thereby heightening the crest of his/her own wave.

In educational administration, there are certain organizational linkages that are absolutely essential. Promoting such essential linkages within a management structure is not a concept unique to educational organizations. An anecdote usually ascribed to the founder of the Marriott organization is especially instructive and bluntly to the point.

Mr. Marriott, it is said, had a habit of reminding his corporate managers of the essential linkage between him, as the CEO, and the on-site hotel manager. All others in between, all of corporate management in other words, is "overhead," he would remind them. He, as the CEO and connection to capital, and the local manager, as the connection to service and revenue, together created profits. Corporate management only consumed revenue and capital. Hence, "corporate" was, essentially, expendable.

The local on-site managers were said absolutely to love hearing Mr. Marriott say this. The CEO was not only recognizing the importance of the hotel manager but he was also recognizing the natural tendency of corporate management to want to reduce the perceived importance of the local manager and enlarge their own importance. Corporate management was being reminded that their role was supposed to be service to the linkage which generated the profits.

Much the same condition exists in educational administration. The essential management linkage is between the CEO—the superintendent, as the connection to the public's purse—and the on-site manager—the principal, as the connection to service. All others in between are overhead. Their role is supposed to be service to the essential linkage.

As in other organizations, it is not unusual to expect that central administration, the educational equivalent of corporate management, will act to insert itself in between. For the superintendent, the ob cycle can serve as the statement about the essentiality of the superintendent-principal linkage.

USES OF THE OB CYCLE IN THE SUPERINTENDENCY

It was lessons such as Mr. Marriott's which taught me, as a superintendent, to use a slightly modified ob cycle with school principals. Regardless of the size of the school district, 5,000 students or 50,000 students, as the superintendent I always conducted day-long observations of school principals.

These observations began as scheduled events, but the principals suggested they become unannounced. They contrasted the personal potential of a full day of the superintendent's individual attention to the irresistible temptation to script a scheduled visit into a schoolwide "circus," as some called it. The school population seemed to assume the entire school was under scrutiny instead of the principal.

Good principals are, I have learned, innately canny. After the first few survived an unannounced day and began to sense from others the view that a "red badge of courage" had somehow been earned, the question of continuing unannounced visits was settled.

Was it difficult? Of course it was difficult, but essentials oftentimes are difficult. District administration can always find important reasons to occupy the superintendent's time centrally. This is to be expected of them, since in order for district management to insert itself into the essential linkage, communications and distance between superintendent and principal should in their view be lengthened. Let me hasten to repeat, this central management attitude derives not from devious motive, but from natural organizational provincialism.

Corporate management, in all organizations, is the creator and keeper of routines. Routine, in the name of efficiency, is central management's *raison d'etre*. It is therefore necessary to central management that principal behavior be routinized. Out-of-routine behaviors by principals must naturally be identified quickly and assigned negative consequences. Thus, before long, if the CEO is not resourceful, his/her own central creation will signal that the desired principal behavior, the behavior that would lead the principal to promotions, is adherence to routine. Creative and, by definition, atypical behaviors that may yield new solutions will be discouraged. Subtly an organization can begin to reward the "warden mentality" and sow its own self-destruction.

The culprit at the root of such a problem can only be the superintendent. As superintendents and other chief executive officers soon learn, others in the organization constantly scrutinize "the boss." What appears to be important to the boss will, very quickly, become important to the organization. If the boss treasures routinization, routines will sprout like weeds. Therefore, it is up to the superintendent to introduce activities that will guard against the strangulation that follows excessive routine.

The ob cycle counteracts what might well be a natural organizational tendency to insulate and separate the essential educational management linkage between the superintendent and the principal. In addition to counteracting this organizational tendency, there is the need to counteract the natural human tendency to shield one's weaknesses from superiors. The cycle, applied horizontally across the organization, can be quite helpful in this regard as well.

A principal, working diligently within the building, will inevitably encounter a new problem. To whom can that principal turn within an hierarchical structure for advice and assistance without risking "exposure?" What provision is made, within the formal organizational structure, to help such a principal? Too often, this sort of assistance can be found only within the informal organizational structure. The principal can turn to another principal, a friend perhaps. But seeking assistance upwardly within the formal structure can be perceived by the principal as risky. In doing so, the principal risks loss of face. As a consequence, it is possible that a principal, reluctant to seek assistance, will dig an ever-enlarging hole which, by the time it becomes evident, requires a steam shovel for assistance.

New principals, with a minimal number of informal connections, with a dedication to keeping all shortcomings and inexperience hidden, are prime candidates for this sort of hole-digging behavior. When the superintendent begins to observe these principals individually, their shortcomings will become evident. There must be a "safe" source to which the principal can be referred for help.

To provide each principal with a safe source for personal assistance, principals in my school districts were divided into "collegial assistance teams" of five principals each. The most senior principals were each assigned to "shepherd" a team. Other team membership was collegial and arranged among the principals as they wished, with the provision that each of the most junior principals served one to a team. The collegial assistance teams were authorized to meet at the call of the senior principal as requested by any member, or at least once each month.

To assure the collegiality of these teams, the senior member was requested to guarantee that no topical records were kept, but one of the five was the "observed" person at each meeting. The senior principal confirmed to the superintendent, monthly, simply that his/her collegial assistance team had met.

These two uses of the ob cycle proved invigorating to all of us. The vertical use, between the superintendent and the principal, certainly invigorated this superintendent and, more importantly, strengthened the requisite linkage. The horizontal use, among principals, provided an organizationally legitimate source for peer assistance and stemmed the career-long tendency toward the self-containment that seems to reside within the position. Structurally at least, both of these applications of the ob cycle tended to reduce the preventative "warden" motivations that may lurk within us all.

Was it 100 percent successful? Of course not. If it were 50 percent effective, then it would be possible to conclude that the effectiveness of administrator-to-administrator supervision had doubled.

Were there unanticipated consequences? Most assuredly.

EXTENSIONS

One of the delightful characteristics of the ob cycle is its tendency, over time, to break out in epidemic proportions. With principals being observed by the superintendent and with principals being observed by colleagues, the suggestion soon followed that "What's good for the goose. . . ." Hence, the ob cycle came into existence for the superintendent. It was decided that, since one of the major tasks of a superintendent was to "teach" in school board meetings, an ob cycle focusing on his/her behavior in these meetings would be of real value.

Logistics for the observation of the CEO proved no more of an obstacle than the logistics related to observation of principals, except perhaps, for duration. It became necessary for the observation of the superintendent at work at a board meeting to stretch over the preparatory weeks preceding the board meeting in which the superintendent was being observed. The pre-observation meeting of the superintendent and the observation team (containing principals and teachers) had to occur at the inception of an item that would appear weeks later before the board. The observation had to include preliminary committee meetings as well as the actual board meeting. Afterwards the ob team conducted its own analysis and strategy session and then met with the superintendent at the superintendent's home for the post-observation conference session. To this superintendent, these "no holds barred" conference sessions were not merely invigorating, they were exhilarating.

In more than a few cases, principals, even those with extensive longevity, remarked that they had never before really understood how a superintendent worked to contribute to the welfare of the children. More than a few of the observing principals must have concluded they themselves could do the job better, because at this writing, some years later, several of them are superintendents.

Are the ob cycle logistics cumbersome? Yes, always. But, they are certainly tolerable, considering the benefit potential.

The detailed preparations for administrative use of the ob cycle are no more encumbering than they are for the cycle's use at the teaching level. With the assistance of a first-rate secretary it is possible for a superintendent's calendar to have one work day out of about five randomly, mysteriously, and covertly appear empty of encumbrances.

In my particular case, information about the assignment often was our last mutual communique of the previous workday, and was accompanied by a map and a warning not to appear at the central office at all but to go the next morning directly to the principal's building. Hence, because school starting times varied as much as an hour between schools so as to accommodate multiple bus usage, the superintendent could find himself at the school in advance of the staff, faculty, and principal. This only added to the folklore about the CEO and generated an atmosphere of simpatico between staff and principal.

Years of association with principals have led me to the conclusion that they are optimists at the very root. One can suppose that nothing challenges an optimistic outlook quite so much as arriving at one's school to see the superintendent there at the door, waiting. On rare occasions, to add to the folklore and because the principal's home was on the route to the school, this superintendent did meet a principal or two as she/he emerged from home.

The pre-observation session between the principal and the superintendent was usually an over-coffee discussion in the principal's office. The question at hand was the principal's calendar for the day, background on events within it, and the principal's definition of what was intended to be accomplished in each situation.

If an observation of a teaching event was not already planned into the principal's day, a request was made that at least one teacher observation be inserted into the day's schedule. The teacher was asked if we could observe. The purpose was explained: the intent was to observe the principal, not the teacher. The purpose was to see what the principal saw, and the measure to which the principal and the superintendent were in agreement about the critical events that occurred between the teacher and the students.

One other modification of the day was always examined. The presence of the superintendent as an observer in some few events could be counterproductive, in a few cases illegal, and sometimes overly confusing. It was the responsibility of the superintendent to ferret out these possible problem events during the pre-observation session and indicate that he would absent himself, spending the time talking with building staff. An example of an event from which the superintendent had to be absent would be the informal first step in a grievance when the contract called for the initial participation of the superintendent at a much later stage in the procedure.

After the completion of the day, a time and a place would be set aside for the superintendent so he could prepare in a strategy session for the subsequent conference session. The principal would be expected to take sufficient notes in the end-of-the-day conference session so as to write it up formally and forward it to the superintendent in the week ahead. If, upon reading the written summary, the superintendent agreed that it contained a clear and accurate summary of the topics discussed, then it was incumbent upon the superintendent to attach his written agreement to the principal's summary so that it could become a part of the principal's yearly record. The primary purpose of the written portion was to reinforce the events and recommendations of the day into the principal's mind.

Toward the end of the pre-observation session the principal was reminded to introduce what would be an abnormally quiet and passive superintendent to people with whom the principal was conversing during the day, and to explain that the superintendent was there observing the principal, not the person with whom the principal was conversing. Principals came to enjoy making this type of introduction. There seemed to be the humorous implication within many of the introductions that the superintendent could be ignored overtly, for the day.

Note taking throughout the day became an important matter. The principal's effectiveness within a building over the course of a full year cannot be impaired by the observation event. A clipboard-carrying superintendent following the principal around all day could subtract from the principal's "face." It was found that yellow-pad paper folded accordion-style so that it could fit easily into an inside jacket pocket would suffice. Inevitably, there were times within the observation when the superintendent could, unobtrusively, remove the folded pieces of paper and write notations. For me, it was found best to record matters chronologically, moving through the notepaper's numbered folds.

After observing a few principals I noticed a consistent interest in the final disposition of the observer's notes at the end of the conference session. The interest could have stemmed from a curiosity about how the observer could have amassed so many precise quotes and facts from the day on what appeared to be so little paper so seldom seen during the day. Each principal may have been interested in developing the technique personally.

Since the closing remarks of the conference were related to a reminder that the principal had to write up and submit the contents of the conference, the interest in the observer's notes may have stemmed from the principal's need to have better notes than he/she actually took during the conference. Over time, principals began to record the conference event, with permission.

On the outside chance that the principal was worried that the supervisor's notes end up in his/her personnel file, the practice was adopted of giving these notes to the principal at the end of the day. The principal was reminded, of course, not to destroy the notes until after agreement was received back that the submitted writeup of the conference accurately summarized its contents.

The observed day in the life of the building was never completely "normal," of course. One could argue that an observed event is never normal, that the very act of observing an event actually changes the event, be it teaching or administering. But the day was always instructive, and over such an extended period of time in a school full of enlivening children, the day always included events that revealed the true instincts of the principal.

On some occasions, though seldom on the first visit, I would take a central office administrator with me. It is possible, when working in central offices, to lose sight of the organization's fundamental purpose. A day at the scene of service delivery can be quite therapeutic. I will give one such occasion here as an example.

One particular elementary principal had become quite notorious within the central administration for never submitting a required report on time. To her second observation of the year I took with me the central office person to whom a majority of such reports usually came due.

In the course of the morning it became quite clear to both of us why the paperwork was always late. The principal was seldom in the office to do the work, spending instead nearly all the time in the building with the teachers and the children.

Children can hardly be expected to conspire in a ruse. If visits from the principal are regular and normal, the children's behavior with the principal will reflect that fact. If the principal is out in the building as an attempt to impress the day's observers, the children, by their spontaneous behavior, will betray the lie. The children were talking with the principal quite naturally, sharing continuing life episodes important to each. The principal easily referenced the earlier applicable episodes and celebrated the accomplishment being shared. Teachers were equally comfortable with the principal's presence, and even participation in the classroom. In some classrooms, there were obvious continuing activities that involved the principal in a role supportive to the teacher and to the students. The principal, the teachers, the students, and the numerous parents simply knew each other too well for what we were observing to have been a scenario created for the observers' benefit. The children were comfortable with adults around. Adults in the school, the children seemed to assume, were all there to participate with them in their very important business of learning.

At the end of the day, the central administrator and I excused ourselves for our analysis and strategy session in preparation for the conference session with the principal. The central administrator, who before that day had been intolerant of this particular principal and a major contributor to the principal's negative reputation developing through the informal central administration network, was insistent upon offering a judgment about the principal. This is something quite inadmissible in the first ten minutes of an analysis and strategy session in which data are the critical ingredients.

The young children of this administrator, it was announced, would be attending this principal's school when they reached school age. So impressed was the administrator with what had been seen that an offer was made to send support out from the central office to the building in advance of report deadlines to help in the preparation. The idea grew in the administrator's mind, and soon it was being examined as a pattern of rolling supportive visits to each school to help by working with building staff in report-preparation skills, perhaps even "retrofitting" some of the report requirements to better fit the school building's life cycle.

On another occasion, in a different district, the value of the collegial assistance team was perhaps best demonstrated in the midst of an observation conducted upon a second year principal of an outlying high school. While working at the desk during the day, the principal described an elaborate plan being concocted, alone, to stop the upward trend of grades on final exams in the schools. Since many of the teachers and students were from the surrounding community, the principal had come to the conclusion that the teachers were inflating grades, in a neighborly fashion of goodwill.

In the conference session, the suggestion was made, forcefully, that the principal first discuss the underlying perception with the secondary school principals on that person's collegial assistance team. Later events showed that this suggestion was followed.

By June of that year the faculty from the various departments of each of the high schools represented on that particular collegial assistance team had gotten together and written common exams for common courses. They had arranged "blind" grading schemes among all of the teachers. Afterwards the papers were regrouped into schools and the results compared. The results demonstrated that the schools were grading similarly for similar student work, and the faculty of this particular principal's school were not at all inflating grades.

Had that young high school principal not had a collegial assistance team on which to rely, and had he sprung, full-blown, a Quixotic plan upon his faculty and community, all blossoming support could have evaporated. Had the superintendent tried, himself, to mandate a plan of common final exams for common courses among high schools, the superintendent might well have been tarred, feathered, and run out of town in short order. But when the idea was locally generated, locally implemented—in short, locally owned—it worked.

Perhaps other CEO's could have accomplished such high school cooperation by issuing an edict. In my case, I benefited from the ob cycle and collegial assistance teams as the medium through which the message could be discovered and embraced with participant ownership. That particular principal and this particular superintendent simply rode the crest of the creative energy.

GERALD D. SKOOG

19

Peer Coaching among University Professors: A Personal Analysis and Commentary

Professors are characterized by diversity in background and interest. Yet they share the common and primary goal of providing instruction that will meet the needs of students and society. Despite increased collegiality in research projects, professors tend to work alone in classrooms and often use inappropriate methods as they teach. Faculty members seldom discuss and critique teaching episodes at the peer level. As a result, they seldom receive concrete feedback about a particular class or even a semester's work. All the same, most professors generally conclude that their teaching has been adequate, appropriate, and understood by the students. However, the perceptions of students and the general public provide more critical and even damning views of the caliber of instruction provided in higher education. A recent Holmes Group Report, in recognizing the problematical status of teacher education, concluded:

> Higher education on the whole is under attack for the poor quality of its teaching. It should be possible to differentiate the teacher education faculty from arts and sciences faculty through their higher quality of teaching. Often, this is not apparent in our institutions. (Holmes Group Board, p. 5)

In an organized effort begun in 1973–74 to improve instruction at the university level and to learn about the improvement process, faculty members in the College of Education at Texas Tech University combined their knowledge and skills in a collegial process using primarily the peer observation model of supervision (Cogan, 1973; Goldhammer et al., 1980). This program had the goals of providing a structure for professional growth, establishing more extensive and productive collegial relationships, and improving instruction at the university level (Skoog and Denham, 1979; Skoog, 1980). As one offshoot of this program, in 1979 ten Texas colleges and universities collaborated through the Texas Teacher Corps Network to form the Collegial Assistance Project which was organized to provide professors with training in the peer observation cycle model of clinical supervision, to generate knowledge about university teaching, and to study the change process in higher education.

In recognition of the need to improve instruction in higher education, this chapter provides descriptive and analytical commentary about the nature and success of these two programs.

HISTORICAL OVERVIEW

When Robert H. Anderson became Dean of the College of Education at Texas Tech University (TTU) in 1973, he established faculty development as a high priority. The peer observation model of clinical supervision became an important vehicle for pursuing this priority. Training sessions and peer observation cycles were led by Dean Anderson and other faculty members in classrooms in the college, elsewhere in the university, and in the public schools. Eventually, a policy was developed mandating that all faculty members in the College of Education (COE) have a teaching session or some other activity (chairing a meeting, advising, counseling, etc.) critiqued by a team using the peer observation model of clinical supervision or an approved alternative at least two times a semester in order to be eligible for merit salary increases and, if appropriate, tenure and promotion.

As can be expected, the policy resulted in supporters, antagonists, and guerrillas who went through the motions without articulating a position. The policy was eventually modified so that only one critique per semester was required. The policy still existed in 1990, but with changing leadership and a different agenda, the policy has been largely ignored since the mid 1980s. Today, an occasional peer observation team meets, but the intensity of the interaction and the significance of data collected seems inconsequential. Despite its status today, the program had, and continues to have, a positive impact on the professional lives of many faculty members.

THE POSITIVE IMPACT OF
THE PEER OBSERVATION PROGRAM

During the early phases of the peer observation program at TTU, there was intense dialogue, self-analysis, and increased collegiality among members in many peer observation teams. Faculty members interested in increasing their teaching effectiveness had access to expert assistance and extensive data about teaching that were collected and analyzed. One faculty member commented wryly that he was suffering from "overkill" inasmuch as he had too much data and feedback to consider. Ownership of common and unique teaching problems was acknowledged more openly. Also, professors who excelled as teachers received peer recognition and acknowledgement as they were observed and as they provided assistance to others on their teams. Instruments were designed to analyze certain problems and collect needed data.

Alternatives to the peer observation cycle were developed and used to critique teaching and, as a result, there was a growing variety of strategies and resources available to individuals seeking feedback about instructional matters. Considerable discussion centered on what kinds of teaching behavior were most productive in achieving certain goals or outcomes. During peer observation cycles, students would sometimes be questioned about areas of concern identified by the professor being observed. Faculty behavior in chairing meetings, providing advisement, and in assuming other professorial roles was observed and critiqued. There was much discussion on how to make conferences and feedback more effective. Attention was given to how "tough" (i.e., sensitive or potentially embarrassing) messages should be delivered. There was concern that self-esteem and confidence could be eroded easily by the presence of two or three colleagues relaying data with negative overtones in an insensitive manner.

Undergraduate and graduate students were provided role models of professors who regularly had their teaching observed and critiqued by peers. Doctoral students were socialized in a nontraditional academic setting as they worked in a collegial relationship with other professors in observing and critiquing the teaching of senior professors. Student teachers sometimes were critiqued by a peer observation team four times a semester. K–12 teachers and other student teachers serving on these teams had opportunities to work with professors in all phases of the process.

Overall, there was considerable dialogue in the COE about teaching, as the doors of previously private classrooms were opened and as faculty members observed and critiqued one another. As a result, new kinds of relationships formed between selected faculty members, students, and administrators. Robert H. Anderson, who provided the leadership, support, and initial training for the project, claimed that the professors in TTU's College of Education "had more knowledge about what can happen in the analysis of instruction than any other group of education professors in the world" (ASCD, 1985, p. 8). To critics of the program within the college, this quote represented hyperbole. However, because of the low level of such activity in other colleges of education and the genuine involvement of a large corps of TTU faculty members in the coaching process, my perception is that Anderson's quote is accurate.

Discussions concerned with the role of peer observations and coaching in improving teaching effectiveness resulted in the development and expansion of additional efforts to improve instruction. In 1976, a program that came to be called University Level Individually Guided Education (ULIGE) was developed and implemented. Thirty-five professors and graduate students worked in teams to provide instruction for three undergraduate education courses during twelve working summer days. Professors and doctoral students from the COE worked with professors from other TTU colleges and other universities to plan and teach the three courses in a collegial manner. Peer observation cycles were a routine and daily part of the program. The following year, a COE team used the ULIGE model to teach a field-based early childhood education block of courses. Later, the COE dean and several faculty members worked with the Lubbock Independent School District to create as part of the desegregation program a K–6 magnet school that emphasized multiage grouping and team teaching. COE faculty members would work as teams one afternoon a week to provide instruction while the school's teachers would meet in their planning meetings. Again, peer observation cycles were a part of the program as TTU professors provided training for the teachers but also used the process to gain feedback about their teaching effectiveness with elementary students.

Professors also were involved in conducting clinical workshops and other inservice programs for K–12 teachers and university faculty members where team teaching, multiage grouping, and peer observation cycles were emphasized and practiced. COE professors skilled in the cycle technology worked with faculty members in other TTU colleges, in other universities, and in attendance at professional meetings in learning how to use peer observation and coaching. Individual professors who were involved in all of the aforementioned projects had extended and repeated opportunities to learn about teaching and learning.

During the most active phase of the program at TTU, the COE dean and a cadre of interested faculty members organized the Collegial Assistance Project (CAP) to pursue a training and research program among the ten Texas colleges and universities that belonged to the Texas Teacher Corps Network. Phase one of CAP involved a training and orientation conference in March, 1980 attended by thirty-nine faculty members and administrators from the ten member institutions. Later that month, two professors from each institution participated in a workshop where they observed and critiqued class sessions taught by professors in Texas Tech College of Education. Later, clinical workshops for faculty members at two Texas institutions of higher education (IHEs) were conducted. With the phasing out of the Texas Teacher Corps Network and the Deans Council, CAP lost its organizational structure. Despite positive evaluations from the clinical workshops and training funds from a foundation, momentum was lost and since no additional institutions opted for training workshops, CAP died.

Despite its shorter-than-desired existence, CAP was successful in engaging faculty members from ten institutions in focused observations, analysis, and discussion of teaching behaviors, and the development of a research plan to evaluate the process and teaching in IHEs. CAP also left behind several unanswered research questions that included the following:

(1) Does participation in peer observation cycles enhance self-supervisory skills and increase the frequency of their use by faculty members?

(2) How are collegial relationships strengthened among faculty members?

(3) What factors are involved in preparing professors to accept and use the techniques of clinical supervision? What kinds of administrative and collegial support are necessary?

(4) How are clinical supervision programs implemented, institutionalized, stabilized, and maintained in colleges and universities?

(5) What institutional norms and expectations exist that either facilitate or inhibit faculty participation in faculty development programs concerned with the improvement of teaching?

(6) What factors are involved in preparing professors to accept and use clinical supervision? What kinds of administrative and collegial support are necessary?

(7) Will professors develop contracts that invite their colleagues to critique important aspects of their teaching behavior? How can we move beyond "show and tell" sessions that involve little or no risk for the observee or the observers? Are professors willing to spend the time and energy needed to help colleagues work toward solving serious teaching problems?

(8) If a professor asks specific questions about a colleague's teaching behavior, will he/she use the same techniques or theoretical framework to critique his/her own teaching behaviors? Can professors gain insight into their own teaching patterns and problems by observing and critiquing the teaching of others?

(9) Do the teaching practices of professors of education reflect applications of educational theory and research to a greater extent than the practices of elementary and secondary school teachers?

(10) What types of professional behavior, in addition to "teaching" (i.e., being in direct instructional contact with one or more students), could profitably be observed and critiqued by colleagues?

Empirical data concerned with the peer observation programs at Texas Tech and CAP activities needed to answer these and other important research questions were not collected. However, anecdotal accounts from the activity in Texas Tech's College of Education provide partial answers to these and other questions.

PERSONAL ATTESTATION

Cross (1987), after a review of 200 articles and books concerned with the teaching effectiveness of college professors, indicated that teachers seldom are asked about what they are trying to accomplish in their own classrooms. She argued that the first step in improving undergraduate education is to attempt to find out what teachers are trying to do. An essential part of the peer observation cycle model used at TTU, and by my regular team, focused on this too-often-missing component of instructional improvement programs. Our team had lengthy discussions of what we were trying to accomplish and whether there was any evidence that desired outcomes were achieved. We worked hard to find ways to collect data to provide insight into questions about our teaching patterns and their effect.

The report *Faculty Development in a Time of Retrenchment* (1974) asserted that "the academic culture is remarkably unreflective" about teaching. Schon (1983), in arguing that research has done little to improve practice in many professions, stated that there was a need "to help professionals gain insight into their practice through an ongoing process of reflecting on what they know, articulating their intuitive thinking, and seeking feedback about the result of practice" (p. 50). In our observation team, we had many intense and lengthy discussions about how we could achieve specific outcomes. Discussion about how our courses were structured in regard to the objectives being stressed, the student assignments, the course content and activities, and how grades were determined were constructive and resulted in change. We also had lengthy discussions about the philosophy and psychology that our teaching behaviors reflected. Over time, common interests became apparent and a sharing process and relationships were shaped that still endure today. For me, the collegial bonds that have continued to exist for nearly twenty years have probably been more important than the direct assistance I received in regard to my teaching. Also, the accretion of new knowledge and the focus on growth rather than correction impacted my teaching in a positive and continuing manner.

The National Board for Professional Teaching Standards, which is currently developing standards for national certification of teachers in twenty or more fields, is operating on the assumption that teaching is context-specific in that teachers instruct particular students in particular skills or subject matter to achieve particular educational objectives. In recognizing the unique aspects of context-specific teaching, Cross (1987, p. 11) suggested that the knowledge gained and exchanged from many "situation-specific classrooms" might "give teachers more useful insight into the teaching/learning process than the search for generalizations across a 'representative sample' of students, teachers, and subject matter."

My experiences support her assertion. As a science educator and program chair of Secondary Education, I served on an observation team with a science educator in Elementary Education and two faculty members from Counseling. I learned much from observing classes in counseling and in K–6 science education, and from sharing techniques and strategies related to our specific fields. I also served on a number of other observation teams both in the College of Education and in other IHEs. As a result, I have observed and critiqued classes in entomology, foods and nutrition, history, clothing and textiles, special education, counseling, child development, teaching methods, and many classes in science grades 7–12 as a supervisor of student teachers in science. Teacher and student behavior in the counseling classes tended to be different from those in entomology classes, which were different from those in the history classes, and so on. Furthermore, there are content-specific methods that are used within a specific discipline or course. For example, the methods used to teach about human evolution may be different from those used to teach about the structure of DNA. Through these diverse and often situation-and-content-specific teaching episodes that I have observed and analyzed, my knowledge of the teaching/learning process has increased and my teaching behavior has been influenced.

Joyce et al. (1990, p. 29) argue that instrument-driven feedback that provides a "mirror" of the professional behavior exhibited does not result in much change in teacher behavior, and that "changes requiring the addition of new repertoire will require more than information about present performance." Much of the feedback I received and gave as a member of many peer observation teams was objective and provided a "mirror" of the professional behavior exhibited. I also participated in a research project as a high school biology teacher where a Flanders Analysis was used to describe and provide a detailed and descriptive "mirror" of twenty-one hours of my teaching. This was followed by involvement in another research project where several hours of my instruction in high school biology was videotaped and analyzed using an expanded version of Flanders Analysis designed to note behaviors associated with inquiry. These videotapes, plus those of other biology and social studies teachers, were viewed, analyzed, and compared in a weekly seminar.

Both of these research projects not only caused me to "look into the mirror," but also involved me in an analysis of my teaching patterns and their similarities and differences with other teachers. I also was in a setting where professional growth opportunities were present and supported. I cannot provide data or evidence of how these research projects changed specific teaching behaviors and enhanced student learning. However, there is no doubt that the data and feedback empowered me with a sense that I could control my teaching behavior and that there was a relationship between my behavior and that of the students.

Participation in peer observation cycles, both as an observer and a subject, has heightened my awareness that teachers can control their behaviors and, in turn, influence student behavior and responses. Though it is well known that teaching behavior can be controlled, many professors have never experienced success in doing so, nor have they observed in classrooms where teaching behaviors were used in a purposeful manner. Looking in a mirror may not assist or change them.

Obviously, what I have learned "looking in the mirror" and analyzing the teaching behavior of others represents a personal journey that is idiosyncratic and may not provide any significant insight to others in regard to developing programs to improve teaching effectiveness. However, it is evident to me that the trail to increased competency as a teacher is lengthy and must be characterized by continual and varying learning opportunities in a culture supportive of teaching. For a brief and exciting time in my career, I had such opportunities and a supportive microculture within my team and a niche in the College of Education. As a result, I was involved in the most intensive study of teaching and learning I have had with my colleagues in higher education during my career of over twenty years.

LIMITATIONS AND DIFFICULTIES

Unfortunately, the intensity and commitment that characterized many of the peer observation cycles that were valuable to me were not sustained as competing priorities became more compelling. Other teams and individuals, perhaps because of a low personal commitment to the process, never experienced a peer observation cycle where the analysis and discussion were conducted seriously and in depth. There were "display lectures and activities" and safe observation contracts. Important steps were eliminated or perverted. Because teaching generally has been seen as a private act that should be immune from scrutiny at the university level, many professors were reluctant to commit to a process where a serious analysis of specific teaching episodes occurred. Likewise, there was a reluctance to enter into questions regarding what should be taught. Despite these limitations, participants even in the least effective peer observation cycles had to observe and think about teaching and undoubtedly gained some insight into the teaching/learning process.

Time, the reward system, and changing institutional norms were major factors that limited involvement and lessened commitment. A complete cycle often required more than two hours. When everyone in a four-member team was observed, critiqued, and given feedback in a comprehensive and conscientious manner twice a semester, many working hours were needed. Many professors chose to use their discretionary time for personal interests or in areas that are recognized most in the reward system and where national reputations can be built. While teaching is generally recognized in the reward systems, research and publication activities are almost universally rewarded. Likewise, national reputations and opportunities to assume an endowed chair or distinguished professorship seldom result from excellence in teaching. As stated in the report "Integrity in the College Curriculum: A Report of the Academic Community," (Association of American Colleges Committee, 1985) "the enemy of good teaching is not research, but rather the spirit that says that this is the only worthy or legitimate task for faculty members" (p. 15). The report concluded that "unless the reward system in higher education measures teaching performance as well as research, all efforts to improve college teaching will be to no avail" (p. 30).

This report deplored and challenged the assumption that college professors need no preparation, no supervision, and no introduction to teaching. However, this assumption is the result of a culture that does not value teaching and accords efforts to improve teaching minimal resources and low priority. My observation team, which was made up of four associate professors who all had solid records of teaching effectiveness, was caught up in an environment of increased expectations for productivity in research and publication. As a result of the need to put our time and best thinking into research and publication, and the resulting peer pressure that grew as a result of mounting faculty opposition and cynicism toward the peer observation policy, we sometimes became involved in hurried and shallow cycles and, finally, none at all. Our team and other teams had worked hard and conscientiously in countless observation cycles, but our ability and motivation were diminished by the lack of a pedagogical culture that supported and rewarded the improvement of teaching.

Also, in the 1980s, life at Texas Tech and other universities began to change as there was a lessening of the sense of common enterprise and collegiality and "more of a sense of campus against campus, segment against segment" that resulted in "fragmentation and internecine warfare" (The Carnegie Council of Policy Studies in Higher Education, 1980, p. 116). In the 1970s, expressions of collegiality were common in the College of Education, both professionally and socially. However, faculty seminars, office visits, long auto trips together to conferences and meetings, eager participation in committee meetings, group picnics and dinners, and athletic teams gradually became less frequent in the 1980s as professors spent more time on their own agendas. Today, professors who once again have their classroom and office doors closed are being asked to collegially define a knowledge base that undergirds and permeates all programs, and then review each other's syllabi to insure that the knowledge base is emphasized. When peer coaching was being used widely and seriously in the college, we had a sense of what was occurring in each other's classrooms and a sense of collegiality that would have facilitated the completion of the aforementioned tasks. Today's fragmented and inward-turning faculty will not approach and achieve these tasks in the same manner.

ROLE OF THE PEER OBSERVATION PROGRAM IN ADMINISTRATIVE DECISIONS

The peer observation system was not intended for use in providing data for decisions about merit pay, promotions, or tenure. However, it seems likely the system did influence these inasmuch as professors observed each other and data collected often became part of official files and portfolios. Peer observation teams were required only to file a report, to verify that a cycle had been completed. No details regarding the data collected or feedback given had to be included (see excerpt six in the Appendix for an example of such a report). However, my regular team usually filed a very complete report that included a summary of the data collected, items discussed, recommendations made, and conclusions drawn. Excerpts from some of the these reports are included in the Appendix. We felt that the data and conclusions that resulted from our observations and discussion would positively influence decisions concerned with merit pay, promotion, and tenure that involved us individually. Thus, we spent the time necessary to write and file a complete report for the Office of the Dean and the program chair. The observee always had the option to modify or reject the report. I do not recall any changes or rejections occurring.

All individuals considered for tenure and/or promotion had been observed previously by one or more members of the Tenure and Promotion Committee that I served on for one year. Also, detailed reports from peer observation cycles were part of the portfolios prepared by the candidates for the committee. The program chairpersons, who were active participants in peer observation cycles, were better able to assess the strengths and weaknesses of faculty members being considered for tenure and promotion. Thus, members of that Tenure and Promotion Committee had considerable data to consider in making decisions about the teaching effectiveness of applicants for tenure and/or promotion.

In my opinion, untenured faculty members were helped and not hurt by the process. They had opportunities to receive continuous feedback about their teaching and to observe and work with senior professors. They had assistance in building a data base and a body of peer judgments that could substantiate their teaching effectiveness. They also had expert assistance available to help in identifying and eliminating weaknesses or problems that eventually could result in the denial of tenure.

CONCLUSIONS

Unfortunately, we failed to seize the opportunity to study and document if and how teaching behaviors and student learning were affected by the peer coaching at TTU. Likewise, solid data concerning faculty interaction, motivation, and interest in teaching were not collected. As a result, it is difficult on the basis of our experiences to counter the arguments of Joyce et al., (1990, p. 29-30) that "the community of practitioners of structured clinical supervision has produced little research" and "it is difficult to estimate the kinds or magnitude of changes it produces." Menges (1987, p. 91) indicates that the "effectiveness of colleagues as consultants in the teaching improvement process has yet to be validated against the criteria of student learning" but participants in programs that use colleagues as consultants "report high satisfaction, more interaction with other faculty members, increased motivation, and renewed interest in teaching." I suspect that any provost, dean, or chairperson would be pleased to identify with and support staff development programs that produce such results. My experience with peer observation and coaching support the conclusions of Menges, and I am convinced that the peer observation model of clinical supervision used at TTU can be a powerful and effective component of staff development programs in pedagogical cultures that value and support teaching and its improvement.

APPENDIX: EXCERPTS FROM SELECTED PEER OBSERVATION REPORTS

Excerpt One from an Observation and Report of a Counseling Class

(1) The pattern of interaction was for the professor to ask for someone to relate the experience they had while practicing active listening in an out-of-school setting. A student would respond and the professor, using techniques of active listening, would respond to the student. The student would then respond and the professor would use more active listening with the student or summarize the experience for the entire class and ask for someone else to relate their experiences.

(2) All students with the exception of one female were attentive.

(3) The professor's wait time after student responses was very short. The relationship between wait time and student response was discussed in the post-observation sessions.

(4) Suggestions were given to the professor on how he could obtain more student-student interaction during the session.

Excerpt Two from an Observation and Report in a Graduate Special Education Class

In this class, the pace of presentation was so fast that students often used recorders to tape the lecture. The professor wanted more interaction with the students. After collecting and analyzing data, the team suggested that the professor:

(1) Arrive at class a few minutes early for informal interaction with the students.

(2) Rather than beginning the class with a brief lecture review of the previous session, review by way of open-ended questions.

(3) Slow down the pace of presentation. Allow students more time to think, question, and comment about the presentation. Pause after rhetorical questions.

(4) Do not precede questions with a specific student's name.

(5) When responding to a student's question, have eye contact with other students also.

Excerpt Three from a Follow-Up Observation and Report of the Session in Excerpt Two

Discussion with the students in the class gleaned the following information, suggested from the first observation. One recommendation was that Dr. X arrive at class a few minutes early for informal interactions with the students. This recommendation did not prove to be feasible in that most students arrived at the last minute and Dr. X's arriving early or late did not seem to affect the opportunity for interaction. However, the class, with Dr. X, negotiated for more time during break and at the conclusion of the class. Therefore, the recommendation of providing more time for informal interaction has been successfully established. A second recommendation involved beginning the class with a review by way of open-ended questions, rather than beginning with a lecture covering new materials, has been followed and supported by students. The third recommendation the team made involved the pace of presentation. The pace of the presentation seemed slower to the observing team, but students indicated that pace had not changed significantly. They still felt very comfortable with the pace provided by Dr. X. Recommendations four and five from the previous observation asked Dr. X to consider using student's name and making eye contact. Students reported that Dr. X does, in fact, use student names appropriately and that her eye contact is very satisfactory.

The information gleaned by the observation team was shared and discussed with Dr. X, who indicated that both observations were beneficial and had resulted in professional growth and development. The observation team also felt that Dr. X was acting upon the recommendations made and was, in fact, utilizing the data in a constructive manner. The process has proved to be a positive experience for all involved.

Excerpt Four from a Team Critique of a Course Syllabus

The team developed the following questions, which were discussed with the faculty member in the post-observation conference.

(1) What is the rationale for the course schedule?

(2) Should the questions on page 2 of the syllabus be recorded in a different sequence?

(3) Should more emphasis be placed on the research and theory base of science education?

(4) What are the distinctions between the syllabi for undergraduate and graduate courses in elementary science methods?

Excerpt Five from a Report of the Observation of a Science Methods Class

Interaction patterns were dominated by student-teacher exchanges. Student-student exchanges did not occur. Wait time was less than in previous observations. Dr. Y tended to incorporate the content of the lesson in his questions and through restructure of student comments. Over one-half of the class participated by asking or answering questions during the observation.

During an interview with Dr. Y out of the classroom, the students reported the expectations and requirements of the course were reasonable and relevant. They thought the contract system was good and fair, and they liked the many facets involved. Some students expressed a need to have more explanations of the requirements for a C contract. The students reported the difficulty level of the course was appropriate for an entry-level course. They indicated the textbook was a good reference but not very useful for the day-to-day activities of the class.

The students spoke positively about how the course was organized and administered. They reported having good experiences. They indicated Dr. Y was flexible, understanding, and came to class prepared.

Excerpt Six Represents the Minimum Requirement for a Report

On March 6, 1986, we conducted a peer observation for Dr. Z. The observation took place from 6:00–6:30 P.M. The observation format was followed. Summary data were presented to Dr. Z during the post-observation meeting.

REFERENCES

Association of American Colleges Committee. 1985. "Integrity in the College Curriculum,"*Chronicle of Higher Education*, 29:12–30.

The Carnegie Council on Policy Studies in Higher Education. 1980. *Three Thousand Futures*. San Francisco: Jossey-Bass, Inc.

Cogan, M. 1973. *Clinical Supervision*. Boston: Houghton Mifflin.

Cross, K. P. 1987. "The Need for Classroom Research," in *To Improve the Academy*, J. Kurfiss, ed., Professional and Organizational Development Network in Higher Education. Stillwater, OK: New Forum Press.

Goldhammer, R., R. H. Anderson and R. Krajewski. 1980. *Clinical Supervision: Special Methods for the Supervision of Teachers*. New York: Holt, Rinehart and Winston, Inc.

The Group for Human Development in Higher Education. 1974. *Faculty Development in a Time of Retrenchment*. New Rochelle, NY: The Group for Human Development in Higher Education and Change Magazine.

1990. "Holmes Board to Develop Strategic Plan for Consortium's Future," *The Holmes Group Forum*, 4(Fall):1–5.

Joyce, B., B. Bennett and C. Rolheiser-Bennett. 1990. "The Self-Educating Teacher: Empowering Teachers through Research," in *Changing School Culture through Staff Development*, B. Joyce, ed., The 1990 ASCD Yearbook. Washington, DC: Association for Supervision and Curriculum Development.

Menges, R. 1987. "Colleagues as Catalysts for Change in Teaching," in *To Improve the Academy*, J. Kurfiss, ed., Professional and Organizational Development Network in Higher Education. Stillwater, OK: Forum Press.

1985. "Profile; Robert Anderson," *ASCD Update*, 27(2):8.

Schon, D. 1983. *The Reflective Practitioner*. New York: Basic Books.

Skoog, G. 1980. "Improving College Teaching through Peer Observation," *Journal of Teacher Education*, 31(March/April):23–25.

Skoog, G. and A. Denham. 1979. "Peer Observation Procedures for Improving the Quality of College Instruction," *Texas Tech Journal of Education*, 6(1):21–29.

20

Peer Coaching in Noneducation Settings

What is a chapter about noneducational uses of clinical supervision with its "ob cycle" doing in a book about education? An educator reading these pages may not be particularly interested in what happens in other walks of life. However, an educator reading the other chapters of this book who remains skeptical about the ob cycle may find it helpful to examine the extent of its applications outside education.

As a superintendent, when I was describing to the board and public the cycle and its planned uses, there arose from among the listeners the not unusual question, "Where else has this idea been used, and has it been successful?" Skeptics must be satisfied. Concerns about trying untried and unproven ideas may fertilize cynicism, but, in the public sector, such concerns must be allayed.

In my experience, if what's being tried is, in fact, unproven and never before attempted, then frankness will usually carry the day. "It's not been tried before and it's not been proven elsewhere; therefore, we are taking these precautions . . ." is a frank statement that can confront skepticism and enlist the support of would-be cynics.

Experience has also shown that if what's being tried is not, in fact, new and untried, then its history had better be known and accurately portrayed. Any inaccuracy about a concept fuels the skeptics and offends the cynics. When it comes to the ob cycle, experience supports the adage, "Know of what you speak, and speak it frankly."

The ob cycle is not, in fact, new, untried, or unproven, as many authors in this volume have shown. Nor is the ob cycle unique to education; it may not even be original with education. Noneducational uses identified here are not, in any way, meant to be all-inclusive. The thread connecting them is my personal experience with each.

A MILITARY EXAMPLE: FLIGHT TRAINING

As a fledgling, frightened, aspiring Marine Corps pilot, I was met every morning at the flight line by an experienced, confident pilot, my flight instructor. Over coffee we would review what had been taught in ground school the day, or week, before. My instructor would review with me that very specific portion of the schooling to which I would be introduced that day, how it would be introduced, when and how I would take over the aircraft to try the new topic myself and, thence, practice it to achieve mastery. When the instructor was satisfied that we shared an understanding of the what, how, where, and why of the topic, he would adjourn the pre-observation conference to the aircraft.

Neither the instructor, the training manual, nor the Marine Corps ever titled that pre-flight event a "pre-ob conference," but that's what it was. On most occasions the pre-flight conference included a mutually understood listing of topics previously learned, which would be reviewed and practiced during the ensuing flight. Frequently the instructor would offer me the opportunity to identify any previously introduced, perhaps even mastered, topics that I might want to practice under his watchful eye. Always I was reminded to expect, in the course of the training flight, the introduction of the unexpected by the instructor in the form of an emergency to which I was expected to respond as practiced in earlier training sessions.

The pre-ob conference included for me the opportunity to introduce topics and skills that I wanted observed and critiqued. "Bonuses" (the term sometimes used to describe extra-contractual feedback topics) were to be included. When the "contract" (i.e., the agreed-upon plan) for the ensuing flight was mutually understood and accepted, we proceeded to the observation event. Again, none of these terms were used, but in fact they accurately describe what occurred. The flight instructor and I had participated in a near classic pre-observation conference.

As the flight progressed, the instructor would introduce the new topic, demonstrate how it was done, call my attention to the changes in the performance of the aircraft as the activity unfolded, and let me ride the controls with him as he did the maneuver another time. He then talked me through it as I did it myself for the first time, watched as I repeated the activity myself, and offered his critique of my emerging skill as I practiced.

The instructor would disengage us from the new topic, have me demonstrate previously learned skills, return us to the new topic of the day, reintroduce it, talk me through it again, have me practice it again, critique me again, and persist. The length of such observation events was not open to contractual agreement, since fuel consumption and capacity had an overriding influence. If, after the instructor had said to me, "O.K., take us home," he sensed I had relaxed my vigilance in the slightest, he would introduce a bonus: an emergency with which I would be expected to cope.

The "observation" event just described was, quite obviously, tailored to the situation. It was somewhat different from what is generally understood to be the pattern experienced by teachers being supervised. Feedback was more immediate (and the instructor's language infinitely more colorful), but the similarities far outweigh the dissimilarities.

Upon landing, and sometimes even before, the instructor would begin his de-briefing. The nature of the topic dictated the often recognizable use of hands depicting aircraft attitude, etc., between two people exiting the flight line. Over coffee the instructor would review the flight, my tendencies, the idiosyncrasies of the aircraft type, the maneuver, the fine points of combinations of activities previously learned separately. He would answer all questions, comment upon bonuses, and prescribe the next steps in the learning cycle, which usually included solo flight time for more practice. This coffee event was never entitled a "post-ob conference," but in essence that's what it was—the instructor having thought through his strategy session on the way home.

Not only were the ob cycle stages carefully scripted into flight training, but so was "coaching," especially during the actual flight. I am assured that, with the exception of the introduction of videotapes and other electronic devices for use in review, the training pattern described here continues.

THE WORLD OF SALES TRAINING

As the spouse of a three-times National Salesman of the Year in three different sections of the United States for two different nationally recognized medical laboratory corporations, the opportunities have been numerous to observe the use of the ob cycle in the training of "salesmen" (the preferred terminology, viewed among them as gender neutral). Again, the wording is occupation-specific, but the cycle is indeed the same.

The use of the ob cycle in sales training appears to divide quite clearly into two versions—a classroom version and a work-with version. In the classroom version, the corporation's salesmen are gathered together at one national site for sales training, usually lasting a full week at a time.

Classroom training divides into three components. The first two components seem generally to be entitled (1) product knowledge, and (2) sales techniques. Each component contains numerous items. For example, within the sales techniques component, one is introduced to the skills related to qualifying a customer, to closing, etc. Likewise, in the other component there are techniques related, for example, to identifying the customer's existing knowledge level so as not to embarrass or offend.

The third component is a trainer-led discussion of the obstacles considered as likely to surface with customers. Ideas are solicited on techniques that might prove successful in overcoming these obstacles, and other impediments anticipated by the national sales manager and/or by the trainer. All of these matters are addressed in classrooms of the sort we would all recognize.

The salesmen then "role-play." In this activity, one of the trainees assumes the role of the customer, and another the role of the salesman. Each customer plays the role to all the salesmen individually, and each event is videotaped. Each customer is coached beforehand in the component obstacle he/she is to raise to each salesman through the series of sales events.

Afterwards, the salesmen are gathered together and the taped events are reviewed by all, along with the national sales trainer. Each then sees how he/she dealt with the various obstacles raised by the customers, and how her/his fellow salesmen addressed the same obstacle. The national sales trainer critiques all events in general terms in the joint gathering, and later critiques them more specifically in subsequent "one-on-ones" with each individual salesman.

In this process we can see the training used, not only for the introduction of new product knowledge and sales techniques, but to establish the terms of the subsequent role-played sales events: the pre-ob event for the salesmen. The contract in this situation is a mutually agreed upon list of techniques to be practiced. The observation sales event(s) are not interrupted at all, as was the case in the flight training episode. They run their course before the camera.

The post-ob strategy session seems to have been muted. In its place is a group critique of the videos. Since salesmen are known for cutting wit, this group event can become, I am told, quite rough. Perhaps, since a salesman must have a thick skin to succeed in the business, there may be a subtle purpose intertwined in this critique. It has to harden the hide, so to speak.

We see the strategy session resurfacing as pre-conference preparation by the national sales trainer for the one-on-one conference event. The conference event also provides the trainer with an opportunity to "reconstruct" any salesman feeling particularly damaged as a consequence of the group critiquing event.

The work-with events occur throughout the year in the salesman's territory, or the field. The national sales manager, the product sales manager, or even the company president—when one is the National Salesman of the Year—will call the salesman to announce that he/she will be coming out into the field to work with the salesman. The regional sales manager has as a regular assignment to work with the salesman.

These events are usually two or three days in length. The visitor goes with the salesman on his/her calls to customers and prospective customers. In the auto during the traveling time between customers, and over dinner when the day's calls are done, the salesman's techniques with each customer are reviewed and critiqued. If the visitor were the product manager, for example, the topics might tend to center around the product knowledge evidenced. None of these work-with activities appear to be unidirectional learning events. The visitor in many cases sees first hand, sometimes for the first time, the customer's actual receptivity to the product and the competition's products. The visitor is knowingly (though occasionally unknowingly) set up by the salesman for a meeting with a customer who has a problem specific to the visitor's special domain. In these cases, the event truly does become a work-with activity, and the salesman does as much post-ob conferencing as does the visitor.

In the work-with version, the formality of the cycle tends to blur as experience among the participants increases and as the mutual experience increases. If there is a decrease in either of these factors, formality resumes. Evaluation visits by the regional manager to a salesman follow the same pattern, but with mutually accepted formality. Evaluations tend to become events added at the end of the field visit, but which still maintain the familiar form of a conference.

THE WORLD OF SAILING

The next example of a noneducational use of the ob cycle moves the scenario from sales to sailing. It was a surprise to me to learn that sailing occasionally receives reference in university courses on clinical supervision. Perhaps it receives attention because of its apparent distance from the classroom setting.

In Europe, and to a lesser measure in Australia and the Pacific Rim countries, there exists a professional sport known as "singlehanded sailing" which, in those locales, rivals our auto racing in popular interest. There is, as might be expected, a consequent professional circuit of races and racers. The sport has not sparked quite the same popular interest in the United States, much to the chagrin of the international sponsors of boats, races, and racers.

Because of a childhood on the Chesapeake Bay, I have had a lifelong interest in sailing. Since this interest was not shared within my family, much of my sailing has been alone, i.e., singlehanded. The temptation to enter the premier race of the professional circuit as an American "amateur" became overwhelming some years ago.

The race in question is from Plymouth, England, across the Atlantic Ocean to Newport, Rhode Island—alone and without stops. Sponsored in Europe by the British *Observer* newspaper and titled in full as the Observer Singlehanded Trans Atlantic Race, it has become known as the OSTAR. Understandably, entry—especially of amateurs—requires substantial solo sailing at sea beforehand to prove to the sponsors that they are not admitting to their OSTAR a guaranteed casualty.

Preparations for such a race are substantial. For earlier amateurs, the race had taken as many as eighty-nine days at sea. Procedures for sustaining life at sea under all possible weather conditions, for both the boat and the sailor, are very rigorous. "How," the question arose, "can one be sure these myriad procedures will work?"

The clinical supervision ob cycle proved a source for a major portion of the answer. After developing the procedures, practicing and improving them alone, an observation team of experienced sailors was assembled to critique the activities. Each request for help went to a sailor who, I am certain, was much better at the sport than I was. Requests were answered in the affirmative immediately. It took some shoreline work to reach a mutual understanding of the cycle's stages before we began. Sailors, I learned, do not come naturally to restrained, passive observation of a fellow sailor with problems, especially when they are all on the same boat.

Finally, however, on an ideally cold, blustery East Coast morning, with five knowledgeable sailors aboard my small boat (each with a clipboard in hand for notes), I moved my boat away from the dock and out into the open Atlantic. The sequence of procedures I would go through had been part of the pre-ob contract. Bonuses, in the form of emergencies, could be introduced at any time. Discussions, if any, were to be between me and the ob team chairman.

For fourteen hours I worked nonstop, setting and resetting sails for all the different possible winds and wind directions, hauling equipment to/from damage sites on the boat, eating, sleeping, cleaning, navigating, repairing, responding to multiple emergencies thrown at me by the ob team. ("They always come in three's," was all the ob team chairman would say.)

For fourteen hours my ob team worked equally as hard, taking copious notes, discussing observations among themselves out of my earshot, comparing, inspecting, and following me around—always with long serious faces. After returning the boat to shore I went below to an exhausted sleep. My ob team went off to prepare for the next day's conference aboard.

Bright and early the next day we began. Better ideas were proffered, implications were studied, third and fourth level consequences yielded to relentless attack. By late in the afternoon, every procedure and every event of the previous day had been examined fully. Afterwards, as we sat about together reviewing our work in the "post-mortem" stage, one of the observers voiced his opinion. "Never," he said, and his team members were quick to agree, "have I learned so much sailing from five others. Don't take me wrong," he continued, "but most especially from my four other team members."

As a consequence of this coaching experience preparatory to the OSTAR I found myself "ob-ing" my activities throughout the subsequent forty-four days at sea. Perhaps this self-observation was merely a delightful mental diversion during the trip. I suspect it was more. I suspect it was an internalization of the process.

This internalization held me in good stead throughout the race, and again when I repeated the competition four years later. Before undertaking an activity, reducing sail in the face of a building wind, for example, my mind quickly reviewed the entire activity. The equipment needed, the sequence to follow, the pitfalls to be avoided—all of these factors passed through my mind in review before any execution was undertaken. My mind required only seconds to do alone what might have taken many minutes to do with others.

A portion of my mind seemed to dedicate itself to recording and, probably because of the flight training experience, critiquing the execution of the activity while underway. After the activity was completed and there was a moment to stop and assess the impact of the change, I reviewed what was done and how it could have been done better.

Besides generating a personal feeling of satisfaction if the activity had been done well, a mental file, so to speak, was created which then became the initial point of review in the pre-ob the next time the activity became necessary. In this fashion the self-coaching (if these two words are not entirely contradictory) worked to continue the improvement long after the real-life peer observation activity was history.

CONSISTENCIES OF NOTE

Among these noneducational uses of the ob cycle, there are some consistencies worth noting—the role of the expert as observer, the candor of the conference, and the internalization process. The contrast to educational uses of the peer coaching process might prove enlightening.

With regard to the severity of the critiquing, more may be at work, and at stake, than the straightforward examination of the immediate activity being observed. In education, we devote substantial attention and concern to the receptivity of the person observed. Learning theory tells us that learning can be blocked by the mind of the observed person in the presence of overly severe criticism. Instead of devoting attention to what should be learned, the mind concentrates on protecting the sensitive psyche.

Maintaining a learning environment for the learner is, indeed, an essential consideration. Comfort with the process is very necessary if the observed person is to be lured back for subsequent coaching events. However, some of the features of group dynamics may also be at work.

If the process is coated with a reputation of severity, there may be a desire on the part of the observed to "survive" the process. The desire to be identified and accepted as a member of an elite group is a strong motivational force. Under these circumstances, the concern for the observed's psyche could be revisited, especially when the process is being used with teachers.

Teaching is not a gentle activity. It requires a toughness of spirit not at all less than the toughness required in sales. Not everyone is cut out to be a salesman, and not everyone can succeed as a teacher. Both are tough occupations.

In politics, the prevailing adage is the "heat of the kitchen." Perhaps the users of the ob cycle in education might investigate uses outside of education, with a view to reexamining the potential in the individual's motivation to be identified as succeeding into membership in a group recognized as elite.

With regard to the expert as an observer, other users provide us in education with an opportunity to contemplate the implications of the phrase peer coaching. The concept of peer in the phrase peer coaching seems to have within it an expectation that the observed person plays a role in the identification and selection of the peer, or, at the least, an acceptance of the peer as worth listening to in the conference. If the observer does choose the peer, that exposes the process to the accusation that the observee selects observers who will do nothing more than pay homage to existing skills, or who may be no more skilled at the activity than the observee. If peer coaching is saddled with the reputation of being no more than a funded "mutual admiration society," then it cannot survive.

The recognized expertise of the observers works to reduce the hazard that the process becomes viewed as "the blind leading the blind." One would not likely fly with a pilot who learned his flying from other student pilots. The salesman application contains an example of how this concern is mooted. The presence and participation of the national sales trainer, a salesman selected into the position because of demonstrated skill in the occupation, seems to remove the concern that arises if there is no recognized expertise on the scene.

There is substantial cost-effectiveness to be realized within peer coaching, which makes this permutation of the original clinical supervision concept more attractive to administrators who must worry about budgets. The use of peers as observers, however, opens the process to the types of accusations described above. Perhaps the salesman example identifies for us a further permutation of the original process that would retain the cost-effectiveness inherent in the use of peers and, at the same time, assuage any concerns about "the blind leading the blind." An additional step in the peer coaching process could be added which would provide for the one associated expert to confer with the observed: a personal conference step added at the end of the peer process.

A SCHOOL DISTRICT EXAMPLE

A somewhat similar problem developed some years ago while we were proposing to our school board in a New Jersey district that they fund a training program within an experimental summer school. The training was to derive from the use of the clinical supervision model throughout the summer school.

Board members and other citizens had an honest worry that the process would result merely in in-breeding of already existing ideas and techniques. In view of the magnitude of funds we were asking from them, they had a right to want an assurance that new ideas would flourish. Those of us who were proposing the clinical supervision model that evening were such evangelists for the classic form of the model that we almost lost the entire proposal for want of a modification that would accomplish what the citizens wanted.

Fortunately, one of my assistants suggested that we lengthen the day, attach a university affiliate to the entire process, give him/her access to all events during the day, and reserve for him/her the final hour in which to present research findings related to matters raised during the day. The idea carried. On-the-spot calculations of the additional costs were amended into the proposal and the board approved it.

The university affiliate did, in fact, contribute the latest research on teaching during the summer. New ideas did flourish. A one-to-one connection between the participation of a university affiliate and the presence of new ideas is hazardous, but the example does support the contention that the classic model can be modified. Local modifications can build local support and acceptance.

INTERNALIZATION AS A GOAL

Finally, the internalization of the process may be worthy of consideration as a long-term goal. Normal people could certainly reach a point where the thinking pattern carried through the original clinical supervision process could become second nature, without having to experience the torture contained within the sailing example. If the immediate purpose of the observation process is the improvement of an existing skill level, *and the process succeeds*, then the question can be entertained: "Does further skill growth depend on the continued application of the entire process?"

When the ob cycle works, must it thereafter be continued? The answer will likely be yes, unless from the outset the process is tailored to lead to something beyond. For those who have internalized the self-analysis thinking pattern that can develop from repetitive use of the cycle, there must be something more. No doubt these people would be the first to want to return to the formal cycle from time to time, in order to hone and resharpen thinking internalized in the original dose.

The recounting of noneducational uses of the process will have served us well if it helps prompt us to think through the implications of success. Perhaps we should be asking, "Clinical supervision: *quo animo?*"

V

DEVELOPING AND
VALIDATING SYSTEMS OF
TEACHER EVALUATION

This section presents procedures and gives selected examples of developing and validating systems of teacher evaluation. The procedures addressed in this section include content validation of the concepts and indicators used in evaluation systems, developing and testing the reliability of observation instruments, norming teacher performance, and testing teacher evaluation systems for predictive validity. Additionally, procedures are outlined in this section for testing the accuracy of data interpretation and the use of observation data in working with teachers towards the improvement of instruction.

The content of this section is limited to the evaluation of teachers in classroom instruction. This limitation is imposed on the premise that teacher performance in the classroom is the second most powerful predictor of student learning. The most powerful predictor is what students know prior to entering the classroom, and that cannot be controlled, at least in most public schools (Soar, 1968; McDonald, 1976; Evertson, 1980; Stallings, 1981). Also, while the summative evaluation of teachers is mandated and is treated in this section, the major focus is on teacher evaluation for purposes of helping teachers improve instruction—formative evaluation.

Examples of the procedures set forth in this section are derived from researches conducted in the development of the Florida Performance Measurement System (FPMS), and the Teaching for Higher-Order Thinking (THOT) system. There are three chapters in this section. The first two chapters are dedicated to the selection, definition, and documentation of the content of teacher evaluation systems, with the remaining chapter explicating procedures for testing system accuracy and application in the evaluation of teachers, particularly beginning teachers.

MARY BULLERMAN
JEAN BORG
DONOVAN PETERSON

21

Research Bases for Enhancing Teaching and Learning: Essential Skills

DEVELOPING A RESEARCH-BASED TEACHER EVALUATION SYSTEM

Major concerns confronting both the educational community and the general public include job satisfaction among teachers, attracting talented young people to the profession, reports of falling test scores, and graduates who are unprepared to live in today's world. Many of these problems are attributed to present-day school systems.

The word "school" may be defined in many ways. In one context it may mean a building; in others, a program of studies, personnel (students and/or staff), or a group with a common outlook on some issue. It may also be used as a verb, meaning to teach or to educate. It is with the teaching function that we are concerned in this chapter.

In an earlier, simpler time the goals of the school were few and clear—to teach the students to read the Scripture for themselves, and to ensure that they would not become a burden to society. Most of their real learning took place apart from the school. Teacher requirements in this era included little beyond the ability to read and willingness to teach. With the increasing complexity of society in terms of ethnicity, mobility, technology, communications, etc., new goals and needs emerged for public schools. The education of teachers required more learning in more areas, and eventually led to tentative attempts to define a methodology of teaching. These methodologies originally came from the disciplines of philosophy and psychology, and later centered on subject-specific techniques. Most recently, the education of teachers has been influenced by research conducted on teacher performance. As the study of teaching progressed, the evaluation of

325

teacher performance has also progressed from ratings based upon high-inference judgments of school board members and/or school administrators using the folklore of teaching, to low-inference, observable performance based on the research on effective teaching.

For several decades, teacher evaluation has been the responsibility of administrators. They had little to guide them, and in most cases depended on their own experience, the experiences of others, or on compliance items such as appearance, punctuality, and cooperation. Purposes of evaluation were not clearly defined, except in extreme cases where blatant incompetence was unmistakably shown. Evaluation was a routine procedure written into the administrator's job description and into the teacher's contract. Administrators set their own criteria, which for lack of anything more concrete, were such high-inference matters as the popularity of the teacher with parents, the number of times help was required with discipline, and a general feeling that "I know good teaching when I see it." Teachers reacted to the process with varying degrees of interest, irritation, or indifference. The results of these evaluations tended to have a very weak (if any) relationship to measures of student learning (Medley et al., 1984).

As "accountability" began to raise its ubiquitous head in the late 1960s and early 1970s, student achievement was its immediate focus, and rightly so, for the mission of the school is the education of students, and most people still perceive achievement as the main mission of the school. It quickly became clear that, since the teacher is the second most important predictor of student achievement (the first predictor is what students know when they enter class), such achievement must depend on improvement in the quality of teaching (Soar, 1968; McDonald, 1976; Evertson, 1980; Stallings, 1981). There were simultaneous efforts to upgrade curricula and to improve teacher performance. The latter took many forms, including curriculum changes in colleges of education and emphasis on staff development in public school systems. Legislatures began to get involved, and teacher certification requirements, especially for those entering the profession, were tightened in many states.

In Florida, a set of twenty-three minimal generic competencies were identified by professional consensus. Temporary certificates, good for one year and renewable for a second year, were issued to beginning teachers. Only on the submission of documentation by the school administrator that the teacher had satisfactorily demonstrated the generic competencies could a regular teaching certificate be issued.

This legislation was to change the whole face of teacher evaluation in Florida. No longer would the traditional items, with their limited impact on students, be acceptable to teachers, to their unions, or to administrators, upon whose decisions careers and livelihoods might depend. A better method must be found to evaluate and improve teacher performance.

The legislation seemed to assume that the competencies as stated were specific enough that there could exist agreement among evaluators as to their presence or absence in the teacher's repertoire. The fact was that although attempts had been made to clarify them by listing subskills, the subskills were not explicated to a degree that would make assessment of them even minimally valid. For example, the competency "Demonstrate the ability to comprehend patterns of physical, social, and academic development in students and to counsel students concerning their needs in these areas" was broken down into subskills, of which the first was: "Demonstrate knowledge of basic principles of human growth and development." Nothing was said about how such a competency was to be demonstrated—whether by examination, written report, observation, or bibliographically. A college transcript showing credit in the subject matter could not fulfill the "demonstrate" requirement of the law. Obviously, much needed to be done to make the competencies specific, observable, and measurable. To do otherwise would establish as many standards of certification as there were administrators documenting compliance or noncompliance with the competencies. Additional work was needed before school administrators could accurately evaluate teacher competencies.

In the past twenty to thirty years a large number of studies known as process/product (what the teacher does/how it affects the student), and experimental research studies have been conducted on teacher effectiveness. These studies identify variables of effective and ineffective teaching that provide concepts and observable indicators that are empirically valid as a basis for teacher education and evaluation. Teaching alone does not determine learning, but, according to Gage and Needels (1989), teachers can, in contrast to unalterable variables such as students' genetic endowment, alter their own practices and behavior. It must be noted that no single indicator has been found to account for significant variance of teacher effectiveness (Borich, 1977). However, when observed in concert, scores derived from combining observations of numbers of indicators increase their discriminatory power, and variations in measures of teacher performance have been shown to significantly relate to student learning (FPMS Predictive Validity Studies, 1987). Thus, in order to be useful in teacher evaluation and for clinical supervision, the concepts of effective and ineffective teaching mentioned above must be identified, defined, classified, exemplified, and documented.

This is the first and most important task in developing a "research-based" teacher evaluation system. Just as the quality of a well-built house depends on the soundness of the foundation, a quality observation system must be undergirded by the gathering and organizing of empirical data and the extraction of items to be observed and coded in the process of evaluation. One example of such an effort is the "Knowledge Base: Domains of the Florida Performance Measurement System" (1983). This document is the culmination of a two-year project in which researchers assembled and organized relevant research on effective teaching. What follows is a description of this process and of the concepts of effective teaching that emerged.

In assembling the domains, the developers of the Florida Performance Measurement System (FPMS) analyzed existing research, studying the relationships between teacher performance and measures of student outcome. Over 300 process/product studies were examined. To be included in this review, each study had to meet the following criteria:

(1) The purpose of the study was to determine the effect of teacher behavior upon student achievement as measured by valid tests, either standardized or constructed by the researcher.

(2) The study was quantitative; that is, its data were derived from measurement.

(3) The results of the study were statistically significant; that is, the results were not attributable to chance.

(4) The study was reported in one or more of the following: (1) refereed journals, that is, journals that subject articles to review by one or more scholars before publication; (2) papers presented at learned societies such as the American Educational Research Association and American Psychological Association; (3) papers and monographs reporting research done at National Research and Development Centers and regional laboratories funded by the federal government through the National Institute of Education; (4) published critical summaries of research by research scholars

(in many cases the original sources were examined as well as the summaries); (5) doctoral studies at major universities.

(5) Advocatory articles and publications and textbooks were not sources.

Once collected, the research findings must be organized into a manageable form. This may be done in two ways. The behaviors identified may be allowed to fall into natural, or familial, clusters, or, a logical organization may be used, with behaviors classified in categories. The six broad categories of instruction that emerged through professional consensus from the literature search were: *Planning, Management of Student Conduct, Instructional Organization and Development, Presentation of Subject Matter, Communication,* and *Evaluation of Achievement.* Under each of these categories, called *domains,* the teacher performance indicators shown by research to affect student learning were organized into *concepts* (definitions of the behavior) and *indicators* (observable specifications of the behavior). The six domains, as finally organized, included thirty-one concepts and one hundred twenty-four indicators.

For each indicator, examples describing its effective implementation were provided, and nonexamples, describing less effective procedures, were given to clarify the attributes of the indicator. Following the presentation of the indicators for each concept, principles formulated from statistical correlations between variables of teacher performance and those of student behavior or achievement were stated in the classic "If . . . then" format: "If the teacher is efficient in the use of class time, then students will spend a high proportion of class time engaged in academic tasks and achievement will likely be higher" (domain 3, concept 1). A review of supportive evidence from the research follows each concept, with extensions and exceptions noted. The domain document thus became a useful tool—practically a textbook—for mastering the advocated teacher skills, understanding the conditions in the classroom to which exceptions and alternatives are applied, and orchestrating all into a smooth and coherent classroom performance.

From the indicators in the domain documents, a formative instrument for each domain and a summative instrument that is used for both screening and summative observations were developed. The screening/ summative instrument combined all of the indicators in thirty-nine abbreviated statements, convenient for making observations. Supervisors use the screening observations to help teachers plan appropriate areas for inservice education and coaching activities, and they use the domain documents to provide specific information about effective pedagogical practices in these areas.

The major purpose of this chapter is to document concepts and give examples of teacher performance such as use of time, handling of materials, questioning, providing feedback, emphasizing, and maintaining discipline. The concepts and examples were extracted from four observable domains (domains 2–5) that make up the FPMS screening and summative instrument. Domain 2, management of student conduct, is concerned with two types of teacher performance: teacher performance that reduces the probability of student disruptions and ways of stopping disruptive conduct once it occurs. Domain 3, instructional organization and development, consists of three components: teacher performance that provides for conservation of class time, skillful management of instruction, and skill in teacher-student interaction. Domain 4, presentation of subject matter, discusses teacher performance that facilitates the acquisition of concepts, laws, law-like principles, rules, and value knowledge. Domain 5, communication, both verbal and nonverbal, is concerned with teacher performance that demonstrates clarity, well-structured discourse, enthusiasm, positive body language, and other communication skills.

INDIVIDUAL DOMAINS

Before proceeding to a discussion of the individual domains, it is important to reiterate that what is presented here is confined to classroom interactions of the teacher with the students. Teachers engage in many other activities as professionals, such as planning for classroom instruction, described in domain 1. This discussion deals only with those performance indicators that are visible, measurable, and have been shown to have an impact on student learning in the classroom. We turn first to an explanation of how teacher performance relates to improving student conduct.

Management of Student Conduct

We usually do not think of student conduct as being the result of teacher performance. Consider these different responses to a common classroom problem, a daydreaming student.

Teacher 1: "Will you please wake up and get going on that assignment? Remember, you want to spend only one year in this grade!"

Teacher 2: "If you get started on your assignment, you may be able to get help with anything you don't understand."

Teacher 3: "Please get started on your assignment, I really get annoyed when you waste time."

The casual observer might not see a difference among the three. Some observers would recognize the technique of Teacher 1 as negative, but would be more likely to support the evaluation in terms of what a teacher ought to be than to any hard data on the use of such methods. It would be even more difficult to distinguish between Teachers 2 and 3 as to the effectiveness of their behavior.

Teacher 1 uses what Kounin (1970) terms a "rough desist"—harsh, punitive, angry. It is readily recognized as inappropriate, for reasons ranging from "creating an adversarial relationship" to "being unprofessional." Research reports show that more disruptive behavior, discomfort among students, and, among high school students, a perception of the teacher as touchy and unfair, accompany this teacher behavior at a statistically significant level.

Teacher 2 has used what Kounin reports as a "task focus desist" (i.e., directing the student to the task at hand). His research reports a positive "ripple effect" with this technique; other students become involved with the task. "Approval focus desist," or conforming because the teacher prefers it, is Teacher 3's response, and usually has little or no effect on students.

Most people, professional and lay, subscribe to the principle that teachers need to be positive with students, praising them for demonstrating desired behavior. Suppose a teacher says to a student, "Bill, what a great day you've had! You didn't disrupt class a single time, and we're really grateful! Aren't we class?" This would seem to be a four star performance for the teacher: direct, sincere, personal praise for good behavior, with peer support added. Research findings tell us, however, that the value of this praise depends on the age of the recipient (Brophy, 1981). If Bill is a first grader, he may decide he'd rather have this attention than a scolding. If he is a sixth grader, a scolding might be preferable to this teacher praise, and to the possible ridicule from other students on the way home.

Thus, research provides a basis for observing teacher behaviors, and shows how and under what conditions these behaviors affect students, individually and collectively. The power of the research-based system lies in the fact that the behaviors are describable; if describable, they are observable; and if observable, they can be learned. After an observation for formative purposes, the observer can say to the teacher, "When you sent each child individually to pick up his/her materials, you were creating a problem for yourself by what we call 'group fragmentation.' Some students become disorderly when they must wait too long for the next activity. Let's look at ways you might accomplish this task in less time by moving subgroups to the cabinets." This indicator is clearly a teacher behavior that is easy to identify, and alternatives can be easily learned. Other examples from the domains follow.

In the Management of Student Conduct domain the eight concepts are: Teacher Withitness, Rule Explication and Monitoring, Group Alert, Overlapping, Desist Techniques, Movement Smoothness, Movement Slowdown, and Praise. Each of these concepts is described by the indicators necessary for its demonstration.

For example, teacher withitness is communicating to the students by skillful words or actions that the teacher is aware of what is occurring in the classroom. Indicators of teacher withitness include immediate stopping of misbehavior before it spreads, selecting the more serious misbehavior for attention when two or more are occurring concurrently, correcting the disruptive students rather than a bystander, and suggesting more acceptable behavior or an alternative task to replace the disruption.

Suppose the teacher observes Jack throwing paper while another student laughs aloud because of Jack's behavior. The effective teacher may immediately say, "Jack, remember you need to complete your math assignment." In doing so, the teacher has quelled the disruption before it spreads, targeted the disruptor, and suggested an acceptable alternative task.

Research supporting teacher withitness includes the Kounin studies (1970) where withitness correlated .615 with work involvement and .531 with freedom from deviancy in recitation settings and .307 and .509 in seatwork settings. Additional studies on this concept include Brophy and Evertson (1974), Borg (1975), and Borg et al. (1975).

A note about the terminology in this domain seems to be in order. There has been much amusement and some resistance to such terms as "withitness," "group alert," and "overlapping." However, these terms label substantive concepts of conduct management. For example, it is clearly understood among students that a teacher who is with it seems to have eyes in the back of his/her head, seems to know what is going on all over the classroom even if he/she is not looking everywhere, and communicates awareness by what he/she says or does to stop misbehavior or to prevent it from occurring. If a teacher disciplines the wrong student for misbehavior, the class knows that the teacher is aware of a disruption but not "with-it." Kounin (1970) found that teacher withitness, if correctly communicated verbally or nonverbally, made a significant difference in classroom management. Much of the research and terminology in this area (including the catchy name withitness) has come from Kounin and supporting studies. There were two reasons for using research terminology. One was that the relationship between the behaviors we discuss in practice and the research that identified them needs to be maintained in this domain, as it is in all of the domains. The second was that while some of the terms sound strange to professional ears, they are clearly specific and not subject to various interpretations nor weighted with unrelated meanings from common usage. Communication among professionals is facilitated by precise terminology.

Instructional Organization and Development

This domain includes variables of teacher performance for establishing academic involvement and maintaining momentum in the classroom. In order to do this, teachers must attend the following concepts: Efficient Use of Time, Review of Subject Matter, Lesson Development, Treatment of Student Talk, Academic Feedback, and Management of Seatwork/Homework.

Glimpses of typical classrooms might reveal the following occurrences:

(1) Mr. Ruff concludes a statement, goes to the cupboard, and counts out worksheets for the practice activity to follow.

(2) Two minutes before the bell rings, Mrs. Abrams, upon concluding discussion of the last step of a seven-step process, says, "All right, class. We'll pick up here tomorrow. Read the rest of the chapter again."

(3) Miss Jurgenson assigns seatwork to her class, tells them to come

to her one at a time if they need help, and begins to look over the homework papers she has just collected.

To most observers, these are normal activities in classrooms of good teachers. Knowledge of research on time management, however, alerts us to loss of momentum in Mr. Ruff's class, as students wait without academic engagement while he is counting worksheets (Fisher et al., 1978; Rutter et al., 1979). Mrs. Abrams, while using most of the class time, fails to provide a concluding review, which research shows to be important to student retention (Wright and Nuthall, 1970). Miss Jurgenson sits at her desk rather than circulating and assisting students doing seatwork (Medley, 1977). None of these behaviors constitutes a severe lapse in effective practice, just as none of them by itself constitutes superior teaching, but by internalizing effective performance of many small matters, teachers become masters of their craft. Effective teachers are aware that time to instruct is the *sine qua non* for good teaching. They complain bitterly when time is lost for what they consider frivolous activities. A period out for a pep rally is readily identifiable, while fifteen hours of instruction, lost at the rate of five minutes a day over a 180-day school year, often escapes notice entirely. Bloom (1976) reviewed fifteen studies of student engagement, finding clear, consistent relationships between student engagement and achievement. The indicators under this concept alert teachers to ways in which they inadvertently lose instructional time, and how to avoid such loss. Beginning instruction promptly, managing transitions from one activity to another without time loss, providing meaningful activities for students who finish assignments before their peers, establishing efficient housekeeping routines, and handling interruptions with dispatch all guard against time loss. The underlying principle simply states that if the teacher is efficient in the use of time, then students will spend a high proportion of class time engaged in academic tasks and achievement probably will be higher.

Teachers also understand the importance of the review of subject matter, but usually conduct reviews in conjunction with tests. Research by Good and Grouws (1979) identifies the importance of incorporation of review: lesson initiating, mid-topic summary, and end-of-lesson review. Of the three indicators, the end-of-lesson review seems to have the most lasting effect on student comprehension and retention of subject matter ($r = .633$). Weekly/spaced reviews were found to be effective (Rosenshine, 1982). The principle derived from these studies states that if reviews are conducted at the end of the lesson and at weekly intervals (or occasionally longer ones), then retention as well as the amount of learning will be increased.

It is generally recognized that students must know what they are to do if learning activities are to be effective. But what teachers are to do in order to make sure that students understand what they are to do and how to do it is not so obvious. Here is where the research has provided know-how. It shows that teachers who use these techniques and who hold students responsible for work are more effective. The amount of lesson structuring is of course partly dependent on the nature of the subject matter, the learners, teaching approach, etc. (Soar and Soar, 1973), but in any event the teacher has an interactive role to perform to keep lessons developing. Extensive research by Bellack et al. (1966), Gall (1970), and many others provides evidence for the use of interactive techniques such as questioning, probing, redirecting, praising, etc., to keep students involved in the developing lesson, which will likely bring positive outcomes.

Three principles emerge:

(1) If the teacher begins lessons by providing orientation and direction and sustains the lesson momentum by providing clear explanations, checking for student comprehension of explanations, maintaining direction by transitions from one part of the lesson to another, and providing practice in unison where it is appropriate, then learning will be increased.

(2) If low order questions are used by teachers of low SES students, then achievement is likely to improve.

(3) If the teacher acknowledges and amplifies student responses, uses their ideas, but organizes instruction around the teacher's questions, and maintains academic focus, then learning increases.

The pedagogical practices discussed in this domain are but a sample of the items that describe teaching and management skills for lesson development. The next domain is concerned with what is taught: that is, the generic teaching skills for handling content. Domain 4 presents conceptual knowledge, explanatory knowledge, rule knowledge, and value knowledge.

Presentation of Subject Matter

Subject matter in this domain refers not to course content as commonly understood, but to four basic forms in which subject matter content may appear. Content, regardless of subject, is expressed in the form of concepts, laws or law-like principles, rules, or value knowledge, and these four forms appear as the concepts of domain 4 in the FPMS.

The first form, conceptual knowledge, in any field provides the objects and ideas on which the understanding and use of the content is built. A concept, by definition, is a mental image, or an idea of what a thing in general should be. Rightly understood, it represents a category with criteria for inclusion, so that one can determine if other objects, ideas, or beings belong to that category.

In teaching concepts, teachers must supply a clear definition, including the concept name, a class term, and critical attributes of the concept. Examples of the concept follow, as well as a number of nonexamples, or items excluded because they lack one or more of the critical attributes. Concepts can, of course, be taught inductively, but the three elements of definition, examples, and nonexamples remain crucial (Tennyson, 1978). The question of how many examples to use has also been studied. Frayer (1970) found that students who were given a concept definition and four examples did just as well in concept learning as students who were given a concept definition and eight examples. This suggests that a few well-chosen examples may be just as effective as a larger number.

The choice of examples is also an important matter. Examples are most effective if they differ widely in variable attributes. Nonexamples are more effective if they exhibit a minimum number of criterial attributes (Klausmeier, 1976; Klausmeier et al., 1974; Tennyson et al., 1972). In addition, teachers test examples by suggesting an item that might or might not be included in the class, and asking students to test it by the attributes of the concept (Smith and Meux, 1967). Finally, Markle (1977) found that distinctions among related, but not identical, concepts must be clarified (e.g., pardon, probation, parole; or taxes, tariffs, fees).

Unless the concepts necessary for dealing with content are well understood, working with other forms of knowledge becomes increasingly difficult.

The second form of knowledge in this domain, explanatory knowledge, includes laws and law-like principles. Laws and principles differ in their reliability: laws are invariably true, with the effect invariably following from the cause, the consequence always following the antecedent, and the conclusion always following the premise; law-like principles are similar statements, but exceptions to the predicted effects do occur. Laws are found mainly in the scientific disciplines, while principles abound in the social sciences.

Teaching explanatory relationships includes a clear statement of the cause and the effect, making explicit the connection between them. This is done by using the scientific language of "If-then," or by using other linking words that clearly connect stated effects of condition A upon consequence B (Rosenshine, 1971).

The indicator, "explicates the cause," describes teacher performance that identifies and analyzes the cause(s), or performance that directs students to do so. This may include identification of the conditions, clarification of definitions, recalling relevant information previously learned, and examining the connection of the cause with the consequence. The third indicator "explicates the effect," applies the same process to the consequence (Smith and Meux, 1967; Ennis, 1969).

Indicator 4, "applies a causal principle," states that the teacher directs students in using a principle to solve a problem or to explain a known effect. It is this provision of practice that makes the principle a permanent and useful part of the student's reservoir of knowledge (Smith, 1970).

Three statements summarize the presentation of explanatory knowledge:

(1) If teachers analyze causal conditions and their effects, then students are more likely to comprehend cause-effect relationships.

(2) If teachers use linking words to connect the conditional part of a principle to the consequent part, then student achievement in explanatory content will be higher than if the connection is made with conjunctions such as "and" or, even less effective, not made at all.

(3) If teachers make applications of laws or law-like principles, then student achievement in explanatory knowledge will increase.

The third form of knowledge, rule knowledge, concerns academic rules that are matters of convention in subjects such as grammar and spelling. Syntax and punctuation are governed totally by academic rules.

Spelling involves a mastery of academic rules and their exceptions, and a word is right or wrong as it agrees with the rule for spelling that word. Rules are also found in reading, physical education, driver's education, and many other areas of the curriculum. Mostly, the teaching of rules is a matter of showing the circumstances to which the rule applies, explicating the rule, and then providing practice in its use.

The fourth form of knowledge in this domain, presentation of value knowledge, has a much narrower definition than that of popularly understood "values." It does not address attitudes, likes, dislikes, preferences, etc., but is concerned with the evaluation of information for the purpose of making judgments and decisions based on relevant criteria.

Value judgments can be found in all academic areas, but are particularly important in areas such as art, literature, music, social sciences, and vocational studies. There are aesthetic objects, such as good art, literature, and music, and virtues, such as honesty, truthfulness, and sincerity, that students should learn to evaluate, to know why these aesthetic objects and virtues are good or desirable.

"Good," "bad," "desirable," "undesirable" are value terms we use to state the worth of things. To decide that something is good or desirable, etc., is to make a judgment. *Gone with the Wind* is a good book. Truthfulness is desirable. The judgments we make do not entail personal likes or dislikes of objects. It is not a contradiction to say that *Gone with the Wind* is a good book, but I did not enjoy reading it. The judgment is based on agreed-upon criteria. However, if we reject something we value, we must have an explanation (Smith and Meux, 1967; Metcalf, 1971).

Students who know the evaluative procedure are ready to explore value questions and make decisions. For example, is it okay to cheat? Which fabric will wear better on my sofa? What kind of car should I buy? What college should I attend?

Communication

The fifth domain presents a critical medium of instruction, the teacher's verbal and nonverbal interaction with students. Aspects of verbal behavior are organized under four concepts: control of discourse, emphasis, task attraction and challenge, and speech. Nonverbal behavior, or body language, is a fifth concept of the domain.

The "control of discourse" studies have consistently shown that teachers who have command of language, who speak clearly and succinctly, are more effective than those who speak vaguely or garble their discourse. Findings by Hiller et al. (1969) and other studies of teacher clarity report significant negative correlations ($p < 0.5$) between teacher use of vagueness words and student achievement. Similarly, studies by Smith and Cotten (1980) and others found discontinuity, another clarity indicator, negatively related to achievement ($p < .01$). A teacher demonstrates connected discourse by making a thematically connected presentation leading to a single point. Failing this, the teacher is guilty of scrambled discourse, which, as its name indicates, consists of discontinuous, garbled verbal behavior that makes no identifiable point and leaves the listener confused and frustrated. Vagueness words contribute to confusion and misunderstanding by using terms with no determinate meanings or references—e.g., "a little," "about," "perhaps" and such terms as "actually," which usually denotes that the preceding statement is inaccurate and is to be ignored.

Two additional indicators, "question overload" and "single questions," are related to each other in the same way as are connected and scrambled discourse—each is the nonexample of the other. Question overload is the posing of several questions in quick succession without allowing for answers, or of asking an unclear question, and following immediately with long, involved attempts at clarification. Single questions, on the other hand, are asked one at a time without rephrasing or giving additional information (Wright and Nuthall, 1970). Question overload, one of the most common problems exhibited by teachers, is negatively related to student achievement ($r = .52$).

Emphasis indicates to the students what is important to be studied. Emphasis techniques include the planned repetition of important points; marker expressions, such as "this is important"; or underlining, starring, or writing key words when using chalkboards or other materials. The principle addressing emphasis states that if marker expressions and techniques are used and main points are repeated at spaced intervals, then students will be aware of important elements of content and achievement will be increased.

Task attraction and challenge (Kounin, 1970) describes teacher behavior that motivates students by demonstrating the teacher's genuine excitement about the task; challenge makes a nondiscouraging statement that an exercise or activity will be hard to do.

Speech or voice characteristics that make up the auditory stimuli as distinguished from the content or message of the discourse are: (1) loud, noisy, or grating voice; (2) shrill, piercing, highly pitched voice; (3) monotone—fails to vary the intensity, rate, and volume of speech; and (4) speaks too softly, almost inaudibly. The principle for this speech concept is stated in less emphatic terms than other principles: If the teacher's speech characteristics, including volume, pitch, etc., are not extreme, then student achievement may not be adversely affected. A number of studies are reported dealing with the effects of these indicators on student comprehension, attitude, and perception of the teacher. We are cautioned that the correlations are not high enough to warrant the use of any single factor or total of speech factors as representative of teaching effectiveness.

Nonverbal behavior or body language, the final concept in the communication domain, is made up of five indicators. "Teacher smiles" include the teacher's facial expressions that give positive feedback—pleasure, friendliness, interest, excitement, surprise—to the student. "Deadpan," on the other hand, indicates lack or concealment of the teacher's feelings. "Teacher frowns" is a facial expression that gives feedback about the teacher's negative affect—displeasure, disapproval, or anger. Posture and movement is seen to indicate the teacher's energy and enthusiasm. Eye contact means that the teacher looks at the students without glaring, suspicion, or anger, but with interest, empathy, and directness. If the teacher demonstrates positive nonverbal (body) communication, then students react favorably and achievement may be increased.

Attempts to increase teacher enthusiasm through training (Collins, 1978) have been positive, but changes in student outcome are mostly attitudinal. Research in this area is sparse, and largely exploratory, so while it is to be taken seriously, it awaits more refined descriptions of the behaviors being studied.

The researches discussed thus far were extracted from the four domains that make up the FPMS screening and summative observation instrument. The knowledge base of essential teacher's skills ("Knowledge Base: Domains of the Florida Performance Measurement System") includes two additional domains—testing and planning. A brief summary of the testing domain follows.

Testing

Observation of teacher behavior in this domain involves noting how the teacher prepares students for tests, how tests are administered, and how feedback on test results is provided.

In preparing students for testing, effective teachers do three things. The first is to orient students to the test, telling them in nonthreatening language the purpose of the test, how the results will be used, and how the results are relevant to them personally. How the teacher introduces a test can influence student performance. For example, Osler (1954) found that students who were discouraged apparently perceived themselves as failures and they scored significantly lower. Kirkland (1971) reviewed seven studies on the relation of expectation of success or failure to successful performance on tests. Expectation determined the amount of time students persisted in attempting to solve problems. Those who had high expectancy of success performed better than those who had low expectations. Also included in preparation for testing is specifying test content (Carrier and Titus, 1981) and instructing students in test taking to insure that students are prepared to utilize the characteristics and format of a test and/or test-taking situation to improve their chances of making a higher score. For example, Kalechstein et al. (1981) found the effects of test-taking instructions raised standardized reading scores significantly ($p < .01$) over the score of the control group. No teaching of the test is in any way implied.

The second concept, the actual administration of the test, is demonstrated by three indicators. The first is the arrangement of the physical setting, in which the teacher does everything possible to provide seating, temperature control, lighting and ventilation, and removal of distractions. The second aspect of physical setting is the provision of a warm and encouraging atmosphere for those being tested. Debilitating anxiety can be induced by the test examiner (Wine, 1971). Finally, the teacher has a responsibility to discourage cheating, or to provide supervision that discourages the use of notes, copying, etc. (Bushway and Nash, 1977). The principles for this concept summarize researches that found:

(1) If tests are administered in a physical setting that is comfortable and free of distractions and opportunities to cheat, by an examiner who is positive and encouraging, then students will have a fair

chance to demonstrate what they know and the teacher will more likely obtain a valid measure of their achievement.

(2) If the teacher is aware of the anxiety caused by tests in some students and refrains from using tests as a threat or from emphasizing the negative consequences of poor performance, then highly anxious students will suffer less anxiety and perform better on tests.

Formative feedback, part of effective testing, provides behaviors that enhance the usefulness of test results for both students and teacher. Formative feedback includes reviewing tests and using test data to identify and correct errors in understanding, and commenting positively on test results, providing expressions of approval of student responses to test items, and discussing responses. The feedback session thus becomes a learning experience, not a punitive session. The principle is that if the teacher provides feedback to students on their tests, then motivation, learning, and retention will increase, and the teacher will be more able to adjust instruction to the needs of the classroom group.

Note that planning is not included in this discussion, because it is conducted prior to instruction, while this chapter focuses only on classroom instruction. Evidence of careful planning emerges in other domains, as when the teacher is able to maintain momentum (domain 3), or has correctly analyzed content and provided appropriate methods for teaching the form of knowledge under discussion (domain 4). This in no way lessens the importance of good planning techniques, and domain 1 of the FPMS Knowledge Base from which this chapter was drawn, is on planning. This domain is recommended as an analytic guide for teachers having difficulty in any area.

CONCLUSIONS AND APPLICATION

Research on teaching has provided the content base for progressing from high-inference ratings to low-inference, observable performance in the evaluation of teachers. Concepts of teacher performance such as rule explication, group alert, review of subject matter, academic feedback, concept development, emphasis, and task attraction and challenge have been extracted from empirical studies on teaching, and organized into domains with definitions, examples, and principles of effective teaching.

From the research, systems of teacher evaluation have been developed. The value of research-based teacher evaluation systems lies in their empirical derivation, explicit definitions and examples, and the documented effects of teacher performance that can be expected if the skills are learned and applied in the classroom. In addition to their usefulness in determining teacher competency, they provide a data base from which to plan coaching and other formative activities for improving teacher performance.

The concepts and indicators identified in this body of literature constitute essential teaching skills. They are the skills that teachers need to manage student conduct, organize and deliver instruction, present subject matter, and communicate with students. Beyond the essential skills, teaching and learning can be enhanced through the teaching of higher order thinking skills, the subject of the next chapter.

REFERENCES

Bellack, A. A. et al. 1966. *The Language of the Classroom.* New York: Teachers College Press.

Bloom, B. 1976. *Human Characteristics and School Learning.* New York: McGraw Hill.

Borg, W. R. 1975. "Protocol Materials as Related to Teacher Performance and Pupil Achievement," *Journal of Educational Research,* 69(September):23–30.

Borg, W. R. et al. 1975. "Teacher Classroom Management Skills and Pupil Behavior," *Journal of Experimental Education,* 44(Winter):52–58.

Borich, G. 1977. *The Appraisal of Teaching: Concepts and Practices.* Reading, MA: Addison-Wesley Publishing Co.

Brophy, J. 1981. "Teacher Praise: A Functional Analysis," *Review of Educational Research,* 51(Spring):5–32.

Brophy, J. and C. Evertson. 1974. *Process-Product Correlations in the Texas Teacher Effectiveness Study: Final Report.* Austin: University of Texas at Austin.

Bushway, A. and W. R. Nash. 1977. "School Cheating Behavior," *Review of Educational Research,* 47(Fall):623–632.

Carrier, C. A. and A. Titus. 1981. "Effects of Notetaking Pretraining and Text Mode Expectations on Learning from Lectures," *American Educational Research Journal,* 18(Winter):385–397.

Collins, M. L. 1978. "Effects of Enthusiasm Training on Preservice Elementary Teachers," *Journal of Teacher Education,* 29(January/February):53–57.

Ennis, R. H. 1969. *Logic in Teaching.* Englewood Cliffs, NJ: Prentice-Hall Inc.

Evertson, C. "Differences in Instructional Activities in High and Low Achieving Junior High Classes," paper presented at the annual meeting of the American Educational Research Association, Boston, March, 1980.

Fisher, C. W., N. A. Filby, R. Marliave, L. S. Cahen, M. M. Dishaw, J. E. Moore and D. C. Berliner. 1978. "Technical Report V-1: Teaching Behaviors, Academic Learning Time and Student Achievement: Final Report of Phase III-B, Beginning Teacher Evaluation Study," San Francisco: Far West Laboratory.

Frayer, D. A. 1970. "Effect of Number of Instances and Emphasis of Relevant Attribute Values on Mastery of Geometric Concepts by Fourth and Sixth Grade Children," *Research and Development Center for Cognitive Learning, Technical Report 116.*

Gage, N. L. and M. C. Needels. 1989. "Process-Product Research on Teaching: A Review of Criticisms," *The Elementary School Journal*, 89(3):253–300.

Gall, M. 1970. "The Use of Questions in Teaching," *Review of Educational Research*, 40:707–721.

Good, T. and D. A. Grouws. 1979. "The Missouri Mathematics Effectiveness Project: An Experimental Study in Fourth-Grade Classrooms," *Journal of Educational Psychology*, 74:355–362.

Hiller, J. H. et al. 1969. "A Computer Investigation of Verbal Characteristics of Effective Classroom Lecturing," *American Educational Research Journal*, 6(November):661–675.

Kalechstein, P., M. Kalechstein and R. Docter. 1981. "The Effects of Instruction on Test-Taking Skills in Second Grade Black Children," *Measurement and Evaluation in Guidance*, 13(January):198–202.

Kirkland, M. C. 1971. "The Effects of Tests on Students and Schools," *Review of Educational Research*, 41(October):303–351.

Klausmeier, H. J. 1976. "Instructional Design and the Teaching of Concepts," in *Cognitive Learning in Children*, J. R. Levin and V. L. Allen, eds., New York: Academic Press.

Klausmeier, H. J., E. S. Ghatala and D. Frayer. 1974. *Cognitive Learning and Development, a Cognitive View*. New York: Academic Press.

1983. "Knowledge Base: Domains of the Florida Performance Measurement System," Chipley, FL: Panhandle Area Educational Cooperative.

Kounin, J. S. 1970. *Discipline and Group Management in Classrooms*. New York: Holt, Rinehart and Winston.

Markle, S. M. 1980. "Teaching Conceptual Networks," paper for Association for Educational Communication and Technology Convention, Miami, 1977, *Review of Educational Research*, 50:55–67.

McDonald, F. 1976. *Research on Teaching and Its Implications for Policy Making: Report on Phase II of the Beginning Teacher Evaluation Study*. Princeton, NJ: Educational Testing Service.

Medley, D. M. 1977. *Teacher Competence and Teacher Effectiveness: A Review of Process-Product Research*. Washington, DC: American Association of Colleges for Teacher Education.

Medley, D. M., H. Coker and R. S. Soar. 1984. *Measurement-Based Evaluation of Teacher Performance*. New York: Longman.

1987. "A Meta-Analysis of Five Predictive Validity Studies," *Florida Performance Measurement System Predictive Validity Report*. Tampa, FL: TEAC, College of Education, University of South Florida.

Metcalf, L. E., ed. 1971. *Values Education*. 41st Yearbook, National Council for the Social Studies. Washington, DC: The National Education Association.

Osler, S. F. 1954. "Intellectual Performance as a Function of Two Types of Psychological Stress," *Journal of Experimental Psychology*, 47:115–121.

Rosenshine, B. 1982. "Objectively Measured Behavioral Predictors of Effectiveness in Explaining," in *Research in Classroom Process*, I. O. Westbury and H. A. Bellack, eds., New York: Teachers College Press.

Rutter, M., B. Maughan, P. Mortimore, J. Ouston and A. Smith. 1979. *Fifteen Thousand Hours*. Cambridge, MA: Harvard University Press.

Smith, B. O. 1970. *A Study of the Logic of Teaching*. Urbana, IL: University of Illinois Press.

Smith, B. O. and M. O. Meux. 1967. *A Study of the Strategies of Teaching*. Urbana, IL: Bureau of Educational Research, College of Education, University of Illinois.

Smith, L. R. and M. L. Cotten. 1980. "Effects of Lesson Vagueness and Discontinuity on Student Achievement and Attitudes," *Journal of Educational Psychology*, 72(October):670–675.

Soar, R. 1968. "Optimum Teacher-Pupil Interaction for Pupil Growth," *Educational Leadership Research Supplement*, pp. 275–280.

Soar, R. and R. Soar. 1973. *Classroom Behavior, Pupil Characteristics and Pupil Growth for the School Year and Summer*. Gainesville, FL: College of Education, University of Florida.

Stallings, J. "Testing Teachers' In-Class Instruction and Measuring Change Resulting from Staff Development," paper prepared for the National Teachers Examination Policy Council, Princeton, NJ, September, 1981.

Tennyson, R. D. "Content Structure and Instructional Control Strategies in Concept Acquisition," paper, American Psychological Association, Toronto, 1978.

Tennyson, R. D. et al. 1972. "Exemplar and Non-Exemplar Variables Which Produce Correct Concept Classification Behavior and Specified Classification Errors," *Journal of Educational Psychology*, 63:144–152.

Wine, J. 1971. "Test Anxiety and Direction of Attention," *Psychological Bulletin*, 76:92–104.

Wright, C. and G. Nuthall. 1970. "Relationships between Teacher Behaviors and Pupil Achievement in Three Experimental Elementary Science Lessons," *American Educational Research Journal*, 7:477–491.

ARTHUR LEWIS
JEAN BORG
DONOVAN PETERSON

22

Research Bases for Enhancing Teaching and Learning: Higher Order Thinking

THOT: BACKGROUND INFORMATION

The teaching of higher order thinking, variously called problem solving, critical thinking, reasoning, and reflective thinking, is largely a matter of identifying and using known thinking procedures in the context of subject areas such as language arts, mathematics, science, and social studies. This chapter describes concepts and indicators of teacher performance found in the research literature associated with student acquisition of higher order thinking skills. The concepts and indicators are organized according to types of problems encountered in everyday life. The descriptions of teacher performance provide a useful guide for clinical supervision designed to enhance the teaching of higher order thinking.

In the preceding chapter, research that shows a relationship between teacher performance and student achievement is cited. Student achievement in these studies generally is in terms of knowledge of subject matter, measured through written examinations. While some items attempt to test application of subject matter, the majority of items on typical examinations test knowledge of subject matter using a multiple choice format for ease of scoring.

Higher order thinking goes beyond the basic acquisition of knowledge and recall or reproduction of the knowledge. It occurs when a person takes new information and information stored in memory and interrelates or rearranges this information to achieve a purpose or solve a problem, for example, establishing a relationship among elements, resolving an argument, or making a prediction. Thinking imposes meaning on or finds structure in apparent disorder.

347

This is not some esoteric activity reserved for the few. All persons need to use higher order thinking as they confront problems in life: where choices have to be made, sometimes with limited information; where the validity of arguments by competing individuals or groups or by merchandisers must be assessed; where generalizations must be made and tested.

Although we frequently find ourselves in situations requiring reasoning skills, some of us are not proficient in such thinking. Limited ability to use thinking procedures interferes with success in all but the most mundane of jobs. Our democratic society is based on the assumption that citizens can and will engage in higher order thinking in making decisions affecting the public welfare. Certainly, a satisfactory personal life depends upon the ability to make sound choices based on thinking. Our society recognizes the need to teach higher order thinking skills in our schools. For example, the National Governors' Association has recommended that as a part of the restructuring of schools, "the curriculum and instruction must be modified to support higher order thinking by all students" (DuPriest, 1990).

The teaching of thinking has received little attention in our schools, partially because of the demand for the teaching of the essential or basic skills and the assessment of those skills on typical classroom as well as standardized examinations. However, another reason that it has received little attention is that generally teachers do not know how to work with students in developing thinking skills. Now there is a research base that describes how teachers can lead students to develop skills in higher order thinking.

There is an empirical body of knowledge from which concepts and indicators of teacher performance that associate with student acquisition of higher order thinking skills may be extracted and used in the training of teachers. A research team reviewed approximately 400 of these quantitative research studies in which the dependent and independent variables were specified. From this review they were able to identify concepts and indicators of teacher performance leading to student acquisition of higher order thinking skills. These concepts and indicators, together with underlying principles and supporting evidence from the research literature, have been published in "Teaching for Higher Order Thinking" (THOT, 1990). This chapter is a condensation of THOT publications.

Certain generalizations, based on the research, guided the preparation of the THOT material. First, the best way for students to learn higher order thinking skills is to be actually engaged in higher order thinking. These skills are reinforced when students observe teachers exhibiting higher order thinking. Second, there must be a content base for higher order thinking—you need something to think about. The research team utilized knowledge of subject matter found in the curriculum as the basis for THOT. Finally, from the research it was found that all students (with few exceptions) at all grade levels are capable of learning higher order thinking skills. Accordingly, the THOT material can be applied in any regular classroom from preschool on.

THE FIVE DOMAINS IN THOT

This chapter documents concepts and gives examples of teacher interaction with students through subject matter as they learn to think for themselves and thus develop higher order thinking skills. The concepts and examples were extracted from five domains found in THOT. These domains, with the exception of domain 1, address different types of problems requiring higher order thinking for their successful resolution. Domain 1, *Developing and Maintaining Flexibility and Student Awareness*, is generic, that is, it is applicable to all situations regardless of the type of problem. It addresses the need to be open-minded, avoid premature conclusions, and be aware of the thinking operations being used to solve problems. Domain 2, *Generating and Validating Generalizations*, is based on problems requiring the development and testing of generalizations. Domain 3, *Assessing Arguments*, helps students solve problems that require the evaluation of arguments, or of what is said or heard. The fourth domain, *Negotiating Issues and Solving Interpersonal Problems*, centers on questions of human conflict, problems that require for their resolution changes in the persons involved in the conflict. Domain 5, *Making Judgments under Uncertainty*, is based on problems whose solutions are uncertain, as in questions whose answers are only probable. A sample of the concepts and examples together with supporting evidence for each domain follows.

Developing and Maintaining Flexibility and Student Awareness

This domain is concerned with improving student ability to modify the method of attack in a problematic situation rather than persevere in an unsuccessful direction. It is a quality of thinking that allows the problem solver to abandon a fruitless approach in favor of a novel way of solving a problem, therefore making a problem solution more likely. Flexibility is enhanced when the problem solver is alert to new approaches to a problem and when new ideas are noted, but not evaluated, in the early stages of problem solving. Teacher instructions to this effect are likely to lead to flexibility in students' thinking.

For example, in a beginning algebra class a teacher challenged his class to find the sum of the interior angles in a polygon. Several possible procedures were suggested by the class, including the use of a protractor. The teacher listed all of the ideas suggested by the class on the chalkboard and warned the group not to discard or to select a procedure until all ideas were listed and reviewed for their potential use in solving the problem. Then one group tested the use of protractors, but found their answers varied due to errors in measurement. At that time the teacher suggested they discard the idea of using protractors and search for a new more productive approach to solving the problem.

Support for warning students against premature evaluation is found in a study by Sappington and Farrar (1982), who compared two groups of students on their ability to generate workable solutions to a problem. Members of one group were instructed to jot down all their ideas and not consider the ideas good or bad. The other group was instructed to carefully evaluate each idea as it was noted. In two experiments, the first group produced significantly more workable solutions, thus lending support to the idea that avoiding premature evaluation can improve problem-solving ability. Goodnow and Pettigrew (1956) also conducted research that supports this concept.

The principle of teacher effectiveness inferred from these and other studies is: if students are instructed to discontinue unsuccessful approaches, to be alert to new ways of solving a problem, and to forego immediate evaluation of ideas for solving a problem, they are more likely to achieve problem solution.

A second concept in this domain is that teachers reduce rigidity and increase pliancy of ideas in students when they provide exploratory material, provide adequate time for students to consider problems (incubation time) and pause during classroom discourse.

Research suggests that the use of concrete exploratory materials is valuable at all ages. The research further suggests that students should be allowed to freely explore the materials with very little imposed structure (Friend, 1971; Peterson, 1978). One study examined the effects of teacher-imposed structure (Cohen, 1984). Two groups of second grade children were provided with concrete materials, but the amount of teacher direction varied. Children in the control group were instructed to work at their desks and manipulate the materials in a prescribed manner. The teacher closely observed individual students in the experimental group who were encouraged to manipulate the materials freely according to their interests. Based on the observations, students were either left to continue, offered alternative activity suggestions, or asked redirecting questions. The experimental group showed significantly more advancement than the control group. Although some of the gain might be attributed to the increased student-teacher interaction, freedom to explore the materials was an important factor.

Teachers can reduce rigidity by allowing sufficient time for students to solve complex problems. For example, a teacher might provide a demonstration or present observations contrary to the students' experience, expectations, or beliefs—a discrepant event—and then say, "I want you to think about the information I have given you until tomorrow and see if you can find some possible explanations." Rokeach's (1950) research showed that when subjects were given a problem to solve, those subjects given the least available time showed the greatest rigidity. Carpenter (1956) and Chown (1959) concluded from their reviews of research that anxiety and increased rigidity go hand in hand. Provision of ample time for problem solving may reduce anxiety and thereby increase flexibility.

Introducing pauses into classroom discourse will reduce rigidity and increase pliancy of ideas in students. In a comprehensive six-year study, Rowe (1974) investigated the influence of the length of time the teacher pauses before soliciting a pupil response on the development of language and logic in elementary science students. Rowe found that teachers typically wait about one second between posing a question and calling on a student. By training, Rowe increased the mean wait time from one second to three to five seconds. Increase in pause time resulted in longer student responses (average shift from seven to twenty-eight words), and a great number of student responses that were unsolicited but appropriate. An increase in wait time led to fewer student failures to respond to a question, and children appeared to be more confident in their answers. Tobin (1987) after a review of the research on wait time concluded that wait time probably affects higher cognitive level achievement in two ways: directly by providing additional time for student thinking, and indirectly by influencing the quality of teacher and student discourse.

The third concept in this domain develops metacognition, based on the principle that if students become aware of problem-solving procedures and their own thought processes, flexibility, and thereby problem-solving ability, are likely to be enhanced. Teachers help students become aware of procedures and thought processes by making explicit statements regarding what is to be learned, modeling problem-solving procedures, using think-aloud techniques, encouraging verbalization, and organizing classrooms into small groups.

The value of making explicit statements regarding content is supported by Duffy et al. (1986). Following four years of classroom-based research, they identified four properties of effective verbal explanation. One of these properties is developing awareness of thinking procedures used to solve problems as an outcome: that is, student awareness of the procedures being taught, when to use them, and how to apply thinking procedures. Effective teachers provide reminders throughout the lesson, and at the end of the lesson, they ask students what they learned, when they will use it, and how they will do it.

Studies of students in kindergarten through college have found that requiring students to verbalize various aspects of a problem situation leads to more effective problem solving. For example, Good et al. (1969) evaluated a four-year high school social studies curriculum designed to teach the skills essential to develop and validate hypotheses about human society. Most lessons were taught by directed discussion in which the teacher's questions elicited student verbalizations and encouraged students to develop and state hypotheses. At the close of the three-year study, students in the experimental group outperformed the control group on a post-test designed to measure a number of inquiry skills.

A number of research studies have examined the effect of group work on students' problem-solving ability. For example, Johnson et al. (1979) found that the discussion process in cooperative groups results in the development of superior cognitive strategies for solving problems. The concepts in this domain are generic to all problem-solving situations. The remaining domains contain concepts teachers can apply to solving various types of problems posed in relation to the subject matter they teach. The first type of problem requires generating and validating generalizations.

Generating and Validating Generalizations

This domain treats the teaching of problems that require the detection and verification of connections between variables, that is, with formulating and testing explanatory generalizations also referred to as hypotheses. The satisfactory solution of such problems requires that students formulate the problem, develop and examine generalizations, and validate conclusions.

The teacher can help students formulate a problem by presenting background information leading to the recognition of a problem or by presenting observations, conditions, assertions, or claims contrary to the students' experience, expectations, or beliefs (a discrepancy). For example, a second grade teacher might hold a glass of water with a piece of paper on top and ask, "If I turn the glass over and hold it upside down, what do you think will happen?" When the students tell her she will spill the water, she tries it and finds that the water stays inside the glass. The teacher may then ask, "What questions would you like to ask about what you have just seen?"

Another method of encouraging problem formulations is to engage students in deciding which elements in a problem are independent variables (causes, reasons) and dependent variables (effects, outcomes). For example, a middle school science teacher may state, "Each group has listed some variables associated with our problem of the declining earthworm population. Now I would like each group to identify the independent variables and the dependent variables. Before we do this, someone please remind us how to tell the difference between the dependent and the independent variable." One of the students responds, "The value of the dependent variable changes as the experimenter changes the value of the independent variable."

The use of analogies in problem solving was investigated by Gick and Holyoak (1983). They found that getting students to search their memory for a useful analogy rather than stumble across one requires teaching. Sometimes the teacher can encourage problem formulation by suggesting elements of the new problem that are like that of some other problem with which the student may be familiar.

Once a problem has been formulated, the teacher needs to provide experiences in developing and supporting explanatory generalizations or hypotheses. This is the very heart of the problem-solving procedure. There are a number of teacher indicators in this domain that provide students with such experience including:

- formulates generalizations from instances
- states alternative generalizations
- clarifies reason and outcome or cause and effect relationship
- decides testability of generalization
- provides example
- states expectations based on generalization
- models "fair test"
- plans and conducts tests of generalizations
- provides evidence to support generalizations

Students gain skill in the development and examination of generalizations as teachers engage them in reasoning that leads from observable facts to an explanatory hypothesis. For example, one elementary school teacher provided a simple demonstration in which she hung a kilogram weight on one end of a stick and a kilogram of grapes in a basket on the other end of the stick. When students were asked what would happen when she placed the stick over the back of a chair, they said it would balance. However, she placed the stick so that the weight was closer to the chair back than the grapes and the stick did not balance. She then said, "Some of you may have an idea about what is happening here so that the stick doesn't balance. Any ideas?" The students were beginning the process of generating hypotheses.

An important aspect of controlled experimentation is the ability to think of alternative explanations for observations and events, rather than accepting the first hypothesis without question. In the balance demonstration cited in the preceding paragraph, after the teacher had received one explanation, she sought alternative explanations by asking "Do any of the rest of you have ideas about what might be wrong?" Case and Fry (1973) attempted to teach high school students of low socioeconomic status the ability to think of alternative explanations. A highly successful treatment involved twelve units spread over twelve weeks. Instruction involved asking students to provide counter-explanations to fact-explanation sequences, designing experiments so that no counter-explanation was possible, and criticizing experimental reports written by others. The instructed students significantly outperformed a control group on a test involving the application of experimental control.

Students can frequently develop several generalizations or hypotheses to explain or predict a given phenomenon. Teachers then need to engage students in developing and applying criteria for judging the quality of their statements. Researchers reviewed in THOT (Quinn, 1975; Pouler and Wright, 1980; Ross and Maynes, 1983) suggest that quality of student hypotheses can be improved by reinforcing only those hypotheses that are acceptable (setting standards), and by giving instructions about criteria for acceptable hypotheses. Teachers can help students apply criteria to generalizations or hypotheses by providing them with samples of testable hypotheses against which to assess their own.

Once a class has agreed that a given generalization meets the criteria they have established, the teacher then needs to engage the students in deducing and stating predictions (expectations, consequences, outcomes, probable effects), assuming the generalization is true. For example, an eighth grade science class studying rate of fermentation developed one hypothesis: given fixed amounts of sugar and water, if more yeast is added then the rate of fermentation will increase. The teacher said, "Now it is your turn to make predictions. Assuming this hypothesis is correct, what would you expect to happen?"

A critical aspect of experimentation is the control of variables. Teachers need to demonstrate tests of a logical or experimental generalization, where all factors that might affect the outcome are constant except the factor in question. Only then can one state with certainty that this variable did indeed cause the observed effect. Research by Wollman and Lawson (1977) showed that students who were taught the concept of performing a "fair test" (one in which variables were controlled) outperformed a control group.

If teachers engage students in using facts to arrive at generalizations, making predictions based on generalizations, developing the concept of "all other things being equal," devising and conducting controlled validation procedures, then students are likely to learn how to formulate and test generalizations. The research literature supports the common-sense view, however, that in order to design and conduct experiments one must have experience in designing and conducting experiments. Accordingly, teachers need to engage students in designing and performing experimental tests of hypotheses, or in gathering evidence both for and against a hypothesis. Research by Linn and Thier (1975) provides support for this indicator of effective teacher behavior. They evaluated a fifth and an eighth grade science program (Science Curriculum Improvement Study) in which students chose major variables in a number of situations and designed experiments to investigate the effects of these variables. The role of the teacher was to guide rather than control. Over 2,000 students participated in this study. It was found that those who participated in the program showed higher levels of logical thinking, in that they were better able to explain the effects of independent variables or dependent variables.

Not all generalizations can be tested experimentally, so evidence must be gathered from resources and then evaluated. An examination of the facts can be a means of testing a generalization, since if an instance is contradictory, the generalization is weakened or possibly shown to be false (Mynatt et al., 1977). This leads to the third concept in this domain: validation of generalizations, which consists of teacher performance that provides experience in evaluating explanatory generalizations and the evidence offered in their support. Through teacher performance, students learn to guard against overgeneralization, to analyze the explanatory power of generalizations, to analyze the relation of generalizations to the relevant body of knowledge, and to evaluate alternative generalizations.

Before an empirical explanation is accepted, competing explanations should be examined. If the competitors are inconsistent with existing data, the explanation is strengthened. In fact, a purpose of evaluating alternative generalizations is to rule out generalizations that are inconsistent with existing data (Ennis, 1969). Teachers concerned with developing higher order thinking skills in their students should engage students in deciding what evidence counts for and against competing generalizations and determining the degree to which these generalizations are supported by evidence.

Generating and validating generalizations constitutes one type of explanatory approach teachers may use in solving problems in their subject areas. Another type of problem we confront every day is assessing arguments. Assessing arguments requires application of thinking procedures and knowledge of subject matter.

Assessing Arguments

An argument consists of premises, plus a conclusion from the premises. Often the premises are not stated, only implied. This is true of many arguments that bombard us every day—arguments that try to convince us to buy a particular product, support an ideological position, vote for a candidate, support a public policy or program, or interpret an event in a certain way. Teacher performance in this domain presents students with arguments and challenges them to accept or reject the arguments on defensible grounds. Students learn to analyze these arguments by identifying the premises, key words in an argument, the line of reasoning used, and the conclusion of an argument. In addition they learn to examine authoritative and observable evidence presented in an argument, and to recognize fallacies. Teacher performance in this domain also leads students to evaluate the conclusions of arguments by checking their logical validity, by testing for overgeneralization, and by comparing the conclusions to what is already known.

Two types of teacher performance help students to analyze arguments. First, teachers engage students in identifying an argument as a discourse that has at least two parts, one of which is given as a reason for the other, as contrasted with statements of explanation, narration, description, or definition. For example, a teacher presents students with excerpts from three letters to editors. Excerpt numbers one and three contain statements of fact and descriptive statements. The students correctly identify these statements as not being arguments. The teacher then asks, "How do we tell the difference between one and three on the one hand, and two, on the other? What are the characteristics of an argument?" A student responds, "An argument has a conclusion." Another student adds, "It has reasons. It moves from evidence to conclusion." The teacher summarizes. "That is correct. An argument has at least two parts, a reason and a conclusion."

Teachers also help students analyze arguments by involving them in activities that require them to distinguish reasons (premises) and conclusions. For example, a teacher might give students a series of statements and ask them to decide which statements are the reasons for the others (conclusions) (Beardsley, 1950).

Students learn how to assess arguments as teachers engage them in evaluating the sources of fact or alleged facts (data) used to support the reasoning of an argument. One way teachers do this is to engage students in examining and weighing the reliability of authoritative sources of alleged facts or observations given in the course of an argument.

Student ability to assess arguments is enhanced when teachers provide experiences in recognizing and avoiding language traps and common flaws in reasoning such as ambiguous language, shifts in definition, black or white fallacy, slanted discourse, misuse of analogy, and post hoc fallacy.

For example, terms used in an argument that can have more than one meaning in the particular context, or sentences in which there is more than one possible way to interpret grammatical relationships are ambiguous. To demonstrate, a teacher helped students learn to spot ambiguous statements by asking them to spot the "cloudy terms" in this statement: "This is the brand recommended more often by doctors." A student responded, "Well, you don't know what 'more often' means — once more? More often than *any* other medication, or *all* other medications, of what? And even 'doctors' isn't really clear because there are so many kinds of doctors."

A final concept in assessing arguments is evaluation of conclusions. This concept relates to teacher behavior that engages students in the process of examining the acceptability of one's own conclusion, or the conclusions of others. Students need to learn to check an argument for logical validity—that is, does the conclusion follow necessarily from reasons presented in the argument, or is the conclusion the equivalent of one of its premises or reasons, or is the conclusion based on a sufficient sample?

In summary, this domain presents a series of experiences teachers can provide to help students learn to assess arguments. If students have experience in recognizing and analyzing arguments, they will improve in ability to respond constructively to contending arguments. If the teacher provides students with practice in the assessment of the factual support of the premises of an argument, they will become more rigorous in their assessment of conclusions. If the teacher provides experience in the analysis of language and ordinary flaws in reasoning, the students will become more effective in recognizing words used to control thought and action and in judging the validity of what they hear and read. And, finally, if the teacher induces students to examine the logical grounds of a conclusion, its consistency with what is already known, and its data base, students will be more skillful in determining the acceptability of conclusions.

While the ability to assess arguments develops personal skill in determining the acceptability of conclusions, the next domain focuses on working with others in arriving at acceptable solutions to problems based on evaluating information relevant to the problem.

Negotiating Issues and Solving Interpersonal Problems

Interpersonal problems occur when the desires or needs of two people, or two groups of people, are in conflict over a matter to be decided. Thus the perplexities in this domain always involve people. Finding a satisfactory solution requires that the viewpoints of all concerned parties be taken into account. Further, the persons affected should participate in finding a satisfactory solution. The arguments used in finding these solutions should be subjected to the same tests of reasonableness as those applied in testing formal arguments. Teacher performance in this area leads students to analyze issues, to develop and elaborate proposals leading to the resolution of a conflict through consensus or compromise, to consider the consequences of these solutions, and to evaluate each proposed solution.

There are several types of teacher behavior that engage students in recognizing interpersonal problems and determining the fundamental nature of such problems. Directing students to consider the differing thoughts, feelings, intentions, and wishes of those involved in a conflict helps students learn to analyze interpersonal problems. For example, a middle school language arts teacher says, "The story we have just read tells how two old friends, the mayor of the town and a leading lawyer, became enemies in a struggle for power. I want you to think about how each of the men viewed the incident that led to their becoming enemies. Then select one of the men and write a two or three paragraph description of how you think he viewed the incident."

An important procedure in analyzing an interpersonal conflict is to validate the components of the conflict. Students learn to validate the components of conflicts as teachers have them discuss whether the assumptions, inferences, and opinions are accurate and well grounded in the information given. After an interpersonal problem has been identified and analyzed, teachers can engage students in the development, discussion, and elaboration of a number of possible solutions to a conflict, rather than just one solution.

Teachers need to provide students with experiences in judging the appropriateness of alternative solutions using criteria such as effectiveness, fairness, reasonableness, and respect for individual rights. The development of proposed solutions and their evaluation is facilitated by interaction within and, in some instances, between groups.

Hirokawa and Pace (1983) analyzed the nature and content of interaction within a number of decision-making groups in an effort to identify consistent differences that might account for variations in the quality of their group decisions. They found that effective groups examined and evaluated the validity of opinions and assumptions introduced into the discussion by fellow members in a rigorous manner, while ineffective groups did not consider the validity of opinions and assumptions. Effective groups were thorough and rigorous in evaluating the consequences of different courses of action, while ineffective groups did not pay close attention to the consequences. Effective groups based their decisions on facts, assumptions, and inferences that appeared to be "grounded" in the information presented in the case study, while ineffective groups based decisions on facts, assumptions, and inferences that were inaccurate, highly questionable, and not well grounded. Both effective and ineffective groups had one or more members who were able to influence the line of thinking and discussion of the group. In effective groups, this influence was positive and facilitative. In ineffective groups, the influence was negative and inhibitive. To summarize, the findings of this and other studies support the importance of interactive group decision making, but teachers must provide specific instruction to teach effective procedure.

Assessing an argument or negotiating an issue may focus on a past, present, or future event. When the problem situation is futuristic, some of the factors relevant to the solution of the problem may not be known. Futuristic problem solving therefore requires making probabilistic judgments under uncertainty.

Making Judgments under Uncertainty

The subject of this domain is the teaching of problems whose solutions are uncertain, as in questions whose answers are only probable. Such problems run the gamut from commonplace questions (e.g., Shall I carry an umbrella today?) to crucial questions (e.g., Shall I drop out of school and get a job?). In every instance, judgments must be made based upon partial information, and the consequences of such judgments are uncertain. An individual confronted with an important decision needs to choose a course of action that has the best chance of producing desired results. To do this requires making an estimation or prediction based on the best available information. Basing predictions on the probability of their occurrence frequently increases their usefulness for making decisions.

The basic concepts of making judgments under uncertainty include the analysis of problems with uncertain solutions; the gathering, examination, and manipulation of information prior to making predictions about unknown outcomes; and rudimentary concepts of probabilistic thinking.

Teachers can help students learn to solve problems by directing them to state problems, alternative solutions to problems, and factors influencing the solution in clear and precise language. For example, Mr. Lawrence, a middle school social science teacher, states: "Our textbook says that one of the effects of increased urbanization has been a general decline in citizen participation in community welfare. We want to examine the question, 'Will citizen participation continue to decline?' Any ideas about how we should proceed to do this?" One student responds, "It seems to me that we have to agree on what we mean by 'citizen participation.' The book supports the claim that citizen participation is declining only on the basis of the percentage of eligible voters who vote. But isn't there more to citizen participation than that?" Mr. Lawrence responds, "Yes, there is. You are right, our first step is to state the question in clear and unambiguous language. We need to agree on what we mean by citizen participation in community welfare."

Once the problem has been identified and analyzed, the teacher and students should gather and examine quantitative and qualitative data and use these data to predict the most probable occurrence of events. In assembling information that pertains to the question under study, the teacher encourages students to use quantitative data when possible. Studies show that students from preschool age through college level can learn to collect information and base judgments on probabilistic thinking. For example, Ojemann et al. (1965), presented probability situations to third grade students where the number of relevant factors to be considered varied. The goal was to get students, when faced with these types of situations, to ask "What information do I have or can I get that will help?" Experiences were planned to develop the following abstractions:

(1) When a random selection is made from a group of equally available alternatives, each alternative has an equal chance of being chosen.

(2) When there are more of one item than another, the former has the greater chance of being selected.

(3) More information about how something works often helps.

(4) It is sometimes possible to gather more information as one engages in probabilistic thinking.

Instruction for the experimental subjects involved discussions, demonstrations with concrete objects, eliciting verbalizations through questioning, and manipulation of materials by the students. Training took place thirty minutes a day for five consecutive days, during which time a variety of problems was presented. Results indicated that the experimental subjects acquired considerable ability to relate their predictions to the probable outcome when the information was available, and to wait before making predictions when only a small amount of information was available and more would be supplied.

Teachers need to help students recognize how estimations of probability can be skewed by basing predictions on memory samples that are biased, by relying on stereotypes, or by giving undue weight to data supporting one's views or wishes. For example, familiar occurrences are recalled more easily than unfamiliar events, and recent occurrences are recalled more easily than earlier occurrences.

The tendency to make judgments based on stereotypes rather than on frequency data can also lead to biased predictions. For examples, Tversky and Kahneman (1974) found that people tend to predict a person's occupation based on the degree to which the person is representative of the stereotype of the occupation. Thus the researchers found that even though subjects had been told that there are many more farmers than librarians in a population, they overwhelmingly predicted that an individual in the population who was described as quiet, thoughtful, and wears glasses was a librarian because he fit the stereotype of a librarian.

Pitz et al. (1967) found that college students were reluctant to revise hypotheses, even when presented with contradictory evidence. The study showed that when evidence is presented that supports the opinion of the subject, the subject became more certain of the previously formed opinion. Conversely, evidence contrary to the subject's opinion did not cause the same degree of change in the subject's previously formed opinion. Thus, encouraging students to revise probability estimates based upon additional information is an important, but difficult task.

Finally, teachers need to help students evaluate judgments by working with them to modify preliminary estimates of probability taking into account the validity and reliability of new information. Beyth-Marom and Dekel (1985) point out that procedures for assessing chances involve various types of errors. They therefore recommend that the final estimate be checked or reviewed against intuition. If intuition does not agree with the final probability estimate, it is a signal that something may be wrong, providing intuition is based on reason and not mere personal bias.

Given the educational priority of developing higher order thinking skills, the clinical supervisor needs to be able to observe and document what the teacher does, and through coaching prescribe the most effective current practices. For documentation, supervisors must have a valid observation system to gather the data that they will use as the basis for assisting teachers. Development of instrumentation for this purpose of assessing essential and higher order teaching skills is the subject of Chapter 23.

CONCLUSION AND APPLICATION

This chapter provides an introduction to effective practice in teaching higher order thinking. Examples of teacher performance, together with citations of the studies from which they are drawn, give the supervisor the practices that associate with student acquisition of thinking skills. Further information may be found by referring to the THOT domains and the research studies cited in this chapter. Two additional general references of particular interest are Nickerson et al. (1985) and Resnick (1987).

One reaction teachers often have when they read the illustrations in this chapter is, "I wish I had students like that in my classes." The examples in this chapter are from actual classroom dialogue, observed and recorded in classrooms of teachers who had been introduced to the teaching of higher order thinking. Most of these classrooms were composed of students in the average range of ability. One of the side effects discovered by the research team in observing lessons designed to teach thinking is that students at risk tend to become far more motivated as their teachers help them develop higher order thinking skills. Furthermore, the teachers reported that they themselves had never been so challenged nor had they ever before found teaching so rewarding.

How may the ideas in this chapter be used to improve the teaching of higher order thinking? One way is for a teacher to take subject matter taught in the regular curriculum and teach it in such a way that students can experience higher order thinking. For example, an eighth grade science teacher taught a unit on the earthworm. However, instead of following her usual procedure of imparting information and having students do an exercise out of the laboratory manual, the teacher was trained and used higher order thinking techniques. This time she introduced the unit with a problem: "Each year I get my earthworms for class work from a certain plot of ground on a friend's farm. This year, when I went to get the earthworms, I found very few. What do you suppose happened to the earthworms?" The students, working in groups, developed a number of hypotheses. The teacher showed them how to state the hypotheses in a clear and precise fashion. She then helped them develop and apply criteria to examine the hypotheses that could be tested, each group of students selected one hypothesis and designed an experiment to test it. Following this they set up and ran their own experiments. And finally, they shared and evaluated the results. Think of the relative sterility of working through a preset experiment in a laboratory manual, where the authors of the laboratory manual did most of the higher order thinking and the students were little more than lab assistants following a set of instructions! In experiencing the higher order thinking procedures, the students became "scientists" and actually worked through formulating and testing a problem and validating their findings.

Another way to improve the teaching of higher order thinking is to work on just one or two of the indicators in this chapter, as appropriate. For example, a teacher could decide to work on increasing the wait time—that is, the time between posing a question and calling on a student. The research by Rowe (1974), previously cited, shows that just this one technique can improve student flexibility in thinking and lead to more thoughtful answers.

One of the most effective ways to use this material would be to combine the special unit approach and the frequent use of one or more of the teacher behaviors. For example, a teacher might teach a unit on assessing arguments. Following the teaching of this unit, as opportunities arose, the teacher could ask, "Is the statement we just read an argument or is it exposition?" This could be followed by such questions as, "Well, if it is an argument, can you find the premises and the conclusion?" The teacher could also lead students in discussing the validity of the argument. Doing this repeatedly, as opportunities arose, would strengthen students' higher order thinking ability.

As this chapter indicates, the teaching of higher order thinking involves a large number of teacher behaviors. Teachers need to recognize that it is better to master a few behaviors at a time. Don't bite off more than you can handle, but at least take a bite, no matter how small.

REFERENCES

Beardsley, M. C. 1950. *Practical Logic*. New York: Prentice-Hall, Inc.

Beyth-Marom, R. and S. Dekel. 1985. *An Elementary Approach to Thinking under Uncertainty*. Hillsdale, NJ: Lawrence Erlbaum Associates, Inc.

Carpenter, F. 1956. "Educational Significance of Studies on the Relation between Rigidity and Problem Solving. III: The Learning Approach," *Science Education*, 40(4):296–311.

Case, R. and C. Fry. 1973. "Evaluation of an Attempt to Teach Scientific Inquiry and Criticism in a Working Class High School," *Journal of Research in Science Teaching*, 10(2):135–142.

Chown, S. M. 1959. "A Flexible Concept," *Psychological Bulletin*, 56(3):195–223.

Cohen, H. G. 1984. "The Effects of Two Teaching Strategies Utilizing Manipulations on the Development of Logical Thought," *Journal of Research in Science Teaching*, 21(8):769–778.

Duffy, G. G., L. R. Roehler, M. S. Meloth and L. G. Vaurus. 1986. "Conceptualizing Instructional Explanation," *Teaching and Teacher Education*, 2(3):197–214.

DuPriest, B. 1990. "The Urban Proving Ground," *ASCD Update*, 32(3):4. Alexandria, VA: Association for Supervisors and Curriculum Development.

Ennis, R. H. 1969. *Logic in Teaching*. Englewood Cliffs, NJ: Prentice-Hall, Inc.

Friend, H. 1971. "A Comparison of the Relative Effectiveness of Two Methods of Teaching the Course 'Time, Space and Matter' to Selected Eighth Grade Pupils," *School Science and Mathematics*, 71(January):69–74.

Gick, M. L. and K. J. Holyoak. 1983. "Schema Induction and Analogical Transfer," *Cognitive Psychology*, 15:1–38.

Good, J. M., J. U. Farley and E. Fenton. 1969. "Developing Inquiry Skills with an Experimental Social Studies Curriculum," *The Journal of Educational Research*, 63(1):31–35.

Goodnow, J. J. and T. F. Pettigrew. 1956. "Some Sources of Difficulty in Solving Simple Problems," *Journal of Experimental Psychology*, 51(6):385–392.

Hirokawa, R. Y. and R. Pace. 1983. "A Descriptive Investigation of the Possible Communications-Based Reasons for Effective and Ineffective Group Decision Making," *Communications Monographs*, 50(December):363–379.

Johnson, D. W., R. Johnson and L. Skon. 1979. "Student Achievement on Different Types of Tasks under Cooperative, Competitive and Individualistic Conditions," *Contemporary Educational Psychology*, 4(April):99–106.

Linn, M. C. and H. D. Thier. 1975. "Effect of Experimental Science on Development of Logical Thinking in Children," *Journal of Research in Science Teaching*, 10(1):83–90.

Mynatt, C. R., M. E. Doherty and R. D. Tweney. 1977. "Confirmation Bias in a Simulated Research Environment: An Experimental Study of Scientific Inference," *Quarterly Journal of Experimental Psychology*, 29:85–95.

Nickerson, R., D. Perkins and E. Smith. 1985. *The Teaching of Thinking*. Hillsdale, NJ: Lawrence Erlbaum Associates, Inc.

Ojemann, R. H., E. J. Maxey and B. C. F. Snider. 1965. "The Effect of a Program of Guided Learning Experiences in Developing Probability Concepts at the Third Grade Level," *Journal of Experimental Education*, 33(4):321–330.

Peterson, K. 1978. "Scientific Inquiry Training for High School Students: Experimental Evaluation of a Model Program," *Journal of Research in Science Teaching*, 15(March):153–159.

Pitz, G. F., L. Downing and H. Reinhold. 1967. "Sequential Effects in the Revision of Subjective Probabilities," *Canadian Journal of Psychology*, 21(5):381–393.

Pouler, C. and E. Wright. 1980. "An Analysis of the Influence of Reinforcement and Knowledge of Criteria on the Ability of Students to Generate Hypotheses," *Journal of Research in Science Teaching*, 17(January):31–37.

Quinn, M. E. 1975. "Teaching Hypothesis Formation," *Science Education*, 59(July/September):289–296.

Resnick, L. 1987. *Education and Learning to Think*. Washington, DC: National Academy Press.

Rokeach, M. 1950. "The Affect of Perception Time upon Rigidity and Concreteness of Thinking," *Journal of Experimental Psychology*, 40:206–216.

Ross, J. A. and F. Maynes. 1983. "Experimental Problem Solving: Instructional Improvement Field Experiment," *Journal of Research in Science Teaching*, 20(September):543–556.

Rowe, M. B. 1974. "Wait-Time and Rewards as Instruction Variables, Their Influence on Language, Logic and Fate Control: Part One—Wait-Time," *Journal of Research in Science Teaching*, 11:81–94.

Sappington, A. A. and W. E. Farrar. 1982. "Brainstorming vs. Critical Judgment in the Generation of Solutions Which Conform to Certain Reality Constraints," *Journal of Creative Behavior*, 16:68–73.

1990. "Teaching for Higher Order Thinking (THOT)," Tampa, FL: University of South Florida, College of Education, Teacher Evaluation and Assessment Center.

Tobin, K. 1987. "The Role of Wait-Time in Higher Cognitive Level Learning," *Review of Educational Research*, 57(1):69–95.

Tversky, A. and D. Kahneman. 1974. "Judgment under Uncertainty: Heuristic and Biases," *Science*, 185(September):1124–1131.

Wollman, W. and A. E. Lawson. 1977. "Teaching the Procedure of Controlled Experimentation: A Piagetian Approach," *Science Education*, 6(1):57–70.

DONOVAN PETERSON
JEAN BORG
THEODORE MICCERI

23

Gathering, Interpreting, and Using Evaluation Data for the Improvement of Classroom Instruction

FORMATIVE SUPPORT FOR BEGINNING TEACHERS

Over the past decade, several states have launched programs of support for beginning teachers in their first year of classroom instruction. Provision of this support involves the observation of classroom performance, the interpretation of data, and the use of observation data in conferring with teachers — in particular beginning teachers — for purposes of improving instruction. This chapter addresses some of the major challenges encountered in attempting to provide accurate formative support for beginning teachers together with procedures and examples of instruments designed for this purpose.

In 1979, the Florida state legislature created a beginning teacher program. This program dramatically changed the manner in which new teachers obtain their initial teaching certificate. Prior to this time, upon graduation from an approved college program, new teachers applied to the Department of Education and were issued a teaching certificate. With the advent of the Beginning Teacher Program, new teachers secure a teaching position, practice for one year, and then receive a teaching certificate through the Department of Education only after verification of successful completion of the first year of practice by the school district.

Florida is only one example. Many states have similar programs. The shift of responsibility in certifying teachers from the universities to the districts appears logical in that it reduces the risk of issuing certificates mainly on the basis of written examinations taken at universities, as opposed to actual tested practice in the classroom. It also decentralizes the power of licensing teachers and places it at the operational level, where beginning teachers can be directly observed and their instruction first formatively and then summatively evaluated. This is a real form of empowerment. However, it adds a heavy responsibility on school district personnel that they did not have previously — a responsibility involving the lives of persons who have invested at least four years in preparing for the profession of their choice.

To err in this responsibility is to deny license to practice. Such denial has legal and professional implications. Deneen (1980) cites four major categories in which problems of teacher evaluation frequently occur: (1) due process, (2) discrimination, (3) validity, and (4) reliability. Knowledge of the problems encountered in evaluating teachers contributes to understanding what must be done to comply with legal and professional standards, thereby avoiding or at least reducing the probability of encountering future problems. Let us discuss each category briefly and then apply these concepts to procedures for gathering and interpreting observation data and using these data in conferring with teachers to improve instruction.

PROBLEMS IN EVALUATING TEACHERS

Due Process

To comply with due process, established rules and procedures must be followed to protect individual rights. Contract wording is important in determining due process, and such wording varies. However, generally accepted procedures that meet due process requirements for evaluating teachers include:

- teacher awareness of the criteria and procedures used for purposes of evaluation
- direct observation of the teacher in the classroom or other teaching situation
- conferring with the teacher, providing data based on observation, and outlining any areas where changes are needed
- assisting the teacher with materials or inservice work that address the area(s) in which the teacher needs to make changes
- provision of sufficient time to make the changes that are needed
- reobservation and evaluation to establish whether or not specified changes have been made

These six steps are stated so as to comply with legal implications of summative evaluation, but logically they also apply to professional practice in the formative evaluation of teachers.

Discrimination

The U.S. Constitution guarantees that no citizen can be discriminated against for beliefs, associates, or personal characteristics. Court cases have found certain tests, interview techniques, and evaluation systems used for selection, promotion, and retention to be racially, culturally, and sexually biased. Only when evaluation criteria are directly *job-related* may they be legally and professionally applied.

Perhaps the best way to establish job-relatedness is to study teachers in classrooms to determine what they do, that is, their performance, and then to relate their performance to measures of student outcome to determine their effectiveness. Such is the content of Chapters 21 and 22, where concepts of essential and higher order teacher performance are identified together with examples of studies showing the relationship of teacher performance to student learning.

Validity

To be valid, an evaluation system must measure the attribute(s) it purports to measure. There are a number of approaches to establishing validity of evaluation systems. The two that most apply in the validation of teacher evaluation systems are content validity and predictive validity.

Content validity, a procedure for determining that items are clearly articulated and represent the concepts to be measured, is established through consensus of knowledgeable people (Kerlinger, 1967; Thorndike and Hagen, 1977).

Predictive validity relates teacher performance to how much students learn. Without some evidence that the scores generated from evaluation systems have a positive relationship to student learning, their use is tenuous.

Reliability

Reliability has legal and measurement implications. Legally the courts are concerned that teachers not be discharged without documented evidence from qualified observers. From a measurement perspective, three questions should be addressed in estimating the reliability of instruments for purposes of teacher evaluation:

(1) To what degree can two or more persons observe the same teacher at the same point in time and independently draw the same conclusions (intercoder agreement)?

(2) To what degree can this be done on various occasions (stability)?

(3) To what degree does the instrument consistently place a teacher on a scale of effectiveness (discriminant)?

Observers are qualified if they can use the instrument consistently and accurately.

To summarize the categories in which teacher evaluation systems experience difficulty, we can say that teachers must be aware of the concepts used in their evaluation, administrators must follow legal and logical procedures in applying evaluation systems, evaluation criteria must be job-related, the instruments must contain valid content that can be consistently observed, teacher evaluation scores must relate to student outcomes, and observers must be accurate in their observations. Let us examine examples of the work required to satisfy these requirements, organized according to procedures for gathering observation data, interpreting observation data, and using observation data in conferring with teachers to improve performance.

GATHERING OBSERVATION DATA

Poorly conceptualized, untested systems of teacher evaluation, and the use of untrained and untested observers/evaluators are obstacles to the effective evaluation of teachers and the improvement of instruction. They are also causes of courtroom battles between administrators and teachers. To avoid these pitfalls, content validation, instrument formatting, and tests of reliability can be applied to the development and validation of teacher evaluation systems prior to their use for gathering either formative or summative evaluation data. Procedures for norming and tests of predictive validity are addressed below.

In the following, we have limited the scope of evaluation to classroom instruction under the premise that teacher performance in the classroom is the most powerful, controllable predictor of student learning.

Content Validity

The process begins with content, i.e., criteria. Content is to an evaluation system as the foundation is to a building. The persons responsible for identifying the content must be knowledgeable. As stated earlier, content validity is established through consensus of knowledgeable people. Persons conducting the validation usually work independently at first to identify the concepts and indicators of effective teaching to be included in the system, and then in concert with other validators to reach consensus on the terms, definitions, examples, and statements of principle that represent effective teaching.

Part of this procedure involves grouping the concepts and indicators of effective teaching into categories. One such division lists planning for instruction, management of student conduct, instructional organization and development, presentation of subject matter, communication, and student evaluation as domains of effective teaching (Knowledge Base: Domains of the Florida Performance Measurement System, 1983). An overview of these domains is in Chapter 21. The domains of the Florida Performance Measurement System include what may be considered essential teaching skills, the kinds of skills that relate mainly to student achievement, i.e., student acquisition of subject matter *knowledge*.

A second grouping of concepts and indicators of effective teaching contains teaching skills that relate to student acquisition of higher order thinking skills, i.e., the use of subject matter in solving problems, critical thinking and reasoning. This division includes developing and maintaining flexibility and student awareness, generating and validating generalizations, assessing arguments, negotiating issues and solving interpersonal problems, and making judgments under uncertainty as domains of effective teaching [Teaching for Higher Order Thinking (THOT), 1990]. An overview of these domains is in Chapter 22.

To be of use to teachers or persons learning to teach, each concept and indicator must be defined and examples of indicators written.

Common questions addressed by external reviewers in the validation of content include:

(1) Is there an empirically established relationship between the teacher performance concepts proposed as criteria for evaluation and measures of student learning?

(2) Are the concepts clearly stated in language useable by practitioners?

(3) Are the concepts accurately interpretated from the literature?

(4) Are the concepts generalizable across various levels and subjects?

(5) Are the concepts representative of the available knowledge on effective teaching?

Instrument Formatting

The next logical step in the process of developing teacher evaluation systems is the drafting of instruments for collecting teacher performance data.

The evaluation instrument is to an educator as a map is to a surveyor or an X-ray is to a surgeon. That is, they serve as records of measurement, and they must be *accurate*. Accuracy in teacher evaluation, whether it be formative or summative, since they both depend on the same baseline data, is dependent upon several factors. A primary factor, and one that is frequently violated, is to separate measurement from evaluation. Ratings of teacher performance based on high-inference judgments by evaluators inextricably interweave the measurement task with the evaluation task and its associated biases. Despite this problem and the lack of relationship between ratings and evidence of teacher effectiveness such as student achievement, rating remains the most commonly used method of evaluating teachers.

An empirical example illustrates the typical positive bias that is associated with teacher ratings. Through examination of teacher ratings in a large school district, we found that approximately 95 percent of the teachers were rated above average leaving only 5 percent of the teachers rated below average. In one school, 100 percent of the teachers were rated as outstanding over a five-year period. This is less than logical given most definitions of the concept of average.

One technique that separates measurement from evaluation requires observing and coding teacher performance without making any evaluative judgments. Measurements of teacher performance are then compared with those of other teachers in like circumstances in order to develop profiles for use in formative evaluation and to arrive at logical and accurate summative evaluations.

Accurate observation of human behavior, however, is difficult to accomplish even in clinical settings, let alone in actual classrooms. Several factors should be considered in attempting to obtain accurate and meaningful results. These factors include the following. First, while research has shown that by combining observations of a number of performance indicators significant relationship may be found with student learning, no single indicator has been found that accounts for significant differences between effective and noneffective instruction. This suggests that observation instruments should include a number of indicators that can be coded to develop a meaningful performance score. Consider also that the frequent use of a few effective behaviors may not prove as effective instructionally as the less frequent use of several effective behaviors, and the scoring system should reflect this.

In formatting instruments, then, it is a matter of selecting concepts from a content valid base that are to be observed, and listing indicators of these concepts on the instrument. Figures 23.1 and 23.2 are examples of instruments. Figure 23.1 is the Florida Performance Measurement System (FPMS) summative instrument, the content base for which is discussed in Chapter 21. Figure 23.2 is the Teaching for Higher Order Thinking (THOT) domain 2 instrument, the content base for which is discussed in Chapter 22.

To use these instruments, observers code in the cell next to each indicator the teacher demonstrates, each time the indicator is observed during a lesson. These codes provide measures of performance, and when standardized for time (i.e., differences in length of lessons) are of use in comparing levels of performance across teachers.

At this point in the development of instrumentation, concern points towards the consistency or reliability of observers in coding observed performance.

Tests of Reliability

Reliability testing is usually conducted using teams of trained observers. The length and depth of training required to obtain acceptable levels of reliability are not well established, and vary according to the complexity of content and instrument formatting.

Training of observers consists of learning the evaluation criteria, examining classroom examples of performance of each criterion, and practicing coding.

In the process of testing reliability, it is possible to incorporate

Number of Students Not Engaged

1 ☐   2 ☐   3 ☐   4 ☐

FLORIDA DEPARTMENT OF EDUCATION
DIVISION OF HUMAN RESOURCE DEVELOPMENT

**FLORIDA PERFORMANCE MEASUREMENT SYSTEM
SCREENING/SUMMATIVE OBSERVATION INSTRUMENT**

DOMAIN		Tot. Freq.	Frequency	Frequency	Frequency	Tot. Freq.	
3.0 Instructional Organization and Development	1. Begins instruction promptly						1. Delays
	2. Handles materials in an orderly manner						2. Does not organize materials systematically
	3. Orients students to classwork/maintains academic focus						3. Allows talk/activity unrelated to subject
	4. Conducts beginning/ending review						4.
	5. Questions: academic comprehension/ lesson development **a.** single factual (Domain 5.0)						5a. Allows unison response
							5b. Poses multiple questions asked as one
	b. requires analysis/ reasons						5c. Poses nonacademic questions/nonacademic procedural questions
	6. Recognizes response/amplifies/gives correct feedback						6. Ignores student or response/expresses sarcasm, disgust, harshness
	7. Gives specific academic praise						7. Uses general, nonspecific praise
	8. Provides for practice						8. Extends discourse, changes topic with no practice
	9. Gives directions/assigns/checks comprehension of homework, seatwork assignments/gives feedback						9. Gives inadequate directions on homework/ no feedback
	10. Circulates and assists students						10. Remains at desk/circulates inadequately
4.0 Presentation of Subject Matter	11. Treats concepts - definition/attributes/examples/ nonexamples						11. Gives definition or examples only
	12. Discusses cause-effect/uses linking words/applies law or principle						12. Discusses either cause or effect only/uses no linking word(s)
	13. States and applies academic rule						13. Does not state or does not apply academic rule
	14. Develops criteria and evidence for value judgment						14. States value judgment with no criteria or evidence
5.0 Communication: Verbal and Nonverbal	15. Emphasizes important points						15.
	16. Expresses enthusiasm verbally/challenges students						16.
	17.						17. Uses vague/scrambled discourse
	18.						18. Uses loud-grating, high pitched, monotone, inaudible talk
	19. Uses body behavior that shows interest - smiles, gestures						19. Frowns, deadpan or lethargic
2.0 Management of Student Conduct	20. Stops misconduct						20. Delays desist/doesn't stop misconduct/desists punitively
	21. Maintains instructional momentum						21. Loses momentum - fragments nonacademic directions, overdwells

Observer's Notes:

NOTE: (Directions for completing the information required on this instrument are in the FPMS Coding Manual)

Copyright
State of Florida
Department of State
1989

State of Florida
Department of Education
Tallahassee, Florida
Betty Castor, Commissioner
Alternative action/equal opportunity employer

Teacher's Name

_____ _____ _____
(Last) (First) (Middle)

SS#_____-____-_____ Inst.#_____

Institution of Graduation_____

Graduated From a College of Education ☐1. YES ☐2. NO
Number of Complete Years of Teaching Experience_____

District Name_____ Number_____

School Name_____ Number_____

Observer's Name

_____ _____ _____
(Last) (First) (Middle)

SS#_____-____-_____

Position ☐1. Principal ☐2. Asst Principal ☐3. Teacher ☐4. Other

Class_____ Grade Level_____ (Specify one level only - For Adult Ed mark Level 13; For Kindergarten or Preschool mark Level 00.)

Subject Area Observed
☐ 1. Language Arts   ☐ 9. Home Economics
☐ 2. Foreign Language   ☐ 10. Other Vocational Ed.
☐ 3. Social Sciences   ☐ 11. Arts
☐ 4. Mathematics   ☐ 12. Music
☐ 5. Science   ☐ 13. Exceptional Stud. Ed.
☐ 6. Physical Education, ROTC ☐ 14. Other (Specify)_____
☐ 7. Business Education, DCT, CBE
☐ 8. Industrial Arts/Education

Type of Classroom/Facility in Which the Observation Occurred
☐ 1. Regular Classroom - Self-contained, Open, Pod
☐ 2. Laboratory or Shop
☐ 3. Field, Court or Gymnasium
☐ 4. Media Room or Library

Total Number of Students in Class_____

Observation Information Date_____

Type of Observation ☐1. Beg. Tchr. ☐2. Dist. Assessment ☐3. Other (Specify)
Screening Obs. ☐1. ☐2. ☐3. ☐4.
Summative Obs. ☐1. ☐2. ☐3. ☐4.

Time Observation Begins __:__ : Observation Ends __:__
Test Begins __:__ : Test Ends __:__

Methods Used in the Observed Lesson
☐1. Lecture
☐2. Interaction/Discussion
☐3. Independent Study/Lab or Shop Work

Teacher's Signature_____

Observer's Signature_____

OTE 349
Exp. 3/31/93

Figure 23.1 Florida Performance Measurement System Screening/Summative Observation Instrument.

Domain 2.0 Generating and Validating Generalizations

Concepts	Indicators	Frequency	Total
Problem Formulation	1.1 Presents background/Uses discrepancy		
	1.2 Cites variables/Eliminates irrelevancies		
	1.4 Poses problem		
	1.5 Uses analogies		
Development of Empirical Explanations and Formulation and Testing of Experimental Hypotheses	2.1/2.2 States generalizations/hypotheses		
	1.3/2.3 Classifies/Clarifies reason/outcome or cause/effect		
	2.4/2.5 Determines testability of hypotheses using criteria/Provides examples		
	2.6 Uses hypotheses to predict		
	2.7 Falsifies a hypothesis/generalization		
	2.8 Models variable control		
	2.9 Plans/conducts experiment/Supports generalization		
Validation of Generalizations	3.1 Guards against overgeneralization/Checks sample		
	3.2 Analyzes explanatory power of conclusion		
	3.3 Relates conclusions to relevant knowledge		
	3.4 Evaluates alternative conclusions		
Notes:			

Domain 1.0 Developing and Maintaining Flexibility and Student Awareness

Concepts	Indicators	Frequency	Total
Flexibility	1.1/1.2 Warns against premature evaluation/Searches for new approaches		
	2.1 Provides manipulative exploratory materials		
	2.2/2.3 Allows thinking time/Pauses		
Student Awareness	3.1/3.2 Models problem solving procedure/Thinks aloud		
	3.3 Makes content explicit: what, when, why, how		
	3.4 Encourages verbalization about thought processes		
	3.5 Uses small groups		
Notes:			

Figure 23.2 Teaching for Higher Order Thinking (THOT).

375

measures of both observer consistency and accuracy. One technique for addressing this issue is the establishment of a set of criteria ("truth") for a measure. Termed criterion-related agreement (Frick and Semmel, 1978, p. 161), in this situation, pre-scored videotapes of teacher performance can be used to measure both observer consistency and accuracy, with the "true" score defined as the number of times the teacher actually demonstrates each indicator in a given lesson.

One method of determining true scores is to average the independent observations of a large number (twenty or more) of observers that have met criteria for reliability to estimate true scores.

Practice exercises using training tapes are important. Observers are nervous at first, and it helps to have a trainer call out the criteria as they are viewed for a few minutes of the first observation followed by paired coding for the remainder of at least the first lesson. Once the observers gain confidence in their coding ability, independent observations are conducted, followed by comparing the number of codes in each cell of the instrument and the resolution of differences through discussion and reviewing of the videotape if necessary. The key is *consensus*. The group may not agree on all items, but consensus on the majority of items coded within a reasonable range is a key to obtaining acceptable levels of reliability.

As mentioned earlier in this chapter, three dimensions of reliability are of interest: (1) intercoder agreement, (2) stability, and (3) discriminant reliability.

Several factors contribute to the reliability of measuring teacher performance. These include having a valid content base so it is highly probable that the criteria may be observed in typical classrooms, formatting the instrument for ease of use, and training observers for accuracy. Two additional procedures may improve the accuracy of performance observations. One is to average observations by two or more independent observers, and the second is to reduce raw frequencies of codes to grouped frequencies, i.e., scaled scores.

We found in testing the FPMS summative instrument that by averaging two observations of each teacher, the coefficient of agreement for intercoder agreement went from $r = 0.64$ to $r = 0.82$, for stability from $r = 0.70$ to $r = 0.81$, and for discriminant from $r = 0.55$ to $r = 0.75$. By averaging in a third observer, however, there was little difference in the coefficients of reliability (Teacher Evaluation Study: Report for 1983–1984).

Trained administrators, clinical supervisors, or peer teachers armed with content valid and reliable instruments are ready to *gather observation data*, but not as yet to formatively, let alone summatively, *evaluate* teacher performance. Evaluations are conducted either using preset standards, or through the use of comparative performance data. Setting standards is risky since it is by nature quite arbitrary. Despite this, it is often necessary. If standards are to be defensible, there must be some indication that they relate to the objective of interest. An alternative to setting standards is the comparison of a teacher's performance against the performance of other teachers.

Caution must be taken, however, in making comparisons of teachers. When making comparisons, a representative sample of the teacher's performance must be observed. This is to prevent use of atypical observations as the norm of performance. As an example, suppose a teacher normally assigns homework and works with students to determine that they understand the assignment and are capable of completing the assignment, but during a given observation they did not do so. Homework, when handled correctly, is a predictor of student achievement, but may not be required every day. By observing the teacher on multiple occasions, homework assignments may be coded, thereby obtaining a more representative sample of the teacher's performance. We have found in using the FPMS to evaluate beginning teachers that performance scores tend to be reasonably stable, and therefore representative, after approximately four observations (Micceri, 1986).

Another pitfall to avoid is comparing teachers where evaluation scores are either influenced or are perceived to be influenced by the context of the observation. Our experience has shown that teachers are very sensitive to being compared, particularly with teachers of other subjects and grade levels, and where differences in student ability may have an effect on teacher performance. Potential differences of this nature may be accounted for through norming. Norming is one of the first procedures necessary for interpretation of observation data.

INTERPRETING OBSERVATION DATA

While determining what to observe and conducting accurate observations is prerequisite to further development of teacher evaluation systems, it is not adequate—the job is not finished. The codes on an observation instrument have some meaning in terms of indicators observed and those not observed, but their complete meaning is not unveiled until comparative performance data across a number of teachers are collected and analyzed and the resulting scores are compared to measures of student outcome. To compare scores across teachers, instruments are normed; and, to estimate score relationships with measures of student outcome, they are tested for predictive validity.

Norming

We generally associate the term *norming* with standardized achievement tests such as the SAT, CAT, or GRE. These tests are normed by obtaining scores from a large number of persons for whom the tests were designed. As a result of norming, ranges of expected scores, averages, and measures of variance are computed and published to provide a basis for comparing scores, i.e., to make the scores meaningful. Scores from subgroups such as sex, race, location, age, and grade level can then be compared to the norms to determine the degree to which subgroup scores are the same or different.

Teacher evaluation systems can and should also be normed. The main purpose of norming teacher evaluation systems is to determine the degree to which a variety of factors influence scores derived from application of the system. If one or more factors contribute significant differences in evaluation scores, then a separate norm group(s) or scoring adjustment(s) should be created. This is done to prevent teachers in one context from having a score advantage over teachers in a different context. For example, many schools group students according to ability in the basic academic subjects. The norming question focuses on whether or not teachers of high-achieving students have a performance evaluation advantage over teachers of low-achieving students, or vice versa.

Although fundamental to the development of meaningful and defensible teacher evaluation systems, few have been normed. A brief summary of the procedures and findings of the FPMS Norming Study (Teacher Evaluation Study: Report for 1984–1985) are provided here as an example.

While the concepts and indicators of teacher performance in the FPMS were drawn from a variety of subjects and grade levels, the degree to which the concepts and indicators were generic (i.e., applicable to all contexts of teaching) was unknown. The effects of factors such as grade level, subject area, and sex were unknown.

The FPMS was normed for the state of Florida. To include a representative sample of teachers, sample strata for this norming study included grade level, subject area, whether the schools were located in urban or rural areas, and the socioeconomic status of students (SES), since SES is a predictor of student achievement. Through application of these criteria, forty-five schools (clusters) were selected from thirteen school districts. All of the teachers in each of the clusters, with the exception of a few absentees, were observed to assure that all frame factors would have a reasonable chance at representation. A total of 1,223 teachers were observed by 117 trained and certified observers using the FPMS summative instrument.

All observations were standardized to thirty minutes and scaled using the interquartile range. Use of the interquartile range converts scores into (1) the lower 25 percent, (2) the mid 25–75 percent, and (3) the top 25 percent. Scores for each item were then summed to create total scores. Using this method, teachers scoring high tended to be those exhibiting multiple performance indicators in several categories, while those scoring low exhibited few performance indicators in few categories.

The independent variables examined in the FPMS norming study were subject; grade level; instructional method; teacher's degree, experience, race, and sex; and student SES. While the indicators appeared generic, it seemed probable to most of the teachers and administrators knowledgeable of the research being conducted that academic teachers may score higher than nonacademic teachers, teachers of high-SES students may score higher than those of low-SES students, and teachers with more experience may score higher than teachers with less experience.

Analysis of variance (ANOVA) procedures were used in determining the degree to which the FPMS summative instrument was generic and generalizable across teaching contexts, and to determine the number and nature of possible norm groups. Due to the large sample sizes and the multiplicity inherent in investigating so many frame factors, the following set of criteria were set to assure that only truly significant and important differences between groups would emerge from the analyses:

(1) Results of ANOVAs had to attain a significance level of .01.

(2) A minimum of one-third standard deviation or 2.15 points difference was measured between groups.

(3) A total of seventy-five or more observations were made for any subgroup.

Results of the norming study showed that only two factors, grade level and instruction format, met the three standards cited above. Analysis of grade level showed a significant difference between elementary (K–5) and post-elementary (6–12) levels, with elementary teachers as a group scoring significantly higher than post-elementary teachers on the FPMS. Two norm groups were created to correct this difference. The second factor, instruction method, was measured by comparing observations where the main method of instruction was (1) lecture, (2) verbal interaction between students and teacher, or (3) independent seat or lab work. The norming study showed that teachers using verbal interaction as the main method of instruction scored significantly higher than teachers using lecture or seat/lab work. Score adjustments were developed for the two lower-scoring methods to control for this factor.

To summarize, norming studies are conducted to test one dimension of validity (i.e., Does the instrument measure what it purports to measure—teacher performance and not context?), to determine the fairness of evaluating teachers teaching in different contexts using the same instrument, to provide a basis on which to create different norm groups, and to provide ranges of scores on which individual teacher scores can be compared. For teacher evaluation scores to be of value, observation scores must show if teachers are performing at a high, mid range, or low level when compared to other teachers in the same norm group.

Norming, however, does not investigate relationships between observation scores and measures of student outcome.

Predictive Validity

Predictive validity is very difficult to establish, since a number of factors influence the dependent variable (student learning) other than the independent variable (teacher performance), not the least of which is what students know prior to being taught by the present teacher. It is, therefore, necessary to control potential sources of error as much as possible. Valid and reliable means are primary concerns.

Length of study may vary, but must be adequate to allow time to teach the concepts to be measured. We have reviewed or conducted studies as short as two weeks and as long as one academic year (Hines et al., 1986; Teacher Evaluation Study: FPMS Predictive Validity Report, 1987). Each teacher must plan to teach the same content during the study period, and the examinations must test the content taught. Reasonable care is required to protect the observations of teacher performance and the student examinations from being altered.

Remember, what students know prior to entering a teacher's class is the best predictor of what the student will know upon completion of the class. Pre-existing differences among students are a major threat to the validity of studies designed to determine the influence of teacher performance on student learning. Random assignment of students to teachers and treatments and the use of pre-/post-testing procedures are frequently used to reduce the influence of this effect on findings.

Five predictive validity studies have been conducted on the FPMS, that include mathematics, biology, and history, at grade levels 2, 3, 5, 6, 8, 10, and 11. In a metaanalysis of these studies, the approximate correlation associated with combined Z scores between FPMS scores and student outcome was $r = 0.28$, $z = 3.09$, $p < .001$.

All of these figures provide a basis for data interpretation. Consider the implications of using a system for which such data are not available. For example, if the criteria of evaluation are not derived from research on teaching, what empirical evidence is there that they are related to the primary job of the teacher, which is classroom instruction? If the instrument and observers have not been tested for reliability and accuracy, how do you know their observations are consistent? How can it be determined that teacher performance scores are not influenced by teaching context if the instrument is not normed? And, the most difficult test of all, are the performance scores of any value if it has not been shown that they are predictive of how much students learn? Legally and professionally, the tests described in this chapter strengthen teacher evaluation systems to withstand challenges of due process, discrimination, validity, and reliability.

Feedback

Providing the foregoing tests have been conducted, feedback containing standardized performance evaluation scores is possible. This is essential to the complete interpretation of observation data. To illustrate, automated feedback reports have been developed for the FPMS (Figure 23.3).

The example feedback report in Figure 23.3 was developed on the basis of averaging two observations of a beginning teacher's classroom performance. Comparative performance scores based on norms for beginning teachers are given for each domain, all of the effective indicators across the domains on the instrument, and the ineffective indicators. These scores are followed by a total performance score. Two or more observations are recommended as a basis for providing feedback to reduce error in the observation process and to provide a more representative sample of the teacher's performance.

Note also that in lieu of listing precise percentile scores, for example, the scores are reported as Level 1 (lower 15 percent of the normed distribution), Level 2 (mid 16 percent–59 percent), and Level 3 (60 percent and above). The purposes of grouping scores are to compro-

Individual Performance Report
Florida Performance Measurement System (FPMS)
Beginning Teacher Program

Name:	John Doe
Social Security Number:	111-22-3333
District:	Edmond
Date of Report:	October 25, 1990
Number of Observations:	2

Performance Scale	Performance Score
Domain 3 ORGANIZATION (items 1-4 and 8-10)	Level 2
Domain 3 DEVELOPMENT (items 5-7)	Level 2
Domain 4 SUBJECT PRESENTATION (items 11-14)	Level 3
Domain 5 COMMUNICATION (items 15-19)	Level 3
Domain 2 MANAGEMENT OF CONDUCT (items 20-21)	Level 1
Effective (left Side Items 1-21)	Level 3
Ineffective (right Side Items 1-21)	Level 3
Total Performance	Level

NOTE: Performance scores are based upon FPMS norm distributions of beginning teachers and are reported as Level 1 (lower 15%), Level 2 (16%-59%) and Level 3 (60% and above). For example, if a teacher received a Level 3 score in Domain 3 it means that at least 59% of the teachers in the norm group earned lower scores in that domain.

Figure 23.3 *FPMS Feedback Report.*

mise some of the error inherent in evaluating human behavior, and in this case to more accurately reflect competence levels.

Using a coded frequency system such as the FPMS facilitates further analysis of feedback reports. In Figure 23.3, the low score in the management of student conduct could be a sign of frequent ineffective performance of the teacher in delaying desists of student disruption, desisting punitively, or losing momentum by fragmenting nonacademic directions or overdwelling. However, it could also mean that in the absence of any student conduct problems during the lesson, there were no disruptions to stop or no call to attend an intrusion while simultaneously maintaining the momentum of the lesson, both of which would be coded on the effective side of the observation instrument. This information would have to be obtained by combining data on the feedback report and the original observation instruments. Both are essential to the analysis of observed lessons which constitutes the data base on which to confer with teachers to improve instruction.

Frame factor information is also essential in working with teachers to improve instruction and in arriving at fair comparative performance scores.

In the case of the FPMS example, three frame factors discovered in the "Teacher Evaluation Study: Report for 1984–1985" are of primary import in the comparative analysis of observation data. They are time, grade level, and instruction format. Time is a factor since the longer the lesson (complete lessons from beginning to end are observed using the FPMS), the more opportunity teachers have to demonstrate codable performance. FPMS observations are, therefore, standardized to a thirty-minute time frame when scored. Teachers in grades K–5 tended to score significantly higher than teachers in grades 6–12 in the FPMS norming study. As a result, two norm groups were created to correct this difference in teaching context. The third frame factor that tends to influence FPMS scores is instruction format. Teachers conducting lessons using an interactive format such as class discussion tend to score higher than teachers using an activity-oriented lesson such as a science lab. A point differential has been developed and included in the automated scoring system of the FPMS to compromise this factor and not penalize teachers for activity-centered lessons such as science labs.

None of the other frame factors significantly influenced FPMS performance scores. Other systems of evaluation may differ, however, so caution is advised in determining frame factor influence on teacher evaluation scores through norming whatever system is used for this purpose. To the need for the observation instruments and feedback reports required for conferring with teachers for the improvement of instruction, we add the need to collect data on frame factors that have an influence on evaluation scores. Attention to the interpretation of observation data is also warranted. It cannot be assumed that given the same data everybody will interpret those data in the same manner.

Data Interpretation

Regardless of who observes a teacher's performance or who conducts the analysis of the observations, both the observations and the analyses should be substantially the same. Accuracy (i.e., reliability and validity) in interpreting observation data is as important as accuracy in the collection of observation data. Both have legal as well as professional implications for formative and summative evaluation.

Research has shown that agreement among observers on how classroom observation data are interpreted can be increased through training (Kessell, 1988). Kessell's findings were consistent with Lawrence (1974), Stallings et al. (1978), Bentzen (1974), and Brophy and Good (1974), in that the provision of multiple training sessions, small group interaction and study, and feedback on performance increased adult learning and improved performance.

Far more study is needed to verify the results of the Kessell study regarding the effects of training and feedback on the accuracy of data interpretation, but the data from this and other studies present a strong case for training persons responsible for the analysis of observation data to improve the accuracy and consistency of their analyses.

All of the foregoing in this chapter is prerequisite to the task of conferring with teachers to improve instruction.

Conferring

The entire fabric of this chapter is woven around the legal and professional requirements of developing and implementing teacher evaluation systems as they apply to both the formative and summative evaluation of teachers' classroom performance.

The preceding are essential. Additionally, conferring is an integral part of the process of improving instruction through the use of evaluation data. In an effort to separate fact from folklore, a search of the literature was conducted for purposes of identifying effective practice of persons who give assistance to teachers on instructional not counseling problems (*Conferring with Teachers*, 1985).

The research indicates that effective conferring requires skilled consultants. We examined sixty-one studies that provided the basis for four major concepts and twenty-five indicators of effective conferring that address this question. The independent variables in these studies were indicators of consultant performance such as body behavior (e.g., expressions of interest, excitement, sadness, boredom), arrangements of space, maintaining a problem focus, listening, clarifying responses, examining observation data, summarizing data, developing a plan, and following up.

The dependent variables in these studies fit one of two categories: (1) opinions of conferrer/client preferences, and (2) process/product research findings on changes in teacher performance following conferences. An example of the first category is a study conducted by Haase and DiMattia (1976) in which they asked persons conducting conferences, and the clients with whom they were conferring, their preferences in the arrangement of furniture. Differences were found in their preferences. For example, the conferrers tended to favor chairs placed side by side at a 45 degree angle, while the clients least preferred this arrangement. An example of the second category is a study by Bergan and Tombari (1976) in which through the use of multiple-regression analysis they found that in solving problems, the identification of the specific problem accounts for almost 59 percent of the variation in the occurrence of planned implementation. They further found that planned implementation accounted for a whopping 95 percent of the variation in problem solving.

Such researches establish relationships, but not cause and effect relationships. When the findings of several such studies corroborate each other, however, the findings gain credibility. Although far from perfect, these studies provide the best information presently available upon which to base decisions about effective and ineffective conferring practices.

With these qualifications in mind, the research indicates four major concepts of effective conferring practice (*Conferring with Teachers*, 1985): (1) development of rapport, (2) interpersonal skills, (3) problem formulation, and (4) development of plans.

Two questions regarding conferring are commonplace. The first is, "Does conferring modify the performance/behavior of the clients?" Studies show that in the majority of cases, conferring does modify performance/behavior. For example Mannino and Shore (1975) in a combined studies analysis found that in 74 percent of the cases change was positive and significant. A second question regards, "Is direct or indirect conferring more effective?" Some studies provide evidence of better results if nondirective approaches are taken—clients do not feel threatened (French et al., 1966; Blumberg, 1968). Other studies, however, provide evidence of better results if the direct approach is taken (Shinn, 1976; Hillery and Wexley, 1974; Copeland, 1980). The direct approach seems to be preferable among inexperienced teachers, while experienced teachers tend to favor the nondirective approach.

The research on conferring is less than conclusive, but some generalizations appear to be in order based upon the review conducted for *Conferring with Teachers*. First, conferring is usually effective in changing performance, and is therefore considered of value in the process of formative evaluation of teachers. Second, whether the direct or indirect approach is used is dependent on the frame factors of the evaluation, in particular the experience of the teacher. Third, the research shows that certain indicators of conferrer performance if practiced improve the chances of making changes in teacher performance. In general, the three most important indicators of effective conferrer practice appear to be : (1) basing the conference on observation data, (2) clearly identifying the problem(s) the teacher is to remediate, and (3) formulating a plan that includes what is to be done, when, and a follow-up time.

SUMMARY

Teacher evaluation, whether formative or summative, may have serious impact on the lives of the persons evaluated. To be legally and professionally viable, the development and implementation of teacher evaluation systems must meet standards of due process, discrimination, validity, and reliability. Preparing a system for the gathering of evaluation data includes searching the literature on teacher effectiveness for concepts of effective and ineffective teaching and content validating the findings of the search, formatting instruments for data collection, and testing instruments for reliability using trained observers.

Interpreting observation data requires norming. Through norming, evaluation scores may be compared across teachers working in various contexts. The ultimate test of an evaluation system is to examine relationships between teachers' scores and measures of student outcome. If the scores are predictive of how much students learn, the system may be considered valid.

Valid and reliable observations, together with normed feedback reports on performance, provide the basis for conferring with teachers for purposes of improving instruction. Effective conferring generally includes an observed data base, clear identification of the problem(s) to be remediated, and a plan including what is to be done, when, and follow-up.

REFERENCES

Bentzen, M. 1974. *Changing Schools: The Magic Feather Principle.* New York: McGraw-Hill.

Bergan, J. R. and M. L. Tombari. 1976. "Consultant Skill and Efficiency and the Implementation and Outcomes of Consultation," *Journal of School Psychology,* 14(Spring):3–14.

Blumberg, A. 1968. "Supervisory Behavior and Interpersonal Relations," *Education Administration Quarterly,* 7:34–45.

Brophy, J. and T. Good. 1974. *Teacher-Student Relationships: Cause and Consequences.* New York: Holt, Rinehart and Winston.

1985. *Conferring with Teachers: Domain 10.* Tampa, FL: University of South Florida, College of Education, Teacher Evaluation and Assessment Center.

Copeland, W. D. 1980. "Affective Disposition of Teachers in Training toward Examples of Supervisory Behavior," *Journal of Educational Research,* 74(September/October):37–42.

Cossairt, A., R. V. Hall and B. L. Hopkins. 1973. "The Effects of Experimenter's Instructions, Feedback, and Praise on Teacher Praise and Student Attending Behavior," *Journal of Applied Behavior Analysis,* 6:89–100.

Deneen, J. R. 1980. "Legal Dimensions of Teacher Evaluation," in *Due Process in Teacher Evaluation,* D. Peterson and A. Ward, eds., Washington, DC: University Press of America, Inc.

French, J. R., E. Kay and H. H. Meyer. 1966. "Participation and the Appraisal System," *Human Relations,* 19:3–20.

Frick, T. and M. I. Semmel. 1978. "Observer Agreement and Reliabilities of Classroom Observational Measures," *Review of Educational Research,* 48(Winter): 157–184.

Haase, R. F. and D. J. DiMattia. 1976. "Prosemic Behavior: Counselor, Administrator and Client Preference for Seating Arrangement in Dyadic Interaction," *Journal of Counseling Psychology,* 17(July):319–325.

Hillery, J. M. and K. N. Wexley. 1974. "Participation Effects in Appraisal Interviews Conducted in a Training Situation," *Journal of Applied Psychology*, 59:168–171.

Hines, C., J. Kromrey, J. Swarzman, M. Mann and S. Homan. 1986. "Teacher Behavior, Task Engagement and Achievement: A Path Analysis," *Florida Educational Research Journal*, 28(Fall):25–40.

Kerlinger, F. N. 1967. *Foundations of Behavioral Research*. New York: Holt, Rinehart and Winston.

Kessell, G. "A Study of the Effect of Training on Observer Agreement in the Interpretation of Teacher Observation Data," unpublished doctoral dissertation, University of South Florida, College of Education, Tampa, 1988.

1983. "Knowledge Base: Domains of the Florida Performance Measurement System." Chipley, FL: Panhandle Area Educational Cooperative.

Lawrence, G. 1974. "Patterns of Effective Inservice Education: A State of the Art Summary of Research on Materials and Procedures for Changing Teacher Behaviors in Inservice Education," ED176424. Tallahassee, FL: State Department of Education.

Mannino, F. V. and M. F. Shore. 1975. "The Effects of Consultation: A Review of Empirical Studies," *American Journal of Community Psychology*, 3:1–21.

Micceri, T. "Assessing the Stability of the Florida Performance Measurement System Summative Observation Instrument: A Field Study," unpublished technical report, University of South Florida, College of Education, Tampa, 1986.

Shinn, J. L. 1976. "Teacher Perceptions of Ideal and Actual Supervisory Procedures Used by California Elementary Principals: The Effects of Supervisory Training Programs Sponsored by the Association of California School Administrators," *Dissertation Abstracts International*.

Stallings, J., M. Needles and N. Stayrock. 1978. "School Policy, Leadership Style, Teacher Change and Student Behavior," final report. Menlo Park, CA: SRI International.

1987. "Teacher Evaluation Study: FPMS Predictive Validity Report." Tampa, FL: University of South Florida, College of Education, Teacher Evaluation and Assessment Center.

1984. "Teacher Evaluation Study: Report for 1983–1984," Document No. SPO 27191. ERIC Document Reproductions Service No. ED22612. Tampa, FL: University of South Florida, College of Education.

1985. "Teacher Evaluation Study: Report for 1984–1985," Document No. SPO 27189. ERIC Document Reproductions Service No. ED226120. Tampa, FL: University of South Florida, College of Education.

1990. "Teaching for Higher Order Thinking (THOT)." Tampa, FL: University of South Florida, College of Education, Teacher Evaluation and Assessment Center.

Thorndike, R. L. and E. P. Hagen. 1977. *Measurement and Evaluation in Psychology and Education*. New York: John Wiley & Sons.

INDEX

BIOGRAPHIES

Robert H. Anderson, coeditor of this volume, is president of Peda-morphosis, Inc., a nonprofit organization promoting educational change through leadership development. He is also a part-time Professor of Education at the University of South Florida. A former teacher, coach, principal, and superintendent, he served as a Professor of Education at Harvard University for nineteen years, and after ten years at Texas Tech University he became Professor and Dean Emeritus in 1983. His work has focused on nongradedness, team teaching, clinical supervision, staff development, and the many dimensions of educational leadership.

John M. Bahner joined the Institute for Development of Educational Activities, Inc., (/I/D/E/A/), in 1968 and currently is its president. Previously, he served as a teacher and school administrator in elementary, middle, and senior high schools. In the early 1960s while a member of the faculty of Harvard's Graduate School of Education, Dr. Bahner was closely involved in the early development of clinical supervision led by Morris Cogan with applications to teaching teams led by Robert H. Anderson. For the past thirty-one years, Dr. Bahner has used clinical supervision as an integral aspect of school improvement efforts he and his colleagues have conducted in schools throughout the United States, Canada, and in American schools overseas.

Jean M. Borg is an instructor and researcher in the area of teacher effectiveness at the University of South Florida, Tampa. For the past nineteen years she has worked on research projects with B. Othanel Smith and with Donovan Peterson to identify the knowledge base for the development of teacher training materials.

Mary Bullerman is retired from the Hillsborough County (Florida) Schools staff development department. While there, she had a major role in designing the Florida Beginning Teacher Program, the program which gave impetus to the development of the Florida Performance Measurement System. She worked with the team that developed and tested the materials for both FPMS and the THOT system, and has done extensive training in FPMS.

Emily Calhoun has taught at the elementary, high school, and university level, and has served as a state regional services agency consultant and as a district language arts coordinator. Currently, she works with schools and school districts to apply knowledge about change to curriculum implementation, staff development, instructional innovations, and action research.

Letitia Carr teaches seventh grade reading and social studies at the Oconee Intermediate School in Watkinsville, Georgia. She completed her doctoral study at the University of Georgia in 1990. Dr. Carr's dissertation focused on the knowledge, skills, and attitudes associated with effective practice by outstanding peer coaches and mentor teachers. Dr. Carr has conducted numerous workshops for teachers who hold leadership positions.

John H. Fitzgerald received a bachelor's degree from York University in 1971, an MS.Ed. from Niagara University of New York in 1976, and a Ph.D. from the University of South Florida in 1991. A professional educator for twenty years, Dr. Fitzgerald has taught in Ontario at all grade levels from kindergarten through grade twelve. He has worked as an instructor and instructor trainer for Performance Learning Systems of Emerson, New Jersey since 1978. Currently, Dr. Fitzgerald is employed by the Carleton Board of Education in Ottawa, Ontario, and teaches graduate courses for the Ontario Public School Teachers' Federation.

Noreen B. Garman is a Professor of Education in the Department of Administrative and Policy Studies at the University of Pittsburgh. Her focus in teaching and research is primarily in clinical supervision and curriculum studies. She has published articles and chapters in both fields. She is also currently teaching and writing in the area of qualitative/interpretive research.

Mary Giella is Assistant Superintendent for Instruction in Pasco County, Florida, and received an Ed.D. in Administration & Supervision from the University of South Florida. Dr. Giella has been an instructional leader and innovator in the Pasco County Schools for over twenty-four years. Her many varied experiences in organizational and staff development have brought her and Pasco County Schools both state and national recognition.

Carl Glickman is the Executive Director of the Program for School Improvement and a Professor in the Department of Educational Leadership at the University of Georgia, Athens, where his work focuses on collaborations with schools on site-based, inquiry-oriented school renewal. He has received broad recognition through his writings on developmental supervision and school improvement.

Nelson L. Haggerson is Professor Emeritus of Education, Arizona State University. During his forty-five years as an educator, he has served as teacher, elementary and secondary school principal, assistant professor, associate professor, full professor, and chair of a department of secondary education. He has won awards for outstanding teaching, research, administration, and community service. His areas of teaching at the university level include curriculum and instruction, secondary education, teacher education, foundations of education, and educational administration. During his tenure as department chair his department's teacher education program won an AACTE Award of Excellence. In 1986 he was a Fulbright Scholar to India.

Douglas D. Hatch is Coordinator of Undergraduate Advising, and an instructor in the Educational Leadership Department at the University of South Florida in Tampa, Florida. He has supervised teacher candidates and published articles on peer coaching and classroom management. His major interests include coaching and teacher education.

Helen M. Hazi became interested in research about supervision and the law in the 1970s while enrolled in a doctoral program in Curriculum and Supervision at the University of Pittsburgh studying under Noreen Garman. While working nearby as a public school supervisor, she was excluded from collective bargaining and wondered how and why teacher contracts controlled her practice. This became her dissertation topic, and since then legal issues that have consequence for instructional supervision and critical incidents of practice have continued to shape and inform her research. She is currently an Associate Professor in Educational Administration at West Virginia University. Having recently studied law, she is currently examining how legal reasoning and qualitative inquiry may be able to provide a vehicle for thinking about (and justifying) professional judgment in education.

Karen Hosack-Curlin has been an elementary school administrator in Pasco County, Florida. She is currently working as an Adjunct Professor at the University of South Florida where she teaches curriculum and instruction and works in a school-university partnership project with Pasco County.

John J. (Jack) Hunt is an Associate Professor at Florida Atlantic University, having gone there from the University of South Florida. A world-class sailor, Jack single-handedly has sailed across the Atlantic Ocean twice in races. He has been a superintendent in three districts in various parts of the country, and was a post-doctorate fellow at George Peabody College of Vanderbilt University.

Robert Krajewski has recently served in a dual role as Dean, College of Education and Dean, Graduate Studies, University of Wisconsin at La Crosse. For more than two decades he has been involved as a scholar, practitioner and author in the supervision of instruction. He has served as a board member of National ASCD as well as an affiliate ASCD board member in three states.

Arthur J. Lewis is Professor Emeritus at the University of Florida. He is coauthor of textbooks and articles on supervision and curriculum development. For the past seven years he has focused his attention on what he considers the most important frontier in curriculum and instruction: how to engage students in higher order thinking.

Theodore Micceri is a Research Associate at the University of South Florida, Tampa. Specializing in performance, courseware, and program evaluation, he has worked jointly the past several years for the College of Education's Teacher Evaluation and Assessment Center and the College of Engineering's Center for Interactive Technologies, Applications and Research.

Lore A. Nielsen is currently Director of Basic Educational Programs for the school district of Pasco County where she is overseeing the restructuring of the district's elementary program into a continuous progress curriculum. She was formerly Supervisor of Staff Development in Hillsborough County Schools, where the research reported in her chapter was conducted.

Edward Pajak is a Professor in the Department of Educational Leadership at the University of Georgia. He has published over thirty articles in professional journals including the *American Educational Research Journal*, *Sociology of Education*, and *Educational Leadership*. He has also authored a book entitled, *The Central Office Supervisor of Curriculum and Instruction: Setting the Stage for Success* (Allyn and Bacon), which focuses on the part played by supervisors in promoting districtwide effectiveness.

Barbara Nelson Pavan was Principal of the Franklin School (Lexington, MA), the first nongraded, team-taught school in the nation and a developmental site for clinical supervision. She has been a classroom teacher, preservice teacher instructor at Queens College (NY) and at Harvard while completing her doctoral study. She is a past president of the Council of Professors of Instructional Supervision. Presently a Professor of Educational Administration at Temple University, Philadelphia, PA, she teaches supervision and conducts inservice for school district administrators.

Donovan Peterson is a Professor of Education and Director of the Teacher Evaluation and Assessment Center at the University of South Florida, Tampa. He is one of the original developers of the FPMS, a research-based teacher evaluation system, and the THOT system, a system for teaching higher order thinking. He writes extensively and makes presentations nationally and internationally.

Jo Roberts is an Assistant Professor of Educational Leadership at the University of Georgia and a Faculty Associate of the League of Professional Schools. Formerly a teacher and secondary school principal, her research on the first-year experiences of principals deals primarily with the areas of culture and change issues. Her current research also is focused on the phenomenon of the instructional conference and related linkages among communication theory, discourse theory, and supervision concepts.

Gerald Skoog is a Professor and the Chairperson of Curriculum and Instruction at Texas Tech University where he has been in an administrative position since 1976. He is an active science educator and served as president of the National Science Teachers Association in 1985–86. His research and publications have centered on the coverage of evolution in high school biology textbooks and the place of evolution in the science curriculum.

Karolyn J. Snyder, coeditor of this volume, is a Professor of Education in the Department of Educational Leadership in the University of South Florida, where she is also Director of the School Management Institute. She and Robert Anderson coauthored *Managing Productive Schools: Toward an Ecology* (Harcourt, Brace, and Jovanovich) and she authored *Competency Training for Managing Productive Schools*. Over 130 published works have grown out of her research and training efforts on leadership, management and supervision.

Myndall Stanfill is Assistant Superintendent for Human Resource Development in Pasco County, Florida. Dr. Stanfill has worked extensively in implementing districtwide collaborative forms of school management, teacher and administrator development, instructional assessment systems, and curriculum development. She earned her doctorate in Ed.D. in Elementary Education at the University of Alabama.

Joyce Burick Swarzman is an Associate Professor and Director of SCATT (Sun Coast Area Teacher Training Honors Program) at the University of South Florida College of Education, a nationally recognized teacher education program. She was a classroom teacher in Chicago, Atlanta, and New York prior to receiving her doctorate from Teachers College, Columbia University.